THE SOUTHERN MIDDLE CLASS
IN THE LONG NINETEENTH CENTURY

THE
SOUTHERN
MIDDLE CLASS
in the
LONG NINETEENTH CENTURY

EDITED BY JONATHAN DANIEL WELLS
AND JENNIFER R. GREEN

Louisiana State University Press
Baton Rouge

Published by Louisiana State University Press
Copyright © 2011 by Louisiana State University Press
All rights reserved
Manufactured in the United States of America
First printing

Designer: Michelle A. Neustrom
Typeface: Minion Pro
Printer: McNaughton & Gunn, Inc.
Binder: Acme Bookbinding, Inc.

LIBRARY OF CONGRESS CATALOGING-IN-PUBLICATION DATA

The Southern middle class in the long nineteenth century / edited by Jonathan Daniel Wells and Jennifer R. Green.
   p. cm.
   Includes index.
   ISBN 978-0-8071-3851-9 (cloth : alk. paper) — ISBN 978-0-8071-3852-6 (mobi) — ISBN 978-0-8071-3853-3 (pdf) — ISBN 978-0-8071-3854-0 (epub) 1. Middle class—Southern States—History—19th century. 2. Southern States—Social conditions—19th century. 3. Southern States—Economic conditions—19th century. I. Wells, Jonathan Daniel, 1969– II. Green, Jennifer R., 1970–
   HT690.U6S69 2011
   305.5'5097509034—dc22

2011011949

To J. Mills Thornton III
and the scholars who have inspired us

CONTENTS

This book recalls for me a moment almost twenty years ago when I presented something of my own at the Southern Historical Association dealing with the rise of the urban middle class, the business elite in particular, in the post–Civil War South. This was the subject of a book I was about to publish and eager to preview to an audience of southern historians. The late Richard Wade was the commentator on the panel, and I remember meeting him for the first time with a mix of awe and joy. I had read Wade's books on western cities and urban slavery with great interest while a graduate student. He had been very influential in my early career as a historian, and it was exciting to finally meet the man behind these books. Any who knew Professor Wade, or saw him perform at a conference, will know what I mean when I describe him as delightfully irreverent in his approach to our sometimes all too serious profession of history. His comments on my paper opened with a recollection of his own graduate student days when one of his professors advised him while preparing for comprehensive examinations that if he ever got stuck for an answer "just talk about the rise of the middle class; it applies to just about any place and period and explains everything."

If I came away a little deflated by Professor Wade's amusing characterization of the rise of the middle class, I was no less earnest in my conviction that the South's urban middle class had been marginalized in the historical narrative of the South. The omission of the urban middle class from the narrative of southern history was, no doubt, testimony to the effectiveness of antislavery propagandists who depicted the North as a society dominated by a robust class of entrepreneurs, merchants, and professionals who imbued the North with the spirit of enterprise and improvement; the South, in stark contrast, was cast as a semi-feudal land dominated by the planter elite. Outside the aristocracy of plantation aristocrats and, of course their slaves, antislavery critics of the South saw only the mass of poor whites mired in poverty and ignorance, victims of slavery in their own right.

This uncomplicated stereotype of the South long outlasted the needs of antislavery critics to demonstrate the deleterious effects of slavery on the region. The idea of two incompatible social and economic systems in the North and South found new life in the early twentieth century with Charles Beard's widely influential economic interpretation of America's past. Beard saw the Civil War as part of a deep conflict between agrarian and industrial interests and emphasized the tariff as an underlying source of conflict, a view that found favor with modern southern sympathizers eager to distance the Confederate cause from slavery. After World War II, the civil rights movement inspired new interest in the moral issues of slavery and racism underlying the sectional conflict, but this revival of interest in slavery focused attention on the plantation, and the urban middle class remained marginal to the main narrative of industrial versus agrarian slave society. Indeed, Wade's book on urban slavery was among the few that distracted attention from the agrarian South.

Eugene Genovese's widely influential book, *The Political Economy of Slavery* (1965), offered a fresh interpretation of the South and its planter elite. Genovese found a planter class imbued with a coherent worldview, one that embraced traditional values of paternalism and inequality that stood in firm opposition to the bourgeois values of the northern middle class, which celebrated the ideals of equality, free labor, and competition. Borrowing from Antonio Gramsci's theory of the cultural and ideological hegemony of ruling classes, Genovese argued that the planter class controlled the ideals as well as the economic wealth and political power of the Old South. In a section on "the subservience of town to country" Genovese argued that middle-class aspirations for industrial development were limited by the planter class's hegemonic control of economic wealth, political power, and ideology. Though his emphasis on paternalism in master-slave relationships drew the most fire from historians of slavery, Genovese's interpretation of the white middle class was no less significant for our understanding of the South, if only because he confirmed the popular understanding of this social element as marginal and impotent within the social hierarchy of the South.

The idea of a subordinate and compliant southern middle class had been central to the interpretation of Barrington Moore Jr., *Social Origins of Dictatorship and Democracy* (1966), a pioneering work in comparative historical social science. Moore argued that the American South followed a "Prussian Road" to modernization; its powerful landed elite, instead of giving way to a rising middle class, managed to ally with them and help build a modern industrial society based on authoritarian social arrangements central to which was the continued subjugation of former slaves. Genovese identified the antebellum antecedents to this class alliance in *Political Economy*, which appeared the following year. In *Social Origins of the New South* (1979) Jonathan Wiener elaborated the theory with a case study of Alabama and its "Black Belt-Big Mule" coalition of planters and industrialists, a southern counterpart to the German "Junker" landed class, which steered the New South toward an oppressive, anti-democratic version of modern society built on unfree black labor and on deliberate under development.

If most historians were willing to view the patterns of politics, violence, and poverty that emerged in the post–Civil War South as a tragic consequence of racism and reaction, it seemed to stretch matters to compare the situation in the American South to the social dynamics that gave birth to Nazi Germany. With all its illiberal manifestations of racism and its many efforts, legal and otherwise, to restrict basic civil rights and political participation, the American South was part of a democratic society whose Constitution at least contradicted the worst tendencies to deny freedoms extended to former slaves after the Civil War.

Despite repeated efforts to restrict the most basic freedoms to move about, change employers, and change locations, the post–Civil War South witnessed massive migration first within and eventually out of the region. Much of this migration involved southerners of both races forsaking rural life for jobs in the towns and cities of the South, and later the North. Not long after the Civil War and Reconstruction, the census revealed a massive and sustained movement from farm to town. During the twentieth century, the decline of European immigration during World War I set off a tremendous inter-regional migration mostly involving rural blacks moving to the industrial cities of the North. Known as the Great Migration, it actually consisted of two waves of movement (interrupted by the Great Depression) that caused about half of America's black population to move from South to North and from country to city.

None of this is to deny that the oppressive legacy of slavery remained evident in the towns and cities of the South long after emancipation. Insofar as segregation, its laws and customs, were largely a product of the South's urban environment, racism was probably more obvious in the daily life of urban southerners than it was for their rural counterparts. Whatever other distinctions marked southern cities, their economic bases, social customs, or politics, the urban South seemed, by and large, to be cut from much the same cloth as towns and cities elsewhere in America. Above all, the southern middle class, with its zealous celebration of individual success, its tireless campaigns for civic improvement, its optimistic boosterism, and, yes, with its racism too, seemed to replicate a quintessentially modern, American type.

This book of essays represents a multitude of fresh insights into the world inhabited by the southern middle class, covering a wide variety of urban settings and a broad stretch of time. It seems unlikely that the historical narrative of the South in the nineteenth century will be allowed to omit the role of the South's urban middle class in light of this achievement.

DON H. DOYLE
McCausland Professor of History
University of South Carolina

THE SOUTHERN MIDDLE CLASS
IN THE LONG NINETEENTH CENTURY

Introduction

JONATHAN DANIEL WELLS AND
JENNIFER R. GREEN

I n one of the most controversial books of the nineteenth century, Hinton Rowan Helper employed a language of class to bemoan the influence of slavery on the South. In *The Impending Crisis,* published in 1857, Helper used the term "class" more than two dozen times to explain the debilitating effects of bondage on the southern economy and society, especially the middle classes, by which he meant the professionals, skilled artisans, and merchants who lived mostly in the urban South. Helper's confidence in employing the term "middle class" reflected a general consensus on its meaning in the nineteenth-century South. By the 1850s, southerners themselves understood such a group to comprise commercial and professional interests, including bankers, merchants, doctors, teachers, lawyers, editors, dentists, and the clergy. In public and private discourse, southerners frequently used the term "middle class," often to assert the vital importance of this social grouping to all societies, free and slave. Indeed, southerners remarked in Fourth of July orations, political pamphlets, commercial reports, newspapers, and literary magazines that republics were particularly reliant on the stable, sober influence of the middle class, which stood between the whims of the mob and the greedy overreaching of the elite.

Despite the belief in the importance of the middle class among nineteenth-century southerners themselves, historians have until recently thought this group largely unworthy of scholarly attention. Frank Owsley's *The Plain Folk of the Old South* (1949) was among the first studies to move beyond the plantation to examine ordinary white southerners. But Owsley focused on rural farmers and yeomen, devoting little space to commercial or professional southerners. In the scholarship of the 1970s and 1980s, the perception prevailed that the region either had no middle class, or that it was, in the words of

Eugene Genovese, "tied to the slaveholding interest," with "little desire or opportunity to invest capital in industrial expansion, and adopted the prevailing aristocratic attitudes."[1] In the 1990s, ground-breaking work, such as Bill Cecil-Fronsman's *Common Whites: Class and Culture in Antebellum North Carolina* (1992) and James Oakes's *The Ruling Race: A History of American Slaveholders* (1998), demonstrated that we still had an incomplete picture of the region's social structure.[2] While Cecil-Fronsman studied plain folk, Oakes sought to refine our understanding of the antebellum southern social hierarchy by emphasizing the fact that many slaveholders were small farmers, owning fewer than five slaves, who sought upward social mobility.

Oakes's contribution was important, for it helped to chip away at the notion that the Old South harbored a truncated social structure of only planters and slaves. Indeed, recent work has suggested that our understanding of the region could be greatly deepened by examining professional and commercial interests more intently. Jonathan Daniel Wells's *The Origins of the Southern Middle Class, 1800–1861* (2004) argued that urban, white professional southerners came together as a self-conscious class by the late antebellum era, with important consequences for the region and the coming of the Civil War. Examining those members who were objectively in the middle of the southern social hierarchy, as well as taking into account the more subjective cultural construction of class, Wells argued that professional and commercial southerners came together ideologically as a self-identified middle class in the 1850s. *The Origins of the Southern Middle Class* concluded that middle-class southerners were shaped by their interaction with northern counterparts as much as they were by internal economic forces. Because of the extensive cultural and intellectual ties with the North, the South did not have to become fully industrialized or urbanized before a middle class could take root.

Several important studies have recently helped to refine and build upon our understanding of the southern middle class while also reigniting the debate over whether the South was capitalist or pre-capitalist. Frank J. Byrne's insightful study *Becoming Bourgeois* (2006) highlighted merchants in the mid-nineteenth-century South as integral components of the increasingly diversified social strata of the region. Tom Downey's *Planting a Capitalist South* (2006) and Bruce W. Eelman's *Entrepreneurs in the Southern Upcountry* (2008) found that the South was already making inroads into industrialization long before the Civil War, a movement exemplified by William Gregg's factory in Graniteville and businessmen in Spartanburg, South Carolina.[3] These works locate southerners who despite slavery managed to encourage economic and cultural modernization. They do not lead us to conclude that the Old South was entirely capitalistic or devoid of pre-modern proclivities. Rather, the notion that the nineteenth-century South harbored considerable differentiation within the white community needs to be incorporated into the broader understanding of the nineteenth-century South.

The notion of a planter or aristocratic hegemony in the nineteenth century has been further eroded by new works that have helped us to refine our knowledge of the South's social structure, culture, and political economy. Path-breaking works such as Johanna Miller Lewis's *Artisans in the North Carolina Backcountry* (1995) and Michele Gillespie's *Free Labor in an Unfree World* (2000) opened up the study of working-class whites and artisans to scholars, and the field continued to grow with the publication of L. Diane Barnes's *Artisan Workers in the Upper South* (2008) and Seth Rockman's *Scraping By* (2009). Social fluidity allowed some of these artisans to enter the middle classes, although recent studies suggest that fewer men could ascend as the antebellum years advanced. Clearly, white and black laborers remained below the rank of middle class.

Recent studies that emphasize internal southern divisions have continued to complicate our understanding of the region's society and political economy. Frank Towers's *The Urban South and the Coming of the Civil War* (2004) and William A. Link's *Roots of Secession* (2003) underscored the geographical divisions within the region. While Towers identified a distinctly urban political culture that was often led by the middle class, Link stressed the East-West divisions of Virginia. William Freehling's recent books also point to significant Upper South/Lower South differences.[4] At the same time, historians are beginning to emphasize divisions within the Civil War and postbellum South. This volume encompasses the war years, although no essay traces the southern middle class during the war, since other studies have recently addressed these divisions.[5] So just as scholars were considering class divisions within the Old South, so too were historians like Link and Towers calling attention to the political divisions that arose over spatial differences. Not surprisingly, professional and commercial southerners were centered in urban areas, although not exclusively. Consequently, most of our essays focus on the urban South, especially in established states, although expanding industry on the frontier was also an important site of southern middle-class development in the antebellum years.

This volume seeks to build on the new scholarship on the southern middle class while also breaking new ground. Class formation, as scholars have discovered, is an evolutionary process. The twelve original essays included here highlight the change over time that allowed men and women sharing certain occupations, status, and ideology—early nineteenth-century southerners in the middle social and economic position—to coalesce into an emerging middle class and eventually a class "for itself."[6] (See Martin Ruef's essay for more discussion of this terminology in the social sciences.) The editors recognize that examining a class means taking a historical snapshot of a group in the process of forming and, thus, constantly in flux. The essays that follow illuminate southerners who did or would comprise the nineteenth-century middle class at specific moments and in specific locations.

The recognition that class formation is a process has led authors, including those in the present volume, to employ terms such as the "southern middle class," "emerging middle class," "middle class*es*," and "middling" ranks. What terminology they use depends on where scholars locate their work within that process, how they define class, and what analyses they are performing. When analyzing segments within the group, as does Ruef in this volume, use of the terminology "middle classes" identifies segments within the class that had their own coherence. Yet all of the terms imply an ideologically cohesive, broader social group that shared cultural and socioeconomic characteristics.

When approaching the southern middle class, scholars face the difficulty of defining the group and the terminology used to do so. In our estimation, the fundamental definition of the southern middle class centers on the categories of occupation, status, wealth, cultural traits, and (in order for complete identification as a class) consciousness. The essays in this volume focus on all or different of these definitional aspects. Many theorists influence our understanding of class, but most significantly the production-based Marxist conception demands scholars examine occupation and resources, whereas Weberian influences direct us to examine status and access to goods. The vast scholarship on the northern middle class (often mislabeled the "American middle class") provides important definitional categories for all scholarship on the national (and regional) middle class.[7] As the first anthology on the southern middle class, this volume hopes to advance the process of defining the group. Presenting a concrete, inflexible definition of the group for all scholars to use in perpetuity would be a wonderful contribution to scholarship but this is as yet impossible; consider that variable definitions of planters, yeomen, and plain folk—social categories that have been under scrutiny for decades—still exist.

Our definitional starting point represents the consensus among contemporaries, such as Helper, as well as among current scholars. Using a definition based on occupation is the most common and the easiest way to trace the middle economic and social ranks. Occupation provided men, their families, and later women with particular levels of status and wealth. Herein, the majority of essays focus on the occupational definition of the southern middle class. Ruef presents a table that indicates the basic occupational categories in use throughout this volume and reflects the available data from the nineteenth-century census (see page 000). The professional, non-manual facets of an occupation certainly mattered, as did its nonagricultural nature, which separated the middle class from yeomen and plain folk. Samuel Hyde Jr. suggested that middle-class antebellum southerners could be part of the agricultural component of the plain folk, and this volume definitionally asserts otherwise.[8] Scholars, including those in this volume, are still analyzing how Oakes's "middle-class slaveholders" with dual agricultural and professional occupations fit into the middle class. Thus relying on occupation to determine class is not entirely without problems. Jennifer Green's essay suggests that some professionals could be planters' sons biding their time until they could afford land and slaves, and Ruef points out that it is nearly impossible to differentiate between some classes or occupations in census data (for example, teachers versus entrepreneurial school owners). Aggregates of occupations provide the best examination of trends (specifically if scholars rely on census data), and we hope scholars continue to fill in the details of those aggregates as these essays do. This volume suggests both ways to expand scholarly consideration of the southern middle class (including factory managers and supervisors) and potentially ways to limit it (evaluating lawyers' or planters' sons' circumstances).

A second definitional characteristic of the group is status, mostly prestige conveyed by occupation and other middle-class traits in the nineteenth century. Resources above those available to plain folk or yeomen contributed to making men middling rank and suggests their status and class position. Ruef successfully uses wealth as a marker of middle-class status as data available from the census; however, individuals in the studies of John Deal, Susanna Delfino, Angela Lakwete, Frank Towers, and Bruce Eelman point to the difficulty in defining members of the middle class when it comes to wealth. Some men problematize simple classification by owning many slaves and possessing wealth that might suggest a class standing well above a middle economic rank. It is important to acknowledge that in the prewar nineteenth-century South economic capital was not the only, nor even the primary, division between the classes. In addition to white racism excluding African Americans from middle-class status before Emancipation, wealth could not gain a man the social status provided by planting. In order to examine the situation of individuals, then, scholars should analyze more than their income or wealth. One aspect of this issue begs the question of the significance of slave ownership to middle-class families. As antebellum southerners, middle-class men generally accepted slavery and some employed slave labor in their commercial enterprises or in their homes; we encourage explorations on how they understood their class position in opposition to these bondspeople and how the possession of human property affected their class ranking.

A final major characteristic of the southern middle class is the exhibition of similar cultural traits. Essays by Jennifer Goloboy, Amanda Reece Mushal, and Sonya Ramsey focus on this aspect of the group across the long nineteenth century; essays by Sally Hadden and Deal examine associational behavior that also reflects those values. Studies of the middle class in the North have well detailed the cultural traits of that group, and the southern part of the class certainly reflected the existence of a national middle class with shared cultural traits.[9] The strength of regional differences within the nineteenth century demands, however, that scholars acknowledge the group's identity as southern, certainly in its proslavery beliefs.

Indeed, the central role religion played in the northern middle class still needs to be explored at the level of class in the South; works such as Christine Heyrman's *Southern Cross* (1997) and Peter S. Carmichael's *The Last Generation* (2005) suggest its presence in the Old South as strongly as in the North. Education was also central to the ideology of professional and commercial

Americans, regardless of location or race. Linking these themes, Beth Barton Schweiger's *The Gospel Working Up* (2000) identifies the importance of education in Virginian ministers' careers and values that coincided with those of the middle class. And in studying the educational experiences, ideological development, and careers of hundreds of military cadets, Jennifer R. Green's *Military Education and the Emerging Middle Class in the Old South* (2008) has added significantly to the reanalysis of class and class formation within the region. Green uses the antebellum South's military schools to add notions of manhood and self-discipline to our evolving understanding of the southern middle class; she demonstrates how important education was in solidifying middle-class values and securing employment after graduation. The social connections formed during years at school were seminal for the emerging middle class in particular, for professional and personal relationships formed at school proved instrumental later in landing business opportunities. We encourage the scholars now addressing the dearth of southern antebellum educational history to explicate education's connections to class development in the South; the work of Kim Tolley and Nancy Beadie has provided a foundation in their examinations of non-elite schooling and teaching.[10]

Literacy formed the foundation for professional careers, especially in the use of practical subjects rather than classical schooling, and both black and white southerners used schooling to attain middle-class status.[11] Building on earlier works, such as James D. Anderson's *The Education of Blacks in the South* (1988), recent studies like Heather Andrea Williams's *Self-Taught: African American Education in Slavery and Freedom* (2007) have stressed the ways in which blacks understood education as the path to social, economic, and intellectual advancement. Sonya Ramsey's *Reading, Writing, and Segregation* (2008) and Adam Fairclough's *A Class of Their Own* (2007) have emphasized education as a fundamentally important path to improvement, as well as a boon to the growing phalanx of middle-class teachers.

Scholarship on the black middle class in the later nineteenth-century South promises equally fruitful paths to understanding the group in its largest scope. Durham, North Carolina, once referred to as "the capital of the black middle class," has been well studied by historians searching for the roots of professional and commercial black southerners. Robert C. Kenzer's *Enterprising Southerners* (1997) and Leslie Brown's *Upbuilding Black Durham* (2008) have added significantly to the emerging historiography on nineteenth-century middle-class African Americans. Kenzer focused on important black businessmen, while Brown's study offered important and fresh insights into the roles of black women. Significantly, Brown also identifies tensions within the black southern social structure, as middle-class notions of respectability allowed them to distinguish themselves from the black working class.

Even with the significant progress made recently in our understanding of the white and black southern social structure, however, much more work remains to be done and fundamental questions persist. Should scholars be examining two parallel social systems, one rural and the other urban? Or does the considerable economic and cultural interaction between rural and urban areas warrant consideration of a single social structure? How large and influential was the incipient class of industrialists? What role did professional organizations such as medical societies, dental societies, lawyers' guilds, and teachers' associations play in the formation of a middle class? For those interested in continuing to facilitate our knowledge of the white southern middle class, opportunities and research questions abound. We still lack even a basic grasp of how the emerging white and black middle classes interacted with each other, or how they shaped each other's formation and development. We also need greater insight into the lives and careers of black professionals; for example, the rich archives of southern black newspapers testify to a vigorous and lively black press. Similar to the avenues still open for exploration on African Americans entering the southern middle class in the postbellum years, the roles of ethnic groups can also expand our knowledge of segments of the middle class. For example, a small Jewish population worked in mercantile and commercial occupations, concentrated in the urban areas where the antebellum emerging southern middle class thrived.[12] We look forward to future studies that illuminate these and other segments of the southern middle class in the nineteenth century and how ethnicity, religion, region, race, and gender shaped people's entrance into and understanding of class and social position.

The hope is that the essays that follow continue to raise our appreciation for analyzing the white and black middle classes of the nineteenth-century South. Drawn from the work of younger scholars as well as established historians and sociologists, the essays provide ample evidence that nineteenth-century southern studies remains a young and lively field, and that the middle class has offered fertile ground for reexamining the nature of race, class, and gender in this complicated region. Arranged chronologically, the essays cover both the Old and New Souths, and a range of topics, individuals, and regions within the South. Much of the evidence in the essays comes from South Carolina, providing case studies of individuals and specific communities in the Palmetto State. As the arch defender of states' rights and secession, that state provides an interesting place in which to study the dynamics of a social system in flux. While the book divides its focus almost equally between the Southeast and the South as a whole, Delfino's and Lakwete's essays in particular offer insight into the vast potential for work on the middle class in the Southwest, border South, and Deep South. Although not fully comprehensive of the southern middle class in the nineteenth century, these essays provide original research as they also suggest new paths for scholarship.

Our first consideration of the southern middle class in the long nineteenth century examines merchants in post-Revolutionary Charleston, South Carolina. Two essays by Sally Hadden and Jennifer Goloboy consider these merchants' position in the incipient middle class. First, Hadden examines the Charleston chamber of commerce to describe the system of arbitration and business organization that commercial men developed after the Revolution. Those merchants worked with planters and wholesaled their rice crops but, as men required to sully themselves in the daily labor of commerce, never attained status equal to that of planters. The merchants' common aspiration to attain plantation and slave ownership suggests their incipient middle-class status, in an era when the middle ranks did not consistently strive to professionalize and legitimate their own values, occupations, and beliefs. These merchants of the early Republic banded together to protect their businesses and reputations, both to separate themselves from lower-status clerks and retailers and to aid their own success.

Investigating some of the same Charleston merchants as Hadden and carrying them into the pre–War of 1812 economic boom, Goloboy stresses the cultural components of the developing middle class. Her investigation problematizes some scholars' general assertions of the virtuousness of the middle class. As the ranks of early nineteenth-century merchants expanded through economic development and success, such businessmen drew criticism over their questionable business practices as well as over their ethnicity and non-southern origin. In this early period, many of the merchants in Charleston were indeed foreigners, seen as outsiders by South Carolinians whether they were British or northern. As planters sought to separate themselves from those of lower status—those men engaged in work or a profession—they focused on that foreignness to denigrate merchants, an image that cast a shadow well into the century.

The next few essays continue to explore the connections and ideologies middle-rank southerners formed in the early decades of the 1800s. Finding members of the class where they were known to exist in northern society, John Deal and Amanda Reece Mushal examine the social worlds of these southerners. Deal describes how middle-class men and women in Norfolk, Virginia, funded benevolent societies to elevate the poor and themselves, demonstrating that the values of the national middle class were found in that southern port city. He suggests that the members of the associations—neither the poor nor the wealthy—joined together to solidify their values and possibly to attempt to inculcate them in others. Deal suggests that the growing southern middle class sought connections within their group and with the rest of their community, particularly in ways that helped their businesses and provided for self-improvement, and that the associations perpetuated their class identity. Similarly using southerners' social world in a smaller urban area, Mushal examines the networks of associations between planters and merchants and those among merchants themselves. Her essay analyzes marriage and social visitation in Camden, South Carolina. Similar to Deal's Virginia findings, Mushal discovers that associations in South Carolina bound middle-class men of similar occupations together and to their social superiors. In particular middle-class merchants found themselves in a unique position, one that seemingly made their connection to the elite both easier and more difficult. Rather than finding strict class boundaries, the number of marriages between commercial and planting households suggests a complex interplay between the groups throughout the antebellum years.

Focusing more on class formation and the manufacturing occupations that make up the antebellum middle class, Susanna Delfino and Angela Lakwete explore the iron, textile, and gin manufacturers of the increasingly industrial South. Together their works illuminate the developing world of industry, with different segments of people working in it and different business and economic structures being developed. Delfino concludes that native-born southern managers, superintendents, and clerks in factories need to be considered as part of the emerging middle class and that they provided occupations for the growth of white-collar workers in the Old South. In both the textile and iron industries, native southerners moved into managerial positions; these men expanded the middle class and southern industry. Lakwete unearths a complicated set of business partnerships and identifies complex economic development in the 1830s, earlier than usually described in scholarship. The Aikin brothers in Mississippi and Alabama succeeded in the professions as manufacturer, merchant, and lawyer, respectively. The brothers most identified with their nonagricultural middle-class occupations regardless of their land and slave ownership. Like Delfino's managers, the middle class of this era centrally defined itself in non-manual, nonagricultural occupations.

Starting from a similar case study of three brothers, Jennifer Green concurs with Lakwete's conclusion that occupation and aspiration should be central to an analysis of the emerging southern middle class. The interconnected relationships of the South Carolina Jenkins brothers lead her to conclude that the development of the middle class was never linear and that professionals in the Old South could have been more connected to their elite kin than to the emerging middle class. Planters' ideals of social status and mobility conflicted with the middle class's rejection of a path to success through land and slave ownership; members of the middle social and economic rank instead began to define social mobility through professional means, just as Lakwete's Aikin brothers did. Thus the essays by Delfino, Lakwete, and Green build a consideration of occupation into that of culture in the examination of the class.

The middle class's political views united the group with similar values and examining their confrontation with secession leads the volume into the Civil War. Frank Towers concludes that southern middle-class men stressed antiparty ideals despite holding office more often in urban areas than their population numbers in the cities might suggest. Their middling status in southern society led them to accept secession, as did the white yeomanry, and to ally more with planters than with the working class from whom they tried to separate themselves. Their influence and participation in politics varied by size of town and the concentration of the class with the location; Towers compares the political situations of middle-class residents in cities, towns, and rural areas. His work again suggests that scholars must consider the group within its regional context and within its national context.

Taking the middle class from the antebellum into the postwar years, Martin Ruef considers entrepreneurial and bureaucratic occupations separately and evaluates the role of geographic location in the class's presence. Employing sociological methodology and statistical data, Ruef sees the formation of a distinctive white southern middle class beginning in the 1850s that had reached maturity by 1890. What made the southern middle class separate from their peers? Ruef focuses on literacy, wealth (real estate and personal assets), and access to schooling and banks. His work provides a bridge across the Civil War from a class "in itself" beginning to coalescence as a class "for itself" and sets the stage for the coherence of the middle class across the regions.

Offering close examinations of the Reconstruction period, essays by Jonathan Daniel Wells and Bruce Eelman show the postwar white southern middle class attempting to reestablish its trade connections to the North and its professional status. Wells illustrates the difficulty the white middle class experienced in making the transition from war to the New South. The postwar atmosphere vacillated between hope for (industrial and commercial) prosperity and resignation. In turn, southerners alternately praised the group for its positive traits, especially its emphasis on hard work, while simultaneously condemning its members as materialistic. Indeed, increasing professionalization troubled southerners—ringing with wartime connotations of "traitor"— but more, the southern middle class demanded the legitimation of the professions and were coming to dominate them rather than planters' sons with agricultural aspirations. Within the contentious atmosphere Wells described, upcountry industry fought to (re)establish itself according to Eelman. He stresses how manufacturers used the traditional southern values of farming to promote their enterprises. Their calls to connect industrial and agricultural interests succeeded with increased industrialization and growth by the late 1870s. Industrialists' mixed views of the Ku Klux Klan—acknowledging how the organization both aided and hindered their aspirations—suggest the difficulties of negotiating the complicated times to restore business and strengthen the developing middle class. The evidence of both these essays demonstrates that no teleological path existed between the antebellum middle ranks and the powerful middle class of the New South, but that continuity certainly existed.

Sonya Ramsey demonstrates how Reconstruction and the last decades of the nineteenth century brought African Americans into the southern middle class. While African American men made gains in the professions, women—especially, but not exclusively, African Americans—found entry into a middle class primarily concerned with occupation difficult. Ramsey investigates the small number of African American women who successfully found their ways into the roles of teachers and community leaders. Seeking to influence society, as the white middle class had been doing for decades prior, these African American women stressed the importance of religion, education, service, chastity, conservative dress, and proper housekeeping standards to mark the cultural boundaries of their middle-class status.

Don Doyle set the tone for the volume by reminding all of us that we stand on the shoulders of important work on class and the South that goes back decades even as we examine new groups and topics. As Jim Oakes notes in his Epilogue, there is much more work to be done to enhance our understanding of the southern middle class and its very southernness holds valuable points of analysis. Furthermore, even as recent scholarship has improved our insight into the lives and careers of middle-class whites, the work to comprehend the developing nineteenth-century black middle class is just beginning.

NOTES

1. Eugene Genovese, *The Political Economy of Slavery: Studies in the Economy and Society of the Slave South* (New York: Pantheon Books, 1965), 20.

2. Of course, other works helped to pioneer southern studies into the social ranks between planter and slave; see, for example, Bell Wiley, *The Plain People of the Confederacy* (Baton Rouge: Louisiana State University Press, 1943); William Kauffman Scarborough, *The Overseer: Plantation Management in the Old South* (Baton Rouge: Louisiana State University Press, 1966); J. Wayne Flynt, *Poor but Proud: Alabama's Poor Whites* (Tuscaloosa: University of Alabama Press, 1989); Charles C. Bolton, *Poor Whites of the Antebellum South* (Durham: Duke University Press, 1994).

3. For further insight into merchant and manufacturing roles during the war, see Harold S. Wilson, *Confederate Industry: Manufacturers and Quartermasters in the Civil War* (Jackson: University Press of Mississippi, 2005). Also see Susanna Delfino and Michele Gillespie, eds.,

Global Perspectives on Industrial Transformation in the American South (Columbia: University of Missouri Press, 2005) and *Technology, Innovation, and Southern Industrialization* (Columbia: University of Missouri Press, 2008), and Sean Patrick Adams, *Old Dominion, Industrial Commonwealth: Coal, Politics, and Economy in Antebellum America* (Baltimore: Johns Hopkins University Press, 2004).

4. See William Freehling, *The South vs. the South* (New York: Oxford University Press, 2001) and *The Road to Disunion: Secessionists Triumphant, 1854–1861* (New York: Oxford University Press, 2008).

5. James Alex Baggett, *The Scalawags* (Baton Rouge: Louisiana State University Press, 2003); Margaret M. Storey, *Loyalty and Loss* (Baton Rouge: Louisiana State University Press, 2004); John Inscoe and Robert C. Kenzer, eds., *Enemies of the Country: New Perspectives on Unionists in the Civil War South* (Athens: University of Georgia Press, 2004); Mark V. Wetherington, *Plain Folk's Fight* (Chapel Hill: University of North Carolina Press, 2005); Hyman Rubin III, *South Carolina Scalawags* (Columbia: University of South Carolina Press, 2006).

6. See, for example, Burton J. Bledstein and Robert D. Johnson, eds., *The Middling Sort: Explorations in the History of the American Middle Class* (New York: Routledge, 2001), and Jonathan Daniel Wells, *The Origins of the Southern Middle Class, 1800–1861* (Chapel Hill: University of North Carolina Press, 2004).

7. Wells, *Origins of the Southern Middle Class;* Stuart M. Blumin, "The Hypothesis of the Middle-Class Formation in Nineteenth-Century America: A Critique and Some Proposals," *American Historical Review* 90 (1985): 299–338 and *The Emergence of the Middle Class: Social Experience in the American City, 1760–1900* (New York: Cambridge University Press, 1989); Michael B. Katz, "Occupational Classification in History," *Journal of Interdisciplinary History* 3 (Summer 1972): 63–88; Jennifer R. Green, *Military Education and the Emerging Middle Class in the Old South* (New York: Cambridge University Press, 2008), ch. 8, 230.

8. Samuel C. Hyde Jr., "*Plain Folk* Reconsidered: Historiographical Ambiguity in Search of Definition," *Journal of Southern History* 71 (November 2005): esp. 813.

9. In recent decades and continuing as a productive field, scholars have produced valuable work on southern manhood, including the differences and similarities between classes and regions; see, among others, studies by John Mayfield, Steven Stowe, Stephen Berry, Lorri Glover, Craig Thompson Friend, Amy Greenberg, and most recently Ami Pflugrad-Jackisch.

10. Tolley and Beadie, "Socioeconomic Incentives to Teach in New York and North Carolina: Toward a More Complex Model of Teacher Labor Markets, 1800–1850," *History of Education Quarterly* 46 (Spring 2006) and, eds., *Chartered Schools* (New York: Routledge, 2002). Most studies of early southern education focus on elite college students; see, for example, Robert F. Pace, *Halls of Honor* (Baton Rouge: Louisiana State University Press, 2004), and Lorri Glover, *Southern Sons* (Baltimore: Johns Hopkins University Press, 2007).

11. Christie Anne Farnham, *The Education of the Southern Belle* (New York: New York University Press, 1995), and Kim Tolley, *The Science Education of American Girls* (New York: Routledge, 2002) excellently detail curricula for southern females, some of whom demonstrated middle-class resources to obtain their education and took courses in the increasingly available practical subjects, such as English and bookkeeping.

12. Recent works on this topic include Marcie Cohen Ferris and Mark I. Greenberg, eds., *Jewish Roots in Southern Soil: A New History* (Waltham, Mass.: Brandeis University Press, 2006), and Mark K. Bauman, *Dixie Diaspora: An Anthology of Southern Jewish History* (Tuscaloosa: University of Alabama Press, 2006).

The Business of Justice

Merchants in the Charleston Chamber of Commerce and Arbitration in the 1780s and 1790s

SALLY E. HADDEN

[handwritten annotation: Really? you're gonna start with "nowadays"? Really]

Nowadays, the chamber of commerce evokes a variety of images—luncheons once a week for car dealers and merchants who own stores, possibly small-town Americans coming together for financial advantages by striking deals behind the scenes. The images are social, deal-making, but hardly legal in nature. There might be a temptation to lump the chamber in with various voluntary associations, like the Rotary or Kiwanis, but those philanthropic groups were born from a very different beginning, a twentieth-century origin that emphasized service to others over profit. Writers like H. L. Mencken and Sinclair Lewis helped create a caricatured vision of clubs that painted all clubmen as shallow conformists, who joined groups for the sake of joining—a vision of club members that persists in some minds to the present day.[1] No matter what image one has of the chamber of commerce, it is probably not a group frequently thought of in association with alternative dispute resolution.[2] The chamber of commerce today, however, is a far cry from the chamber of commerce as it existed in the eighteenth century.[3] In Charleston, South Carolina, merchants of the early national period turned to the chamber to mediate both local and long-distance financial quarrels. They did this so that they could avoid the costly proceedings of local trials that would only tie up their capital and prevent them from making more profits as quickly as possible. Their reliance on the chamber to resolve disputes was rooted in centuries of tradition, and was likewise an expression of the growing importance of civil society in early America.[4] It also reflected a desire for stability in a changing milieu of economic growth, one fraught with bankruptcies and pitfalls that businessmen had to avoid, if, as commercially wary men, they were also to take advantage of new, emerging trade opportunities.

awful sentence

Whether establishing a chamber of commerce could increase commercial stability in a time when currency fluctuations and business failures were common was a gamble, one that wealthier merchants may have been willing to take.[5] Some, perhaps, knew of similar mercantile associations that had long existed in Europe.

Merchants in Europe had well-established trading networks and business associations by the Middle Ages and had likewise developed the *lex mercatoria,* laws that effectively bound traders to certain standards of reciprocal good behavior.[6] The "law merchant," as it was known, "governed a special class of people (merchants) in special places (fairs, markets, and seaports); and it also governed mercantile relations in cities and towns," sustaining commercial courts and setting out rules of acceptable trading behavior.[7] The "law merchant" eventually came to serve as a foundation for modern commercial law throughout the Western world. In Europe, the good will engendered by traders who respected each other and traded fairly became the root of trust behind *lex mercatoria,* and Charleston merchants, particularly those who traded overseas, knew the "law merchant" as a body of principles guiding their conduct. In areas where the *lex mercatoria* did not reach, coalitions of traders operated with agents, relying upon the benefits of membership in the coalition to guarantee for proper conduct in trades present and future.[8] Establishing a reputation for fair dealing brought in additional trading partners, despite long distances between both buyers and sellers. The uncertainty and complexity of trade could be limited or done away with if known associates were employed or men traded only with individuals who demonstrated that they could be trusted. When they could not find reliable trading partners (and sometimes even if they could), merchants spread their risks by diversification.

The quest for reliability and a steady return on investments marked the behavior of merchants through the centuries, while preventing or circumventing litigation was almost as commonplace. Traders wished to avoid going to court to resolve trade disputes, for litigation was costly and time-consuming, and assumed that an unfaithful trading partner (who might long before have skipped town) was still in place to be brought to justice.[9] Advice manuals and business handbooks for merchants in the seventeenth and eighteenth centuries, printed in many European countries, counseled against lawsuits and legal entanglements as both expensive and detrimental to the greatest profits.[10] As trade networks spread across the Atlantic in the early modern period, merchants and dealers on both sides of the Atlantic depended upon the basic concepts found in *lex mercatoria*.

Merchants did not rely upon the "law merchant" alone to safeguard their investments; they began to create trade associations that crossed traditional guild lines, allying commercial dealers of many commodities for their mutual trading benefit. The first group to be called a "chamber of commerce" appeared in Marseilles in 1599.[11] In France, most major trading cities established chambers of commerce during the eighteenth century, often at the behest of the royal government.[12] Similar associations began to appear elsewhere, as merchant traders organized into protective groups that also engaged in self-policing. Through the seventeenth and eighteenth centuries, in growing cities along the Atlantic rim, like New York, Boston, Philadelphia, and Charleston, the largest merchants realized that one or two deals poorly handled could give their trading center a negative reputation. A few bad apples might detract from the quality or quantity of deals to be made. Reputation had to be safe-guarded among high-profile merchants, like wholesalers, for a positive reputation for fair dealing could attract new business, while a negative reputation would quickly repel potential business deals.[13] First in New York, then Boston and Philadelphia, and later Charleston, eighteenth-century merchants banded together to form the earliest chambers of commerce in America.

This chronological development is somewhat odd. Charleston was, in the seventeenth century, the largest city in North America, surpassed by Boston in size at the start of the eighteenth century. Philadelphia and New York eventually overtook both Boston and Charleston by mid-century, with New York clearly pulling ahead in population by the 1790s. A survey of dwellings in major American cities in 1786 reported that Philadelphia had 4600 homes, New York 3500, Boston 2100, and Charleston 1540.[14] One can only speculate about why New York's merchants chose to organize themselves so much earlier than their counterparts in larger cities, but it may have been the presence of active Dutch traders interacting with a large body of English traders that spurred them into action.[15] Philadelphia's concentrated population of Quaker merchants, who were already familiar with arbitration through the Society of Friends for the resolution of interpersonal disputes, quite logically gravitated to the creation of a chamber in the eighteenth century for similar reasons.[16]

Boston apparently formed a trade association of merchants in order to protest imperial trade regulations, and many city-based merchants in the American colonies were beginning to exhibit group consciousness about the benefits to be derived from acting collectively by the time of the Revolution.[17]

A possible reason why Charlestonian merchants took so long to create a chamber of commerce—formed in 1773 and becoming consistently active only after the Revolution in 1784—may have been because of the region's export monoculture: rice.[18] So long as the port's largest traders were focused upon one principal export crop, this may have precluded the need for a chamber to develop.[19] With a limited number of rice wholesalers on both sides of the Atlantic, it may have been marginally easier for merchants to assess the creditworthiness of and prevent mistakes with their trading partners, even at a distance. Charleston's network of ties to Barbados, Liverpool, and London through families in trade may have also delayed the development of a chamber, for family ties would enhance the likelihood that business disputes could be resolved outside of the formal channels associated with courts.[20] Approximately three hundred merchants lived and worked in Charleston in the latter part of the eighteenth century.[21]

Following the American Revolution, when Charleston was no longer occupied by British military forces, normal, prewar trading patterns that favored the large-scale import and export of staple products began to resume. In Charleston, merchants who engaged in commercial trade on a grand scale re-formed the chamber of commerce in 1784.[22] The first gathering of this re-established group occurred January 23 at six o'clock at the City Tavern, and was open to both "former members, and other Merchants, who are Citizens of America, and the Merchant subjects of our foreign allies."[23] It is unclear whether they were inspired by the activities of the chambers formed in other American cities or abroad, but these merchant men desired to restrict their membership to those engaged in friendly, not hostile, shipping. Following the tradition of European merchants who had banded together for mutual aid and support for hundreds of years, these Charlestonians sought the assistance of other traders to resolve problems and grant legitimacy to their activities, while simultaneously promoting the fortunes of all. As they wrote in their founding statement and list of rules, "any attempt to extend Commerce, encourage Industry, and adjust disputes relative to Trade and Navigation must deserve the approbation of every well wisher to his country." They therefore agreed to gather the largest merchants for monthly meetings where they could debate important questions, collect money that could then be lent out on interest, and resolve disputes that were put into their care. The chamber's founders intended to offer their arbitration services to nonmembers as well as each other. The chamber began meeting monthly in the Exchange Coffee-House, on the bay, on Wednesdays. Quarterly sessions featured business meetings that started at eleven in the morning, with dinner served afterward, at three in the afternoon. In later years, anniversary dinners were held at the beginning of the year to commemorate the first founding meeting.[24]

Originally, the group had a restricted membership, thirteen men in all, for only the largest and best-established merchants decided to join, which was slightly different from the practice in other American cities.[25] In New York, as in Boston, the chambers of commerce attracted many members, often with triple the numbers of those admitted to the Charleston chamber. The chamber of commerce in Charleston may not have served precisely the same social function as the chamber in New York, which was far more inclusive and took in merchants who were not at the very top of the trading community. Had sociability been paramount, the Charleston chamber would undoubtedly have contained more members. The original thirteen members in Charleston comprised the elite of the mercantile community; although these men were merchants, not planters in the grand style, they were far from the petty traders or common dealers in household wares.[26] Ten of the original thirteen chamber members would serve a term or more in the South Carolina House of Representatives, or the state Senate, an honor reserved by South Carolinians for the most influential men in their state.[27]

Chamber membership was a means of demarking status within the ranks of commercial traders, to distinguish those men in the upper echelon.[28] Charleston's lowly peddlers and simple shopkeepers, who numbered in the hundreds, were not permitted to join the chamber. The restrictive aspect of membership set apart the upper tier of merchants from those below them, suggesting that chamber members wished to be considered better than those simply "in trade." Import/export wholesalers, who comprised the chamber's earliest members, typically had the closest contact with planters—the state's upper class—and well-to-do slave owners who resided in town. Among the chamber's charter members were several slave owners, and even traders in slaves, like John Lewis Gervais, Daniel Bourdeaux, and William Logan.[29] Gervais and Bourdeaux owned land outside Charleston and speculated in the land market, but made their year-round homes in the city and acquired their fortunes through commerce. Logan, another founding chamber member, was owner of seven trading ships and partner in two more, but owned only fifteen slaves at the time of his death, despite having traded slaves extensively prior to the Revolution. Joseph Atkinson, a former business partner of Bourdeaux's, was likewise a large land owner outside Charleston and owner of more than sixty slaves. Like so many of these merchants, another chamber member, Robert Pringle, practiced several occupations at once—overseas trader, physician, and politician—but he derived the bulk of his wealth from his overseas trading connections.

All of these men had close ties to the planter class. For instance, John Lewis Gervais supervised Henry Laurens's estates when the Revolutionary leader was absent from South Carolina at the Continental Congress.[30] Through their trade and personal relationships with planters, these chamber members developed extensive contacts in the backcountry and earned the trust of residents there, such that they were regularly elected to the state assembly. As the legislature met in Charleston, city residents were frequently called upon to represent a remote district; on the part of voters, this was not only an exercise in parsimony, but required faith in the judgment of the men chosen as well as some sense of their moral character. As such, election represented a tacit approval by other members in society that these men were considered upright, fair in their dealings, and knowledgeable about affairs outside of Charleston.

Yet chamber members were not on par with the planters, whose interests they often served publicly in the legislature and privately through the administration of their estates or the provision of goods or slaves to support their plantations. Among all occupations in eighteenth-century South Carolina, planters could earn the greatest return on their wealth (through their slaves' labor), while not having to "dirty their hands" in the business of daily commerce. The removal of planters from the day-to-day activities of commercial life formed a dividing line—of occupation, outlook, and behavior—between that group and the men who were full-time merchants regardless of the riches they accumulated. In southern society, planters were the men of the upper class; merchants, even the wealthiest who became chamber members, remained among the middling sort, or incipient middle class, due to their occupation and work practices.[31] Planters could afford to hire overseers, leave a plantation in the hands of a third party, and expect to reap a profit from the agricultural labor of their slaves. Merchants might trade in slaves, and even own groups of them, but rarely did chamber members possess the large work gangs necessary to staff and work a plantation under an overseer's watchful eye. Though some planters did work hard, many of them did not supervise their plantations or slaves on a daily basis the way that merchants managed the personnel and business of their warehouses and shops.

To become a planter was the aspiration of almost every southern merchant: the money accumulated year after year in trade might slowly be converted into land and slaves, or could be transformed within a single year, but most if not all merchants of South Carolina did not crave to remain commercial traders their entire lives. They sought to become gentleman planters if circumstances permitted; their ultimate goal was to leave the (overtly) commercial realm and live upon the agricultural labor of others. The wealthiest South Carolina merchants invariably retired from trade and became plantation owners, increasing their stocks in land and slaves to demonstrate their continuously rising wealth and improved social position.[32] The men who made up the chamber had not yet attempted this transition; they might later become planters, and their membership in the chamber marked them out as the elite within a commercial group that was routinely considered by white South Carolinians as middling, or middle class.[33]

Membership in the Charleston chamber clearly carried with it some degree of prestige, in a town where civic memberships were the coin of both entertainment and access to the ranks of the rich and powerful.[34] When the group began to expand from its original thirteen founders in later years, many chamber members wanted to restrict membership to those solely engaged in the large-scale import and export business. The largest wholesalers marketed commodities like rice abroad, while providing slaves and plantation supplies domestically; ties to the planter class required merchants at this level to have sufficient capital to offer credit seasonally to their best customers. Men in this mercantile group were much smaller in number, and their solid economic standing was well known to local residents as well as traders in other cities.

They were completely unlike the small peddlers and fly-by-night shopkeepers who flocked to every seaboard town, whose creditworthiness was much harder to ascertain. Excluding these individuals from their gatherings was an early decision taken by the "Gentlemen in Trade," as members of the chamber described themselves at their initial meeting.[35] To restrict membership monetarily, they set the entrance fee high: 10 pounds, with 10 shillings paid quarterly thereafter. Membership cost enough to keep out the small-time general storekeepers, and became a marker of distinction between those merchants who could afford chamber dues and those who could not.

Nonetheless, the chamber was besieged by men who desired entry, but who were admitted slowly.[36] Typical membership of the Charleston chamber hovered between fifteen and twenty in the forty years that the group maintained membership records. The ability to meet and associate with others must have been important to men who toiled in separate, insular warehouses and shops, seeing only customers day after day. A small, regular club that gathered men with similar interests, levels of wealth, and goals could serve many purposes simultaneously. While increasing their capital was an obvious goal, meeting in fellowship with likeminded men created a social outlet for individuals who might otherwise remain somewhat isolated due to the nature of their daily work. The men, whose ages ranged from twenty-nine to fifty-seven, were all roughly in the prime of life, with many years of commercial activity ahead of them.[37] The chamber allowed them to swap news about trade, and eventually gave them enough influence to establish (and publish) exchange rate standards for the various currencies passing through Charleston, which fluctuated increasingly in the 1780s and 1790s. The economic dislocations of those decades may have also spurred some men to join (or attempt to join) the chamber, in hopes that membership might protect them, either through more timely, accurate commercial information or through the enforcement mechanism offered by arbitration to chamber members. Business collapses and increasing numbers of bankruptcies became common in the 1780s, leading some states to create bankruptcy statutes, as Pennsylvania did in 1785.[38]

To exit the mercantile ranks, eventually, and avoid the snares of business failure, merchants looked to increase their revenue returns by any means possible. If time was money, these merchants could speed up the return on their investment capital by encouraging each other to use the chamber for the resolution of legal disputes. If one member brought a dispute with a second member to the chamber, both agreed that the resolution was binding on both parties, and that they would not litigate their differences in court. Preventing waste was essential, and wasting the time of chamber members was to be discouraged. Therefore, chamber members also agreed that ongoing litigation would not be dragged before the chamber for arbitration, but that the court system would have exclusive jurisdiction over contests first taken to the judiciary. One example of the chamber's refusal to act occurred when Joseph Abadonne and Henry Putnam appeared to discuss their disputed accounts in June 1785. Abadonne pointed out that the dispute "had previously been referred to a court of law & private arbitration." Upon receiving that information, the chamber cited its 1784 rule that barred the chamber from hearing such disputes, and informed the parties that the chamber could not resolve their difficulties.[39] In April 1784, the group had concluded that "this chamber will not receive any Business of Arbitration that has been referred to any Court of Law or private arbitration," possibly following the lead of New York City's chamber, which used a similar rule.[40]

Although the chamber would not intervene when a lawsuit had already commenced between members, the normal rule was that "all disputes relative to commercial matters between any of the members of the chamber, shall be referred to the chamber for their determination." This principle would promote amity and friendship among members, while speeding up the process of assessing claims. Surprisingly, chamber members did not want the public to know of their disputes; in an honor-based culture like the South, the public's attitude toward questionable behavior marked it as honorable or dishonorable. The merchants shunned lawsuits and open squabbles among themselves.[41] Instead, preserving decorum between members was paramount. Should any member refuse to let the chamber arbitrate, the penalty was severe: "the party refusing shall be no longer considered a member."[42] Expulsion from the group was a high penalty, but the chamber's records give no indications that such an extreme measure was ever invoked for refusing to arbitrate. A rule in favor of forced arbitration obviously could have dire effects for legal professionals—fewer suits meant fewer fees—if members of the chamber abided by this regulation, which they apparently did most of the time. What is striking is that this rule was not repealed in later years, although other rules about residency and citizenship agreed upon by the original chamber members were open to discussion and even revoked.

While Charleston chamber members followed New York (and possibly Philadelphia) merchants in the area of arbitration, they did not share exactly the same legal milieu. In other regions, eighteenth-century arbitration processes became "increasingly legalistic and inflexible." Legal historian Bruce Mann has argued that, in Connecticut, merchants pressed the colonial assembly to enact a statute that would routinize and structure the arbitration process, so that in the end, reliable and enforceable judgments could be rendered. Through the mid-eighteenth century, this methodical attack on arbitration's loose processes made using arbitration look more and more like going to law.[43] However, in South Carolina, no such legislation was enacted. Merchants in Charleston appear to have sought no formal enforcement mechanisms for their arbitration awards, asking for no mechanisms to sustain the arbitration method and outcomes. Perhaps these businessmen were more trusting that, in the close-knit world of face-to-face trading, they could continue to rely upon honor and family bonds to recognize (and avert, if necessary) impending financial distress among their number. Certainly, the importance of honor should not be discounted in evaluating why southern merchants were willing to place faith in the arbitration decisions of their fellow commercial traders. Honor was not the exclusive concern of planters, but ran in strong currents through all levels of southern society by the end of the eighteenth century. The value of both upholding family names and individual reputations probably convinced some southern merchants to trust arbitration to yield fair results, even as the postwar economy became increasingly bleak and some business deals turned sour. In the 1780s and 1790s, a number of disputes were taken to the chamber for resolution.

The first such dispute arose only three months after the organization held its inaugural meeting. Alexander Rose, who was not yet a member of the chamber but would later become one, and a "Mr. [John] Kirk," asked the chamber to settle their dispute in April 1784. The chamber established a committee to investigate the matter and present their report, which laid out the details of the two merchants' differences. Unlike the New York chamber, the Charleston chamber had not already established an arbitration committee at its outset, but it would quickly see the need for a standing arbitration committee to be established.[44] Kirk claimed that Rose had stood as guarantee for a Mr. Tetley in a purchase of goods from Kirk, and Tetley had defaulted on repayment. The committee "lent an attentive ear to the allegations of the parties" and reviewed the "papers & proofs produced to them," which suggested that Kirk's allegation was correct: Rose owed Kirk nearly 350 pounds plus 7 percent interest for the intervening 4 years since the transaction took place. The real dispute, however, arose in how to calculate the depreciation in currency that had occurred between 1780 and 1784, and whether Rose's offer to pay in 1782 with highly devalued paper currency should be taken into consideration. The committee of merchants set the rate of depreciation at 75 for 1, and urged that Rose's earlier offer to pay in devalued Continental dollars should be dismissed, for by that time "paper currency was cry'd down in Philadelphia, then the seat of Congress, and almost totally annihilated in every other state." They thus calculated that the balance due in local, current currency was more than 9500 pounds, or in sterling, 1357 pounds, 14 shillings, and 3 pence, along with costs of suit.[45] What is most interesting is that Alexander Rose chose to join the chamber after this adverse decision—his respect for the men in the association seems not to have been diminished despite losing the suit.

What remains unknown about this judgment is the methods and reasoning the committee used to render its final decision. Although the principles and procedures called for by *lex mercatoria* were known to businessmen operating in Charleston, the committee left no records behind to demonstrate how they reached their ultimate decision. Indeed, the membership on the committee appeared to rotate every few months, suggesting that the burden of being on such a committee was too onerous to bear for a year, or even a half a year; this may have been true elsewhere also, for the New York chamber's arbitration committee changed membership every month.[46]

Although the means used to reach their decision remains shrouded in mystery, the chamber committee did render a final verdict in the Kirk and Rose dispute that concluded the affair. The acceptance of Alexander Rose into the chamber's membership a few months later indicates that he did not attempt to undermine their decision by continuing the case before a court of law. It also suggests that nonmembers took advantage of this new forum for alternative dispute resolution; arbitration was not limited to chamber members alone. Whether many or most merchants were willing to forgo their official legal remedies in return for the swifter justice of the chamber, however, remains unknown. Nonetheless, individuals who attempted to ask for justice from both the law courts and the chamber's members ran the risk of being labeled time-wasters, for the effort needed to evaluate witnesses and review ledgers of complex business transactions would not be undertaken lightly by chamber members if they believed that the same dispute would be heard a second time by either state or federal courts sitting in Charleston. Indeed, unless one received an extremely adverse decision from the chamber, no merchant was likely to try both forums for justice unless he wanted to lose access to the chamber on a permanent basis. If a chamber member had done such a thing, it might have been received badly: such a double move could be considered a breach of the code of behavior tacitly agreed to by all members to steer their squabbles out of the public view and into the closed chamber meeting room.

A willingness to render judgments against its own members might run somewhat counter to modern-day expectations, but the second suit heard by a chamber committee in June and July 1784 did just that when it reached a similar result to the Kirk-Rose dispute. When Henry Mounier, "a subject of France," had a difference of opinion with James Neilson, a Charleston merchant and chamber member, the association investigated. The chamber's arbitration subcommittee reviewing the matter discovered that Mounier had entrusted Neilson with money to be invested at the Continental Loan office in 1779, but that Neilson failed to act, and was only now offering to give Mounier his money in Continental Loan certificates dated for 1784. After a lengthy calculation of the difference in value between the certificates from 1779 with those of 1784, the committee concluded that Neilson owed Mounier a total of 1037 pounds, 8 shillings, and 11 pence. The arbitration committee then reviewed a recent piece of state legislation that allowed debtors to repay their creditors slowly over time, and urged that "as Mons. Mounier is a foreigner and it will probably be very prejudicial his waiting that long period for payment, we could wish and recommend it to Mr. Neilson to wa[i]ve the benefit of the said act." This would not only help Mounier, but by so doing "every foreigner will be convinced that strict justice is to be had and administered in this state." The committee's report was unanimously endorsed by the chamber.[47] Mounier and Neilson each wrote individually to the chamber later that month, probably to complain that the award was either too low (Mounier) or too high (Neilson), but neither man persuaded the chamber members to change their minds; the only reply made by the association was that their award was "final and conclusive."[48]

The act that the chamber wished Neilson to forgo the benefit of had been created by the South Carolina General Assembly in the postwar period, when the economic situation of the states was highly volatile. Prior to the war, South Carolinians could attach the goods or chattels of an absent debtor, if the debtor himself could not be found; land could also be attached and sold for debts contracted and not paid. Given the large number of absentee land-lords, these laws were invoked again and again for the payment of outstanding accounts.[49] The colony also had a rather unusual bankruptcy scheme, which granted only a twelve-month stay of execution against creditors, but also "discharged only those debts owed to creditors who accepted a dividend from the debtor's estate."[50] The instability of paper currency in the 1780s throughout the new nation was a hardship that some businessmen accepted as a form of patriotism; depreciation taxed those who held or accepted money that was issued by the Revolutionary government. In response to the economic upheavals the fluctuating currency created, some states required the paper money be accepted at par, regardless of how much the currency had depreciated.[51]

The instabilities of currency and the economic shocks that immediately followed the war's termination led South Carolina lawmakers, like those in other states, to enact additional legislation in the early 1780s that blocked lawsuits for the collection of debts contracted during the war.[52] These so-called stay laws prevented creditors, frequently foreign, from extracting specie that hard-pressed merchants could ill afford to part with. The title of one such law, passed in 1782, was "An Act to prevent the commencement of suits for the recovery of debts," which conveys the legislature's intention quite clearly. Stay laws were supplemented by installment payment laws that permitted debtors to extend the period of time for legal payment over a period of years. The chamber intended Neilson to forgo using the new law, which would have given him an advantage over the foreign-born Mounier, who would be kept out of his money for months, if not years.[53]

None of the earliest disputes brought before the chamber was for a small sum of money. The third one in 1784, a controversy between William Miller and Samuel Courtauld, two nonmembers of the chamber, was for $525, relating to a disputed charter party. The chamber ruled in Miller's favor.[54] The four cases that the chamber heard in the first six months of 1785 involved a dissolved partnership and its collective debts, disputed accounts, and other typical matters over which traders might quarrel. What distinguished these suits was their size: all of them were for significant amounts in excess of 100 pounds, which suggests that the chamber best served individuals who wanted to resolve quickly disputes that tied up large sums of capital. The sluggish economy of the 1790s may have also sparked greater interest among members in making Charleston appear a safe place to engage in fair trade. Indeed, although chamber members routinely lost disputes that were heard by their fellow members, it may have been that the speed of dispute resolution made those losses bearable; if a decision by the chamber was less than a person might have lost by appearing in a law court, then even a loss before fellow chamber members might seem preferable to a lengthy lawsuit with an potentially worse outcome before the regular tribunals of justice.[55]

Very little publicity attended the arbitration of mercantile disputes in Charleston in the 1780s and 1790s. Only one of the cases that it handled ever attracted wider notice from local newspapers, and that occurred when merchants felt their reputations were at hazard if they did not speak out. In 1785, A. E. Van Braam Houckgeest paid for a lengthy advertisement in the *Columbian Herald* to lay before the public his version of a commercial imbroglio that was brewing. Van Braam, a Dutch man residing in Charleston, was an investor in the joint venture of Van Braam, Johnston and Joyner, a partnership dissolved by the chamber early in 1785. Johnston and Joyner published a notice at the beginning of June 1785 that stated the partnership was dissolved because Van Braam had not complied with the articles of the partnership, and Van Braam retaliated by publishing, in full, the chamber's decree sundering the partnership (giving costs and percentages to be charged on both sides) and stating that as of January 1, 1785, he had not received "a single farthing remittance," suggesting that he was the wronged party in the transaction. In August, Van Braam paid for another "NOTIFICATION" in the *State Gazette* to inform the public that despite the chamber's orders, Johnston and Joyner had failed to make a final settlement with him on June 20. Having received no money, Van Braam laid claim to "every debt still existing to the aforesaid property, as his only property" and requested customers and other merchants not to make any payments to Johnston and Joyner (contrary to the original order of the chamber of commerce).[56] Only then did Johnston and Joyner break their silence, venting some spleen about Van Braam's actions. After advising debtors that they could only receive a complete discharge of debts if they paid Johnston and Joyner, the pair then asserted that their business failure was "owing entirely to the designing deception of the self-created Dutch Consul" Van Braam. He had promised to supply them annually with goods worth "ten or twelve thousand pounds sterling" plus a vessel that would ply between Amsterdam and their shop in Beaufort, but both promises were false, and the goods he did supply were unsuited to the climate and thus had been returned. They entreated their debtors to pay promptly after the next harvest, so that they could conclude all business with Van Braam. After this last advertisement, the dispute dropped from public notice. Interestingly, Johnston and Joyner operated a shop in Beaufort, but the dispute with Van Braam was settled by the chamber in Charleston, suggesting that its reach, and possibly prestige, extended beyond the immediate Charleston vicinity.[57]

Of course, the chamber was not the only group that could resolve disputes, and the process of private arbitration had a long history both in Charleston as well as in colonial America and England.[58] Indeed, binding private arbitration was quite common among some religious groups active in commerce in early America. The Society of Friends, commonly called Quakers, included a rule in their Discipline that required all disputes between Quakers to be resolved without recourse to law courts. Quakers followed the precepts of Matthew 18:15–17, which required that a debtor should be admonished by his creditors and his friends to pay what he owed, and only after such admonishment could a creditor commence legal process to collect a debt. Quakers disdained participating in public legal disputes with one another, for fear that it might bring about greater conflict and discord in the wider community, as well as bring disrepute down upon their religious denomination. Hence, they stayed away from formal proceedings in law courts and opted for their own methods of dispute resolution. Members of a local monthly meeting chapter would speak to any persons who had a dispute, whether commercial or noncommercial in nature, and try to resolve the problem amicably. If, after repeated efforts by individuals in the local meeting had been made, both parties could not be reconciled, the dispute could be referred to a committee of Quakers to hear all aspects of the dispute. If one of the parties did not accept the resolution offered by the committee, he could appeal their decision to the quarterly (district) meeting, and even to the yearly (regional) meeting. Such hearings were common, particularly in areas with a high concentration of Friends such as Pennsylvania, Delaware, and New Jersey. However, any Friend who chose to disregard the findings of the meeting and who pressed for a legal hearing of his rights could find himself banned from the society. Being barred from religious gatherings of the faithful might seem a harsh penalty, but it was effective in pushing many Quakers toward the private, religiously based arbitration system. In Charleston, the monthly meeting records reveal no such arbitration system in use, but the records of the Friends in Charleston are remarkably spartan in appearance; it may well have been the case that they engaged in private arbitration but did not record it.[59] The use of private arbitration, by Quakers and others, flourished in the eighteenth century.

Arbitration was only one part of the chamber's regular business, along with answering correspondence and lobbying politically on both state and national levels for regulations that would favor their commercial interests. While they were in correspondence with other chambers of commerce in New York and Philadelphia about trade wars with other countries in the 1780s, and were answering Thomas Jefferson's queries from Paris about the quantities of goods shipped out from Charleston and their destinations, the Charleston merchants took steps to ensure that only loyal Americans could have access to their group. In June 1784, they passed a resolution that members must be residents and citizens of South Carolina.[60] They also tried to regulate various charges that were fixtures of the mercantile trade: commissions on sales should be 5 percent; procuring freights should be 5 percent; paying insurance on the ship and cargo of another should be worth half a percent on the amount insured; exchange and re-exchange of bills protested in Europe was worth 15 percent of the original bill; and collecting money using a power of attorney or other authority was worth 5 percent.[61] These charges were comparable to those that attorneys in the colonial and early national periods attempted to set in many urban areas, so as to prevent any one attorney from charging the lowest fees and gathering in the most business. Fortunately, many of the fees that the chamber agreed to were already considered standard ones in the eighteenth century.

The appearance in the 1780s of a renewed and invigorated chamber in

Charleston that assumed responsibility for arbitrating disputes between merchants adds some credibility to Eben Moglen's assertion that Morton Horwitz may be in error in his assessment of what merchants wanted from American courts in the late eighteenth century. According to Horwitz, "one still has the strong sense that resorting to arbitration among New York merchants had begun to decline after 1795."[62] An overall reduction in enthusiasm for and use of arbitration was suggested by Horwitz for the late eighteenth century, but in Charleston, arbitration appears to have been alive and well during that time period among merchants, at least. While arbitration had been known in Charleston prior to the Revolution, it gained momentum in the 1780s and into the early 1790s with the formalized structure of the chamber to sustain it. A South Carolina justice of the peace manual from 1788 included multiple references to the legality and utility of arbitration, as well as providing all the forms for drawing up binding bonds of arbitration.[63] In New York, efforts continued until as late as the 1840s to make it mandatory in their organization, as well as through legislation, for the chamber to handle *all* commercial disputes between merchants—an effort that enjoyed great support among merchants but that failed to find favor with state legislators until the 1860s.[64]

In Charleston, the chamber's members continued to serve as state politicians: indeed, there was enough overlap through the years between the chamber and the state legislature that the odds of passing similar legislation would undoubtedly have been excellent. Yet no legal requirement about binding arbitration ever became law in South Carolina. Beyond politics, the chamber as a group became solidly entrenched in Charleston's antebellum society. In 1844, merchants of the chamber began spending their surplus funds to create a mercantile library, open to all traders in the city; clerks from shops across the city flocked to become members of the library. Likewise, chamber members considered purchasing a building to house both the library and "Committees of Arbitration" that were still being convened.[65] Details about those meetings, however, are more difficult to ascertain. Membership records of the Charleston chamber continue into the 1820s, but the minutes for their monthly gatherings and arbitration reports, which start off with such fullness and promise, come to an abrupt stop in 1794.[66] By 1820, the chambers numbers were still small—only thirteen members—but they had buried some forty members, all of considerable economic and political stature, in the intervening years.

What these arbitration proceedings do tell us is that, North or South, merchants in the 1780s and 1790s sought alternative methods to resolve their disputes without recourse to the legal system. For these men, chambers of commerce provided speedy resolutions to tangled business dealings for a fraction of the cost of a regular lawsuit, and the decision makers would be men of business like themselves—individuals who they could trust. Speedy resolutions, knowledgeable assessors, and the chamber's desire to maintain a positive reputation for local trade kept commercial arbitration alive among the city's merchant middle class for decades. The relative decline of mercantile arbitration during the nineteenth century is a story for another day; at the end of the eighteenth century, and particularly in the wake of war against the British, newly minted American businessmen demonstrated their willingness to rely on the judgments of other traders and merchants to resolve their business problems outside of Charleston's courtrooms.

How is this essay relevant to the southern middle class?
They're trying to say that the SMC wasn't just planters.
Okay, but all the SMC wanted to become planters.

NOTES

1. Jeffrey Charles, *Service Clubs in American Society: Rotary, Kiwanis, and Lions* (Urbana: University of Illinois Press, 1993), 1–8; Jack Ross, *An Assembly of Good Fellows: Voluntary Associations in History* (Westport, Conn.: Greenwood Press, 1976), 141, 147, 178. Earlier fraternal organizations (for example, Odd-Fellows, Masons, Knights of Pythias, Woodmen) began in the early nineteenth century, largely among men of the middle class. During a period of industrial upheaval and uncertainty, these groups offered the reassurance of insurance, retirement homes, and death-rite protection to members of similar middling social status (only the Masons did not provide housing). Charles, *Service Clubs in American Society*, 10–17. Short-term loans and financial support during illness were common among these associations, particularly in England, where they had a long history. P. H. J. H. Gosden, *Self-Help: Voluntary Associations in the 19th Century* (London: B. T. Batsford, 1973), 2–4. The U.S. Chamber of Commerce, which works on a national level, developed at the end of the nineteenth century. Richard H. Werking, "Bureaucrats, Businessmen, and Foreign Trade: The Origins of the United States Chamber of Commerce," *Business History Review* 52 (1978): 321–41.

2. Many definitions have been given to the term "alternative dispute resolution." For the purposes of this essay, it will include arbitration and the settlement of conflicts without the use of judicial process.

3. Charleston was not the only city of early America to host an active chamber of commerce. On the activities of the New York City chamber of commerce, particularly during the American Revolution, see John A. Stevens Jr., *Colonial Records of the New York Chamber of Commerce, 1768–1784 with Historical and Biographical Sketches* (New York: John F. Trow & Co., 1867); Wil-

can't make up the rest next.
the point of the past.
This isn't about the South except the plantation.

liam C. Jones, "Three Centuries of Commercial Arbitration in New York: A Brief Survey," *Washington University Law Quarterly* (1956): 193–222; Eben Moglen, "Commercial Arbitration in the Eighteenth Century: Searching for the Transformation of American Law," *Yale Law Journal* 93 (1983): 135–52; New York Chamber of Commerce, committee on arbitration, *Earliest arbitration records of the Chamber of Commerce of the State of New York, founded in 1768: Committee minutes, 1779–1792* (New York: Press of the Chamber, 1913).

4. From the 1780s to the end of the nineteenth century, Americans formed voluntary associations for social, political, and economic ends. Following in the footsteps of Alexis de Tocqueville, numerous scholars have elaborated on or challenged his early definition of civil society, most notably Mary Ryan, "Civil Society as Democratic Practice: North American Cities during the Nineteenth Century," *Journal of Interdisciplinary History* 29 (1999): 559–84; John Ehrenberg, *Civil Society: The Critical History of an Idea* (New York: New York University Press, 1999); John Brooke, "Consent, Civil Society, and the Public Sphere in the Age of Revolution and the Early American Republic," in Jeffrey Pasley, Andrew Robertson, and David Waldstreicher, eds., *Beyond the Founders: New Approaches to the Political History of the Early American Republic* (Chapel Hill: University of North Carolina Press, 2004), 207–50; and Albrecht Koschnik, *American Conceptions of Civil Society, 1730–1850* (forthcoming).

5. Whether the chamber might also be used to broker partnerships and encourage the making of new deals is not contained in the group's records. That this essay focuses upon the disputes within the chamber should not overshadow the organization's potential for deal making and cooperation.

6. Harold Berman, *Law and Revolution* (Cambridge, Mass.: Harvard University Press, 1983), ch. 11; Leon Trakman, *The Law Merchant: The Evolution of Commercial Law* (Littleton, Colo.: Fred Rothman & Co., 1983), ch. 1. Even among African traders, a form of merchant law was adhered to by Maghribi merchants as early as the eleventh century. Avner Greif, "Contract Enforceability and Economic Institutions in Early Trade: The Maghribi Traders' Coalition," *The American Economic Review* 83 (1993): 525–48, esp. 543. On English reception of and mutation of the "law merchant," see Mary Basile, Jane Bestor, Daniel Coquillette, and Charles Donahue, eds., *Lex Mercatoria and Legal Pluralism: A Late Thirteenth-Century Treatise and its Afterlife* (Cambridge, Mass.: Ames Foundation, 1998), esp. 179–88. On the reception of European "law merchant" in America, see Bruce L. Benson, "Justice Without Government: The Merchant Courts of Medieval Europe and Their Modern Counterparts," in David T. Beito, Peter Gordon, and Alexander Tabarrok, eds., *The Voluntary City: Choice, Community, and Civil Society* (Ann Arbor: University of Michigan Press, 2002).

7. Berman, *Law and Revolution,* 341.

8. Avner Greif, "Reputation and Coalitions in Medieval Trade: Evidence on the Maghribi Traders," *Journal of Economic History* 49 (1989): 859; see also Greif, "Contract Enforceability and Economic Institutions in Early Trade," 529–30.

9. Greif, "Contract Enforceability and Economic Institutions in Early Trade," 529.

10. Daniel A. Rabuzzi, "Eighteenth-Century Commercial Mentalities as Reflected and Projected in Business Handbooks," *Eighteenth-Century Studies* 29 (1995–96): 171, 178.

11. Lee M. Friedman, "The First Chamber of Commerce in the United States," *Bulletin of the Business Historical Society* 21 (1947): 137.

12. Amalia Kessler, *A Revolution in Commerce: The Parisian Merchant Court and the Rise of Commercial Society in Eighteenth-Century France* (New Haven: Yale University Press, 2007), 245; Gail Bossenga, "Protecting Merchants: Guilds and Commercial Capitalism in Eighteenth-Century France," *French Historical Studies* 15 (1988): 699.

13. Greif, "Reputation and Coalitions," 868, and "Contract Enforceability and Economic Institutions in Early Trade," 532.

14. *State Gazette of South-Carolina,* September 14, 1786 [accessed through Early American Newspapers Series 1–5, 1690–1922, URL: www.infoweb.newsbank.com (hereafter EANS), September 5, 2008]. The article author extrapolates from this census by multiplying all houses by 7 inhabitants for the following population estimates: Philadelphia, 32,205; New York, 24,500; Charleston, 10,780.

15. Earlier scholars have suggested that the relatively easy transition from Dutch to English law in New York may have been a result of the use of the "law merchant," with which both commercial agents in both European nations were familiar. Herbert Johnson, *The Law Merchant and Negotiable Instruments in Colonial New York, 1664–1730* (Chicago: Loyola University Press, 1963), 16. On the presence of Dutch traders and arbitration, see Friedman, "The First Chamber of Commerce," 137, and J. R. Aiken, "New Netherlands Arbitration in the Seventeenth Century," *Arbitration Journal* 29 (1974): 145–60.

16. On arbitration among the Quakers, see George S. Odiorne, "Arbitration and Mediation among Early Quakers," *Arbitration Journal* 9 (1954): 161–69, and "Arbitration under Early New Jersey Law," *Arbitration Journal* 8 (1953): 117–25. Arbitration was not limited to commercial disputes, but could be used by the Quakers for all manner of conflicts, including the resolution of family quarrels.

17. Robert East, "The Business Entrepreneur in a Changing Colonial Economy, 1763–1795," *Journal of Economic History* 6 Supp. (1946): 25–26.

18. Peter Coclanis, *The Shadow of a Dream: Economic Life and Death in the South Carolina Low Country, 1670–1920* (New York: Oxford University Press, 1989); S. Max Edelson, *Plantation Enterprise in Colonial South Carolina* (Cambridge, Mass.: Harvard University Press, 2006), 54. A similar possibility is that prior to the rise of rice's dominant export role in South Carolina trade, the number of merchants in the town may have been too small to sustain a chamber of commerce.

19. The effects of commercial specialization after 1750 appeared in Philadelphia for the dry goods and provision trades, according to Thomas M. Doerflinger, "Commercial Specialization in Philadelphia's Merchant Community, 1750–1791," *Business History Review* 57, no. 1 (1983): 20–49. Doerflinger posits that only the very wealthiest merchant traders could afford the geographic and commodity diversification typically (and erroneously) ascribed to all traders during the eighteenth century.

20. Debt in the seventeenth century was more likely to be contracted locally, and local debts seemed to attract less legislative attention. As trade networks expanded, debts traveled as well, and the need to protect far-away creditors may have created a greater need for both protective legislation and a chamber of commerce structure to enforce good behavior. Bruce Mann, *Republic of Debtors: Bankruptcy in the Age of American Independence* (Cambridge, Mass.: Harvard University Press, 2002), 47–48.

21. Jeanne Calhoun, Martha Zierden and Elizabeth Paysinger, "The Geographic Spread of Charleston's Mercantile Community, 1732–1767," *South Carolina Historical Magazine* 86 (1985): 186.

22. This runs contrary to the example of the New York City chamber of commerce, which in fact became more active during British wartime occupation. Moglen, "Commercial Arbitration in the Eighteenth Century," 145.

23. *South-Carolina Gazette and General Advertiser,* January 6–8, 1784, EANS [accessed June 15, 2008].

24. Charleston Chamber of Commerce bound volume, 1784–1794, February 1784 meeting, n.p., South Carolina Historical Society (hereafter Commerce volume). The close connection between coffeehouses and trade associations or merchants was well established by the seventeenth century. Ross, *Assembly of Good Fellows,* 215–220. *South-Carolina Gazette and General Advertiser,* April 29–May 1, 1784. Anniversary dinner announced in *City Gazette and Daily Advertiser,* February 6, 1792, EANS [accessed June 15, 2008].

25. Although its members comprised the largest, wealthiest traders of the city, the New York chamber of commerce's forty members also included a sea captain, an auctioneer, a banker, and small retail traders. Friedman, "The First Chamber of Commerce," 138. Creating distinctions between merchants based upon the scale, destination, and cargos traded was common in other parts of the Atlantic world as well. Susan Socolow, "Economic Activities of the Porteno Merchants: The Viceregal Period," *Hispanic American Historical Review* 55 (1975): 2–4.

26. On the feeling of social superiority that wholesalers and planters felt toward small-scale retailers, see Henry Laurens to Richard Oswald, July 7, 1764, in *The Papers of Henry Laurens,* ed. George C. Rogers et al. (Columbia: University of South Carolina Press, 1968–2005), 4:332–33.

27. Of the thirteen, only John Dawson, John Lloyd, Daniel Hall, and Samuel Legaré did not serve in government. For all others, see Walter B. Edgar and N. Louise Bailey, eds., *Biographical Directory of the South Carolina House of Representatives,* 5 vols. (Columbia: University of South Carolina Press, 1974–) or N. Louise Bailey, Mary Morgan, and Carolyn Taylor, eds., *Biographical Directory of the Senate of South Carolina,* 3 vols. (Columbia: University of South Carolina Press, 1986).

28. Here we do well to heed Peter Stearns's nuanced description of multiple middle classes. Stearns, "The Middle Class: Toward a Precise Definition," *Comparative Studies in Society and History* 21 (1979): 392.

29. Bailey, Morgan, and Taylor, *Biographical Directory of the South Carolina Senate,* 1:161, 560; 2:944. These three men were not full-time slave traders, but were heavily involved in the importation of five to fifteen shiploads of slaves.

30. Raymond Starr, ed., "Letters from John Lewis Gervais to Henry Laurens, 1777–1778," *South Carolina Historical Magazine* 66 (1965): 15–37.

31. On the need to consider occupation, mentality, inter- and intra-class conflict, behavior, and wealth when describing the "middle class," see Stearns, "Middle Class," 377–96. On occupational structure and mobility, see Michael Katz, "Occupational Classification in History," *Journal of Interdisciplinary History* 3 (1972): 63–88.

32. On motivations as a class behavior marker, see Stearns, "Middle Class," 382. One such individual who "parlayed a fortune trading rice and slaves into a private plantation empire" was Henry Laurens, who made that transition in the 1750s. Edelson, *Plantation Enterprise in Colonial South Carolina,* 200.

33. The existence of the chamber might be said to indicate some consciousness of class divisions between the upper and middle classes by Charlestonians, but lacking any definitive statement about such consciousness in the sources, I have not used the chamber as a stand-in for the middle class per se, since the members chose to exclude other merchants whose wealth might well have placed them in the middle class. Rather, I have focused upon the divide between merchants more generally and planters, a gap in social and economic status and daily behavior that white men in the period would have recognized.

34. Nicholas Butler, *Votaries of Apollo: The St. Cecilia Society and the Patronage of Concert Music in Charleston, South Carolina, 1766–1820* (Columbia: University of South Carolina Press, 2007).

35. Commerce volume, February 1784 meeting (quotation), April 21, 1784 meeting, n.p. A similar delay occurred in New York, where the group was incorporated in 1770 but held no meetings between 1775 and 1779. Friedman, "First Chamber of Commerce," 142.

36. Five in the next three months alone, all of whom were elected: Harry Grant, James Simons, Felix Warley, John McCall, and John Edwards Jr. Edwards and Simons both served in the state House of Representatives. Edgar and Bailey, *Biographical Directory of the South Carolina House of Representatives*, 4:648–50, 209–10.

37. Charles suggests that a similar goal motivated Paul Harris, the founder of the Rotary Club, in the early twentieth century. Charles, *Service Clubs in American Society*, 9–10. The youngest member was Robert Pringle (twenty-nine), and the eldest was William Logan (fifty-seven). Four men were of unknown age in 1784; the others were mostly in their thirties. Data compiled from Richard N. Cote and Patricia Williams, *Dictionary of South Carolina Biography* (Easley, S.C.: Southern Historical Press, 1985), volume 1.

38. *State Gazette of South-Carolina,* March 11, 1785, EANS [accessed June 15, 2008]. These exchange rates received public approbation. See John Wray's complaint about William Rogers, *City Gazette and Daily Advertiser,* December 9, 1788, EANS [accessed June 15, 2008]. On the multiple reasons for economic dislocation in the 1780s and 1790s, see Mann, *Republic of Debtors*, 172–205.

39. The combination of social, economic, and legal parallels between medieval or early modern guilds and the chamber of commerce bears further investigation. On guilds, see generally Joseph P. Ward, *Metropolitan Communities: Trade Guilds, Identity, and Change in Early Modern London* (Stanford: Stanford University Press, 1997), and Antony Black, *Guilds and Civil Society in European Political Thought from the Twelfth Century to the Present* (London: Methuen, 1984). Commerce volume, June 8, 1785 meeting, 28 (quotation).

40. This is in direct contrast to how large land owners initiated lawsuits (strategically abandoned later) to encourage parties to arbitrate in other countries, such as France, in roughly the same period. Rafe Blaufarb, "Conflict and Compromise: Communauté and Seigneurie in Early Modern Provence," *Journal of Modern History* 82 (September 2010): 519–45.

41. Whether the chamber functioned as a moral arena for transmitting acceptable community values and establishing virtuous behavior could be debated. The chamber's desire to appear "respectable" placed it on par with other Charleston social groups, such as the St. Cecilia Society or Hibernian Society, but the chamber did more than promote social cohesion. Its willingness to arbitrate disputes between members suggests that it wished to achieve an air of calm in what might otherwise be considered a rough-and-tumble profession. For more on the values transmitted by Charleston society memberships, see Butler, *Votaries of Apollo*.

42. Commerce volume, April 14, 1784 meeting, 4. Only one man voluntarily resigned his chamber membership; for details, see the Van Braam dispute, below.

43. Mann, *Republic of Debtors*, 160 (quotation), and Mann, *Neighbors and Strangers: Law and Community in Early Connecticut* (Chapel Hill: University of North Carolina Press, 1987), 111, 127–33.

44. Friedman, "First Chamber of Commerce," 139.

45. Commerce volume, 1784–1794, May 12, 1784 meeting, 6.

46. A similar absence is clear upon examining the New York chamber's records. Stevens, *Colonial Records of the New York Chamber of Commerce,* and Chamber of Commerce, *Earliest arbitration records of the Chamber of Commerce;* Friedman, "First Chamber of Commerce," 140.

47. Commerce volume, July 7, 1784 meeting, 11.

48. Commerce volume, July 28, 1784 meeting, 14.

49. "An Act for the better securing the payment of debts due from any person inhabiting and residing beyond the sea or else where without the limits of this province of South Carolina, and to subject a feme covert that is a sole trader to be arrested and sued for any debt contracted by her as a sole trader," December 12, 1712, in Thomas Cooper, ed., *The Statutes at Large of South Carolina,* 10 vols. (Columbia: A. S. Johnston, 1837), 2:588–93. The law permitting land to be sold was enacted in Great Britain under the title "An Act for the more easy recovery of Debts in his Majesty's Plantations and Colonies in America," 5 George 2, ch. 7 (1732), reprinted in ibid., 10:571–83.

50. Mann, *Republic of Debtors,* 183. If a creditor refused to become part of the bankruptcy group settlement, he risked seeing all the debtor's assets disappear into the hands of the other creditors first. In a game of debtor-creditor "chicken," this law urged creditors to accept a percentage of the money owed in order to release the debtor from all his creditors' obligations and wipe the slate clean in a single action. See also Peter J. Coleman, *Debtors and Creditors in America: Insolvency, Imprisonment for Debt, and Bankruptcy, 1607–1900* (Madison: University of Wisconsin Press, 1974).

51. Mann, *Republic of Debtors,* 172–75. Similar "tender laws" appeared in multiple states.

52. "An Act respecting suits for the recovery of debts," enacted February 26, 1782, renewed March 16, 1783, *Acts and ordinances of the General Assembly of the state of South Carolina, passed in the year 1783* (Charleston: Miller, 1784). The law was renewed again in 1784. "An Ordinance respecting suits for the recovery of debts," *Acts and ordinances of the General Assembly of the state of South Carolina, passed in the year 1784* (Charleston: Miller, 1784). Both laws reprinted in Cooper, ed., *Statutes at Large of South Carolina,* volume 4.

53. Similar stay laws were reenacted by the South Carolina legislature in 1787 and 1788, each time with the same title. "An Act to regulate the Recovery and Payment of Debts," in Cooper, ed., *Statutes at Large of South Carolina,* 5:36–38, 88–91.

54. A charter party was the one-time, one-trip agreement made between a ship owner and men who hired the ship to transport goods overseas. Commerce volume, August 11, 1784 meeting, 15.

55. It is possible that the disputes resolved by the chamber followed the pattern set by other non-court bodies that arbitrated problems. See Nelson, *Plymouth Court,* on trends of church courts in the seventeenth century; disputes heard before church courts were for larger amounts than those heard in regular trials. Thanks to John Wertheimer for this suggestion. Small sums

could be sued for before a justice of the peace (40 shillings), or before two justices and three freeholders (20 pounds) in the pre-Revolutionary era; Charleston later established its own Court of Wardens to resolve disputes under 20 pounds for city residents.

56. *State Gazette of South-Carolina,* September 19, 1785, EANS [accessed June 15, 2008].

57. Van Braam later resigned his membership in the chamber.

58. Merchants' willingness to resort to arbitration can be positively measured by the frequency with which preprinted legal forms were readily available for purchase at local printers' shops, and the inclusion of numerous arbitration forms (for example, bonds, releases) into local justice of the peace practice manuals. Forms can be located through the Early American Imprints database, URL: www.infoweb.newsbank.com.

59. On members excluded from the Society of Friends for failure to agree to arbitrate, see Jack Marietta, *The Reformation of American Quakerism, 1748–1783* (Philadelphia: University of Pennsylvania Press, 1984) and unpublished computer records, the Friends Historical Library, Swarthmore College. Society of Friends, Transactions 1719–1769, Charleston, South Carolina (collection 34/157), South Carolina Historical Society.

60. Queries from New York and Boston merchant associations, receipt of letters recorded in Commerce volume, May 1785 and July 13, 1785 meetings, 27 and 29; Jefferson's query, ibid., July 28, 1784 meeting, 13; the chamber's detailed reply, ibid., October 15, 1784. Commerce volume, June 2, 1784 meeting, 9.

61. Commerce volume, June 23, 1784 meeting, 9.

62. Morton Horwitz, *The Transformation of American Law 1780–1860* (Cambridge, Mass.: Harvard University Press, 1977), 149, as cited by Moglen, "Commercial Arbitration in the Eighteenth Century," 148.

63. *The South-Carolina justice of peace, containing all the duties, powers and authorities of that office, as regulated by the laws now of force in this state, and adapted to the parish and county magistrate. To which is added, a great variety of warrants, indictments and other precedents, interspersed under their several heads, and a summary of several of the decisions which have been had in the courts of this state. Entered in the secretary's office of the state of South-Carolina, 11th October, 1788, agreeable to the act of Assembly in that case made and provided, entitled "An act for the encouragement of arts and sciences." Ratified the 26th of March, 1784.* (Philadelphia: R. Aitken & Son, 1788), 35–37, 47. Accessed from Early American Imprints, series I (Digital Evans), doc. 21472 [accessed October 7, 2007]. The same information was reprinted in 1796 (Philadelphia: R. Aitken & Son, 1796). Accessed from Early American Imprints, series I (Digital Evans), doc. 30519 [accessed October 7, 2007].

64. New York Chamber of Commerce, *Earliest arbitration records of the Chamber of Commerce,* 124–25.

65. *Southern Patriot* [Charleston], August 7, 1844.

66. The ongoing military conflict between England and France that punctuated the Napoleonic era played havoc with trade relations for merchants across America. This may have also affected the ability or willingness or some merchants to allow their financial disputes to be resolved by the chamber of commerce. For a review of the effects of war on merchants in another trading seaport, see John D. Forbes, "European Wars and Boston Trade, 1783–1815," *New England Quarterly* 11 (1938): 709–30.

Strangers in the South

Charleston's Merchants and Middle-Class Values in the Early Republic

JENNIFER L. GOLOBOY

One of the great mysteries of South Carolina history is why merchants were considered an important component of the elite class before the Revolution, but by the early nineteenth century had moved into a middle class disdained by the aristocracy. A diarist visiting the city in 1809 wrote that "the planters consider themselves much above the merchants,"[1] a sentiment embodied in patrician Hugh Legaré's later comment, "The *town bourgeoisie* is *so* odious! . . . Alfred Huger's remark always occurs to me, that the greatest absurdity in the world is a 'Liverpool Gentleman.'"[2] Historians have identified two sources for this distaste: an influx of foreign merchants after the war and "a notion universally shared by the planting and professional classes that the pursuit of gain was vulgar." Scholars have often remarked on this important cultural and ideological shift in perceptions of the merchant class, but basic questions remain unanswered.[3] Why did an elite that prided itself on its cosmopolitanism resent the influx of foreign merchants? And how could mercantile behavior become perceived as "vulgar" in a matter of a few decades?

Americans like to blame economic busts on speculators and outsiders. Planter bias against the merchants originated during a bubble, mostly forgotten by historians, which took place in Charleston, South Carolina, between the 1790s and the beginning of the War of 1812. City directories suggest that the number of merchants in Charleston more than doubled between 1790 and the high point of the boom in 1807. The way that these merchants recklessly pursued wealth, ignoring the restraints of ethics and law, should make us rethink our image of the early American middle class as sober, diligent, and virtuous. After the bust came, embarrassment over economic instability and the resumption of the slave trade caused planters to describe the mercantile middle class as a group of deceitful, immoral strangers. This saved planters from having to question their own role in the debacle, especially as importers of slaves, and enabled them to think of themselves as genteel aristocrats.

Charleston's boom shaped stereotypes about merchants throughout the antebellum South. Historian Frank Byrne has discovered that southerners believed that most merchants were foreigners and Yankees—an inaccurate description of the makeup of the southern mercantile population, but a fair one of pre–War of 1812 Charleston. The middle class would find it difficult to fight its portrayal as an alien parasite in the plantation paradise.

The term "middle class" is used to mean many different things, often at the same time. Sometimes the term describes an economic class, which according to Max Weber's definition was based on the individual's likelihood of "procuring goods," "gaining a position in life," and "finding inner satisfactions," "which derives from the relative control over goods and skills and from their income-producing uses within a given economic order."[4] In this sense, the middle class refers to people in the professions, manufacturing, and business who have enough money to live without want and with some luxury. (What luxury means, of course, is always a matter for debate.) In the late eighteenth and early nineteenth centuries, most artisans found it increasingly difficult to earn enough to remain middle class. Middle-class income became associated with non-manual work, which implied education in literacy and numeracy.[5]

But "middle class" also refers to a "status group," which as Weber explained was unified by "an effective claim to social esteem in terms of positive or negative privileges," based on "formal education," and "hereditary or occupational prestige," and especially "style of life." Weber concluded that a class and a status group were not quite the same thing, though they were related. "Money and an entrepreneurial position are not in themselves status qualifications . . . and the lack of property is not in itself a status disqualification."[6] As many historians have pointed out, the bourgeois "style of life" is socially constructed, and has changed at different periods in time. In Germany, for example, middle-class men frequently engaged in dueling to defend their honor, while their British peers disdained the practice.[7] Nevertheless, there were some constants in the middle-class "style of life." The early American middle class was unified by the self-perceived possession of various Franklinian traits: "frugality, temperance, chastity, silence, tranquility, humility, cleanliness, moderation, order, resolution, sincerity, justice, and industry." Wealthy and poor Americans believed themselves to be middle class because they valued self-control and diligent, steady work at a non-manual profession.[8] For this reason as well as their occupation, though Charleston's merchants came from diverse origins and found varying levels of success, they could generally be described as middle class.

Take the example of Christopher Fitzsimons, an Irish immigrant who became a slave trader, distiller, and general merchant. Fitzsimons was a very wealthy man; as an awestruck local diarist noted, "[O]ne of his daughter married lately—he gave her *merely as a nuptial Present*—130,000$ . . . The Parson who married them had 500$ sent him the next morning in a silver cup." Nevertheless, Fitzsimons felt it was important for his son, Cashal, to learn how to be a good merchant. As a boy, Cashal was given a barrel of rice on one of his father's voyages. Fitzsimons encouraged his son to reinvest the proceeds and watch his capital grow, writing, "I wish him prepared for mercantile pursuits."[9] No matter how rich the Fitzsimons family grew, Cashal's father believed that his son needed to know how to work for a living—a very middle-class sentiment. Even wealthy merchants like Fitzsimons considered themselves to be middle class, both culturally and socially separate from the plantation elite.

A final complication in defining the middle class is that middle-class culture and the rise of middle-class professions antedated both a consistent terminology and a sense that society was best defined as three competing groups. Americans knew that there was a distinctive culture that belonged to "independent trading households," but they lacked a common term for it until well into the antebellum era.[10] The term "middle class" seems to have appeared in print in the 1830s, and to have become common in the 1850s.[11] Furthermore, the idea that society was divided into thirds, and that the three classes had conflicting interests, lagged behind the birth of this trading culture.[12] It is only in the nineteenth century that bourgeois culture became associated with the middle third of American society, and this middle third saw itself to be in conflict with lazy, amoral, and disdainful elites and rowdy, uncontrollable workers. By this point, however, centuries of bourgeois life had given the new class a set of values and acceptable occupations that could be modified but never completely discarded.

Between the 1790s and the War of 1812, prosperity swelled the ranks and transformed the membership of Charleston's mercantile population. Investing in government securities, neutral trading (shipping opportunities that opened to Americans as neutrals during the European wars), cotton exporting, and the brief, legal revival of the international slave trade promised optimistic young men wealth and independence.

Finance gained importance for Charleston's merchants in the early Republic. A branch of the Bank of the United States was founded in Charleston in 1791, and the Bank of South Carolina was chartered the following year.[13] Beginning in the 1790s, Charlestonians eagerly bought and sold government securities and bank stock. Merchants were disproportionately involved in trading federal bonds, holding 27.4 percent of accounts registered in the state between 1790 and 1797, and 38.6 percent of the value of bonds purchased in the state. Bank of South Carolina stock also found ready buyers, with stock price averaging about $77 per share between 1797 and 1811.[14]

The European wars also boosted the fortunes of Charleston's merchants. As neutral carriers, Americans were permitted to ship colonial produce between the West Indies and Europe during the Napoleonic Wars, as long as the captain stopped at an American port. Charleston was well placed for this purpose, because it was so close to the Caribbean.[15] The merchants took advantage of the war in less legal ways. Contemporary observer E. S. Thomas said that in 1795, "[t]he forced and smuggling trade to the then Spanish and Portuguese South American colonies, in British manufactures, was immense, and extremely lucrative, bringing in return large quantities of specie, and innumerable cargoes of coffee, cocoa, and sugar, which were re-shipped to Hamburg, Bremen, Amsterdam, &c."[16]

At the same time, international industrial development drove demand for cotton and for slaves. For a brief period before soil exhaustion set in, South Carolina was at the center of American cotton production. In 1811, 75 percent of the cotton grown in the United States came from South Carolina and Georgia, and 50 percent from South Carolina alone.[17] A contemporary analyst calculated that between 1791 and 1803, at least 11 percent of total national exports left through South Carolina, peaking between 1800 and 1802 at 15 percent. After this, the state's percent of national exports slowly dipped to 5 percent in 1812.[18]

Although exports declined, Charleston's merchants were kept busy by the overseas slave trade. Reopened on December 17, 1803, the international slave trade flourished in Charleston until the federal Constitution definitively ended it on January 1, 1808, because South Carolina was the only state to permit the trade.[19] South Carolina's legislators seem to have been eager to supply laborers for the state's expanding cotton production—perceiving African slaves as more docile than native-born ones—and also to provide slaves for the newly acquired Louisiana Territory.[20] James McMillin recently estimated that 74,500 people were brought to South Carolina as slaves between 1800 and 1810, or about 68 percent of the 109,200 slaves imported nationally in that decade. During this period Charleston was "one of the great slaving ports of the world."[21]

Though local directories were quite inaccurate, the number of merchants listed in each year in Table 1 indicates the timing of the boom and bust. From a nadir in 1782 during the British occupation, the number of merchants in Charleston built to a peak in 1807, declined sharply during the War of 1812, boomed again after the war, and dropped back to its pre-boom numbers by 1825. The increase in the number of men entering commerce, and their equally rapid exit, is clear.

TABLE 1   Number of Merchants Listed in Charleston Directory

YEAR	MERCHANTS
1782	135
1790	199
1794	214
1796*	241
1803	336
1807	472
1813	247
1819	429
1822	355
1825	214

*Some pages missing from this volume.

The length of time that these men were listed in the directory indicates whether they were newly arrived in the city, or local men who had changed careers (for example, from a retail shopkeeper to an overseas-trading merchant). The 1794 city directory recorded 214 men as merchants (see Table 1). About 51 percent of them had been listed in the 1790 directory, and only about 11 percent of them had been in Charleston in 1782 during the Revolution.

Similarly, in the 1807 city directory, the last full year that the international slave trade was legal, the number of men listed as merchants reached its zenith at 472, more than twice as many men as had been listed 13 years earlier. Again, only about half of them were listed four years earlier. The number of merchants in Charleston grew rapidly, promoted by immigration from Great Britain, France, Germany, and elsewhere in America.[22]

Merchants rarely stayed in Charleston for very long. In 1796, there were 241 merchants listed in the directory. Seven years later, in 1803, less than half of them remained.[23] In 1807, there were 472 merchants in the directory. Six years later, in 1813, only about 41 percent of those men remained. Though the first block of time stretched through the boom years, and the second included the wartime depression, merchants were nearly as transient under both conditions. In general, Charleston's merchants seem to have tried their fortunes in the city for a brief period, and then left to retire or try again elsewhere.

Contemporary observers often complained that very few local boys grew up to be merchants. E. S. Thomas listed the proprietors of the twenty-one most important firms in Charleston in 1795, then mentioned that "[n]ot one of the above was a native of South Carolina, except for Mr. Stoney."[24] J. B. Dunlop, who visited Charleston between 1810 and 1811, concluded that "The young men are either bred to the Law enter into the army or Spend their days in Idleness and they leave the profits of Commerce to be enjoyed exclusively by Strangers: It is a rare thing indeed, for a Carolinian to follow the avocation of a Merchant."[25] These complaints seem to have been accurate. In this period, most of Charleston's merchants originally lacked strong local ties; they were typically men who came to Charleston to export cotton, to ship Caribbean produce to Europe, or to import slaves.

The same observers noticed the ethnic diversity of many Charleston merchants. A visitor said that he saw in Charleston the "mixture and jostling together of men of all classes and nations . . . the desperate slave trader, privateer, and pirate from Cuba and the Spanish main, the keen Jew from Poland, and the keener Scotchman from the Clyde," and many others.[26] Scottish merchants came to Charleston to profit from the boom years; one merchant joked during an epidemic that "the City is Cleared of all the young Scotchman" who would ordinarily be engaged in trade.[27] The number of Jewish merchants also surprised visitors, because Charleston between 1776 and 1820 was home to more Jews than "any other city in America."[28] This ethnic diversity may have contributed to a perception that nearly all merchants were foreign, with little rootedness in the community, regardless of whether they intended to remain in Charleston.

Charleston notables criticized merchants for being "mere *Birds of Passage*,"[29] but merchants were not the only skilled workers who drifted throughout the Atlantic World to wherever the prospects seemed best. Historian T. A. Milford has noted the itinerant careers of lawyers in the pre-Revolutionary period. Foreign-born artisans increasingly brought their skills to antebellum America; as Bruce Laurie noted, "in every major Northern city by 1860 just about a third of the printers, almost half the building tradesmen, and nearly three-fourths of the shoemakers, tailors, and cabinetmakers were foreign-born."[30] In general, we have not paid enough attention to the numbers of foreigners who worked in the white-collar and well-paid blue-collar occupations that became defined as the American middle class.

In the nineteenth century, Americans and Europeans often claimed that the middle class had a moral sense superior to that of other classes. As one Virginian wrote, "The middle class in every community . . . being equally removed from the temptations of poverty and the allurements of great opulence, is uniformly the most virtuous."[31] Middling comforts, according to a British analyst, promoted middle-class engagement in civic improvement. "The middling class, those who are above want and not exposed to luxury, are comparatively . . . moral, commanding their passions, and endeavouring to diffuse happiness around them."[32] This link has endured in modern historiography. Many historians have placed the middle class at the center of the humanitarian projects of the nineteenth century, such as abolitionism.[33]

Recent scholarship has questioned the purported virtuousness of the middle class through a closer look at business behavior in the early Republic. British colonial economic strategy had been rooted in mercantilism: while promoting financial and industrial development in the mother country, it restricted the colonies to agricultural production.[34] The Revolution liberated Americans to engage in previously discouraged occupations such as the international slave trade, manufacturing, and banking.[35] The post-Constitution boom, in common with the relaxation of governmental authority after the Revolution, freed trade from many of the ethical scruples that had once bound it. Seemingly staid occupations were actually thoroughgoing examples of aggressive capitalism. Banks loaned recklessly to insiders and blanketed the country with worthless notes.[36]

Even trades that had existed before the war showed the new spirit. Retail trade was especially corrupt.[37] Swindling clerks jousted with haggling customers in "a contest of knavery" on retail streets in every urban center. Customers demanded to look at all the goods in the shop, in hopes that the beleaguered clerk would offer them a discount. Meanwhile, clerks offered flattery while concealing the poor quality of their goods.[38] In a contemporary short story, a storekeeper tells his new clerk that he hires young men "trained . . . to industry, perseverance, honest frugality, and the duties of a Christian man." The clerk agrees that he does, indeed, embody all these middle-class virtues. Then the storekeeper outlines what the clerk's job entails: "If a woman asks whether four-penny calico, or six-penny delaines will wash, say 'yes, ma'am, *beautifully;* I've tried them, or seen them tried;' and if they say, 'are these ten cent flannels real *Shaker flannels?* or the ninepence hose *all merino?'* better not contradict them . . . when you make change, never take a ten cent piece and two cents for a shilling, but give it as often as practicable . . . in measuring, always put your thumb *so,* and when you move the yardstick forward, shove your thumb an inch or so *back;* in measuring *close* you may manage to squeeze out five yards from four and three-quarters, you understand?"[39] In short, the clerk's job was to lie to his customers, and to steal from them.

The letters of Charleston's merchants reflect the rough-and-tumble nature of antebellum business, and suggest that the virtuousness of the nineteenth-century middle class has been greatly exaggerated. Though merchants were trustworthy and reliable with close friends and family members, they were not "the most virtuous" members of society with casual customers and the government. As England became an industrial giant, the need to feed the machines drove demand for slaves and cotton. Well aware that the boom could end at any time, Charleston's merchants were willing to do nearly anything to fill these demands. They cheated their customers, cheated the government, and only behaved ethically with their friends and family. Such a system was functional because everyone knew what to expect: *caveat emptor.*

Charleston's merchants often overcharged short-term customers. Jacob Rapelye asked his relative Paul in New York to send some kitchen equipment to his landlady, telling him, "you can charge twenty five percent [commis-sion] by making out a ficticious Invoice."[40] The retail shops that lined King Street provided ample opportunities for fraud. A young Yankee in Charleston commented on the lack of ethics he witnessed as an employee of E. L. Miller, dry goods merchant: "I've to sovereign a contempt for the, <u>low art, Finesse, cunning & sarvility</u> mde use of now a days in the dry goods trade—<u>those are but other words for swindling</u> Miller tried to persuade me it was indispens-ably necessary if one intends to live in the business—if thats the case think I I'll not live by it." The young man added, "I would think my own Father an accomplish'd knave if he had been any time, & made money in the dry goods line in <u>King St.</u>"[41] Charleston's merchants believed that customers knew what they were in for when they went shopping. If they were cheated, they had only themselves to blame.

The government and police force in post-Revolutionary Charleston did not protect citizens from swindling. Modern Americans take the police force for granted, but it functioned quite differently in the early Republic. Though a constabulary existed in Charleston, historians agree that as in other major cities, it cared more about "social order" than "the apprehension of criminals." Charleston patrollers, like those elsewhere in the South, particularly focused their efforts on repressing the slave population.[42]

One example shows how crime was treated in post-Revolutionary Charleston. In early 1804, merchant John Day loaded trunks with gold in Charleston and shipped them to Savannah. But the boat was becalmed, and the passengers disembarked, including the man charged with watching the trunks. When the passengers returned, the gold, not surprisingly, was gone. Day had left Charles-ton by the time the theft was discovered. Confronted with an unhelpful police force, Day entrusted several friends with the task of tracking down the gold.

In particular, Day became convinced that an old German man who worked for his friends Alexander Ewing and James Ross was the thief. So Ewing and Ross came up with a plan to determine the old man's guilt or innocence. At three in the morning, Ross woke the old man, holding a gun to his chest. Claiming the man had confessed to the crime in his sleep, Ross threatened to shoot him unless he gave up the location of the gold and his accomplice. But the old man "evinc'd no symptom of guilt," Ross and Ewing explained, and "we feel satisfied of his innocence."[43] There was an undercurrent of danger and lawlessness to

*Cause they're all
shady thiefs*

business in Charleston. Like cowboys in a Western movie, Charleston's merchants resorted to violence because they knew the state would not help them.

Because they expected so little from the government and so many of them had only weak ties to South Carolina, many merchants had absolutely no ethical qualms about cheating either local or national governments. Thomas Henry Hindley, a regular mercantile visitor from Great Britain, was about to ship cotton to a British client when he learned of the imminent approach of the 1808 Embargo. In his eagerness to fulfill the contract, he snuck onto the ship with a pilot before dawn, hoping to launch the ship unnoticed. However, "we were not fortunate enough to get . . . over the Bar, before we were boarded by the Revenue Cutter, who fired three shot into us, and I have nearly got into great difficulty for making the attempt to get the vessel out." Untroubled by his close brush with the armed forces of the custom house, Hindley cheerfully told his clients that he would try to sneak the cotton onto a British ship that was about to get under way.[44]

In general, merchants responded to restrictions on trade with increasingly sophisticated attempts at smuggling. During the Non-Intercourse Act and the War of 1812, Charleston's merchants shipped cotton to British customers through Spanish Amelia Island.[45] The trade continued even though merchants complained about Spanish corruption and ineptitude. Bribing the customs agents there was part of the cost of doing business. An agent explained how he had been able to reduce the duties on his customer's cotton "through Mr. Clough's Influence with the Collector at Amelia & a Doubloon or two's assistance."[46] Merchants smuggled cotton to Europe because of industrial demand, regardless of the desires of the "wiseacres at Washington."[47]

After the opening of the international slave trade, merchants traded slaves illicitly with customers in the Caribbean. Fitzsimons suggested that it might be profitable to ship slaves from Charleston to Havana, if a war took place between England and Spain. He added that "there is a difficulty attending the shipping of Slaves from the United States, an act of Congress which Prohibits that Trade, under *severe Penalties*—as yet it has not been noticed but was Slaves Shipped off, in large Numbers—it would be attended with danger."[48] Slaves were valuable, made more so because their transportation was frequently interdicted by state or national governments. Smuggling was an understandable response to governmental restrictions.

A picture emerges from mercantile letters of the middle-class values merchants themselves most esteemed: energy, cunning, diligence, and reliability. What a man wanted was a partner who was willing to brave the cannons of the revenue cutter, lie about the illicit origins of a slave, bribe a customs officer, or smuggle goods out through a purportedly closed port. Hard work was at the center of middle-class identity, and virtue was much further down the list of valued assets in a trading partner. As they would have seen it, the goal was to run a business, not a Sunday school.

Despite all the short-term thinking and blatant fraud, the boom years still promoted improvement and modernity in Charleston, especially in the financial sector. For the remainder of the antebellum period, merchants and former merchants worked at local banks and also invested heavily in government securities.[49] William Lee, for example, was a merchant and slave trader who became a teller for the Bank of the State of South Carolina. Josiah Smith, who had been a merchant in Charleston before the war, served as cashier of the local branch of the Bank of the United States.

George Nelson's letters document why merchants became so interested in banking. He commented to a friend in 1794 that it was a good time to leave the retail and wholesale trades and to speculate in U.S. Bank stock instead; "if you was out of business [i.e., trade] and had the Command of Cash . . . you would be sure to do well with prudence & with less anxiety then being in business."[50] Nelson expected to make money both as a short-term speculator, benefiting when stock prices rose, and as a recipient of dividends. He claimed that a South Carolina bank regularly gave dividends of 15 percent, "which is very handsome."[51] Because banking was a more conservative form of enterprise in Charleston than in the North, it served the same purpose that manufacturing did for the merchants' Bostonian peers: a way for well-capitalized men to be semiretired and still have a regular income stream.[52] The boom may have been overheated, unfettered, and temporary, but some of its consequences were beneficial. Unfortunately, some were not.

Scholars agree that merchants were not always viewed negatively in South Carolina. Through the Revolution, they were part of Charleston's elite. Men like Henry Laurens, inspired by British writers who flattered the middle class for its cosmopolitanism and practicality, believed that even though a merchant could never be a member of the aristocracy, he could be refined into gentility by his occupation.[53] But by 1800, as historian George C. Rogers Jr. noted, "the merchants were declining, the men who had imported not only goods, but ideas . . . who had brought a sense of struggle and competition, who represented the thrust of the new middle class."[54]

References to merchants as members of a distinct middle class—and of this class being less worthy and refined than the planter elite—multiplied around the War of 1812. E. S. Thomas claimed that in 1795, "Charleston was the most aristocratic city in the Union . . . The door of the '*St. Cecelia Society*' was shut to the plebian and the man of business, with . . . two exceptions."[55] Henry Gourdin, a planter's son, felt uncomfortable in the "civilization of the life" of the retail trader who was his first master. "Their sitting room, dining and breakfast room were one, and opened immediately into the store. To be put to bed at night on a mattress dumped upon the floor of this room when the family had retired, and stirred up in the morning by the broom of the house maid of all work to prepare it for breakfast, was . . . 'tight lines' for one born and nurtured" in the planter class.[56] Refinement, as Gourdin knew, demanded separation of the social and functional spaces of the house into parlor and kitchen. The visible presence of work was not genteel. Furthermore, a gentleman required private space to prepare to be sociable.[57] Most merchants accepted that they were not elegant. Thomas Smith wrote that, unlike the "fashionable people" who attended parties and flirted with ladies, "we of Manchester Hall do not . . . rank as fashionable, confining our attention too exclusively to Cotton Bags & our visits to the Wharves."[58] Merchants saw themselves as too awkward and rough for the genteel social sphere, and the local planter elite agreed.

Why did planters decide they were superior to the merchants who had previously been their peers? Charleston's planters accurately claimed that trade could be debasing, and they were probably also correct to impugn the morality of many postwar merchants in comparison to their more staid colonial predecessors. Merchants knew that at least two types of business were only temporary—the slave trade ceased in 1808 and the neutral trade finished with American entry into the war—and entered into them with a frenzy that belied ethics and good judgment.

Nevertheless, planters were not disinterested parties. By removing the British "*de jure*" aristocracy from the top ranks of the social world, the Revolution made room for local "*de facto*" aristocracies.[59] Great wealth, political control, and the stability that came from the intermarriage of a small number of families formed the primary sources of the planters' power. As one observer wrote, Charleston's social leaders were a "few old patrician families, into which 'novi homines,' unless distinguished by great personal merit, find it extremely difficult to gain admission." But the planters also wished to believe that their status rested on their inherent aristocratic qualities. Like other post-Revolutionary elites, planters sought to consolidate their social power through their claims to refinement: "travel (especially travel to Europe), education, manners, and mastery of genteel skills such as dance and dress."[60] The luxurious homes and artworks that these men acquired advertised their elegant taste and intellect. As Frederick Law Olmstead wrote, "there is less vulgar display, and more intrinsic elegance, and habitual mental refinement in the best society of South Carolina, than in any distinct class among us." Another British visitor praised them as "a genuine aristocracy."[61] Charleston's merchants—precursors of the Age of Barnum—were increasingly out of place in this self-consciously genteel world.

Historians have found many ways that the southern elite distinguished itself from the middle class. Elite white southerners upheld honor culture, rejecting Christian-inspired morality, self-control, and self-discipline.[62] But in South Carolina, it may have been gentility that became the most important fault line between merchants and planters. Charleston's elite maligned mercantile behavior less because it was dishonorable than because it was inelegant.

Furthermore, planters benefited from making economic turmoil and the resumption of the slave trade someone else's fault. The War of 1812 ended Charleston's boom years. Neutral trading was shut off, and the overseas slave trade had already come to a close. Financial institutions were damaged by the war, and the Bank of South Carolina stock dropped in value. Averaging $77 per share before the war, from 1812 to 1825 the price dropped to an average of $66 per share.[63] It took a longer time for the cotton trade to show this downward trend. Following a wartime slowdown, high cotton prices prevailed between 1815 and 1819. After 1819, however, cotton prices declined again. Charleston's preeminence as a cotton port ended as it was replaced by cities with better connections to the backcountry and hinterlands with fresher soil. From 472 merchants in the 1807 city directory, the number dropped to 247 in 1813. After a rebound in 1819 to 429 merchants, the number declined again to 355 in 1822 and 214 in 1825. As other businesses became unprofitable or illegal, a merchant's job was reduced to exporting cotton, and to a lesser extent, rice. Ambitious young men went elsewhere. As one historian put it, "After nearly twenty-five years of prosperity, a long period of economic stagnation and a mood close to despair were setting in."[64]

Though the economic decline probably hurt planters less than merchants, it did make planters fear that their region was falling behind its peers to the north.[65] Charlestonians knew exactly who to blame for the economic turmoil: strangers. These "foreign" merchants were believed to be un-southern in their behavior. According to Frank Byrne's study of merchants, antebellum North and South Carolina newspapers identified merchants as following "cunning Yankee practices" and "values alien to Dixie" that risked disrupting the community. Newspapers commonly contained stories of predatory merchants who cheated naive customers.[66] While analysis of the city directories shows that most merchants were strangers to Charleston, Charlestonians emphasized their foreign behavior because that meant that economic misjudgments could be placed at the feet of outsiders.

The temporary revival of the international slave trade also decreased mercantile status. Despite South Carolina's economic dependence on slavery, the decision to legalize the slave trade was controversial within the state, especially in the lowcountry. As Jed Shugerman found, "Of the twenty-five lowcountry representatives who voted to reopen the trade, fourteen were not returned to the house next year [1804]." Four others, responding to their constituents, reversed their positions.[67] A congressman from South Carolina said that merchants who attempted to extend the international slave trade past its deadline were "so taken up with their idol, Mammon, with their zeal after profit, that they cared not what became of the country if their coffers were filled."[68]

As the only state to open the international slave trade, South Carolina was reviled by other Americans. Southerners worried that South Carolina's action would trigger a Haiti-like uprising. The *Raleigh Register* described it as "a detested short sighted policy, which in order to increase the wealth of a few can impose upon the state the greatest calamity with which any nation has ever been afflicted." Northerners were often troubled for moral reasons. Pamphleteer Ann Alexander, a Philadelphian, was horrified that "a custom, so barbarous as well as so repugnant to every principle of humanity and justice, as the African Slave-Trade, should be continued in this or any other nation."[69]

The more that Charleston's planters could make the responsibility for the slave trade's magnitude either foreign or northern in origin, the more morally pure they themselves would appear to be. In the face of northern criticism that South Carolina had stood alone to open the slave trade, the *Courier* pointed out that "of the six American ships that were on the coast of Africa in February [1806], only one was owned by a Charlestonian. The rest belonged to citizens of Philadelphia, Boston, and Newport."[70] This sort of statement was true, but also incomplete. As James McMillin has pointed out, Charlestonians had plenty of involvement in the slave trade, even if they were not merchants. "Planters [and] farmers . . . poured into the city to purchase the Africans. To pay for the slaves, planters and farmers sent more than $18,000,000 in rice, tobacco, and cotton to the port." The beneficiaries of the slave trade also included lawyers, clerks, innkeepers and many other tradesmen.[71] In short, white Charlestonians from all walks of life profited from the boom; slave trade business did not only earn money for strangers.

Slave-trading merchants may also have been less foreign than merchants in general. Of the merchants in the 1807 city directory found on James McMillin's list of slave traders, about 64 percent had been there in 1803, and about 59 percent remained in 1813, 38 percent in 1819, and 31 percent in 1822.[72] For merchants in general in the 1807 city directory, about 50 percent had been there in 1803, and about 41 percent were still there in 1813, 29 percent in 1819, and 25 percent in 1822 (Table 2). Slave-trading merchants seem to have been less transient than the average merchant, which might have been due to the greater wealth of slave-trading merchants. Because men who sold slaves were supposed to extend a considerable amount of credit to their customers, it was a trade that was only open to the successful.

TABLE 2   1807 Directory-Listed Merchants, Percent Listed in Previous and Following Years

YEAR	SLAVE-TRADING	NON-SLAVE TRADING
1803	64	50
1813	59	41
1819	38	29
1822	31	25

Even after the international slave trade was banned, Charlestonians continued to insist upon the primary culpability of foreign merchants. Senator William Loughton Smith told the Senate in 1820 that most slave-trading merchants were British or Yankees. He added, "those [New England] people who most deprecate the evils of slavery and traffic in human flesh, when a profitable market can be found, can sell human flesh with as easy a conscience as they sell other articles."[73] One visitor was told in the mid-1820s, "There was formerly a considerable trade in slaves carried on from Charleston, most however by foreigners."[74]

Though the slave traders were purportedly "foreigners" who had left town, Charlestonians had a superstition about their children. "It was a common saying in Charleston, that 'the curse of God stuck to all slave-traders and their children,' who never prospered finally. There seemed to be one, and I was told only one, exception to this rule, in the person of a very benevolent gentleman, the son of a slave trader. But during my residence in South Carolina, this exception ceased to exist; for the person alluded to failed in business, and 'the curse' at last fell upon him."[75] Contradictions to this "curse," such as Nathaniel Russell, Adam Tunno, and Christopher Fitzsimons, all of whom died wealthy, are easy to find. Fitzsimons, for example, married one of his daughters to Wade Hampton's son, and another to James Henry Hammond. But apparently ashamed of their slave-trading past, Charlestonians wished to make transgressions disappear, as if by the hand of God. At the same time that mercantile practices became most embarrassing, the middle class vanished from the mental map of elite Charleston.

As a leader of cultural thought in the antebellum South, Charleston's bias against merchants shaped the status of the middle class throughout the Cotton Empire. For example, Byrne has pointed out that the idea that "most merchants operating in the South hailed from Europe and the North—that they were 'Jews' and 'Yankees'" was a "commonly held misconception."[76] While the stereotype failed to fit most of the antebellum South, it was an accurate depiction of the mercantile population in pre–War of 1812 Charleston. A bias against foreign merchants, based on a desire to seem aristocratic, a reaction to a particular economic bubble, and the controversial status of the slave trade in antebellum America, shaped the treatment of the middle class throughout the antebellum South.

What is especially ironic about the wide spread of anti-mercantile thought in the South is that Charleston's merchants actually regained some of their status in the 1830s and 1840s, as Charlestonians fought to improve the local economy.[77] Defenders of the rejuvenated mercantile population endlessly repeated that they were a new breed of merchants, and that unlike their predecessors, they could boast local ties. (This may not have been true—a contemporary visitor claimed that five-sixths of local merchants were strangers.[78]) A South Carolina newspaper proclaimed that Charleston's "most eminent men are placing their sons in counting houses on both sides of the Atlantic." Merchant Henry Gourdin's brother wrote that when his brother entered trade in 1819 he was the "first planter's son who embarked in a business upon which the elite of the community looked down," ending a period when "the trade and commerce of Charleston lapsed into the hands of strangers, Northerners and foreigners." Interestingly, Gourdin's brother seems to have forgotten that their uncle and grandfather were also merchants in Charleston.[79] Charleston's merchants enjoyed their renewed status until the economic chaos of the Civil War brought new and sometimes justified allegations of profiteering.[80]

Business ethics during the boom years of the 1790s and early 1800s should make scholars rethink what we mean by "middle-class values." Rather than being moral exemplars, or hypocrites, Charleston's merchants believed that the world was an untrustworthy place. As realists, they gave their loyalty to those who might return it: their families and business partners. Most customers and the state and federal governments were not included. Participants in the market understood the prevailing atmosphere of deceit, and took measures to protect themselves.

The brief legal reopening of the international slave trade and the excesses of the boom years before the War of 1812 had readily apparent effects on the status of the middle class in South Carolina. As elite Carolinians liked to tell the story, deceitful foreigners had swept into South Carolina and then left again with their ill-gotten gains. The mercantile middle class was nonexistent or dying out. But this story was popular because it excused Charleston's planters for their promotion of the boom and bust. When we hear contemporary speakers say that the southern middle class was disappearing, we should wonder how they benefited from saying so.

NOTES

1. Maurie McInnis, *The Politics of Taste in Antebellum Charleston* (Chapel Hill: University of North Carolina Press, 2005), 25.

2. William W. Freehling, *Prelude to Civil War: The Nullification Controversy in South Carolina, 1816–1836* (New York: Oxford University Press, 1992), 13; Frederick Cople Jaher, *The Urban Establishment: Upper Strata in Boston, New York, Charleston, Chicago, and Los Angeles* (Urbana: University of Illinois Press, 1982), 337–38.

3. See previously listed books as well as Rosser H. Taylor, *Ante-bellum South Carolina: A Social and Cultural History* (Chapel Hill: University of North Carolina Press, 1942), 43–45; George C. Rogers Jr., *Charleston in the Age of the Pinckneys* (Columbia: University of South Carolina, 1980), 52–53.

4. Max Weber, "Status Groups and Classes," in *The Essential Weber: A Reader,* ed. Sam Whimster (New York: Routledge, 2004), 176.

5. Stuart Blumin, *The Emergence of the Middle Class: Social Experience in the American City, 1760–1900* (New York: Cambridge University Press, 1989), esp. ch. 3.

6. Weber, "Status Groups and Classes," 179–80; Max Weber, "The Distribution of Power in Society: Classes, Status Groups, and Parties," in *The Essential Weber,* 188.

7. Ute Frevert, "Honor and Middle-Class Culture: The History of the Duel in England and Germany," in *Bourgeois Society in Nineteenth-Century Europe,* ed. Jurgen Kocka and Allen Mitchell (Providence, R.I.: Berge Publishers, 1993), 208–10.

8. For a more thorough analysis of this issue, see Jennifer L. Goloboy, "The Early American Middle Class," *Journal of the Early Republic* 25 (Winter 2005): 537–45.

9. July 30, 1817 entry (first quotation), Davis Thacher Papers, South Caroliniana Library, University of South Carolina (hereafter SCL); C. Fitzsimons, Charleston, to Captain Silvanus Rich, on board Brig Plough Boy Charleston, February 13, 1805, April 18, 1805; C. Fitzsimons, Charleston, to Peter Thomas Ryan, on board Brig Plough Boy, Charleston, June 1, 1805; [Christopher Fitzsimons], Charleston, to John Gernon Esqr, December 20, 1805 (second quotation), Christopher Fitzsimons Letterbook, vol. 2, SCL.

10. Jonathan Barry, "Introduction," in *The Middling Sort of People: Culture, Society and Politics in England, 1550–1800,* ed. Jonathan Barry and Christopher Brooks (New York: St. Martin's Press, 1994), 2–3, 15.

11. Jonathan Daniel Wells, *The Origins of the Southern Middle Class, 1800–1861* (Chapel Hill: University of North Carolina Press, 2004), 68, 86–87; Blumin, *Emergence of the Middle Class,* 1–2.

12. Burton J. Bledstein, "Introduction: Storytellers to the Middle Class," in *The Middling Sorts: Explorations in the History of the American Middle Class,* ed. Burton J. Bledstein and Robert D. Johnston (New York: Routledge, 2001), 3–7; Barry, "Introduction," 3.

13. Jaher, *Urban Establishment,* 344.

14. Robert E. Wright, *One Nation Under Debt: Hamilton, Jefferson, and the History of What We Owe* (New York: McGraw-Hill, 2008), 246–51, 317, 332. Stock prices calculated by the author using statistics from Richard E. Sylla, Jack W. Wilson, and Robert E. Wright, "Price Quotations

thanks Goloboy for waiting until your 4 to make a 4th to last thesis-like definitive, statement.

in Early United States Securities Markets, 1790–1860" [www.eh.net/databases/early-us-securities -prices, accessed May 28, 2008].

15. Eli F. Heckscher, *The Continental System* (Oxford: Clarendon Press, 1922), 102–3.

16. E. S. Thomas, *Reminiscences of the Last Sixty-Five Years*, 2 vols. (Hartford: Case, Tiffany, and Burham, 1840), 1:35.

17. Stuart Bruchey, *Enterprise: The Dynamic Economy of a Free People* (Cambridge, Mass.: Harvard University Press, 1990), 231.

18. Jennifer L. Goloboy, "Success to Trade: Charleston's Merchants in the Revolutionary Era" (Ph.D. diss., Harvard University, 2003), 41.

19. Jed Handelsman Shugerman, "The Louisiana Purchase and South Carolina's Reopening of the Slave Trade in 1803," *Journal of the Early Republic* 22 (Summer 2002): 264; Walter J. Fraser, *Charleston! Charleston!: The History of a Southern City* (Columbia: University of South Carolina Press, 1991), 188.

20. Shugerman, "Louisiana Purchase and South Carolina's Reopening of the Slave Trade in 1803"; Patrick S. Brady, "The Slave Trade and Sectionalism in South Carolina, 1787–1808," *Journal of Southern History* 38 (November 1972): 601–20.

21. James A. McMillin, *The Final Victims: Foreign Slave Trade to North America, 1783–1810* (Columbia: University of South Carolina Press, 2004), 48, 94.

22. These calculations are based on my analysis of Charleston city directories. I count as merchants any men who used the word "Merchants" to describe themselves, including "Hay Merchants," "Lumber Merchants," "Wine Merchants," and an "Importer French Goods" from 1825. I exclude "Shopkeepers" or "Factors" as merchants. In determining their tenure in town, however, I count men who at one point called themselves merchants regardless of their later identification. Thus, a merchant in 1803 with a different occupation in 1807 would be included as a merchant for 1803 and would only be included in calculating merchant retention in 1807.

Because of many sources of error, these numbers should used as a suggestion of population trends rather than as an accurate count of the total number of merchants in Charleston. Directory tabulators often left people out, especially merchants who only spent part of the year in Charleston. Since different men assembled the directories, types of omissions probably varied from year to year. The common eighteenth- and nineteenth-century practice of reusing first names for sons and nephews probably means that I inaccurately combined listings for close relatives. Merchants may have been listed twice, under their firm names and under their own names; I choose to include both listings to avoid combining listings for men with the same last names. Finally, I use James Hagy's transcriptions of the city directories, rather than the original directories.

23. This count is based on a copy of the 1796 directory with missing pages, so is probably slightly low. However, this should not increase the retention percentage.

24. Thomas, *Reminiscences of the Last Sixty-Five Years*, 1:40–41. Thomas's list: "Nathaniel Russell, Kirk & Lukens, Mann & Foltz, James & Edwin Gardiner, Robert Hazelhurst & Co., Vos & Graves, Whitfield & Brown, Jennings & Wooddrop, Campbell, Harvey & Co., J. & J. Hargraves, Casper C. Schutt, Charles Banks & Co., Williamson & Stoney, John Brownlee, William Turpin, Allan, Mason & Ewing, Frederick Kohne, William & James Thayer, Tunno & Cox, E. Coffin, Thomas Tunno."

25. J. B. Dunlop Diary, 1810–11, New-York Historical Society (hereafter NYHS).

26. "Notes on America, No. I: Charleston, South Carolina," *The Albion: or British, Colonial, and Foreign Weekly Gazette,* July 28, 1832, vol. 11, no. 8, 61. This observer visited Charleston in the mid-1820s.

27. Seth Lothrop, Charleston, to Mr. Sylvanus Keith (Brother), Providence, September 29, 1807, Sylvanus and Cary Keith Papers, Rare Books, Manuscript and Special Collections Library, Duke University.

28. Marcie Cohen Farris, *Matzoh Ball Gumbo: Culinary Tales of the Jewish South* (Chapel Hill: University of North Carolina Press, 2005), 37; Jaher, *Urban Establishment,* 337.

29. Jaher, *Urban Establishment.* Also see Adam Smith, *The Wealth of Nations,* book III, ch. 4. [http://ibiblio.org/gutenberg/etexto2/wltnt10.txt, accessed April 20, 2003.]

30. T. A. Milford, *The Gardiners of Massachusetts: Provincial Ambition and the British-American Career* (Lebanon: University of New Hampshire Press, 2005), 10; Bruce Laurie, *Artisans into Workers: Labor in Nineteenth-Century America* (Urbana: University of Illinois Press, 1997), 103–4.

31. Wells, *Origins of the Southern Middle Class,* 86 (quotation), 137; see also Dror Wahrman, "'Middle-Class' Domesticity Goes Public: Gender, Class, and Politics from Queen Caroline to Queen Victoria," *Journal of British Studies* 32 (October 1993), *passim.*

32. Wahrman, "'Middle-Class' Domesticity Goes Public," 412.

33. These historians have also acknowledged that the middle class may have chosen its favorite causes for self-aggrandizing reasons. Thomas L. Haskell, "Capitalism and the Origins of the Humanitarian Sensibility, Part 2," in *The Antislavery Debate: Capitalism and Abolitionism as a Problem in Historical Interpretation,* ed. Thomas Bender (Berkeley: University of California Press, 1992), esp. 153–55. See also earlier treatments of the "social control" thesis, which linked the middle-class claim to morality with power over the working class, discussed in Haskell's "Capitalism and the Origins of the Humanitarian Sensibility, Part 1" in ibid., esp. 110–12.

34. Peter A Coclanis, *The Shadow of a Dream: Economic Life and Death in the South Carolina Lowcountry, 1670–1920* (New York: Oxford University Press, 1989), ch. 1.

35. Ronald W. Bailey, "'That Gainful Branch': South Carolina's Henry Laurens and the Political Economy of the Slave(ry) Trade," unpublished paper, Carolina Lowcountry and Atlantic World conference, March 26, 2008; Lawrence A. Peskin, *Manufacturing Revolution: The Intellectual Origins of Early American Industry* (Baltimore: Johns Hopkins University Press, 2003); Bray Hammond, *Banks and Politics in America: From the Revolution to the Civil War* (Princeton: Princeton University Press, 1957).

36. Stephen Mihm, *A Nation of Counterfeiters: Capitalists, Con Men, and the Making of the United States* (Cambridge, Mass.: Harvard University Press, 2007), 56; Naomi R. Lamoreaux, *Insider Lending: Banks, Personal Connections, and Economic Development in Industrial New England* (New York: Cambridge University Press, 1996).

37. Brett Mizelle, "William Frederick Pinchbeck and the Strategy of Exposure: A Prehistory of the Antebellum Culture of Deception"; Paul J. Erickson, "Narratives of Antebellum Commercial Deception"; and Wendy Woloson, "Hammer Time: Spurious Auctions and the Public Spectacle of Antebellum Deception," papers presented at the Society for the Historians of the Early American Republic, Montreal, Canada, 2006.

38. Erickson, "Narratives of Antebellum Commercial Deception."

39. Jonathan F. Kelley (Kelly), "Wanted—A Young Man from the Country," in *The Humors of Falconbridge: A Collection of Humorous and Every Day Stories* (Philadelphia: T. B. Peterson, 1856), 332–34.

40. J Rapelye, Charleston, to Mr. Paul Rapelye, New York, November 16, 1815, Napier, Rapelye, and Bennett, SCL.

41. Davis Thacher Diary, October 1818 entry, SCL.

42. William H. Pease and Jane H. Pease, *The Web of Progress: Private Values and Public Styles in Boston and Charleston, 1828–1843* (Athens: University of Georgia Press, 1991), 100–101; Sally E. Hadden, *Slave Patrols: Law and Violence in Virginia and the Carolinas* (Cambridge, Mass.: Harvard University Press, 2001), esp. 57–58, 84.

43. A. Ewing & J. Ross, Charleston, to Mr. John Day, Messrs. Taylor & Scarbrough, Savannah, January 31, 1804, Ferguson & Day and successor companies, NYHS.

44. Thos. Hy. Hindley, Charleston, to Messrs. Ferguson & Day, New York, January 7, 1808, Ferguson & Day and successor companies, NYHS.

45. Hindley & Gregorie, Charleston, to Messrs. Ferguson & Day, New York, September 27, 1809, Ferguson & Day and successor companies, NYHS.

46. Henry Lord, St. Marys to Messrs. Ferguson & Day, May 19, 1809, Ferguson & Day and successor companies, NYHS.

47. Hindley & Gregorie, Charleston, to Messrs. Ferguson & Day, New York, December 29, 1809, Ferguson & Day and successor companies, NYHS.

48. CF [Christopher Fitzsimmons], Charleston, to Mr. Patrick Welsh, Havana, February 14, 1805, Christopher Fitzsimons Papers, SCL.

49. Jaher, *Urban Establishment*, 344–45; Wright, *One Nation Under Debt*, 246–51, 317.

50. Geo. Nelson to Mr. Samuel Bellamy, July 28, 1794, George Nelson Letterbook, Southern Historical Collection, University of North Carolina (hereafter SHC).

51. GN [George Nelson], C'ton, to Mr. [Samuel] Bellamy, March 2, 1796, George Nelson Letterbook, SHC.

52. Jaher, *Urban Establishment*, 348; Robert F. Dalzell Jr., *Enterprising Elite: The Boston Associates and the World They Made* (Cambridge, Mass.: Harvard University Press, 1987), 52–54, 63–67.

53. On gentility among non-elites, see Milford, *Gardiners of Massachusetts*, 24–25.

54. George C. Rogers Jr., *Evolution of a Federalist: William Loughton Smith of Charleston (1758–1812)* (Columbia: University of South Carolina Press, 1962), 373; Rogers among others often made this argument; see Rogers, *Charleston in the Age of the Pinckneys*; Richard Waterhouse, *A New World Gentry: The Making of a Merchant and Planter Class in South Carolina, 1670–1770* (New York: Garland Publishing Inc., 1989); Mark Dementi Kaplanoff, "Making the South Solid: Politics and the Structure of Society in South Carolina, 1790–1815" (Ph.D. diss., University of Cambridge, 1979).

55. Thomas, *Reminiscences of the Last Sixty-Five Years,* 1:33–34.

56. Robert Newman Gourdin, "Gourdins of Charleston: A Family Notable in Social and Commercial Life," in *The Gourdin Family,* comp. Peter Gaillard Gourdin IV (Easley, S.C.: Southern Historical Press, 1980), 534–35.

57. Richard L. Bushman, *The Refinement of America: Persons, Houses, Cities* (New York: Knopf, 1992).

58. Thomas Smith to John Ferguson Esq. [dear Ferguson], Messrs. Ogden Ferguson & Co., New York, January 13, 1827, Ferguson Papers, New York Genealogical & Biographical Society.

59. Daniel Kilbride, *An American Aristocracy: Southern Planters in Antebellum Philadelphia* (Columbia: University of South Carolina Press, 2006), 2.

60. Kilbride, *American Aristocracy*, 18, McInnis, *Politics of Taste in Antebellum Charleston*, 24. Planters were not always successful in appearing genteel; some felt that they were "crude, debauched, money grubbing, and patriarchal" compared to their northern elite peers; Kilbride, *American Aristocracy*, 47.

61. McInnis, *Politics of Taste in Antebellum Charleston*.

62. Jennifer R. Green, *Military Education and the Emerging Middle Class in the Old South* (New York: Cambridge University Press, 2008), 102–7; Wells, *Origins of the Southern Middle Class*, esp. part II; Kilbride, *American Aristocracy*, 44–45.

63. Wright, *One Nation Under Debt*, 332. Calculated by the author using statistics in Sylla, Wilson, and Wright, "Price Quotations in Early United States Securities Markets."

64. Fraser, *Charleston!* 194–95, 197, 198 (quotation).

65. Jaher, *Urban Establishment*, 341.

66. Frank J. Byrne, *Becoming Bourgeois: Merchant Culture in the South, 1820–1865* (Lexington: University Press of Kentucky, 2006), 66–67.

67. Carl Harrison Brown, "The Reopening of the Foreign Slave Trade in South Carolina, 1803–1807" (M.A. thesis, University of South Carolina, 1968), 8; Shugerman, "Louisiana Purchase and South Carolina's Reopening of the Slave Trade in 1803," 286–87.

68. Rogers, "Evolution of a Federalist," 369.

69. Brown, "Reopening of the Foreign Slave Trade in South Carolina," 46, 48, 49.

70. Ibid., 50.

71. McMillin, *Final Victims*, 95–96.

72. This does not include merchants in the directory who had names similar to those of slave traders, but whom I could not positively identify. I use the entirety of McMillin's list for this calculation, which extends from 1783 to 1807 for Charleston. McMillin, *Final Victims*, 124–31.

73. McMillin, *Final Victims*, 88–89.

74. "Notes on America," 61.

75. Ibid.

76. Byrne, *Becoming Bourgeois*, 41.

77. For the political background of this change, see Joseph J. Persky, *The Burden of Dependency: Colonial Themes in Southern Economic Thought* (Baltimore: Johns Hopkins University Press, 1992), 63–66.

78. Jaher, *Urban Establishment*, 338–39, 343–44.

79. Freehling, *Prelude to Civil War*, 304 (first quotation); Gourdin, "Gourdins of Charleston," 534, 535, 545 (second quotation).

80. Byrne, *Becoming Bourgeois*, 172–73, 180, 187, 189.

Bonds of Marriage and Community

Social Networks and the Development of a Commercial Middle Class in Antebellum South Carolina

AMANDA REECE MUSHAL

Ah, good. South Carolina. Again.

In early June 1844, Camden, South Carolina merchant Eli Whitney Bonney reflected with satisfaction on the recent success of his dry goods business. "I am now in the old store I occupied when you were here," he wrote to his aunt Lucy Carpenter in Massachusetts. "I have purchased and improved it very much since you saw it—next week the carpenters are coming to put 35 feet more on its length." Bonney, who had once been in business with Lucy's son Penuel, had good reason to be proud. Carpenter & Bonney had opened its doors in the early 1830s, when South Carolina was reeling from Nullification upheavals, plummeting cotton prices, soil exhaustion, and a steady stream of outmigration by planters seeking the main chance in more fertile regions to the West. When the Panic of 1837 hit, its ripples spread into a state already struggling from a string of economic troubles; aftershocks struck the region well into the 1840s. Yet a few years later Bonney's stock of goods was growing, his business was improving, and he was planning additions to the store.[1]

In many ways, Eli Bonney epitomized an emerging southern middle class. An independent, upwardly mobile merchant, thoroughly commercial in his outlook, he married the daughter of another local merchant, made regular buying trips to the Northeast, joined the Presbyterian church in the early 1830s, and lived—unlike his parents' generation—in a house separate from his place of business. By the early 1850s, his children had become active in the local temperance movement, espousing in their turn the reform and improvement impulses of their northern middle-class counterparts.[2]

Shifting the lens slightly, though, blurs the picture of a middle class neatly distinguished by occupation or mentality. Bonney owned not one residence but two, the second a summer home in the sandhills just north of town, where he counted among his neighbors some of the wealthiest planters in the district. He was well connected not only to members of the local commercial community, but also to acquaintances and extended family among the South Carolina elite. And like many other southern merchants he was a slaveholder, owning nine slaves on the eve of the Civil War.[3]

As Bonney's situation suggests, attempts to define a middle class, difficult everywhere, are particularly bedeviled when historians turn their focus to the antebellum South. Much of the region lacked the large-scale processes of industrialization and urbanization that drove class formation in the Northeast and Britain. The relatively small proportion of the southern population living in urban areas meant that fewer still were employed in the nonmanual occupations that were becoming a marker of middle-class status elsewhere. At the same time, southern planters remained economically and politically powerful throughout the first half of the nineteenth century, so that securing landed wealth evidently remained an important aspiration of many of their upwardly mobile neighbors.

Despite these differences, southerners built and promoted towns, funded railroads and other internal improvements, embraced reform efforts, promoted domestic manufacturing, and consumed increasing quantities of manufactured goods. Jonathan Wells has focused attention on a middle class of merchants and professionals emerging from these changes, defined in part by status and occupation, and in part by their shared commitment to forms of economic development and cultural reform inspired by their northern counterparts. The South's commercial men were central players in these changes. Similar to Wells, but taking the South's merchants as his focus and extending his study through the Civil War years, Frank Byrne has argued that southern merchants developed a cohesive identity through their espousal of these market relations and bourgeois cultural values, as well as through their realization that such values often ran counter to those of their agricultural neighbors.[4]

Relations between merchants and agricultural southerners could indeed be strained by divergent economic interests, particularly when it came to questions of personal indebtedness and public spending. Yet during the first half of the nineteenth century such divisions were frequently balanced by networks of kinship and association that bridged social hierarchies and helped mitigate the development of rigid class identities. Catherine Kelly has found that in provincial New England, small community sizes alone helped limit the development of class distinctions, as residents shared bonds of family, friendship, and associational life across lines of wealth and occupation. A close study of similar networks within a southern community—the town of Camden, South Carolina—suggests that they played an analogous role in shaping antebellum southern society.[5]

Camden, the administrative seat of Kershaw District and an important piedmont cotton transshipment center, was not a large town by the standards of nineteenth-century urbanization. Its official boundaries encompassed a mere 1149 free and 472 enslaved souls on the eve of the Civil War—not counting residents of a small unincorporated suburb who were participants in the town's social networks—compared with the 22,316 residents who were the subject of Mary Ryan's study of middle-class Utica, New York. Yet as the fifth largest town in the state, Camden remained more typical of the South's many small urban communities than were the few large cities in the region. The town's residents participated in many of the changes sweeping the region in the nineteenth century: extensive emigration to the southwestern frontier; the advent of the railroad; the incorporation of banks and new mercantile firms; and the establishment of intellectual, religious, and benevolent institutions. Local social life was further shaped by interactions between planting families, some of whom had lived in the area for several generations, and merchants who were often newcomers to the region.[6]

Many of South Carolina's antebellum merchants had been born elsewhere and arrived with relatively few ties to their new communities. In 1850, fewer than half of the forty-five residents recorded as "merchants" in the federal census for Kershaw District—nearly all of whom lived in and around Camden—were natives of the state. A handful had been born in the Northeast, but 40 percent of the town's merchants hailed from the Caribbean or Europe, the majority of the latter from Scotland. The proportions were similar elsewhere in the state. In Columbia, capital city and hub of the state's inland transportation networks, a mere 39 percent of the town's 160 merchants were native Carolinians in 1850, while Europeans, primarily of British or German birth, accounted for an almost equal percentage of the group. Approximately one out of six Columbia merchants had been born in the Northeast. Clerks were less often outsiders than were their employers: in both Camden and Columbia, nearly three out of every five clerks were native to South Carolina by 1860. Several of these were the sons of established merchants, suggesting the coalescence of class along family and occupational lines, yet others were the sons of prominent planters and professionals. All would have grown up sharing their parents' bonds to the surrounding community, bonds that newcomers were compelled to forge for themselves.[7]

Successful mercantile newcomers, however, soon forged such connections. It was not uncommon for such merchants to acquire planting kin—and with them land and slaves—through marriage. Questions of class and occupation were further complicated by the status of professionals in southern towns. Several Camden doctors kept small drug stores, a necessary professional sideline in a region where apothecaries were few, but one that nonetheless compelled physicians to straddle the worlds of commerce and the learned professions. In Camden as elsewhere, planters' sons might train in medicine or law—legal training frequently serving as a springboard to political life—as did the sons of successful merchants who were leaving behind the world of ledgers and shop inventories for the scalpel or the bar. On the other hand, the sons of prominent planters and professionals occasionally turned to trade, while planters themselves might diversify their interests by investing in mercantile or manufacturing enterprises. Marriages among young merchants and their professional and agricultural neighbors added new layers to already complex social networks.[8]

Marriage, though a matter of romantic attraction as well as economic interest, had ramifications for the community at large, creating and extending networks of material resources and influence. Thus a rising merchant or professional's acceptability as a marriage partner suggests his social success, and marriage patterns may be seen as key indicators of merchants' integration into their surrounding communities. Between 1830 and 1839, twenty-eight marriages were announced in the Camden newspapers in which the occupations of both the bride's family and the groom can be identified, and in which at least one party was a resident of the town. Of these, two commercial men married into planting families, as did six young professionals—medical men, lawyers, editors, and one minister. Two additional professionals, a minister and a naval officer, married the daughters of planters who also ran mercantile establishments in town. During the same period, six additional marriages took place between commercial and professional families, while only a third of the town's marriages occurred between families of shared occupational backgrounds.[9]

Several planters who watched their daughters marry non-planters had strong commercial connections themselves. James Chesnut's father had gotten his start in life as a clerk; Chesnut later witnessed one daughter marry an attorney and newspaper editor, another a doctor who kept a small drugstore. Chesnut himself sat on the board of one of the local banks, and both sons-in-law subsequently became involved in banking. Planter Benjamin Haile, whose daughter married merchant William Kennedy, later became a bank director as well. Other planters seemingly had little connection to the commercial worlds of their new sons-in-law, although in at least one instance, the bride's commercial connections initially failed to reconcile her father to the match: planter James Barkely disowned his daughter when she married one Camden merchant. Yet his own son had been the young man's business partner, and the rift was later healed, the groom becoming a respectable bank director and elder in the Presbyterian church. Even among families linked to trade, southern attitudes toward commerce—and toward the South's young commercial men—were often complex and contradictory, a mirror of the region's deeply conflicted attitudes toward commercial society.[10]

A generation later, marriages continued to cross occupational lines. Out of twenty-nine marriages taking place between 1850 and 1860 in which both parties can be identified, one bookkeeper married the daughter of a prosperous farmer, while another wed a young woman whose brothers included a carpenter, a saddler, and a machinist. Two professional men married the daughters of commercial men, while five professionals—including the sons of a bank president and a hotel-keeper—married into planting families. And while two commercial men saw their daughters marry young clerks, another gave his blessing to his daughter's union with a Charleston manufacturer. A senior bank officer saw his daughter wed the local Baptist minister. Although a number of young people married within their own or their parents' occupational groups, unions among families of differing occupational backgrounds continued to occur frequently enough, within a small community, to suggest the ongoing fluidity of social boundaries across occupational lines.

Like many southern communities, Camden underwent a profound change in the antebellum period. The town, which initially developed around the

backcountry branch of a Charleston mercantile firm, grew with the proliferation of short-staple cotton beginning in the 1790s. As the cotton trade tied the
piedmont more closely to Atlantic ports, planters in the region built themselves into a class that more nearly resembled the aristocracy of the coastal
lowcountry than had their cattle-raising parents. Beginning in the 1820s and
1830s, banks, improved transportation networks, and the development of increasingly rationalized and depersonalized institutions of credit assessment
incorporated the community ever more closely into the national economy.
Yet because the community remained small, these changes were experienced
through the medium of the same personal interactions that had shaped social,
economic, and political life in the past.[11]

A close examination of two local families' social activities illustrates the
networks of marriage, sociability, and civic involvement binding southern society together across occupational lines and generations. James Kershaw was
the son of merchant, land speculator, and planter Joseph Kershaw, around
whose store and flour mills the settlement of Camden developed in the latter
half of the eighteenth century. Physician William Blanding and his brother
Abram moved to South Carolina from Massachusetts early in the nineteenth
century. While Abram became prominent in state banking and political circles, William built up a medical practice in the Camden area, where he also
opened a small drug store and cultivated friendships with his fellow merchants and a correspondence with nationally renowned naturalists. Both Kershaw and the Blanding family left letters and journals documenting the development of social networks and class distinctions from the last decade of the
eighteenth century through the first half of the nineteenth century. Patterns
of marriage and social visiting, which helped maintain and define these new
networks, figure notably in both men's writings. Although both Kershaw and
Blanding were prominent members of local society, their writings reveal networks that encompassed both the local elite and their more humble neighbors,
providing a window into the development of these networks over time.[12]

As Camden grew with the cotton boom, and the surrounding district became more closely tied to the lowcountry, members of the Kershaw family
remained leaders within the community. Prior to the Revolution, Joseph Kershaw had constructed a substantial two-story frame house on a knoll over-
looking the town. Built in the style of a lowcountry great house, the residence

announced Kershaw's wealth and, more important, his familiarity with the culture of aristocratic Charleston. Kershaw's two eldest sons, James and John, continued their father's efforts to convert economic clout into social and political influence. Father and sons took up the mantle of civic leadership, becoming executive officers of the Camden Orphan Society, a local benevolent society and money-lending institution whose monthly meetings and Fourth of July celebrations were important features of the town's social life. John was also active in the early establishment of the town's Presbyterian church and later became a judge and congressman. His brother worked to develop the town's cultural life, serving on the organizational committee of the local Thespian Society and stepping onto its stage in *Love a la Mode, School for Scandal, Revenge,* and other plays from London's Drury Lane.[13]

While his brother turned to law and politics, James focused on planting, and by the late 1790s employed sixteen slaves in the cultivation of indigo, flax, and cotton. He also cultivated social connections to the town's planters and rising merchants, jotting in his diary the names of those who called on him or whose entertainments he attended. Rarely did his memoranda include details of the entertainments; rather, they read more like an accounting of social honors and obligations, a ledger that today provides a remarkable sketch of the social networks in which he was involved.[14]

Social calls figured prominently in the lives of early Camden residents, reflecting and reinforcing networks that spanned social rank. Even those of limited means could and did maintain their social connections by making the rounds of their acquaintances. James Kershaw recorded receiving calls from "Mrs. Adamson," wife or daughter-in-law of planter and prosperous merchant John Adamson, as well as middling tavern-keeper Jonathan Eccles, New Jersey-born merchant Phineas Thornton and his wife, jeweler and bookseller Alexander Young, and Irish-born teacher and druggist Joshua Reynolds. Although the men's visits in particular might have combined business transactions with neighborly sociability, some calls unmistakably involved social dimensions, as when "Joshua Reynolds dined here," in early October 1814. Other visits were explicitly structured around labor: one September day in 1794, James Kershaw recorded that his sister Mary had attended a "Quilting frolic" at the home of planter William Lang, a custom that lasted into the following decade as Camden's women gathered to share time-consuming tasks among themselves.[15]

Lang and other prominent members of the community also hosted more formal entertainments. Both Kershaw and the Blandings were present at two wedding balls in 1808. "A splendid Ball" followed by an "Elegant supper" marked the marriage of Bermuda-born planter Henry H. Dickinson to Martha Brevard, while John Chesnut, a rising planter who had once clerked for Joseph Kershaw, impressed William Blanding's young wife by hiring musicians from Charleston to celebrate his daughter Margaret's union with planter James S. Deas.[16]

Not all formal entertainments were restricted to members of the local elite; rather, both guests and hosts were often persons of middling means. At the turn of the century, only a few local residents could boast houses spacious enough to accommodate such large gatherings. Other dances were held at a local tavern, where physician Isaac Alexander's wife later recalled that "all Camden" assembled in the early nineteenth century. Friends evidently pooled their resources to host entertainments: in early 1799, planter William Lang, merchants Alexander Matheson and John Ker, and a man identified only as "Gow" jointly hosted a dance at Dinkin's Tavern; two weeks later planter-merchant John Adamson or his son William, merchant Lewis Ciples, one of the mercantile Arrants brothers, and Thomas Dinkins (perhaps the tavern-keeper's son) held another dance.[17]

As Camden grew and its planters prospered, however, many sought to distinguish themselves from their neighbors. The Kershaws found themselves at the crux of these changes. In the 1790s, they, along with planters John Adamson, Dan Brown, Isaac Dubose, and William Lang, took turns hosting St. Cecilia Society gatherings, emulating the most exclusive of Charleston's private social organizations. They also attended dinners given in private homes. In one of James Kershaw's earliest diary entries, he recorded that he had "suped at Lang's"—"Lang" being planter William Lang, who even before the cotton boom owned forty-six slaves. Several years later Kershaw dined at Isaac Dubose's home, and, a few days later, attended a dinner at the home of Duncan McRae, part owner of a large lumber- and gristmilling operation, where he was introduced to the new Mrs. James Chesnut. Members of these families would be, by the late antebellum period, among the most prominent in the district, culminating a process of distinction begun much earlier in the century.[18]

Even as he dined with the region's rising planter elite, however, Kershaw hints at a growing differentiation between the wealthiest planters and their neighbors in his diary. For the most part Kershaw recorded social events matter-of-factly. But one visit elicited a stronger response: when Isaac Dubose and planter-attorney Dan Brown took tea with him in 1793, the diarist felt moved to comment dryly that the event was "a wonder indeed." Though he had served with Dubose for several years as an officer of the Orphan Society, dined at Dubose's home a month earlier, and socialized with both Brown and Dubose at the St. Cecelia's Society functions, Kershaw's words suggest that he recognized the visit as a mark of particular condescension. Sometime later, when he found himself excluded from a "dance at Mrs. Cantey's," the snub likewise was keen enough to merit note in his diary.[19]

Though a number of rising planters maintained strong mercantile ties, many began to emulate members of the Charleston and European aristocracy in assuming a prejudice against "the shop." Zach Cantey's emporium dominated trade in Camden's commercial center even as he increased his plantation holdings and his wife cut James Kershaw from her entertainments. Yet some years later, according to diarist Mary Boykin Chesnut, the Kershaws too participated in this distancing, recalling that the first John Chesnut—whose descendents were now among the most prominent planters in the district—had gotten his start as a clerk in Joseph Kershaw's store. "The Kershaws . . . have that fact on their coat of arms," she commented caustically. If the Kershaws made a point of reminding the Chesnuts of their commercial roots, the Chesnuts returned the compliment. "In the second generation the shop was so far sunk that the John Chesnut of that day refused to let his daughter marry a handsome dissipated Kershaw," the diarist wrote. Although the senior Chesnut's opinion was perhaps based more on the unidentified Kershaw's character than his commercial origins, the diarist's reference to "the shop" suggests that as they rose to social prominence, even planters of mercantile backgrounds made a point of distancing themselves from trade.[20]

By the 1830s, efforts by at least a few of the elite to accentuate emerging social distinctions had become more pronounced. Shortly before his marriage to Susan Witherspoon, merchant William McDowall received a letter from his prospective father-in-law warning him to expect hostility from the community. "After the *anonymous* letter . . . to Dr. George Reynolds & Miss Mary Chestnut [sic] to break off their union, and to Mr. Martin of Charleston touching his marriage—*all* in the *same handwriting*," wrote John Wither-spoon, himself a planter and Presbyterian minister, "I should not be surprised at anything of this kind, with regard to *your marriage with Susan*." George Reynolds, a doctor and druggist, was well on his way to becoming a pillar of the community when he married Mary Chesnut. He had recently become an elder in the Presbyterian church and had studied under a well-regarded local physician; his uncle had married into an old mercantile family with planting connections. Yet, like McDowall, he was connected more directly to the re-gion's mercantile and professional families than to its planting elite, of which the Chesnuts were now established members. Though a single person had penned all three letters, Witherspoon believed they betrayed a wider prejudice among the town's elite. "We have amongst us, even in high places, many . . . too degradingly mean in all their monied aristocracy; to know & feel what *true virtue* is," he averred.[21]

As members of the planting elite began to distinguish themselves from their neighbors, Camden's merchants in turn created networks that would later form the core of a recognizable middle class. By the early 1820s, William Blanding found himself part of a closely knit enclave of merchants residing and keeping shop in the district of Camden known as Logtown. "Dinned at Mr. Clarks," Blanding recorded in his journal one November evening. Like Kershaw, he offered no description of the meal or its presentation, but listed the company present, among them "Mr. and Mrs. Abbott, . . . Miss Eccles, . . . Mr. Clarks famely and Mr. Murray," his terse, unemotional private notes bely-ing the density of ties that bound the dinner companions to each other. The friendship between Blanding and merchant James Murray was so close that Murray later named two of his children for Blanding and his wife. James Clark and Henry Abbott, both merchants, lived and kept dry goods stores nearly opposite each other in Logtown. Social intercourse between Blanding and the Clark family stretched back at least to 1807 and occurred with a frequency that revealed the closeness of the connection. Only four days previous to the din-ner in 1822, Blanding had joined the Clarks for dinner at the home of Phineas and Elizabeth Thornton, whose guests were also part of the Clarks' social net-works. New Jersey-born Thornton was Mrs. Clark's brother and uncle to the Miss Eccles with whom Blanding and the Clarks would dine a few nights later. He had moved to Camden to work for a mercantile brother-in-law, and then leveraged his success to become a small shopkeeper and the town postmaster. Although Thornton's business evidently never grew very large, he and his wife would continue to exchange regular visits with their more prosperous relatives. James Clark's niece, "Miss Eccles," was the daughter of Jonathan Eccles, whose tavern and store stood less than a block from the site of the evening's dinner party. The closeness of these ties suggests the development of strong connections binding Camden's commercial families to each other.[22]

Commercial relations could simultaneously bring these same men into conflict with their planting neighbors. Calls for William Blanding's services as a physician had taken him into the homes and slave quarters of some of the district's most prominent families; in the 1830s, when he had removed to Philadelphia, more than $8000 in unsettled accounts took him back every winter to demand payment for past services. But by 1834, as South Carolina staggered under the effects of tightening currency and several years of bad harvests, Camden and its dunning doctor were losing patience with each other. After a long day of collections, Blanding once exclaimed to his wife that he had received "only Notes . . . all good when I get it!" He recorded his elite debtors' profligate amusements with some disgust: when planter William Adamson hosted a dinner lasting into the wee hours of the morning Blanding wrote grumpily, "Toward morning the dinner party came in town—, eating drinking and playing cards 13 hours—Genl. J. W. Cantey and John Boykin staid it out and lost not a little, each. They were all *mighty* drunk tis said." News of their gambling losses perhaps caused Blanding particular annoyance since he had long struggled to collect cash from at least one of the revelers. A day later, when General Cantey had presumably sobered up, he paid Blanding $6.50 in interest on a note Blanding held, a fact that prompted Blanding to write sarcastically to his wife in Philadelphia, "so much saved you may now go to market tomorrow morning." And Blanding increasingly received blunt refusals of payment, followed by a pointed "when are you going home?"—a further reminder of the distance separating him from his powerful debtors. While planters might extend credit to establish social and political relationships, debt primarily represented a more straightforward economic obligation for mercantile men, and one that their own tenuous finances required them to pursue. Although he was a man of learning and cosmopolitan connections, Blanding's determination to collect outstanding obligations reinforced barriers to his acceptance as a full equal by those who paid "debts of honor" promptly but dragged their well-shod feet over the tradesman's bills.[23]

If resentments arose over unpaid debts, however, such tensions could be offset by social connections. In another letter in which he described pursuing payments from several of the planting Canteys, Blanding also recorded making calls on acquaintances who ranged along the social scale, from his old friend Elizabeth Thornton (wife of shopkeeper Phineas Thornton) and merchant James Murray's daughter Sally, to Mary Kershaw, James Kershaw's unmarried sister, and "Mrs. Cantey," the wife or sister-in-law of General Cantey. Unlike the calls Blanding paid on his male debtors, which he concluded by tallying monies received, his account of calls on the women made no mention of business, suggesting that these were explicitly social visits. The visit with Mrs. Cantey in particular, following as it did the calls for money from her male relatives, suggests that Blanding sought to preserve his social connections to the elite despite financial tensions.[24]

Other mercantile Camdenites evidently enjoyed less troubled relationships with their planting neighbors. On the eve of one departure for Philadelphia, Blanding reported "great doings" at the home of one of the planting Boykins, to be followed by an entertainment hosted the next night by Blanding's good friend and fellow merchant James Douglas. Though Blanding attended neither function, the Douglases partook fully of the Boykins's hospitality: when Blanding paid a farewell call the next day, he found the family "a little dull, too merry last night at Mr. Boykins no doubt." Three of Douglas's daughters later cemented the family's social connections by marrying into the planting elite.[25]

A fundamental shift took place in the culture of Camden's commercial community over the course of the 1830s and 1840s, as the community became integrated more fully into an increasingly institutionalized national economy. The roots of change lay in the preceding decade, when in 1823 a branch of the state bank was established in Camden, and in fact may date to the late 1810s, when local planters and businessmen laid plans to develop the Orphan Society, long a modest source of backcountry credit, into a full-scale lending operation. Suddenly debtors discovered how much more pressing institutional obligations could be than those owed to friends and community members. By the early 1830s, struggling debtors told William Blanding, "No, I can't pay you, I have a Note in Bank and that *must* be paid." As institutionalized credit relationships began to underwrite an increasing volume of southern business, southerners relied on indefinite extensions of credit from individuals while they repaid institutional debts.[26]

Chronic debt had long permeated all levels of the South's commodity economy. Merchants purchased on credit from wholesalers, many of them based in the cities of the Northeast, and in turn extended credit to their own customers. They then tried to collect these accounts each winter after crops had been sold. Yet as overproduction drove prices down, and as the seaboard states struggled to compete with virgin soils of the Southwest, collections became increasingly difficult. Rather than suing for their debts, which might send debtors into bankruptcy and yield only a small settlement for each creditor, many wholesalers continued to grant credit extensions to troubled merchants, hoping to collect at a future date.[27]

In 1837, this credit bubble collapsed, and the resulting panic reverberated throughout the nation. In the wake of the panic, northeastern wholesalers experimented with a number of measures designed to guard against future disasters. Many wholesale firms shortened the time permitted for payment; others purchased the services of new credit-reporting agencies such as the New York-based Mercantile Agency.[28]

The Mercantile Agency received its first reports on Camden merchants in 1845. The widespread availability of credit information, collected and distributed anonymously, represented a major departure from older business practices. No longer were wholesalers compelled to rely on personal acquaintance or recommendation when deciding which merchants to do business with or what length of credit to extend to customers. Utter strangers could trade with each other on the strength of anonymous credit reports. Yet at the same time, those reports relied on the same measures of credit assessment, gathered at the local level, which had served as the basis of earlier transactions. Within the Camden banks (a second local bank was chartered in 1836), customers turned to friends of good financial repute to provide security on notes when demanded by the banks. Such security could permit renewals when a bank might otherwise demand immediate payment.[29]

The Camden economy became further integrated into the national market with the completion of a railroad connection in 1848. Where earlier internal improvements, including river dredgings and the chartering of steamboats, had slowly improved the speed of transportation, the railroad increased business dramatically. "It is pleasent to see [rail cars] come in loaded with merchendize, and many comforts formaly rare here," one observer wrote. Merchants capitalized on these advantages, not only providing a wider array of goods to customers, but also playing on townspeople's excitement about the new connection. "Just received per Rail Road, And expected to be sold with Rail Road Speed," crowed one advertisement for dry goods at the town's new Palmetto Cash Store. As they became more closely linked to national networks, Camden's stores gave a new generation entrée into a developing commercial society and simultaneously connected them to broader cultural trends.[30]

Like their elders, the younger generation of merchants and clerks built friendships among themselves and with local professional men, but also formed lasting and significant alliances with the families of local planters. Even as Blanding worked to cash out his South Carolina assets, his nephew Penuel Carpenter moved to Camden to set up a dry goods business with cousin Eli Bonney. Penuel attended the marriage of future bank clerk Alexander Johnson to the daughter of a prominent local planter, while Bonney and fellow merchant Jim Bryant served as groomsmen for one "Wilky" Barnes, who later became a prosperous farmer in Sumter District. Bryant sent news of local parties and courtships to merchant William McDowall, in Charleston on business, who was himself about to marry into a planting family. "We have had one or two parties since Miss Boykin's wedding," Bryant reported, referring to the marriage of James Taylor to planter Burwell Boykin's daughter Charlotte. Bryant had also attended a party given by bank president Thomas Salmond, and Bryant and clerk Hall McGee regularly squired McDowall's betrothed around town, riding with her and laying plans to make Christmas eggnog. Among themselves the festivities often turned boisterous: toasts to schoolteacher Henry Hatfield's pending nuptials were so liberal that McDowall had had to be carried home from the party, "and by one probably as far gone as yourself," Bryant laughingly recalled. As they corresponded with each other, drank together, and stood beside each other at the altar, Camden's younger mercantile and professional men developed their own set of middle-class connections, but simultaneously cemented their ties to their more prosperous agricultural neighbors.[31]

As he adapted to the changing business culture, Eli Bonney built his store—

the additions to which he reported so proudly to his aunt—into a thriving business. In 1835, he and Penuel advertised their enterprise as a "Cash Store," selling goods at a discount to those willing to pay cash for them. By 1842, Bonney conceded that he would extend his low prices to "punctual customers." His caution paid off in the new world of institutionalized credit: when the Mercantile Agency received its first Camden reports in early 1845, Bonney was unequivocally rated "one of the best business men in the place," and a few years later, "good for [his] contracts." By 1850, he was doing more than $4000 annually with the Bank of Camden and serving as an agent for both banks in town, while his sons Usher and Charley were members of Camden's Cadets of Temperance.[32]

By the late 1840s and 1850s, Camden had developed a recognizably urban social life, yet it was one in which planters as well as their mercantile and professional neighbors participated, and in which distinctions among occupational groups were partially obscured by close social connections. In the winter of 1849, Bonney played host to Penuel's mother Lucy Carpenter, who was William Blanding's sister. Lucy had lived in Camden for several years while her son was alive, and then maintained connections to friends there through letters and visits after his death in 1836. Almost immediately upon her arrival, Lucy was greeted with a rush of calls from old friends. Her visitors crossed lines of status and occupation, many of them bound together by long years of association. Among her first callers were "Mrs. Lee and Eliza," a merchant's widow with whom Lucy had once boarded and her unmarried daughter, and William Blanding's old friend James Douglas. Having made his fortune in the mercantile line, Douglas was by the late 1840s a leader in the town's social and civic life, an elder in the Presbyterian church, president of the Camden Bible Society, and an active member of the local temperance movement.[33]

By the late 1840s, Douglas's children, as well as those of the Lee family, were consolidating their parents' positions in the town's developing middle class, and in several cases, moving into the planter class. Whereas Mrs. Lee's husband had been a druggist, all three of her sons eschewed mercantile enterprise, pursuing professional training instead. The eldest, Joseph, became a dentist, his brother Thomas first an attorney—a profession in which he was later joined by James Kershaw's nephew—and then a Louisiana planter, while Francis attended seminary and secured a position as rector of Camden's Episcopal church. The daughters of successful merchants likewise often married into the ranks of planters and professionals. Two of James Douglas's five daughters married planting brothers William and Thomas Ancrum, while another wed Lynch Horry Deas, a physician and scion of an old lowcountry planting family. Douglas's youngest daughter allied herself with James Kershaw's nephew, attorney Joseph Brevard Kershaw. Catherine Clark, daughter of William Blanding's old friend and mercantile neighbor James Clark, followed a similar course, wedding Mrs. Lee's dentist son. When the daughters of successful merchants married other merchants, their new husbands were often closely connected to the bride's family in other ways: Rebecca Lee, for instance, married Eli Bonney, further strengthening the longstanding bonds of affection between the two families. This second generation maintained close ties to their parents' social circles: all joined their parents in Lucy Carpenter's parlor or received calls from her in the weeks after her arrival.[34]

The family history of nearly every one of Carpenter's visitors reflected equally closely woven connections and patterns of social mobility among the town's merchants. Ann Cook Salmond, a physician's wife and daughter-in-law to a bank president, had been born to carriage-maker Henry Cook; Sarah Ciples, a planter's daughter, had married merchant Lewis Ciples and become a close neighbor of the Bonneys at their summer residence; and "Mrs. McDowel" had been Susan Witherspoon, daughter of minister and struggling planter John Witherspoon, who had figured in the correspondence of her merchant husband's friends thirteen years earlier.[35]

Longstanding patterns of sociability were reinforced and replicated by drawing unwed members of the next generation into their parents' social circles. Until her marriage, Eliza Lee dutifully followed her mother on calls around Camden. When fourteen-year-old Rebecca Lee (niece of Eliza and the Rebecca who had married Eli Bonney) accompanied her mother on a call to Lucy Carpenter, her younger siblings stayed behind, suggesting that such calls marked Rebecca's introduction to her parents' social world. The widowed wife of doctor and planter Alfred Brevard brought several of her daughters to call on Carpenter in a visit that might have coincided with calls from Sarah Ciples and prominent planter Daniel DeSaussure, both of whom waited on Lucy Carpenter that same day. Like Eliza and Rebecca Lee, the young Brevard women were learning to take their place in Camden's social networks.[36]

As Camden became increasingly integrated into a national economy, its residents nonetheless maintained the closely overlaid interpersonal networks of a small community. Even as formerly backcountry planters built themselves into a powerful elite, and the merchants and professionals of a developing middle class sought to consolidate or improve their positions, social connections among occupational groups helped mitigate the formation of rigid class distinctions. Relations between rising merchants and their planting and professional neighbors could be complex and contradictory, marked by growing social divisions and friction over financial obligations. Yet within a closely knit community, such rifts were partially offset by networks of marriage and association reinforced daily through visits among kin and neighbors. Similar networks, involving many of the same individuals, developed around churches, benevolent associations, and civic institutions. The experience of Camden's commercial community suggests that not only did networks of kinship and friendship play a critical role in antebellum southern class dynamics, but that new economic relations also developed alongside older patterns of association. Even as Eli Bonney and his commercial neighbors adapted to a modernizing national economy, they did so while preserving personal connections to their kin and customers.

This is kind of contradictory to what the prev. essay says. This says they get on fine. the other said there was disdain.

NOTES

1. Eli W. Bonney (hereafter EWB), Camden, SC, to Lucy Carpenter (hereafter LC), Rehoboth, Mass., June 7, 1844, William Blanding Papers, South Caroliniana Library, University of South Carolina (hereafter SCL); *Camden Journal and Southern Whig,* January 17, 1835.

2. EWB, Camden, to LC, Pawtucket, R.I., May 20, 1840; Rebecca A. Bonney (hereafter RAB), Camden, [to LC, Rehoboth], March 19, 1850, both Blanding Papers, SCL; Thomas J. Kirkland and Robert M. Kennedy, *Historic Camden, Part Two: Nineteenth Century* (Columbia, S.C.: State Company, 1926; reprint, Columbia: State Printing Company, 1973), 404; *Minutes and Register of Members of the Presbyterian Church at Camden, S.C. from 1806 to 1833,* W.P.A. Project 2004, transcr. Maude Gardner, 1937, 28, Bethesda Presbyterian Church (Camden, S.C.), SCL; *Camden Journal,* April 12, 1850. On the contemporary development of a distinct northern middle class, see especially Stuart M. Blumin, *The Emergence of the Middle Class: Social Experience in the American City, 1760–1900* (New York: Cambridge University Press, 1989), Paul E. Johnson, *A Shopkeeper's Millennium: Society and Revivals in Rochester, New York, 1815–1837* (New York: Hill and Wang, 1978), and Mary P. Ryan, *Cradle of the Middle Class: The Family in Oneida County, New York, 1790–1865* (New York: Cambridge University Press, 1981).

3. EWB, Camden, to LC, Pawtucket, May 20, 1840; EWB, Camden, to LC, Rehoboth, June 7, 1844, both Blanding Papers, SCL. Members of the Blanding family had married into the prominent DeSaussure family. Kirkland and Kennedy, *Historic Camden*, 2:382–85. One out of every three Camden merchants owned slaves in 1860. *Eighth Census of the United States, 1860,* Population and Slave Schedules, Kershaw District, South Carolina.

4. Jonathan Daniel Wells, *The Origins of the Southern Middle Class, 1800–1861* (Chapel Hill: University of North Carolina Press, 2004); Frank J. Byrne, *Becoming Bourgeois: Merchant Culture in the South, 1820–1865* (Lexington: University Press of Kentucky, 2006).

5. Byrne, *Becoming Bourgeois,* 26–27; Wells, *Origins of the Southern Middle Class,* 134–42; Catherine E. Kelly, "'Well Bred Country People': Sociability, Social Networks, and the Creation of a Provincial Middle Class, 1820–1860," in Scott C. Martin, ed., *Cultural Change and the Market Revolution in America, 1789–1860* (Lanham, Md.: Rowan and Littlefield Publishers, 2005), 127. On the role of kinship connections in shaping social institutions and economic life see J. F. Bosher, "Huguenot Merchants and the Protestant International in the Seventeenth Century," *William and Mary Quarterly* 52 (1995): 77–102, and Edward E. Baptist, *Creating an Old South: Middle Florida's Plantation Frontier before the Civil War* (Chapel Hill: University of North Carolina Press, 2002).

6. Joseph C. G. Kennedy, *Population of the United States in 1860; Compiled from the Original Returns of the Eighth Census, under the Direction of the Secretary of the Interior* (Washington: Government Printing Office, 1864), 337, 452; Ryan, *Cradle of the Middle Class,* 5; J. D. B. DeBow, *The Seventh Census of the United States: 1850* (Washington: Robert Armstrong, Public Printer, 1853), 339; Thomas J. Kirkland and Robert M. Kennedy, *Historic Camden, Part One: Colonial and Revolutionary* (1905; reprint, Charleston: Booksurge for the Kershaw County Historical Society, 2004), 9–12; Kirkland and Kennedy, *Historic Camden,* 2:22–56, 114, 277–308; Judith Jane Schulz, "The Rise and Decline of Camden as South Carolina's Major Inland Trading Center, 1751–1829: A Historical Geographic Study" (M.A. thesis, University of South Carolina, 1972).

7. U.S. Census, 1850, Population Schedule, Kershaw and Richland Districts, South Carolina; 1860, Population Schedule, Kershaw District, South Carolina. Of the thirty-eight clerks in Camden in 1860, at least six were following in the footsteps of older mercantile relatives, while three were the sons of planters and professionals.

8. *Camden Journal,* June 3, 1826. As Ford has noted, merchants sat with planters and professionals on the boards of banks and internal improvement corporations; they also joined churches and other organizations together. Lacy K. Ford Jr., *Origins of Southern Radicalism: The South Carolina Upcountry, 1800–1860* (New York: Oxford University Press, 1988), 232. For local planters who invested in mercantile and manufacturing enterprises, see Kirkland and Kennedy, *Historic Camden,* 1:289–90, 388; *Camden Journal,* March 14, 1840.

9. On marriage in the antebellum South, see Charlene M. Boyer Lewis, *Ladies and Gentlemen on Display: Planter Society at the Virginia Springs, 1790–1860* (Charlottesville: University Press of Virginia, 2001), 175–86; Byrne, *Becoming Bourgeois,* 89–92; Elizabeth Fox-Genovese, *Within the Plantation Household: Black and White Women of the Old South* (Chapel Hill: University of North Carolina Press, 1988), 207–9; Suzanne Lebsock, *Free Women of Petersburg: Status and Culture in a Southern Town* (New York: W. W. Norton and Company, 1984), 18–30.

Marriages are from Brent Holcomb's *Marriage and Death Notices from Camden, South Carolina, Newspapers, 1816–1865* (Greenville, S.C.: Southern Historical Press, 1978). Fifty-five announcements of marriages taking place "in Camden," or involving at least one party from Camden, were published between 1830 and 1839, and forty-seven from 1850 to 1860. Unless otherwise noted, identifications of individuals throughout this study have been compiled from federal census returns, Kirkland and Kennedy's *Historic Camden*, Charleston city directories, and business notices in the Camden newspapers. When multiple persons of the same name lived in the Camden area, I have taken into account age, household status, dates of marriage, and other relevant factors. In categorizing parties as commercial or professional, I have relied primarily on the classifications employed by Wells, although I have kept manufacturers in a separate category. Wells, *Origins of the Southern Middle Class*, 239.

10. W. A. Clark, *The History of the Banking Institutions Organized in South Carolina Prior to 1860* (Columbia, S.C.: State Company for the Historical Commission of South Carolina, 1922), 201–2, 207–8; Katherine Barnes, *John Rosser, Gentleman of the Old South* (Nashville: by the author, 1984), 13–31; *Minutes and Register of Members of the Presbyterian Church at Camden*, SCL.

11. Rachel Klein, *Unification of a Slave State: The Rise of the Planter Class in the South Carolina Backcountry, 1760–1808* (Chapel Hill: University of North Carolina Press for the Omohundro Institute for Early American History and Culture, 1990), 31–32, 35, 37, 247–68.

12. Kirkland and Kennedy, *Historic Camden*, 1:376–81, 2:100–103; *Camden Journal*, June 3, 1826.

13. Minutes of August 9 and September 20, 1786; August 8, 1787; and July 9, 1794, Camden Orphan Society Records, SCL; Kirkland and Kennedy, *Historic Camden*, 2:294–95; James Kershaw Diary, February 1 and March 15, 1793; December 7, 1796; March 3, 1797; and August 17, 1798, James Kershaw Papers, SCL. On the significance of houses as markers of a rising gentry, see Richard Bushman, *The Refinement of America: Persons, Houses, Cities* (New York: Alfred A. Knopf, 1992), 3–21.

14. U.S. Census, 1800, Kershaw District, South Carolina; James Kershaw Diary, August 1, 1796, March 13, and May 25, 1797, Kershaw Papers, SCL.

15. Kershaw Diary, September 17, 1794, December 29, 1798, July 28, 1800, March 5, 1809, May 11, 1810, February 20, 1813, October 1, 1814, Kershaw Papers, SCL; Kirkland and Kennedy, *Historic Camden*, 2:19. In her study of one contemporary Maine community, Laurel Thatcher Ulrich found that men and women maintained extensive but separate networks of economic exchanges, many of which evidently took place during the apparently social visits that midwife Martha Ballard recorded in diary notations similar to James Kershaw's. Ulrich, *A Midwife's Tale: The Life of Martha Ballard, Based on Her Diary, 1785–1812* (New York: Alfred A. Knopf, 1990), 75–94, esp. 75–77, 86.

16. Kershaw Diary, December 1, 1808, November 9, 1808, Kershaw Papers, SCL; Susan Blanding, Camden, to Blanding Family, n.p., December 2, 1808, Blanding Papers, SCL.

17. Sarah Alexander, 1857, quoted in Kirkland and Kennedy, *Historic Camden*, 2:18–19; Kershaw Diary, March 20, 1794, January 3, 1799 and January 14, 1799, Kershaw Papers, SCL.

18. Kershaw Diary, October 16, 1792, March 26, 1793, November 20, 1796, and November 27, 1796, Kershaw Papers, SCL. For St. Cecelia Society gatherings, see entries for October 1, 8, 22,

and 29 and November 5, 1793, and January 23, 1794. The original diary has deteriorated to a point where the entry for October 16, 1792, is not legible, but a transcription survives in an appendix to Kirkland and Kennedy, *Historic Camden,* 1:405. U.S. Census, 1790, Camden District, South Carolina; Nicholas Michael Butler, *Votaries of Apollo: The St. Cecilia Society and the Patronage of Concert Music in Charleston, South Carolina, 1766–1820* (Columbia: University of South Carolina Press, 2007).

19. Kershaw Diary, July 24, 1793, August 27, 1793, November 24, 1801, Kershaw Papers, SCL; Minutes, 1786–1794, Camden Orphan Society Records, pp. 68, 95, 108–9, SCL. By 1800, John and James Kershaw each held 16 slaves, while Isaac Dubose owned 105 and Zach Cantey 86. U.S. Census, 1800, Kershaw District, South Carolina.

20. William M. Shannon, "Old Times in Camden: Pen Pictures of the Past," ed. Harvey S. Teal (Camden, S.C.: Kershaw County Historical Society, 1996), 27; Mary Boykin Chesnut, *Mary Chesnut's Civil War,* ed. C. Vann Woodward (New Haven: Yale University Press, 1981), 816.

21. John Witherspoon, Camden, to William D. McDowall, Charleston, December 11, 1835, Witherspoon and McDowell Family Papers, Southern Historical Collection, Wilson Library, University of North Carolina at Chapel Hill (hereafter SHC), emphasis original. Kirkland and Kennedy, *Historic Camden,* 1:74, 86, 99–103, 399–403, and 2:425–26; *Minutes and Register of Members of the Presbyterian Church at Camden,* SCL. On Reynolds's relationship with the Chesnut family, see George Reynolds, Camden, to Colonel James Chesnut, n.p., February 4, 1832, Williams-Chesnut-Manning Family Papers, SCL. On the reputation of Dr. E. H. Anderson, under whom Reynolds trained, see "The Camden Debating Club Anniversary Celebration," *Camden Journal,* March 9, 1842. It seems likely that "Martin" was Charleston factor Robert Martin, who had recently married Serena M. Daniel of Camden. Holcomb, *Marriage and Death Notices,* 41; Morris Goldsmith, *Directory and Stranger's Guide for the City of Charleston, and Its Vicinity* (Charleston: Printed at the office of the Irishman, 1831), 92.

22. William Blanding Diary, November 26, 1822, July 15, 1807, November 22, 1822; William Blanding (hereafter WB), Camden and Charleston, to Rachel Blanding (hereafter RB), Philadelphia, April 11–16, 1832 (April 13); WB, Camden, to RB, Philadelphia, November 29–December 6, 1834; Lucy Carpenter Journal, November 20 and December 7, 1848, all Blanding Papers, SCL; Holcomb, *Marriage and Death Notices,* 32, 52, 117; Schulz, "Rise and Decline of Camden as South Carolina's Major Inland Trading Center," 57, 112, 114; Kirkland and Kennedy, *Historic Camden,* 2:22, 436–38; Probate Records Office, 1:2 (1825), Kershaw County Courthouse; "Items from the Reminiscences of Mrs. Phineas Thornton," Thornton Family File, Camden Archives, transcribed from original at SCL; *Camden Journal,* April 8, 1826. The Thorntons owned no real estate and no slaves in 1850; U.S. Census, 1850, Population and Slave Schedules, Kershaw District, South Carolina.

23. WB, Camden, to RB, Philadelphia, April 5, 1834; WB, Camden and Charleston, to RB, Philadelphia, April 11–16, 1832; WB, Camden, to RB, Philadelphia, April 23–28, 1834 (April 25), emphasis original, and March 21–24, 1834 (March 22), Blanding Papers, SCL; Byrne, *Becoming Bourgeois,* 26–27; Bertram Wyatt-Brown, *Southern Honor: Ethics and Behavior in the Old South* (New York: Oxford University Press, 1982), 345.

24. WB, Camden and Charleston, to RB, Philadelphia, April 11–16, 1832 (April 13), Blanding Papers, SCL; Holcomb, *Marriage and Death Notices,* 51; Ulrich, *Midwife's Tale,* 75–94.

25. WB, Camden, to RB, Philadelphia, April 11–16, 1832 (April 14), Blanding Papers, SCL; Kirkland and Kennedy, *Historic Camden*, 2:389.

26. Clark, *History of the Banking Institutions*, 201–2; Report on Funds, July 3, 1816–May 20, 1818, and Scheme of Finance, May 20, 1818, Camden Orphan Society Records, SCL; Bruce H. Mann, *Republic of Debtors: Bankruptcy in the Age of American Independence* (Cambridge, Mass.: Harvard University Press, 2002), 17–18; WB, Camden, to RB, Philadelphia, March 21–24, 1834 (March 22), Blanding Papers, SCL.

27. Lewis E. Atherton, *The Southern Country Store, 1800–1860* (Baton Rouge: Louisiana State University Press, 1949), esp. 113–29.

28. Ibid., 114–28; Lewis E. Atherton, "The Problem of Credit Rating in the Antebellum South," *Journal of Southern History* 12 (1946): 534–56, esp. 540–41; Bertram Wyatt-Brown, "God and Dun & Bradstreet, 1841–1851," *Business History Review* 40 (1966): 432–50.

29. See, for example, reports on Paul F. Villispigue and William Anderson, South Carolina, vol. 11, p. 33, and South Carolina, vol. 11, p. 56, both R. G. Dun & Co. Collection, Baker Library Historical Collections, Harvard Business School (hereafter HBS). On the use of sureties, see Mann, *Republic of Debtors*, 17–18; Minutes of April 17, 1854 (e.g.), Bank of Camden (S.C.) Records, SCL.

30. *Camden Commercial Courier*, May 6, 1837, and June 24, 1837; Kirkland and Kennedy, *Historic Camden*, 2:37–41; LC, Camden, to WB, [Rehoboth], January 23, 1849, Blanding Papers, SCL; *Camden Journal*, January 9, 1850.

31. WB and Penuel Carpenter, Camden, to RB, Philadelphia, November 19, 1834; WB, Camden, to RB, Philadelphia, April 23–28, 1834 (April 25), both Blanding Papers, SCL; Jim F. Bryant, Camden, to William D. McDowall, Charleston, November 2, 1835; Hall T. McGee, Camden, to William D. McDowall, Charleston, December 7, 1835; Jim F. Bryant, Camden, to William D. McDowall, Charleston, December 14, 1835, all Witherspoon and McDowell Family Papers, SHC. Bank clerk Alexander Johnson married Sarah Joanna Perkins, daughter of planter Benjamin Perkins. Clark, *History of the Banking Institutions*, 201–2 and 207–8; "From Notes of William E. Johnson III, October 31, 1880," W. E. Johnson Family, unaccessioned file, Camden Archives; Will of Benjamin Perkins (transcr.), Probate Records Office, 56:1947 (1841), Kershaw County Courthouse; U.S. Census, 1850, Population and Slave Schedules, Sumter District, South Carolina; Holcomb, *Marriage and Death Notices*, 65.

32. *Camden Journal and Southern Whig*, January 17, 1835; *Camden Journal*, January 5, 1842, January 12, 1850, and April 12, 1850; credit report of Eli W. Bonney, South Carolina, vol. 11, p. 33, R. G. Dun & Co. Collection, HBS; Minutes of January 9, March 13, April 24, June 12, September 18, October 16, and November 20, 1850, Bank of Camden (S.C.) Records, SCL.

33. Abram Blanding, Columbia, to WB, Philadelphia, April 23, 1836; Caroline Blanding, Camden, to LC, Brooklyn, June 1, 1841; EWB, Camden, to LC, Providence, September 19, 1847; Carpenter Journal, November 20, 1848, all Blanding Papers, SCL; *Camden Journal*, December 23, 1840; Kirkland and Kennedy, *Historic Camden*, 2:388–90, 404–5.

34. Carpenter Journal, November 20 and 26 and December 4, 1848, and January 3, 1849, Blanding Papers, SCL; Kirkland and Kennedy, *Historic Camden*, 2:360, 389, 404–5.

35. Kirkland and Kennedy, *Historic Camden,* 2:24, 427; Joan Inabinet, "A Wateree River Plantation Journal: 'Rosny' from 1815" (Camden, S.C.: Kershaw County Historical Society, 1997): 8; EWB, Camden, to LC, Pawtucket, May 20, 1840, Blanding Papers, SCL.

36. LC, Camden, to WB, Rehoboth, November 23, 1848, and January 11, 1849; Carpenter Journal, November 26 and 28, 1848, all Blanding Papers, SCL; Kirkland and Kennedy, *Historic Camden,* 1:326 and 2:24, 404–5; U.S. Census, 1850, Population Schedule, Kershaw District, South Carolina.

4

Middle-Class Benevolent Societies in Antebellum Norfolk, Virginia

JOHN G. DEAL

Thank God uc are out of SC for now.

D uring the two decades prior to the Civil War, voluntary organizations were central to cultural life in American cities and towns. Benevolent, fraternal, intellectual, and reform organizations not only served specific goals, but also acted as crucial and very public institutions of an emerging middle class of merchants, proprietors, white-collar businessmen, and professionals. Beyond a financial status that bound them together, these middling sorts believed in thrift, industry, sobriety, and piety, and shared similar consumer habits. They also participated in a culture of association membership that provided a means to rationalize their environment, promote their values, socialize prospective members, engender a sense of community, and connect them with like-minded persons beyond the town's borders.

Really?

Many studies have addressed the middle class in the antebellum urban North, and some scholars have simultaneously maintained that a southern middle class emerged only after the Civil War.[1] In recent years, historians examining the Old South have described a middle class with similar characteristics, despite a lack of large urban centers, manufacturing, and immigration, and despite the presence of slavery, which, according to one line of thinking, made the plantation South antithetical to the North's free-labor meritocracy. In Norfolk, Virginia, a middle class of merchants, proprietors, white-collar businessmen, and professionals emerged to shape the antebellum cultural environment, especially through the medium of voluntary associations. This essay examines benevolent societies, one category of voluntary organization, and their middle-class members during the two decades preceding the Civil War to demonstrate how these charitable organizations helped unify the middling sorts and promote their ideals.

Situated on the Elizabeth River lying south of the Chesapeake Bay, Norfolk is one of Virginia's oldest cities, dating to 1680. On the eve of the American Revolution it was the eighth largest city in the colonies and a primary commercial port.[2] Norfolk continued to prosper commercially during the early Republic, but like other southern ports it became increasingly dependent on northeastern cities for its commercial livelihood between the War of 1812 and the Civil War and was steadily marginalized in the national economy.[3]

Instead of the cotton or tobacco staple crops of Charleston, Mobile, or Savannah, Norfolk's commercial life centered on a thriving produce trade. In New York and Baltimore the Virginia port was referred to as the "Atlantic Garden" where fruits, vegetables, and grains grew in the rich Tidewater soil and shipped out of Norfolk. The city's market garden economy created similar limitations as did staple crops in that the products directly or indirectly affected most local businesses and the city shipped little directly to foreign ports. Having by far the lowest level of manufacturing of any major city in the South, Norfolk possessed few industries of any magnitude and those that did exist were small and generally limited to agricultural processing.[4]

Given this economic composition, it is not surprising that the city reflected its region's investment in slavery. In 1840, it housed 10,920 residents, including 3709 slaves (34 percent) and 1026 free blacks (9.4 percent), and a decade later Norfolk's total population consisted of 14,326 souls, including 9075 whites (63.3 percent), 4295 slaves (30 percent), and 956 free blacks (6.7 percent). By 1860, the region had suffered through a horrific yellow fever epidemic that killed more than 2000 residents and reduced the net population gain; Norfolk's resultant population was 14,620, including 10,290 whites (70.4 percent), 3284 slaves (22.5 percent), and 1046 free blacks (7.1 percent).[5]

Within the city's social structure was a middle class that established voluntary associations. A sample of four hundred association members between 1845 and 1854 illustrates that benevolent, improvement, cultural, and fraternal organizations were dominated by native, married, middle-aged (in their thirties and forties) merchants, proprietors, white-collar businessmen, and professionals with families, who owned slaves, and who possessed modest—but not extreme—wealth.[6] Fewer older men of "gentlemanly" wealth or land ownership entered the organizations. The majority of the sample possessed real estate and personal property upon which they were taxed, but their financial holdings did not rise to the level of wealth enjoyed by elite planters. The average and median real property levels fall far below $10,000, a conservative estimate for elite wealth in antebellum America.

Forty-year-old tailor William Dey exemplifies the members of the socio-economic upper end of the middle class who most often served as association office holders. Possessing $40,000 in real estate property and 6 slaves, he was a longtime member and one-time president of the Norfolk Humane Association, as well as a manager of the Seamen's Friend Society, an executive committee member of the Norfolk Tract Union, and a member of a Democratic Party Vigilance Committee. Also representative is Richard H. Chamberlaine, a 43-year-old married father of 6 children, who served as a cashier with the Norfolk branch of the Farmers' Bank of Virginia and as a councilman. A vice president of the Norfolk Humane Association, he possessed $17,500 in real estate and owned 19 slaves. He also was a member of the Norfolk Provident Society, and a manager of both the Seamen's Friend Society and Norfolk Tract Union. Multiple office-holding was prevalent among this group and many, like Chamberlaine, used this experience to prepare them for public office.

At the lower end of the middle-class spectrum were men like Moses P. Robertson, a 28-year-old merchant with one child but no real estate or slaves. Still, he was engaged as a solicitor assigned to the first ward for the Humane Association. Similarly, William P. Stewart, a 49-year-old merchant with only $50 in real estate and 1 slave, served as a Humane Association manager for 4 years and as a Master Mason with the Norfolk Lodge for 7 years. Between these property-holding extremes were many men such as Thomas D. Toy, a 36-year-old druggist/merchant who owned $3500 in real estate and 4 slaves. A solicitor and visitor for the Humane Association, he was also a secretary for the Seamen's Friend Society, a vice president for the Norfolk Musical Association, and a manager for the Norfolk Tract Union. Despite being lower on the socioeconomic scale, these men still possessed essential middle-class characteristics of a family and a white-collar job, which engendered stability and a better potential to improve oneself financially, morally, and intellectually.

As these men demonstrate, slave ownership was neither necessary for—nor antithetical to—association membership, even in benevolent societies that might be tied to northern cities. John G. H. Hatton, a 40-year-old teller at the Norfolk branch of the Farmers' Bank of Virginia, owned many slaves and also $10,000 in real estate property. He served as treasurer and secretary of the Norfolk Humane Association, as well as manager of the Seamen's Friend Society, and was president of the select council in 1852. Similarly Nathaniel Nash, a solicitor with the Humane Association and a Master Mason, was a 36-year-old carpenter/proprietor who possessed $9000 in real estate and 29 slaves, who probably labored in his shop.

These Norfolk men, a selection of the four hundred that provide the source base for this essay, reflect the traits of other association members in the era. For example, Norfolk reformers owning slaves confirms that benevolent and temperance societies existed in the Old South despite their potential connection to northern abolitionism. In his regional comparative study John W. Quist finds that in antebellum Tuscaloosa County, Alabama, temperance and evangelical benevolent reform societies existed on a level similar to that in Washtenaw County, Michigan. Accentuating the lack of cause and effect that the peculiar institution had on reform activities, Quist found that most of the leaders, directors, contributors, and volunteers to such endeavors were slaveholders. Membership rolls in both areas revealed a parallel of sorts in that abolitionists dominated Washtenaw's temperance proponents in comparison to their overall presence in the community, just as slaveholders dominated the ranks of temperance organizations in Tuscaloosa. Quist concludes that the intensity of benevolent activity related more to economic fluctuations than to the existence of slavery or perceptions of these endeavors as subversive northern causes.[7]

Thus this middle class of proprietors, merchants, professionals, and white-collar businessmen established a steady stream of benevolent societies during the two decades preceding the Civil War. Often inspired by the reforming impulses of the Second Great Awakening, charitable associations in both regions were essential to assisting those in physical distress with relief beyond what local governments would or could render.[8] Throughout the South municipalities had limited resources; the funds that did exist mostly were allocated to commercial improvements in streets, docks, market houses, canals, and railroads, rather than to provide for care of the needy.[9] In his examination of *Welfare and Charity in the Antebellum South,* Timothy J. Lockley points out that southern state and local officials did not mind providing public assistance in the form of poorhouses and asylums to those who were truly in dire straits, such as the elderly and orphaned. These institutions also temporarily housed the indigent or intemperate, however, and officials worried that such aid provided no reason to change wayward behavior, negatively influencing the truly destitute, especially children. These issues and the limited public assistance left room for private organizational assistance.[10]

Not everyone who required assistance received it, however, as benevolent societies increasingly gave only to those deemed to be the "worthy poor." Misfortune, unemployment, loss or death of a breadwinner, and other external factors could explain penury but personal failings often disqualified the rest. Quist explains that prior to the Civil War benevolent societies existed in the North and South to dole out assistance to this "worthy poor" of the community, such as women who were elderly, infirmed, or widowed and thus deemed not responsible for their predicament. In Baltimore the bourgeoisie directed benevolent societies to assist families and petitioned the city to provide firewood to "poor and worthy citizens" during the winter. In Boston assistance was temporary, only directed to the poor who deserved it, and conducted in a context of maintaining social stability and religious obligation. In contrast, benevolent societies in Charleston provided relief to those who required it within a context of paternalistic noblesse oblige and personal obligation.[11]

These associations improved a person's material condition but also endeavored to instill middle-class values of industry, thrift, sobriety, and self-discipline. Paul Boyer writes that when establishing the New York Association for Improving the Condition of the Poor (AICP) middle-class leaders believed that poverty was a result of character failings that led to moral depravity and threatened society. Financial assistance and counseling from the AICP instructed the "morally bankrupt" poor to improve their character and instill in them industry, thrift, and sobriety. Lockley concludes that southern benevolent societies not only hoped to improve the individual for his or her own sake, but they also aimed to create a better citizen who would contribute positively to the larger community rather than be a financial drain on the town.[12]

Alabama's benevolent workers believed that by attacking poverty with their programs they were aiding in the spiritual growth and economic development of the individual and by extension even that of the national economy. In Jacksonville, Illinois, civic boosters pushed for elevation of the lower orders that would enable the poor to contribute to the town's economy and growth, but also help to mediate internal conflict by creating a sense of community among the divergent populations.[13] Underlying this framework for charity was a certain degree of social control. As urban society advanced and correspondingly harbored increasing numbers of poor and needy, the middle class and its associations sought to bring order and stability to this changing urban landscape.

In Norfolk the Humane Society (or Association as it was sometimes styled) was the primary organization devoted to assisting the poor or those in distress during the antebellum period. Although it addressed specific relief efforts throughout the year, generally it would lie dormant during the spring through autumn months and then become more active in November to provide assistance for the upcoming winter. Prior to each year's reorganization meeting the managers placed notices in the local newspapers asking for contributions and inviting those who were interested in assisting the poor to attend. The society's officers divided the city into wards for the purposes of soliciting contributions and formed committees to carry out specific tasks, such as purchasing and distributing wood.[14]

In pleading for donations, a letter writer to the Norfolk *American Beacon* late in 1840 extolled the role of the Humane Society in helping the unfortunate of the city, especially women, children, and widows in need. In the same edition William E. Cunningham, editor of the *Beacon,* called attention to the organization and appealed to those who would waste money on luxuries to donate to philanthropic causes, such as the society, instead. In encouraging the public to alleviate the suffering of the poor and destitute, Cunningham explained that charity began at home and reminded those who were better off financially that their situations could change quickly and that they could require assistance. He also preached that while riches were fleeting, those who gave to the poor would be rewarded in the hereafter.[15]

About the time of the 1841–42 winter meeting a long commentary in the *American Beacon* reiterated the society's good works and urged citizens to support the association on behalf of the poor. The anonymous writer argued that the most useful undertaking that an individual could perform was to relieve human distress. The author, perhaps a leader in the organization, explained that when virtuous philanthropists reviewed what they had performed in their lives, those who garnered the greatest pleasure were those alleviators of human misery. Even in hours of sadness, the contributor emphasized, donors could reflect upon the deeds that sprang "up before the mind, like a green and refreshing oasis, in a wasted and weary land."[16]

One of the highest priorities for the Humane Society was extending relief to the oft-called "widowed friendless mother." Widows were described as barely surviving during the summer and during the harsh winter months their needs were even greater. The society furnished needed relief that supplemented what little the city doled out. The *Beacon* observer hoped that the liberality of the people would move them to support the cause, proclaiming that the society "invites the confidence of the public, and affords a channel for their charity, free of objection, and certain of reaching worthy recipients."[17]

Despite such assurances, questions regarding the quality of charity recipients and philanthropy would plague benevolent endeavors throughout the antebellum period. Prior to the winter of 1849 a declaration by a letter writer identified only as "C" appeared in the Norfolk *Daily Southern Argus,* calling for an improved and systematic plan for aid distribution to Norfolk's poor because of the perceived unsatisfactory results in past years. There was an "uncertainty as to the worthiness of the recipient; [an] inability on the part of the benefactor to trace the blessing of his charity in the physical or moral improvement of the individual; there is, oftentimes, the actual encouragement of idleness, vagrancy, drunkenness . . . indiscriminate alms-giving is far more productive of evil than good." These actions, the letter asserted, caused many Christian philanthropists to stop giving to the relief of the poor. The solution was to develop a system that would both provide physical assistance and elevate the moral health of those who were needy and worthy recipients.[18]

Using the New York Association for Improving the Condition of the Poor as a guide, "C" proposed the formation of a Norfolk organization based upon the AICP's three fundamental principles. The first stressed the sound and judicious discrimination in affording relief, meaning that no persons would receive aid without "an intimate acquaintance with their character, history, and habits of life." It further meant that the association would provide only necessary items of food, fuel, and clothing, rather than money, which could be abused. Assistance provided would be inferior to what could be acquired by labor and could be cut off if there were no improvement as a result of the aid provided. Perhaps most important, "never, under any circumstances" was aid to be given "to the street beggar or vagrant."[19]

Another principle stipulated that aid should be donated through a systematic unity of action so that services could be provided by numerous sources, thoroughly organized and working in concert, thus spreading out the division of labor. The last fundamental principle stated that assistance would be provided via personal interaction with the needy in their homes by dividing the city into districts and appointing visitors to interview those requesting assistance and provide written reports to solicitors and managers. As evidenced by the New York AICP, "C" argued, this system had been tried with success in other cities.[20]

In addition to knowledge of northern relief organizations, the letter demonstrates familiarity with many associations' structures and routines. When the New York AICP was established in 1843, middle-class bankers, professionals, and merchants developed a system whereby visitors went into assigned districts to determine who received aid—usually those perceived as destitute for reasons beyond their control—as well as counseling and instructing the bankrupt poor to improve their character. Boyer writes that with this systematic rational approach "the AICP represented an institutional mechanism for transmitting the values of the city's middle and upper strata downward into the ranks of the poor." Quist explains that from 1853 to 1867 members of the Tuscaloosa Female Benevolent Society collected money from middle-class and elite women to buy goods for the "worthy poor" of the community. Members would evaluate those needing assistance and later follow up on their situation.[21] At least one reformer in the late 1840s Norfolk publicized his desire to see similar principles and procedures brought to local charitable organizations.

In December 1848, Samuel T. Sawyer, editor of the *Daily Southern Argus,* commented on the plight of the poor and the new plan developed to assist them. He wrote that the proudest cities and societies provided services to their less fortunate citizens by private or public ventures. Implying a necessary worthiness in those the society aimed to help, he further insisted that the situation continued year after year as vice and intemperance were inflicted upon "our innocent mothers and helpless children." Less subtle was his assertion that one of the merits to this reorganization plan was that the association would provide for the *"virtuous poor,"* which meant an individual who was in need because of situations beyond his or her control (illness, loss of a spouse, joblessness) and who needed a temporary helping hand. Although it would sometimes be difficult to escape the deceptions of the impostor (who might be poor for reasons of character such as intemperance or who did not want to work), he emphasized that even this occasional deception was better than any individual of merit suffering on account of a lack of food, shelter, and clothing. Another positive element, Sawyer explained, was that the Humane Association was not bound by any single religious denomination but was "as broad and bounding as charity itself."[22]

The *Argus* editor continued by asserting that the association had been formed under favorable conditions with earnestness, a kind spirit, and judicious officers with only the best motives to discharge their duties. The real question, he asked, was if and how the citizens of Norfolk would respond to the call to assist the virtuous poor, not only with their verbal encouragement but also with their monetary contributions. Explaining the benefits of charity to the recipient, the benefactor, and the larger society, Sawyer proclaimed—in true booster fashion—that "every act of generous philanthropy, while it tends to promote the happiness of others, likewise contributes to the advantage, and ennobles the person who bestows—yields an inestimable consciousness of internal excellence and dignity, and is the best proof of public spirit and patriotic views."[23]

As a result of society members' dissatisfaction with the current system and dwindling public contributions, and no doubt spurred on by newspaper editorials and letters, the Norfolk Humane Society was reborn late in 1848 as the Norfolk Humane Association for the Relief and Improvement of the Poor. Complete with a new constitution and by-laws, its managers emphasized assisting only the virtuous, industrious poor and stressed systematic service provision by dividing the city into twelve wards, each with a committee of solicitors and visitors. Similarly, those in distress had to apply to their ward visitor for aid and be interviewed in their homes to determine if assistance could and should be provided. Only with a written report by the visitor would relief be provided in the form of food, clothing, wood for fuel, and dry goods. A final significant improvement was that the new system of assistance would not be confined to the winter months alone but would continue throughout the year.[24]

At the regular meeting of the board of managers in January 1849, the organization's financial difficulties occupied the agenda as distributions had already exceeded half the funds collected and it was still early in the winter season. In an effort to rally support and raise more money, the association called on the citizens of Norfolk through pleas in the newspapers. Editors like Samuel Sawyer wrote columns explaining that during the harsh winter months when the poor and destitute suffer the most, the community, known for its benevolent and charitable liberality, must be generally ignorant of the conditions of poverty in their city. When made aware of the situation, however, he believed Norfolk citizens would rally to relieve the suffering and necessities of the needy.[25]

Despite such public entreaties the situation only got worse as outlays exceeded contributions by a significant margin over the next two years. Still, the society continued to assist many individuals; in December 1848 and January 1849, the visitors granted relief to 281 families totaling 599 persons and distributed 200 cords of wood and groceries valued at $143, including dry goods, clothing, and shoes. In one ward alone during the winter of 1850 the society provided relief to 113 families with contributions of 250 cords of wood and 36 orders for groceries.[26]

By the end of 1850, the organization's financial health declined to the point that the Humane Association was unable to continue its attempt at year-round assistance. Managers reemphasized the temporary, helping-hand nature of assistance (to the worthy) in a public notice asking for contributions, explaining that "The design of the Association is not to support the poor of the city, but only to give the relief and assistance from time to time. Persons who have no means of subsistence . . . must be entrusted to the care of their friends and relatives, or be sent to the Alms House."[27]

Throughout the remaining antebellum years, the association operated on the same principles and methods, hibernating, as it were, during the spring and summer months and reviving when the cold winds blew into the city. During the winter leaders continually asked for contributions through the efforts of solicitors and newspaper articles and notices. The society also held benefits, including panorama shows and musical concerts, to raise funds. The general tone of giving stressed not only what it would do for the needy, but also what contributing could do for the donor who would demonstrate "all the nobler attributes of our nature."[28]

In terms of practical operations the Humane Association exemplified middle-class ideals of order, frugality, and efficiency. Advocates described the society as improved, systematic, sound, and judicious; it rationalized an organization comprising a board of managers, solicitors and managers in their

respective wards, and committees carrying out certain functions such as purchasing and distributing wood. Calculated for maximum efficiency, assistance
was doled out relative to the needs of the individual or family as determined by
the visitor. The two-step process of deciding on aid—the initial visitor report
and subsequent board of managers evaluation—assured that the visitor had not
made an unwise decision. Applicant evaluations and subsequent monthly reports ensured that recipients used the assistance wisely, that they continued to
live appropriately (including abstaining from liquor), and that support continued to match the relative needs of the family. Assistance in the form of wood,
food, and clothing rather than money guarded against wastefulness or inap-
propriate purchases. Such characteristics of the Humane Association guaran-
teed, at least on paper, that only the virtuous, industrious poor received aid.[29]

Accentuating the middle-class values emerging during this time was the
1848 rebirth and renaming of the Humane Society as the Norfolk Humane
Association for the Relief and Improvement of the Poor. The new title "Association" clearly indicated a more structured and formal organization, which
reflected the increasing bureaucratization of white-collar work and significance of order and efficiency. At the same time, "relief" and "improvement"
highlighted the association's intention that aid would be merely temporary;
those citizens requiring more than short-term assistance would be banished
to the almshouse. These words stressed the organization's appreciation of the
values of progress and improvement.

Essential to middle-class ideology was the belief that helping and improving others enhanced the life of the donors as well. As exemplified in numerous
editorials and letters, those who gave to Norfolk's suffering poor felt themselves closer to God. Giving offered benefactors identifiable moments of their
lives when they elevated the condition of someone in their community and
by extension their own condition as well. Present in this context was a not-
so-subtle implication that the most virtuous individuals in the community
donated to benevolent causes and that the final reward would be greater for
those who gave rather than those who did not. Many entreaties in local newspapers appealed to individuals to spend their extra monies on philanthropic
causes. The members of the Humane Association, especially those visitors and
solicitors who were most directly responsible for the provision of assistance,
were saluted as being among the most virtuous citizens in the community.

Additionally, local leaders exemplified by *Argus* editor Samuel Sawyer and local historian William Forrest believed that the donation process reflected positively on the city as a whole as residents were portrayed as benevolent persons. In a context of boosterism Norfolk could join other proud cities that provided for the less fortunate of their citizenry.[30]

While Norfolk's men directed good works with the Humane Association, the city's women developed their own organizations devoted to helping the destitute. Throughout the North and South women established a number of benevolent societies to serve the needy. As Timothy Lockley explains the major difference between the two regions, beyond the sheer number (which is explained in part by the North's larger cities), is that southern women did not establish abolitionist organizations. He also argues that during the first half of the nineteenth century, women dominated the private provision of benevolent aid and charity in America. Service provision was a natural extension of caring for one's family and also fit into a paradigm of republican motherhood in which those who were a drain on society were elevated to useful members of the community. Importantly, male community leaders accepted women's participation in this aspect of the public sphere. Frank J. Byrne argues that merchant wives often moved beyond the proscribed role of domestic caretaker by joining voluntary organizations such as benevolent societies. He further explains that most public roles assumed by antebellum southern women related to imparting knowledge in some form or fashion, including instructing values of hard work and thriftiness or practical skills like sewing in classroom venues or in the community through voluntary organizations.[31] The wives of Norfolk's mercantile and professional middle class likewise entered and founded aid societies.

The Dorcas Society in Norfolk, established in 1811, dedicated itself to alleviating the needs of the "suffering poor" during the winter months and in times of crisis. Consisting of "charitable ladies," many the wives of civic leaders and from all religious denominations, its members visited the homes of the afflicted and suffering, often weekly, to supply their needs. They provided clean clothing (frequently what they had made themselves), food, medical assistance, and religious ministering. The latter was of the utmost importance as the group provided temporal comfort as well as endeavoring to "impress upon the minds of the poor the necessity of religion, and to put their trust and confidence in God." Further echoing the improvement goal of their work, members reported that they hoped those being assisted would find their way to God.[32]

Beyond the Dorcas Society, women became involved in church auxiliaries that met regularly and raised monies for a variety of congregational and community-related causes. Working as individual church auxiliaries or in concert with other churches and even denominations, the chief method of fundraising was the fair and feast. The goals of the fairs ranged from church renovations or new sanctuaries to charitable endeavors such as aiding the poor and destitute, orphan asylums, and local voluntary militia companies including the Norfolk Light Artillery Blues.[33] These ladies' fair events included simple occasions where the auxiliaries sold baked goods, foodstuffs, and homemade fabric items, as well as grand celebrations like that hosted by the Ladies of the Freemason Street Baptist Church in April 1850. The auxiliary presented the Norfolk Sacred Musical Society, which conducted a benefit concert at Mechanics' Hall with a program of Mozart and Hayden, along with various hymns and religious anthems.[34] That same month the ladies of St. Patrick's Church held a Catholic Fair, which proudly counted General Winfield Scott as an attendee.[35]

These occasions helped to create a sense of community among the women's auxiliaries as different churches and denominations assisted each other in organizing events. Perhaps more important, the Dorcas Society and church-oriented ladies' auxiliaries provided paths by which antebellum women could be active beyond the domestic sphere. Indeed, Norfolk resident Mary McPhail Smith wrote to a friend that she did not correspond more often because she was involved in too many activities, including the Education Society on Mondays, a Bible class on Tuesdays, the Dorcas Society on Wednesdays, and preparation for her Sabbath School class on Saturdays. Still, she admitted that although she had little free time, "I know that I daily spend too much in idle thoughts which should be better employed. I often feel unhappy to think how many thoughts are given to the world and how few to God."[36]

The fairs also created a larger sense of community within the city as a whole. When the Ladies of the Freemason Street Baptist Church hosted their 1850 celebration to raise money for a new sanctuary, *Daily Southern Argus* editor Sawyer observed that residents "should attend this entertainment, where they will not only be served with all the delicacies in the edible line at the hands of the 'fairer portion of our creation,' but regale themselves with an hour or two of delightful sociability."[37] Certainly this comment was directed toward men and the opportunity to hobnob with the women organizing and attending the fairs. It also suggests, however, a larger context of sociability whereby likeminded members of the community with similar beliefs and socioeconomic levels could fraternize, incorporate new residents, and form business contacts. Ultimately, these ladies' organizations engendered a sense of commonality within and between their own groups, while also mediating class conflicts in the larger community.

Throughout the antebellum period local women's organizations assisted many benevolent institutions. Among the most popular to receive aid, because they were continually in need, were the various orphan asylums of Norfolk. Benefits to raise money for these asylums included dramatic performances, musical events, pleasure excursions, and fairs conducted by the ladies' church auxiliaries as well as female schools and seminaries.[38] The Female Orphan Asylum organized a benefit in 1847 to repair its deteriorating building. To raise the estimated $4000, the ladies of the different religious denominations combined to hold a Union Fair. An anonymous letter writer commended the ladies for their "patient industry and generous devotion of time, labor, and money."[39]

Similar to the goals and actions of the Humane Association, providing assistance for orphans reflected middle-class values. In contrast to those who were poor because of bad habits, children were considered innocent victims of circumstances. Closely connected were ideals of improving the children through the inculcation of industry and religious virtue. Similarly Norfolk women focused on selecting appropriate aid recipients, as did female benevolent societies in Baltimore, Charleston, Nashville, New Orleans, and Savannah that limited service to the "worthy poor."[40] Echoing such sentiments in 1840, *American Beacon* editor William Cunningham wrote that giving necessary assistance to children was a fine action, but that "to bestow it, as a reward, in some measure, of industry, taste and skill, is better."[41] In March 1842, he called for asylum donations by writing that "There could scarcely be devised a more effectual plan for relieving the wants of the poor, and encouraging the growth of virtue in that class. To instill in [the orphan's] soul the purity of principle, moral and religious, and imbue its mind with the elevation of knowledge" was a privilege.[42]

Simply providing a place for orphans was not enough, however. Without parents the child would be at risk of becoming intemperate, lazy, morally bankrupt, and areligious—in short, a danger to society. The orphan asylums took the place of the departed parents and taught the children society's conventions. They would mold their charges into industrious, virtuous, useful, and intelligent members of society, which reflected both orphans' eventual need to work for a living and the values of the primarily middle-class groups supporting the institutions.[43]

Some in the community favored even more practical means of improvement, such as a correspondent to the *American Beacon* in April 1847 who suggested that a large lot be purchased and a new building erected. The Orphan Asylum could subsequently use these facilities to cultivate a vegetable garden that older orphans could farm for themselves. This would enable the institution to support itself and perhaps even be able to accept more orphans to house and educate. The new asylum in Richmond, it was believed, had adopted a similar plan.[44]

As the Humane Association and the various women's clubs and auxiliaries provided aid to the city's "worthy poor" and needy, one of the most enduring of Norfolk's benevolent associations was organized during an especially dark period of the city's history. In the summer of 1855, Norfolk suffered a terrible yellow fever epidemic that was so overwhelming it required citizens to ban together in special organizations. From June until October nearly ten thousand people, about two-thirds of the population, contracted the disease and more than two thousand perished.[45] Informally established in August 1855, but formally reorganized in September with a constitution and bylaws, the Howard Association was the most important organization established to alleviate the suffering from the epidemic.[46] It turned Norfolk's largest hotel into a hospital, set up other medical facilities in buildings at a race course several miles from the city, distributed vast amounts of monies (about $160,000) and supplies sent from all over the country, and built a new orphan asylum to house children who lost parents in the epidemic. The association also paid for burials and the following winter it distributed food and fuel relief to about five hundred families.[47]

After the crisis had passed, the Howard Association evolved into a benevolent society attending to the needs of the poor year-round by using the remaining funds left over from the epidemic contributions (about $67,000). Out of this sum, the association's officers invested $50,000, using the interest to pursue its charitable endeavors well into the twentieth century. The association devoted the remaining $17,000 to maintain the Howard Asylum and fund the education of children orphaned by the epidemic. The asylum continued until 1861, when expenses became prohibitive and the remaining twenty-nine orphans were turned over the Norfolk Female Asylum. The Howard Association contracted to support the orphans in the asylum until they were eighteen years old (or adopted).[48]

Even though the Howard Association directed many good works during the yellow fever epidemic, some observers believed that the organization did not receive its fair recognition. In an early 1856 letter to the *Daily Southern Argus* a person identified as "Refugee" wrote that the association had been slighted and not appreciated for its work helping others during the epidemic, especially in light of the public praise that had been heaped on others. Undoubtedly someone who received aid, "Refugee" wrote that the group deserved an ovation of some kind, but that the public had subjected the association to contemptible taunts and jeers. Some who received assistance even criticized the organization as "miserably incompetent to transact its peculiar duties" in aiding the suffering, displaced, and poor.[49]

The Howard Association was important because it was one of the few, if not only, charities to dispense assistance without any preconceived notions concerning the worthiness of the recipients as it doled out fuel and food to about five hundred families during the winter of 1855–56. Perhaps this could be explained by the fact that the yellow fever was so devastating, striking Norfolk residents of all backgrounds, wealth, and occupations, that aid simply could not be held back from those normally considered unworthy. Given the magnitude of the tragedy, everyone was worthy at this particular time.[50]

In this context, it is arguable that some of the criticism directed toward the Howard Association came from those who believed that assistance should have been more selective, thus allowing for more resources to be given to the perceived better elements of the community. Middle-class ideals were not entirely divorced from the organization, however, as it received positive recognition when the asylum children were taken to an Episcopal church, a middle-class behavior that promoted piety. On one occasion in January 1856 at St. Paul's Church, the seventy-eight boys and girls were described as very beautiful and reported to be neatly dressed and happy. On another occasion in May fifty orphans attending St. Paul's were described as healthy, tidily groomed and dressed, and exhibiting "orderly and correct behavior . . . [evincing] the good effects of the parental care bestowed upon them," which included a matron.[51] With an emphasis by commentators on the children's robust and neat demeanor, the implication arises that if the orphans attended church in a disheveled, ill-mannered, or slovenly appearance, then the association's orphanage would have failed.

Norfolk's middle-class residents supported a network of benevolent associations during the antebellum years as the Humane Association, Dorcas Society, ladies' auxiliaries, and the Howard Association provided physical assistance to the needy. They did so predominantly in a context of middle-class beliefs, stressing not only the improvement of the physical well-being of the individual, but also the moral and spiritual elevation of the person's character. With the exception of the Howard Association and its extraordinary circumstances, assistance was provided only to those people the groups identified as the "worthy poor" and needy. Civic boosters viewed charitable giving as a way to elevate the status of the city in concert with the elevation of the needy. For those volunteering their time to benevolent societies or making contributions, these efforts not only elevated feelings of self-worth, they also reinforced one's public standing and improved one's chances for a later reward in heaven. In turn, these voluntary organizations helped to cultivate a cohesive middle class and promote values of industry, thrift, sobriety, and improvement among their number, those they assisted, and in the community at large. The nascent middle class of merchants, proprietors, professionals, and white-collar businessmen emerged in antebellum Norfolk, regardless of the city's lack of size, industry, and immigration, and despite the presence of slavery, and laid the foundation for a full flowering of the middle class during the postwar New South era.

NOTES

1. These "new men" were described in Don H. Doyle, *New Men, New Cities, New South, 1860–1910* (Chapel Hill: University of North Carolina Press, 1990). Similar middle-ranking businessmen and professionals controlled political power in Birmingham, Alabama, during the city's first half-century from 1871 to 1921; Carl V. Harris, *Political Power in Birmingham, 1871–1921* (Knoxville: University of Tennessee Press, 1977).

2. H. W. Burton, *The History of Norfolk, Virginia: A Review of Important Events and Incidents which occurred from 1736 to 1877* (Norfolk: *Norfolk Virginian*, 1877), 1; Andrew Morrison, *Norfolk, Portsmouth, and the Tidewater Country* (Norfolk: George Engelhardt, 1889), 29; Robert W. Lamb, ed., *Our Twin Cities of the Nineteenth Century: Norfolk and Portsmouth, Their Past, Present, and Future* (Norfolk: Barcroft, 1887), 6–8; *Virginia Gazette* (Purdie), February 9, 1776.

3. Burton, *History of Norfolk*, 4–5; Lamb, *Our Twin Cities of the Nineteenth Century*, 9–10; Thomas C. Parramore, Peter C. Stewart, and Tommy Bogger, *Norfolk: The First Four Centuries* (Charlottesville: University Press of Virginia, 1994), 75, 86–94; Morrison, *Norfolk, Portsmouth, and the Tidewater Country*, 28; William S. Forrest, *The Norfolk Directory, For 1851–1852: Containing the Names, Professions, Places of Business, and Residences of the Merchants, Traders, and Manufacturers Mechanics* (Norfolk: William S. Forrest, 1851), 114; W. H. T. Squires, *Through the Years in Norfolk: Historical Norfolk—1636–1936* (Norfolk: Norfolk Advertising Board, 1936), 122–23. The marginalization of other southern ports is discussed at length in David R. Goldfield, *Cotton Fields and Skyscrapers, Southern City and Region, 1607–1980* (Baton Rouge: Louisiana State University Press, 1982), esp. 6–8, 29–79.

4. W. Eugene Ferslew, comp., *Vickery's Directory for the City of Norfolk, to Which is Added a Business Directory for 1859* (Norfolk: Vickery & Company, 1859), 25–26; David R. Goldfield, *Urban Growth in the Age of Sectionalism: Virginia 1847–1861* (Baton Rouge: Louisiana State University Press, 1977), 238; U.S. Census Office, *Statistics of the United States, Including Mortality, Property, &c., in 1860* (New York: Norman Ross Publishing, 1990), xviii; Forrest, *Norfolk Directory*, 114; Parramore, Stewart, and Bogger, *Norfolk*, 189, 192.

5. U.S. Census Office, *Compendium of the Enumeration of the Inhabitants and Statistics of the United States, as Obtained at the Department of State, From the Returns of the Sixth Census* (New York: Norman Ross Publishing, 1990), 32–34; *The Seventh Census of the United States, 1850* (New York: Norman Ross Publishing, 1990), 258; and *Population of the United States in 1860* (New York: Norman Ross Publishing, 1990), 519. For comparison, state neighbor Richmond's 1860 population was 37,910, ranking it third in the South behind New Orleans (168,675) and Charleston (39,870).

6. This sample was taken from membership rolls, newspapers, organization records, and local histories. Age, nativity, marital status, children, occupation, real estate wealth, and slave ownership were collected using the 1850 manuscript and slave censuses, 1850 personal property tax returns, and city directories. Although not an exhaustive collection, the sample does reflect the general characteristics of association members during the antebellum period in Norfolk.

7. John W. Quist, *Restless Visionaries: The Social Roots of Antebellum Reform in Alabama and Michigan* (Baton Rouge: Louisiana State University Press, 1998), 1–21, 38–39, 100–101, 195–96, 210, 234, 302.

8. Camilla Townsend, *Tales of Two Cities: Race and Economic Culture in Early Republican North and South America* (Austin: University of Texas Press, 2000), 101–10; Clyde Griffen and Sally Griffen, *Natives and Newcomers: The Ordering of Opportunity in Mid-Nineteenth-Century Poughkeepsie* (Cambridge, Mass.: Harvard University Press, 1978), 40; Mary P. Ryan, *The Cradle of the Middle Class: The Family in Oneida County, New York, 1790–1865* (Cambridge: Cambridge University Press, 1981), 236–37; Paul Boyer, *Urban Masses and Moral Order in America, 1820–1920* (Cambridge, Mass.: Harvard University Press, 1978), 1–15.

9. John S. Gilkeson Jr. argues that middle-class associations acted as surrogates for the weak governmental authority that existed for much of the nineteenth century; Gilkeson, *Middle-Class Providence, 1820–1940* (Princeton: Princeton University Press, 1986), 7–10, 55–56.

10. Timothy James Lockley, *Welfare and Charity in the Antebellum South* (Gainesville: University Press of Florida, 2007), 28, 32–35, 42–43, 59.

11. Quist, *Restless Visionaries*, 81–86; Townsend, *Tales of Two Cities*, 102–3 (quotation); William H. Pease and Jane H. Pease, *The Web of Progress: Private Values and Public Styles in Boston and Charleston, 1828–1843* (New York: Oxford University Press, 1985), 145–52.

12. Boyer, *Urban Masses and Moral Order in America*, 86–94; Lockley, *Welfare and Charity in the Antebellum South*, 213–14.

13. Quist, *Restless Visionaries*, 71–77; Don H. Doyle, *Social Order of a Frontier Community: Jacksonville, Illinois, 1825–1870* (Urbana: University of Illinois Press, 1983), 64, 225–26.

14. *American Beacon*, January 14, November 19, 29, 1839, January 14, February 4, December 11, 18, 1840, November 3, December 19, 1842, December 19, 1843, December 11, 13, 1845.

15. Ibid., December 22, 1840.

16. Ibid., December 12, 1841.

17. Ibid.

18. *Daily Southern Argus*, November 27, 1848.

19. Ibid.

20. Ibid.

21. Boyer, *Urban Masses and Moral Order in America*, 86–94, 91–92 (quotation); Quist, *Restless Visionaries*, 81–86.

22. *Daily Southern Argus*, December 5, 1848; italics original. Norfolk Catholics established their own charitable association, styled the St Patrick's Society, in January 1852. It stressed the duties of man as required by religion, morality, and humanity; Burton, *History of Norfolk*, 257.

23. *Daily Southern Argus*, December 5, 1848.

24. Solicitors asked for contributions while visitors examined the needs and circumstances of the poor, provided the necessary relief, and presented monthly reports to the managers. Ibid.; Forrest, *Norfolk Directory*, 96–97.

25. *Daily Southern Argus*, January 9, 10, 1849.

26. Ibid., February 21, 1849, March 16, 1850.

27. Ibid., December 14, 1850, December 18, 1850 (quotation).

28. Ibid., December 8, 1851, December 20, 1853 (quotation), December 22, 24, 1853, January 16, 1854, December 11, 13, 16, 1854, January 21, 24, 26, 1856.

29. *Daily Southern Argus*, December 5, 1848; Forrest, *Norfolk Directory*, 96–97.

30. Ibid. Also see *American Beacon*, December 22, 1840.

31. Lockley, *Welfare and Charity in the Antebellum South*, 60–63, 69–78; Frank J. Byrne, *Becoming Bourgeois: Merchant Culture in the South, 1820–1865* (Lexington: University Press of Kentucky, 2006), 81–87. As Jonathan Daniel Wells points out, women in southern towns also broke out of gender roles limiting self-expression by establishing literary and debating societies, often modeled after those of their male counterparts, which nurtured their intellectual growth and served as a means for socialization; Wells, *The Origins of the Southern Middle Class, 1800–1861* (Chapel Hill: University of North Carolina Press, 2004), 102–5.

32. Goldfield, *Urban Growth in the Age of Sectionalism,* 161–62. The Dorcas Society received much support from local newspapers. Abram F. Leonard, editor of the *Daily Southern Argus* by the early 1850s, often wrote of the society's fairs and benefits and called for the community's generous support; *Argus,* October 15, 1851, November 12, 1851 (quotation), January 3, 12, 1856.

33. *American Beacon,* June 13, 22, 1841, June 20, 1842, April 19, 1844, February 5, 6, April 26, 1847; *Daily Southern Argus,* January 6, 9, 10, April 10, 1849, June 27, 1851, October 22, 1852.

34. *Daily Southern Argus,* April 1, 1850. Lockley describes similar fairs occurring throughout the antebellum years in Mobile and Savannah, specifically imitating fairs held in Baltimore, Boston, and Washington; Lockley, *Welfare and Charity in the Antebellum South,* 87.

35. *Daily Southern Argus,* April 24, 25, 1850. These fairs could be very successful, such as when the Ladies and Friends of the Methodist Protestant Church held a fair at the Mechanics Hall to raise money for a new church and raised $1000; ibid., May 24, June 2, 1854.

36. Mary (McPhail) Smith to Mary Venable Carrington, Charlotte Court House, January 30, 1832, Carrington Family Papers, Section 26, doc. 55, Virginia Historical Society.

37. *Daily Southern Argus,* April 1, 1850.

38. Burton, *History of Norfolk,* 223–26. An 1855 fair to benefit St. Mary's even published a daily newspaper for the six-day event, entitled *The Fair Offering,* with literature, instruction, and amusement; *Daily Southern Argus,* May 16, 1855. Fairs announced in *American Beacon,* March 22, 1839, May 3, 4, 1841, May 6, 28, 1842, September 2, 1846, April 5, 9, 13, 16, 1847; *Daily Southern Argus,* October 20, 1853, January 7, November 9, 15, 16, 1854.

39. *American Beacon,* January 27, 1847, March 22, 1847 (quotation).

40. Lockley, *Welfare and Charity in the Antebellum South,* 97–103.

41. *American Beacon,* May 6, 1840, May 8, 1840 (quotation).

42. Ibid., March 5, 1842.

43. The operations of the orphanage reflected the changing nature of public institutions as asylums, penitentiaries, almshouses, and orphanages emerged by the antebellum era. David Rothman explains that these institutions not only existed to reform the "inmates," but also to serve as a model for a well-ordered republican society. Using similar program models for criminals, the insane, the poor, and orphans, these institutions provided shelter, daily routines, discipline, and authority that transformed inmates' character and made them respectable citizens; Rothman, *The Discovery of the Asylum: Social Order in the New Republic,* rev. ed. (Boston: Little, Brown, and Company, 1990), 3–35, 56–84, 103–8, 133–42, 180–84, 206–24.

44. *American Beacon,* April 12, 1847.

45. Modern studies of the epidemic include David R. Goldfield, "Disease and Urban Image: Yellow Fever in Norfolk, 1855," *Virginia Cavalcade* 23 (Autumn 1973): 34–41, and Charles A. Nicholson, "The Tragic Summer of 1855 at Norfolk and Portsmouth, Virginia," *Genealogical Society of Tidewater, Virginia Bulletin* 10 (December 1979): 171–88. Contemporary accounts include George D. Armstrong, *The Summer of the Pestilence: A History of the Ravages of the Yellow Fever in Norfolk, Virginia, A.D. 1855,* 3rd ed. (Virginia Beach: W. S. Dawson & Co., 1994); William S. Forrest, *The Great Pestilence in Virginia: Being an Historical Account of the Origin, General Character, and Ravages of the Yellow Fever in Norfolk and Portsmouth in 1855; Together with Sketches of Some of the Victims* (Philadelphia: J. B. Lippincott, 1856); and Norfolk Committee to Investigate the Cause and Origin of the Yellow Fever of 1855, *Report on the Origin of the Yellow Fever in Norfolk During*

the Summer of 1855, made to City Councils by a Committee of Physicians (Richmond: Ritchie and Dunnavant, 1857).

46. Named after British social reformer John Howard (1726–90) these associations developed in the first half of the nineteenth century in most major cities around the country, including Boston (established in 1812), Washington, D.C. (1825), New Orleans (1837), New York (1843), and Philadelphia (1858), and concerned themselves with issues related to prison reform, crime, and especially public health. See Sidney Lee, ed., *Dictionary of National Biography*, vol. 28 (New York: MacMillan and Co., 1891), 44–48; Flora B. Hildreth, "The Howard Association of New Orleans, 1837–1878" (Ph.D. diss., University of California, Los Angeles, 1975), esp. 48–69; Goldfield, *Urban Growth in the Age of Sectionalism*, 162–63.

47. *Report of the Howard Association of Norfolk, Va., to all Contributors Who Gave their Valuable Aid in Behalf of the Sufferers from Epidemic Yellow Fever During the Summer of 1855* (Philadelphia: *Philadelphia Inquirer*, 1857); Nicholson, "Tragic Summer of 1855 at Norfolk and Portsmouth," 172; Edward Wilson James, ed., *The Lower Norfolk County Virginia Antiquary*, vol. 5 (Baltimore: The Friedenwald Company, 1904), 24–25; *Daily Southern Argus*, October 26, 1855; C. W. Tazewell, ed., *Vignettes from the Shadows—Glimpses of Norfolk's Past* (Norfolk: W. S. Dawson Company, 1992), 46; Parramore, Stewart, and Bogger, *Norfolk*, 176–90.

48. Except for limited funds from private sources, the Howard Association appropriation would be the only monies received by the Norfolk Female Orphan asylum during the war years; Tazewell, *Vignettes from the Shadows*, 46; Burton, *History of Norfolk*, 223–24; see also Goldfield, *Urban Growth in the Age of Sectionalism*, 162–63.

49. *Daily Southern Argus*, January 18, 1856 (quotation), January 24, 1856. Reverend George Armstrong also recognized the Howard Association on behalf of his Presbyterian church, writing that the "members of the Howard Association, left nothing undone which they could do for us"; Armstrong, *Summer of the Pestilence*, 52.

50. Indeed, one resident wrote that the fever had taken physicians as well as African Americans and noted that "by degrees some of the most enterprising of the Norfolk merchants are dropping" and that "nearly every person you see at the post office now seem[s] to have had the fever. The white people of Norfolk seem to be at present a regular set of invalids"; John Shanks to Debree Taylor, September 20, 1855, Virginia Historical Society.

51. *Daily Southern Argus*, January 29, 1856, May 6, 1856 (quotation); Armstrong, *Summer of the Pestilence*, 59–60. Timothy Lockley explains how important the cleanliness and dress of orphans was to judging the quality of their care; Lockley, *Welfare and Charity in the Antebellum South*, 105–6.

Too long sentences
Weird wording.
overexplained a little

5

Running Southern Manufactories

The Antebellum Origins of Managerial Professions

SUSANNA DELFINO

In their attempt to demonstrate the South's inadequacy to carry on a genuine process of modernization, antebellum northerners often contended that its society and culture did not possess either the technical expertise or the managerial skills necessary to run successfully southern manufactories. According to them, exceptions made for the few commendable examples of achievement below the Mason-Dixon line were to be catalogued under the rubric of northern ingenuity and spirit of enterprise migrated to the South. So assumed Englishman James Montgomery, long a resident of the United States, and the author of essays and books on textile manufacturing.[1] Moreover, in his view, even the most competent northerners could fail when confronted with an inhospitable environment. "There is a prevailing impression among mill managers," he wrote in an 1859 article, "that the proprietors of Southern factories invariably refuse to pay their superintendents such high salaries as are paid by Northern manufacturers. Hence, they, employing cheap men, may only expect cheap management." According to Montgomery, the making of an accomplished mill manager required not only a long "practical experience with all kinds of machinery," but also the support of a whole community network that "some of the Southern States" did not seem to provide.[2]

The persistence of the opinion—well into the twentieth century—that even the managerial structure of antebellum northern industrial concerns was very simple, coupled with the widespread belief that southern manufactories were usually small enough to be personally managed by their owners, long discouraged investigation of the diversity of ownership formulas adopted by southern industrialists.[3] As a consequence, the professional figures of southern origin who were engaged in the variety of managerial and, generally speaking, white-collar occupations attendant to the operation of a manufactory have also been

for
dear *?*

neglected. In this essay, I will outline the shaping of such professions that have long been perceived as largely alien to the antebellum southern industrial experience, unless performed by northerners who offered their services for dear. Notwithstanding Montgomery's contention that the managerial cadres of southern manufactories were overwhelmingly of a northern provenance, evidence illustrates that, during the last two antebellum decades, southern industrialists were increasingly able to tap into an available pool of local and regional skills and abilities to fill managerial and clerical positions at their manufactories. By employing native southerners, they implicitly acknowledged the coming to maturity of an indigenous industrial tradition.

Apart from the rather more obvious case of corporations, neither partnerships nor individual or family proprietorships were exempt from the need to resort to managerial support. In many instances, the role of general manager, or superintendent, was performed by someone holding a personal stake in the concern, such as a partner or a younger family member. However, the very diversity of the operations carried out at a manufacturing establishment invariably prompted the recruitment of lower-rank managers to supervise each of the several processes involved.[4] Job opportunities were thus open to, and well sought after by, ambitious individuals of even modest means who were anxious to promote themselves, sometimes in the secret hope of eventually making themselves proprietors. Only a limited number of them were, however, able to crown that dream. In fact, as the industrial phenomenon grew in proportion and importance in the South from the 1830s, chances for rags-to-riches careers in the field of manufacturing decreased correspondingly. As a result, manager remained a permanent profession for many, while for others it turned out to be the endpoint of a career path that had not infrequently evolved from some sort of manual, albeit skilled job.

Largely focused on Tennessee and Kentucky, this essay also draws upon a number of sources related to North Carolina and Georgia to provide a broader, regional perspective on the antebellum shaping of managerial professions in the iron and the textile industries. Given the limited space, the present essay cannot offer an exhaustive treatment of such a heretofore neglected subject. It nonetheless aims to establish the meaningfulness of pursuing a line of investigation—the rise of managerial professions in southern industry—which adds an important facet to the delineation of the contours of the antebellum southern middle class. By documenting the social transformations engendered by industrialization, such an effort contributes an important chapter to the history of the modernization and class development of the antebellum South.

On February 13, 1818, Charles Wilkins, a Lexington merchant and industrial promoter, formed a partnership with Ruggles Whiting and Jacob Holderman for the purpose of erecting and operating a furnace in what was then Hardin County (Hart from 1819), Kentucky.[5] The article of agreement specified that, whereas the three men were the joint owners of Aetna Furnace, Jacob Holderman was entrusted with its "management and direction." Besides being attributed "entire control" of the furnace, of all the persons employed, and of the proceeds of the production, he was also empowered to collect debts and make all the necessary contracts, and "do and perform all the duties of a manager, subject however to the instructions of a majority of the owners of Said Furnace."[6] For his services, Holderman was to receive, besides the boarding for himself and family, "the sum of one thousand and one hundred dollars annually"—a remarkable amount of money for those times—which he was to withhold from the proceeds of the furnace.[7]

It was indeed mere coincidence—although fortunate for this essay—that the following day, February 14, 1818, the directors and stockholders of the Sanders Manufacturing Company, a textile manufactory promoted by Kentuckian William McRobb Sanders, convened for the first time in Lexington and listened to the keynote address given by George Lockerbee, a gentleman boasting thirty years of experience "in a variety of branches, both in the cotton and woollen manufactories."[8] Starting from the premise that waste of materials and time, and the destruction of machinery, were the order of the day at most American manufacturing establishments, because of neglect on the part of the operatives and disinterest on the part of the agents and overseers, Lockerbee placed "proper management" at the center of his speech.[9] From that perspective, he argued for the desirability of having someone holding a personal stake in the concern to perform that delicate and crucial function. Although his views may have been overly influenced by his firsthand experience, which suggested to him that "a few wandering individuals . . . not stationary enough to improve anything," could not be depended upon "for either knowledge or virtue," Lockerbee perfectly hit the core of the problem. Given the well-known resistance shown by factory hands in every part of the country to submit to work discipline, the quality of supervision and managerial control was essential in determining the success of an industrial enterprise. The more so "where a large number of strangers of all habits and dispositions is collected together in a large building," such as a textile manufactory.[10]

The Aetna contract and Sanders board meeting address a number of important issues connected with the subject of the present investigation. First of all, they indicate the diversity of proprietary formulas adopted by southern industrialists at an early time in the development of American manufactures. Whereas the former—an iron-manufacturing venture—was a simple partnership between three people, the latter—a textile enterprise—was a corporation. Underlying the difference, which was not by any means the rule, were the special requirements in capital outlay commanded by the nature of the two enterprises, respectively.[11] While a large part of the capital needed to set up an iron-making establishment consisted in land (to make charcoal and to extract limestone and mineral ore), an asset that was mostly available to southern industrialists, in the case of textile manufacturing the heaviest capital outlay required was for the purpose of purchasing very expensive machinery, usually from the Northeast.[12] As a consequence, whereas the former type of enterprise could be realized in the shape of a simple partnership thanks to the involvement of a few local landowning investors, the latter entailed the pooling of much vaster financial resources, such as a corporation could best provide. Even as industrial concerns owned by a single family existed in both branches of industry throughout the antebellum era, from the 1840s many of them became less and less able to weather competition and, in order to survive, were forced to procure fresh capital by forming partnerships with wealthy people.

Second, the two documents suggest that the iron and the textile industries, respectively, posed different problems in terms of management. The former involved a number of independent steps taking place over remarkable stretches of land: from wood cutting to coaling, to digging for limestone and ore, to hauling, to making pig iron, and to the several operations required to obtain semi-finished and finished products (bar and wrought iron, castings, sheet iron, nails, and rails, among others). Although interlocked and needing a good deal of coordination, each of these separate procedures relied on the expertise of highly skilled workers in charge of specific operations who would know when exactly to intervene in the process and how to direct their own assistants accordingly.[13] At any rate, the pace of work at an iron-making establishment was largely controlled by human agency. Not so in a textile factory, where it was mostly determined by the machines. The organization of production at the Sanders cotton factory contemplated a number of procedures (picking, drawing, roving, stretching, winding bobbins, stripping and dressing cards, carding, and spinning), which required a high level of coordination as well as close supervision, the more so in view of the fact that, as Lockerbee had remarked in his speech, they implied the concentration of many hands, seventy-three in the case of the Sanders Company, in one single, closed-in space: the factory. Such a work dimension was largely unknown to the antebellum iron industry.[14]

The type of technology used also influenced the issue of management and supervision. Textile technology was in constant evolution from the late eighteenth century and, much as the British had been very jealous of their own inventions and innovations in the field, northeastern Americans were not inferior to them in their reluctance "to have the details and results of their operations exposed" and shared with manufacturers in other parts of the country.[15] The following report of the vicissitudes encountered by the Kentucky Society for the Encouragement of Manufactures in the late 1780s to secure a manager, adequate machinery, and skilled workers well illustrates the difficulties that early southern industrial pioneers might face. In 1789, the newly founded society had contacted one Mr. Welsh, a man who "had long acted as manager for the Philadelphia Cotton Society," inviting him "to undertake the whole management" of the textile manufactory they were in the process of establishing. Having accepted the job, by mid-May Welsh left Philadelphia with a party including his family, a number of skilled workers, and machinery. However, to the utmost astonishment of everybody, he was arrested and brought back to Philadelphia, while the rest of the group proceeded to their destination. Eventually, by the middle of October, Welsh was released from jail and reached Danville, where he took up his new position as manager. Upon further investigation, it turned out that his prosecution had been "malicious & only supported by perjury," and very probably inspired by jealousy and desire to punish him for his decision to quit his old job, thus depriving the Philadelphia industrial community of his highly valued mechanical and technical expertise.[16]

Even though during the following decades southern manufacturers were less and less likely to confront such melodramatic situations, they continued to depend heavily on the greater mechanical skills that northerners had built up over time. However, thanks to the resolute commitment of people like New York-born and Georgia-transplanted textile manufacturer James Merrell, during the latter part of the antebellum era the shaping of "a southern-based network of knowledge and . . . of a southern technical community" was well under way, and industrialists were able to avail themselves of the services of native technicians and superintendents, as well as to purchase machinery built in the South.[17] Indeed, except for some innovations in the smelting of iron, and for the increasing use of steam power, few technological advances occurred in iron manufacturing in pre–Civil War America, either North or South. As a result, southern ironmasters were not closely dependent on northern technological know-how and could rely much earlier than textile manufacturers on a regional body of experts to operate and manage their manufactories.[18]

In light of the fact that westward migration was closely intertwined with the territorial structuring of the United States, it is not surprising that in early nineteenth-century Kentucky those skills and abilities still had a largely eastern derivation. As Lockerbee's speech reminds us, from an early time southern manufacturers assigned a central importance to competent management, no matter how expensive. Consequently, much as in 1789 the directors of the Kentucky Society for the Encouragement of Manufactures had agreed to hire Mr. Welsh on "terms equal to what he at present receives," in 1818 the two partners of Jacob Holderman did not hesitate to pay him quite a handsome annual salary, and the Sanders Manufacturing Company relied on the experience of a gentleman who had long operated in the northeastern, and probably the British, textile industry.

The case of Jacob Holderman constitutes an excellent starting point to explore the genesis and development of factory management as a profession in the Tennessee/Kentucky iron-making district, an area lying between the courses of the Tennessee and Cumberland rivers.[19] To begin with, what was exactly the nature of his participation in the founding of Aetna Furnace? Considering that by the time Holderman entered the partnership with Whiting and Wilkins in 1818, he was already a middle-aged man—having been born in Chester County, Pennsylvania, around 1773—he may have accumulated some wealth over time and possibly contributed some capital to the enterprise. However, it is plausible to surmise that, what made his participation in the undertaking so desirable, to the point of being worth such a high compensation, was his expertise in iron making which, assumedly, his two partners lacked. Biographical information reveals in fact that, although he may have been a man of limited financial means, Holderman boasted a long record of activity in the field. In 1806, he had married into a Pennsylvania family of iron masters, the Vanleers (or Van Leers), and, soon after, had moved with his bride to Ohio, a promising state for an enterprising would-be industrialist. Apparently, however, his business was not successful enough, for, in the span of less than a decade the couple relocated in Kentucky, first in Clark County and finally in Green County, where Holderman operated a furnace and a forge with reported dissatisfaction because of the poor quality of the ore. So, in 1818, he was ready for a new industrial venture, and perhaps gladly agreed to undertake it in partnership with Wilkins and Whiting. Undoubtedly, this start firmly set him on the road to riches. When Whiting dropped out some time later, he was not replaced by a new partner, thus suggesting that Holderman and/or Wilkins had bought out his interest. Finally, when Wilkins died in 1827, Holderman became the sole owner of Aetna Furnace, a property including at least 10,500 acres. In the span of less than a decade, he had been able to build up a fortune, which included the ownership of fifty slaves.[20]

Holderman's story not only illustrates how brisk opportunities were for economic and social mobility in semi-frontier Kentucky in the early decades of the nineteenth century, but also allows us to introduce an important phenomenon in the history of southern manufacturing: the migration of people experienced in the business of iron making from the eastern seaboard states to Tennessee and Kentucky between the late eighteenth and the early nineteenth centuries. Although in all probability a self-made industrialist, Holderman was, nonetheless, brother-in-law of Anthony Wayne Vanleer, who had migrated from Pennsylvania to Middle Tennessee to become perhaps the most substantial iron manufacturer in the area. There, Vanleer had established business relations with other ironmasters such as the Napiers from North Carolina, the Stackers from Pennsylvania, and the three Hillman brothers from New Jersey, as well as with local entrepreneurs and investors. Such encounters, not infrequently sealed by marriage ties, gave rise to a complex network of powerful connections and alliances that resulted in the shaping and development of perhaps the most extensive and thriving iron-making district known in the Old South.[21]

From the 1830s, the most enterprising Middle Tennessee-based iron manufacturers began to expand their activities into west Kentucky. The Stackers invested in Caldwell and Trigg counties, where they built Stacker Furnace. The Hillman Brothers built Fulton and Center furnaces in Lyon County, and in 1845 Daniel Hillman founded the Tennessee Rolling Mills, a giant industrial complex, which would long survive the Civil War. To give a measure of the extent and profitability of the iron-making business in the region, in 1860 the Hillmans were, reportedly, the richest family in Tennessee, while the Vanleers were reputed to be no less than the wealthiest family in the entire South.[22]

The legal framework through which the Tennessee/Kentucky iron manufacturers mostly operated was the partnership. Indeed, they created a vast system of them through which individual shareholders held interest in multiple concerns. By making such assets as land and slaves important and highly valued contributions to an industrial enterprise, this form of joint ownership could partly obviate the well-known dearth of circulating medium that afflicted antebellum industrialists. For this reason, iron manufacturers were usually the owners of many slaves whom they largely employed as manpower in their industrial concerns.[23] Partnerships were formed, changed, and dissolved with high frequency, as circumstances demanded, to release capital for new ventures, to pay for debts and liabilities of different sorts, or, more simply, due to the withdrawal or the death of one of the partners. C. E. Hillman kept an "interest book" in which he took note of all the partnerships in which he was involved between 1837 and 1879: eight of them. One of these companies, Hillman, Vanleer & Co., operated the Tennessee Rolling Mills, in Kentucky, from 1846 to 1854, when the Hillmans bought out the interests of the other partners for the sum of $500,000, thus becoming the sole owners of that imposing industrial complex.[24]

In Middle Tennessee, Woods, Yeatman & Co. was by far the most important iron-making company: the owner of the renowned Cumberland Iron Works.[25] After Thomas Yeatman's death, in June 1833, his widow Jane Erwin married John Bell, the well-known Whig politician and future founder of the Constitutional Union Party, who soon acquired interest in the company.

Following the division of the Yeatman estate, the shares were redistributed among his heirs, and between the 1840s and the 1850s the company underwent a number of reorganizations. In 1859, the business was so thriving as to show the impressive annual profit of $20,948.80.[26]

Although similar examples abound, the few offered above well illustrate that between the late 1810s, when Holderman began his career as an iron manufacturer, and the middle of the century, when iron manufacturing was in full bloom in the Tennessee/Kentucky district, both the scale of the industry and the size of individual enterprises had grown so much as to render the services of full-time, professional managers mandatory. This would have increasingly been the case when owners were involved in multiple ventures.[27] But even in cases of smaller-size concerns, in which the general managerial role could be performed by either the single owner or one of the partners, the need to improve managerial efficiency was increasingly felt by the 1830s, when mounting competition began to demand the imposition of tighter controls over the quantity and quality of production.[28]

The new opportunities appealed to a variety of southerners. Young men belonging to families of manufacturers who did not yet own independent property could find in this kind of employment a way to exploit their knowledge of and familiarity with the iron business to emancipate themselves economically and to start building their own fortunes. Such was the case with Levin D. Goodrich, Daniel Hillman's grandson, who began his career as a manager at Aetna Furnace in Dickson County, Tennessee.[29] But there were also instances in which personal expertise in iron making turned out to be a real blessing if, despite the existence of family ties with prominent people in the business, one was not to inherit interest. "Captain" Mockbee was among this number. The son and nephew of men involved in the building and management of ironworks, Mockbee had been orphaned of his father when only five. For the following ten years he resided at Randolph Furnace, the property of his mother's brother. Then, he removed to Carroll Furnace, which was run by his cousin. He there trained in the iron business until old enough to earn a living "about the furnaces in that section" as a manager, a profession he pursued until the Civil War broke out, when he enlisted in the Confederate Army.[30]

Sometimes, tense relations within a family resulting from disillusionment for expected but not received recognition combined with a rebellious and capricious personality could jeopardize a man's opportunities in the iron industry. Such seems to have been the case with George Erwin, a brother of Jane Yeatman Bell. Besides being substantial farmers in Bedford County, the Erwins were also in the iron business with the Yeatmans and their associates. It is thus no surprise that, between 1832 and 1837, young Erwin was employed in some managerial role at Dover Furnace, which was part of the Cumberland Iron Works complex.[31] However, in 1843 we find him in charge of the organization and management of a Barren County, Kentucky salt works that his nephew William Yeatman had acquired one year earlier and in which his own brother, Andrew Jr., also held an interest. Although we do not know exactly the reasons for his leaving the Cumberland Iron Works, we may surmise that the change might have been dictated by some sort of uneasy relation with the Yeatmans following the patriarch Thomas's death. Perhaps, on account of his seniority, George Erwin had expected to accrue increased authority as well as a more prestigious role in the family iron business. Instead, he found himself superseded by the heirs of his deceased brother-in-law. Embittered, he therefore seized the opportunity that was extended to him: to organize and manage the Barren Salt Works. Apparently, Erwin had promised to make the salt works operative in the span of one year, but such was not the case. So, when Yeatman manifested disappointment for the waste of time and loss of money resulting from the delay, Erwin took the comments as a personal offense and reacted disproportionately. Yeatman responded in a conciliatory tone but, upon Erwin's polemic insistence, cut it short. "I believe," Yeatman wrote his uncle, "that I was offering you an excellent opportunity of promoting your interest . . . but if your views are opposed to a continuation with me . . . I hope you will let me know immediately."[32] From this incident we may surmise that difficult interpersonal relations compounded by an intractable character had lain at the basis of the decision to remove Erwin from the management of Dover Furnace. Possibly, however, the real issue had been his unfitness for that role. If such was the case, Erwin's story cannot but suggest that, when it came to deciding who was to run their industrial concerns, southern manufacturers were ready to privilege competent management over family ties.

From the 1840s on, a growing demand for managerial and clerical positions began to create new opportunities for enterprising individuals who were unrelated to ironmasters' families. Evidence for the four Middle Tennessee

not okay

counties of Dickson, Hickman, Montgomery, and Stewart allows us to glimpse the contours of a fairly articulated managerial structure: At the top stood a general manager, followed by those in charge of the several departments in the production line, and, finally, by those who supervised the external operations. Apparently, such positions were mostly filled by native Tennesseans or by individuals originating from southern states boasting a tradition in iron manufacturing, such as North Carolina and Virginia, while the presence of northern or European-born managers was comparatively small. Four of six managers employed at Stewart County ironworks were native Tennesseans and the other two had been born in Virginia.[33]

It is hard to tell whether the more detailed description of managerial occupations provided by the 1860 census, as compared with that of the previous decade, should be ascribed to increased precision on the part of the census takers in securing and reporting information or, more ambitiously, reflected an actual evolution that had occurred in industrial management; either way, industrial professions had clearly become more established and better defined in the span of a decade. Information for 1860 outlines the structure of the managerial cadres operating in the iron industry. For example, Thomas H. Hinson was reported as being an "Iron Works Manager" in Dickson County, and Thomas W. Dickson as the "manager for Anthony W. Vanleer," thus suggesting the top-level ranking of their employments. Other people filled instead more circumscribed managerial roles in the iron-making process proper: Henry Irwin was in fact a "furnace manager" at the Cumberland Iron Works, and one William H. Easley a "manager of forge" in Hickman County. Finally, other individuals were in charge of external operations as either "coaling ground" or "ore bank" managers. Except for Hinson, who had been born in North Carolina, all the other managers included in this group were native Tennesseans.[34] Some evidence of continuity in the profession is also available. William Boyd, who in 1850 was a "manager" in the employ of Thomas Kirkman, ten years later was a "coaling ground manager" working elsewhere. James H. Gossitt, a "manager" at C. B. McKernan's Carroll Furnace in 1850, ten years later was reported to manage an ironworks located near Palmyra, still in Montgomery County. We also know that, for most of the 1850s, John B. Evans was a "furnace manager" at William Kelly's Union Forge, in Lyon County, Kentucky.[35]

The establishment of a strict correlation between age and managerial ranking is quite problematic. Reference to individual cases may nonetheless help
make sense of the sometimes wide age variation found among factory managers. For one thing, family background was crucial, and may account for the
young age of some of the top-level managers. People like the aforementioned
Goodrich and Mockbee, who had been raised within families of ironmasters
and specifically trained in a managerial perspective, undoubtedly enjoyed an
advantage over self-taught individuals. Both of them were in fact enabled to
enter the profession when in their early twenties. Other examples, however, be-
speak the fact that even individuals who, as far as can be ascertained, were un-
connected with ironmasters' families could make early careers as well. James H.
Gossitt was twenty-three years old when he became the manager of Carroll
Furnace, and two more managers employed in Stewart County were aged, respectively, twenty-three and twenty-nine. Perhaps, these people were the offspring of skilled ironworkers, and had thus benefited from their fathers' jobs to
obtain an early introduction to the business. More simply, they may have been
especially gifted in the mastery of that branch of manufacturing. We cannot
know. Conversely, other mangers had to build their own careers from scratch,
probably beginning with some kind of manual, although skilled job, and rose
to managerial positions at an older age. Take, for example, thirty-one-year-old
William C. Holland, who entered the employment of D. & D. Hillman's Center
Furnace in 1856 as a "worker in iron," and made his rise to management there
after the Civil War.[36] On the other hand, the existence of a clear connection
between the performing of a skilled job and the assignment of lower-rank
managerial responsibilities is supported by the case of Michael Coreran who,
in 1842, was hired as a superintendent of the nail factory by the High Shoals
Manufacturing Company, located in Lincoln County, western North Carolina,
on the proviso that he would be "working on one machine himself."[37]

So far, our attention has concentrated on managerial positions only. However, the running of an industrial concern also required the full-time services
of clerks and bookkeepers to whom was entrusted the delicate function of
keeping complicated records related to a variety of transactions—purchases
and sales of raw materials, machinery, provisions, and so on—as well as of the
monies disbursed in the form of wages and salaries. Although not directly
concerned with the technical workings of an industrial enterprise, these some-

what less visible professional figures were necessarily knowledgeable in the business because, as James Montgomery remarked, "no business, where the books are not kept in good order, can prosper."[38] As such, they enjoyed a rather prestigious status among the cadres of a manufactory and, as white-collar workers, could claim middle-class membership. All in all, one important question we want to ask is: How remunerative were managerial positions in the iron industry in the late antebellum era? And what was the salary differential between them and the clerical ones? It is clear, in fact, that the levels of income earned by the people engaged in those professions both revealed their social status and shaped their self-perception of their relative position among the managerial cadres.

The value of real and personal properties reported by the managers so far identified, supplemented by a few more examples, allows us to attempt a few guesses. James Gossitt, an apparently property-less manager at Carroll Furnace in 1850, 10 years later reported a personal property valued at $2000. Charles Dudley, a 41-year-old manager at Peytona Furnace in 1850, 10 years later was a retired ironmaster reporting $800 worth of real estate and a personal property valued at $9500. While Gossitt's case reiterates the existence of a relatively high rate of permanency in the profession among factory managers, that of Dudley suggests instead that, toward the end of a career a man may have attempted to set up his own independent manufacturing business, although probably unsuccessfully in Dudley's case, judging from his early retirement at age fifty-one. Both cases hint, however, at the high level of remuneration that such employments could command, especially when combined with more than a decade of work experience. Three more managers employed at ironworks located, respectively, in the counties of Dickson and Montgomery, reported real estate values ranging between $1000 and $4000.[39] Particularly intriguing is the case of Henry Irwin, a 33-year-old "furnace manager" at the Cumberland Iron Works, in Stewart County, who reported the remarkable value of $7450 of real estate. Considering his age and work place, and in light of the well-known unreliability of antebellum censuses as for the spelling of names, could not his be a case of name misspelling? Perhaps he was an "Erwin," instead of "Irwin": the son of Andrew Erwin Jr. and nephew of George Erwin, whose involvement in the iron business has been described above, which would account for the high value of real property he reported.[40]

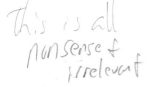
This is all nonsense & irrelevant

Apparently, bookkeeping and clerical positions also paid well, for the values of personal property reported for individuals employed in such capacities in the Middle Tennessee iron industry ranged between $1800 and $4000. Moreover, much as was found about managers, figures suggest a lack of correlation between nativity (either southern or non-southern) and remuneration levels. The values of property owned by such professionals compared well, on the average, with those of managers. Yet, white-collar workers below managers may have perceived their social status as somewhat inferior, due to the non-decision-making nature of their jobs as opposed to those of the latter, and the possible lack of technical knowledge of the production process, which may have limited their career potentials, at least as far as the iron industry was concerned.[41]

In the 1850s, managerial and supervisory professions in the iron industry were not perhaps as lucrative as they had been forty years earlier. This fact suggests the shaping of a relatively wide job market for positions which, judging from the fair amount of property (either real and/or personal) reported, seem to have been quite profitable. Nonetheless, the sometimes wide variation in property values is confusing as one tries to find evidence of gradation in income levels as related to the several managerial and clerical roles. Ostensible inconsistencies could be explained by a number of variables. First, a family background in farming may have been crucial in determining property holding, including through inheritance, and may have accounted for some of the highest values of real estate reported, as in the case of Henry Irwin/Erwin. Second, the priorities each individual assigned to spending his income, such as the purchase of a house and land as opposed to the acquisition of property in slaves, may also have played a role in determining the sometimes remarkable disproportion observed between the values of their real and personal properties. One could even guess that the high values in personal property reported by some of the managers may have been largely determined by their slave-owning status. Yet, the fact remains that most of the people who performed managerial and clerical jobs connected with the iron industry earned enough money to be able to acquire some kind of property or to increase their previous holdings. At this point, one still wonders what approximately their remunerations amounted to, and the census data do not reveal that. The case of Jefferson F. Gentry can help us form an idea.

Possibly a farmer of some substance in Stewart County during the 1850s, Gentry wanted nonetheless to become an iron manufacturer. With this outlook, in 1853 he purchased an "undivided ¼ interest of Valley Forge, Montgomery County," for the sum of $2000 in cash, plus two installments of $1500 before January 1, 1855.[42] The next year, Gentry formed a partnership with three more investors under the title of Gentry, Gunn & Co. for the purpose of building an ironworks in Trigg County, Kentucky, which would become known as Laura Furnace. According to the terms of agreement, Gentry was to manage the business at an annual salary of $1200, Gunn would dispatch clerical duties for the annual sum of $600, and McCaughan was supposed to perform sundry chores for the latter compensation.[43] Perhaps, the three partners had miscalculated the amount of money needed to start the ironworks vis-à-vis their initial investment. Be it as it may, at some point they were forced to sell the entire concern. After that failure, however, Gentry did not go back to farming, but continued as factory manager under the new owners, initially in Kentucky, and later in Tennessee, where two of them were from. In fact, the 1860 census listed him as a "furnace manager" residing in Stewart County, Tennessee.[44]

Gentry's case well illustrates the reverse path that unsuccessful manufacturers were sometimes forced to follow but, what most matters, indicates the sum of $1200 as the annual remuneration commanded by a general manager and that of $600 as the one accruing to a clerk or bookkeeper. The annual salary received by Gentry roughly corresponded to what Jacob Holderman had earned some thirty-five years earlier, although the purchasing power of that amount of money must have been lower in the 1850s. Even conceding that the three partners in the ownership of Laura Furnace were sovereign in determining the pecuniary worth of their own services, it is hard to believe that they must have done so in complete disregard of current standards of remuneration. To cross check the reliability of the above figures, we will consider a few more examples. The first of them comes from Washington County, East Tennessee, and relates to the Pleasant Valley Iron Works, a handsome iron-making complex including the second largest rolling mill in the state. After the original owner's death in 1846, the works' ownership changed hands several times until, in October 1858, Robert and William Blair formed a partnership with Addison Threadway of Tennessee and Charles W. Meek of Virginia to launch the Pleasant Valley Iron Manufacturing Company. According to the terms of agreement, the two Blairs were by far the majority shareholders, own-ing ten out of twelve shares in the concern, while Threadway and Meek each acquired one of the two remaining shares. As specified in the agreement, the two new partners performed the role of manager for the annual sum of $600 each, thus totaling a combined compensation of $1200. William and Robert Blair instead received, jointly, $600 "for the attention they may bestow to the business of the concern."[45] Apparently, in this case, managerial work and re-sponsibility were traded for the modest capital contribution that Threadway and Meek brought to the enterprise. Given the disproportion existing between their shares and those held by the Blairs, it is plausible to surmise that the latter's intention was to secure competent and responsible management for their industrial enterprise through the involvement of minority partners en-gaged for the purpose. The Blairs did not mean, however, to become absentee owners. In fact, the 1860 census listed Robert Blair as a "superintendent of ironworks," and his two sons, Samuel and John, as clerks.[46] A second example is offered by the already mentioned Michael Coreran, whose salary as super-intendent of the nail factory at High Shoals amounted to $600 plus board, a sum that is consistent with the range of remunerations so far ascertained.[47]

From all these examples we could perhaps conclude that the annual sal-ary commanded by managerial positions in the iron industry ranged between $1200 for general supervisory roles and $600 for more circumscribed ones, especially if performed in conjunction with a skilled job, as in Coreran's case. This was indeed a good amount of money, considering that the arrangements always included board. Although evidence in this regard is much thinner, the example of Gentry, Gunn & Co. would safely place the sum of $600 a year as the highest compensation for clerks. Of course, remuneration levels could be influenced by conditions attendant to geographic location, including the availability of liquid capital, scale of operations, access to markets, and trans-portation networks. In East Tennessee and western North Carolina, salaries seem in fact to have been lower than those prevalent in the Middle Tennessee/ Kentucky iron district.

South of the iron-making district of upper Middle Tennessee, textile mills appeared with increasing frequency. In the counties of Hickman and Lawrence cotton manufacturing reached a prominent position, ranking second among all industrial activities in 1860.[48] Following a pattern that was widespread not only in the United States, but also in England up until the 1850s, these textile mills were small-to-medium size concerns owned by a single family or by two partners, and employing between twenty-five and seventy-five hands. They were nonetheless thriving industrial enterprises that sometimes continued in activity for many decades after the Civil War. Different from the iron-making establishments in the area, which heavily employed enslaved labor alongside white workers, some Middle Tennessee textile manufactories made use of a totally white workforce. Among them was the mill village of Pinewood, in Hickman County, established in 1848 by North Carolinians Samuel Lowry and Richard Graham, two former merchant tailors of small means. In the beginning, the factory employed some eighteen people, but the business was thriving and in full expansion. So, sometime during the 1850s the Grahams hired J. M. Meacham as a clerk. By 1860, the mill village, at the center of which stood the factory consisting of a four-story brick building, surrounded by a number of workshops and a grist mill, employed 40 people, and its production was valued at $27,000.[49]

The highest concentration of textile mills was found, however, in Lawrence County. In 1860, the 6 active mills mostly resorted to a combination of enslaved and white labor for a total of about 240 people.[50] Among them, most important was Hope Factory, established in 1823 by William and Thomas Parkes. In the 1840s at least three more cotton mills started: Glen Factory, also owned by the Parkes, William Simonton's Crescent Mills, and Clay Factory. In the following decade, Crowson and Eagle Mills were erected, plus at least two woolen manufactories. Except for Englishman James Sykes, the owner of Crowson Mills, all the other manufacturers in the county were natives of the South, the Parkes and two more being from Tennessee, Simonton and two wool manufacturers from North Carolina, and a third from South Carolina.[51]

As a British immigrant, Sykes exemplifies the case of an outsider who, although lacking the advantages of an established family in the area, was able to build a career in textiles from a managerial position to an independent manufacturer. And his career was quite an adventurous one. Before landing in Tennessee, sometime between 1843 and 1845, Sykes had long been looking for opportunities elsewhere in the United States. Once settled in Lawrence County, he exploited his competence in textile manufacturing to find employment as a manager at some local mills, and became well respected as such in the community. Apparently, however, his work experience was marked by friction with his employers—a circumstance not unusual in southern manufacturing.[52] Sometimes, these periodical tensions climaxed into acute crises. One such event occurred in December 1846, when Sykes "left Clay Factory," where he seems to have been working, took "a spree," and, "stunting to Decatur," entered the Simonton & Henderson Factory, all the while being determined to set up his own independent business.[53] Evidently, his hope was fulfilled for, three years later, he appeared in a partnership in a textile mill, and in the early 1850s he finally established a manufactory of his own, Crowson Mills.[54]

The general supervisory functions at the textile mills located in Lawrence County were largely performed by the owners themselves, sometimes with the help of younger family members. Despite his young age of seventeen, William H. Sykes became the superintendent of his father's factory in the 1850s. However, as argued above, external managerial support was often unavoidable, especially when in view of expanding operations.[55] Some correspondence related to the Hope and Glen factories sheds light on the complex articulation of the managerial structure of southern textile mills. Although Hope Factory had been active since the early 1820s, Glen was erected by the Parkes in 1846, possibly indicating that considerations connected with economies of scale prevailed over the choice simply to enlarge their old mill. The management of the two factories seems, however, to have been performed jointly: Joseph L. Campbell acted as general superintendent, and Daniel Gustine and Peter Seales were agents in charge of reporting to the owners problems in the staffing of both Hope and Glen factories and, especially, in the performance of the hands who, as it appears, were partly white and partly slave. In fact, in October 1849 Gustine wrote Thomas Parkes of Mr. Campbell's request "to have two of his Blk. [sic] Girls (spinners) to go down to the Glen and . . . to furnish him with two white girls in their place."[56] Down the managerial chain, Colonel Billy McKisacs (or McKisack) and one Mr. Baker worked as superintendents—they were primarily in charge of the machinery—and, as such, directed and controlled the work of skilled hands. Finally, John Clegg was probably an overseer in charge of the "spreader room." In February 1849, Peter Seales reported to Thomas Parkes of General Superintendent Campbell's disappointment about the performance of Baker in the "spreader room," and of John Clegg's being "much dissatisfied with the way Mr. Baker is managing," because of his unwillingness to give him "any direction about the spredder room." Apparently, Baker had a "bilious" character and had insulted Colonel McKisacs several times. As Seales reported to Parkes, Campbell thought he had better talk to him personally to overcome the crisis.[57]

Much attention was devoted to the performance of laborers, a very delicate and crucial aspect in textile manufacturing. For example, Gustine also reported to Parkes that all hands were "attending cloc [sic] to the business," at both Hope and Glen factories, as confirmed by Campbell and McKisacs. Diverging evaluations concerning the performance of factory hands could, however, generate tensions between the several levels of management. So, on one occasion, Gustine confessed to Parkes that it had been "with a good deal of reluctance" that he had written him a previous letter denouncing the inadequate performance of the laborers, but he "could not get clear of Campbell conveniently." Expressing his belief that Parkes would understand that letter had been "dictated by Campbell," Gustine urged him to come and see with his own eyes and, further commenting on the performance of the white employees, added: "my opinion is that they are all doing as well at this time as could be expected of a set of men who has nothing at stake but their wages and have never been in the habit of doing business for their selves."[58]

The need to secure a well-articulated body of managers to run properly the several departments of a textile mill of even moderate size is confirmed by the case of the Lenoir Manufacturing Company, a cotton mill located in Roane County (later Loudon), East Tennessee. In 1840, the Lenoir Mills employed some thirty people in the factory proper, thirteen of whom were whites and the remainder were a portion of the fifty enslaved workers owned by William B. Lenoir. However, considering the enterprise's external operations related to agriculture, grist and saw milling, commerce, and trades carried on in the village, the total number of laborers might have easily approached fifty. Ten years later, the company's activities had further expanded, with a possible increase in workforce. So, despite the fact that all three of his sons were engaged as superintendents in the family's industrial concern, Lenoir contracted with one Presley L. Amos to be "a hand and manager in his factory for one year"; Amos agreed "to attend faithfully and to the best of his skill and judgement to the machinery and hands under him . . . and . . . to endeavour to advance said Lenoir's interest in every thing pertaining the factory." Amos was supposed "to manage and carry on said business under the direction and control of William Lenoir, who has the superintendency [sic] of that factory . . . then under any other superintendent who may be employed."[59]

The terms of Amos's contract were essentially similar to those agreed to by North Carolinian Michael Coreran with the High Shoals Manufacturing Company, thus suggesting that, in both iron and textile manufacturing, the performing of a skilled job could be a joint requisite for employment in a supervisory capacity. Amos's example also suggests that managerial careers in the textile industry were as open to men with some mechanical skills and a good deal of determination as we have been able to detect in the iron industry.[60] We may therefore hypothesize the existence of similar trends of continuity in career patterns across the Civil War as we have been able to ascertain for the iron industry.[61]

In light of the remarks made by James Montgomery in the article that opened this essay, perhaps an even closer connection existed between floor training and managerial careers in the textile industry than was true in the iron industry. As a consequence, the prestige attached to the position of skilled mechanic was probably even higher in the former industry than in the latter. Such assumption seems to be supported by evidence related to the Rockford Manufacturing Company, a corporate enterprise established in 1852 in Blount County, East Tennessee, out of a textile mill previously owned and operated by Alexander Kennedy since 1845.[62] Despite his being the son of the mill owner, twenty-four-year-old Arthur A. Kennedy was listed as a "mechanic" in the 1850 census. Ten years later, when the concern had become a corporation in which the Kennedys held majority shares, he was reported as a "miller," although of substantial property, thus suggesting that he was being trained in the several departments pertaining to the overall management of the enterprise.[63]

Conventional wisdom has long maintained that, because of their inexperience in textile manufacturing, southern industrialists were forced to resort to the services of northern or British superintendents. Although this may have also been the case, the hypothesis holds true that many of them moved south, attracted by the new opportunities existing in the region and, consequently, by the high prestige attached there to their profession as compared with the northeastern states. However, as Montgomery implicitly hinted, sometimes these professionals of a northern origin were not of the best variety being, rather, fairly young, incompletely trained "adventurers" who expected to get rich fast by offering their services to southern manufacturers. As such, they were largely unprepared to handle the special problems connected with the running of a factory in the South.[64] Among other things, sometimes they miscalculated the extent of competition they might face from native southerners, for, as numerous cases throughout this essay have shown, both industries attracted southerners as managers, superintendents, and bookkeepers. In late 1850s Lawrence County, two of three factory superintendents were Tennesseans, and a third was from New York. In North Carolina, although a factory located in Richmond County hired "a gentleman from the North" as superintendent, two Lincoln County textile mills employed natives of the state. During the 1850s, southern-born managers also asserted themselves in Georgia.[65]

Just as both industries employed native southerners, they offered comparable pay. Although slightly lower, textile industry salaries are consistent with those found for the iron industry. According to an investigation conducted by *DeBow's Review* in the early 1850s on the textile mills of Columbus, Georgia, the general superintendent at the Coweta Falls Manufacturing Company earned $1000 per year and the one at Howard Factory received annual compensation of $900. On the other hand, even a manager of such a high reputation as Henry Merrell earned a constant annual salary of $1000 during his six years of work at the Roswell Manufacturing Company.[66] In some areas like East Tennessee and western North Carolina, income levels could be influenced by factors such as the dearth of circulating medium and the limited scale of operations due to the small size of the market. Therefore, one would expect to find decidedly higher remuneration levels in the textile-manufacturing districts of Georgia that, during the 1850s, were in full expansion and had attained national prestige. Instead, the property values reported for Georgia factory superintendents of lower rank seem to suggest that their incomes must not have been much higher than that earned by Presley Amos at the Lenoir Mills in East Tennessee: $200 annually, part in money ($100) and part in kind (1000 dozen thread), plus board.[67] The above reported examples for East Tennessee, western North Carolina, and Georgia also indicate that managerial professions in textile manufacturing must have commanded somewhat lower salaries as compared with those prevalent in the iron industry. Although working under a similar contract, which also involved the performance of a skilled job, Presley Amos earned $200 in textiles, while Michael Coreran made $600 in the North Carolina iron industry.

Property values reported by the census for factory superintendents would further support the inference. In Muscogee County, three superintendents reported values of personal property ranging between $100 and $350 and no real property whatever, while a fourth employed in Baldwin County owned a personal property valued at $1500, perhaps suggesting his higher ranking in the managerial chain. Additional data for Clarke County also suggest that the salaries earned by northern or British-born superintendents were no higher than those commanded by their southern-born counterparts. The lower property values for managers in the textile industry suggest their overall lower compensation compared to those employed in the iron industry.[68]

During the last three decades of the antebellum era, industrial development fostered the emergence of new, white-collar professions in the South. Even as managerial and supervisory positions resulted from a variety of career paths, floor training was highly valued, if not a pre-requisite to run a manufactory in the "proper manner." While the engagement of managers coming from the Northeast or from Britain persisted, especially in the textile industry, by the 1840s southern industrialists were increasingly able to tap a regional pool of skills and expertise, thus implicitly acknowledging the coming to maturity of an autochthonous industrial tradition. Even as the occupations and incomes of the managerial and clerical cadres of southern manufactories classified them as members of the middle class, how these people perceived their own social position in relation to the upper classes is hard to tell. We know, however, that despite declining opportunities for industrial ownership, during the last two antebellum decades a good many of them continued to cherish the American—and southern—dream of economic independence through proprietorship.[69] While only a limited number of individuals succeeded, the vast majority of them probably began to work out a group identity as permanent professionals within a dynamic and expansive southern industrial economy.

As many authorities have remarked, the middle classes of nineteenth-century industrializing societies tended to borrow the systems of values subscribed to by the agrarian elites and used their accumulated wealth to acquire landed property and establish themselves as country squires.[70] As far as the American South is concerned, this implied adhesion to the ideals of a slaveholding republic as opposed to the advancement of an alternative, middle-class culture of a modern description. However, as important scholarly work has argued, the wide support offered by the southern middle class, both rural and urban, to the slave regime did not necessarily define them as groups opposed to modernization. Quite the contrary, they were largely in the forefront of a reform movement aimed at transforming the economic and cultural institutions of the southern region.

Because the majority of the manufacturers considered in this essay were slaveholders, it is not improbable that slave ownership was part of their managers' expectations of self-improvement. The economic milieu seemed to suggest that slavery and industrialization were not incompatible, and some of the factories demonstrated that fact. However, it is also likely that, when it came down to supporting the project for an independent, southern slaveholding republic, the issue of slavery must have been as deeply divisive among the managers as it turned out to be for the manufacturers. The impending threat of secession involved ~~theretofore~~ unimagined issues of group identity, both economic and social. In April 1861, when an Alabamian told Samuel L. Graham that "they" did not want manufactures, "that it brought about a rabble that had no sympathy with the planters," the owner of the Pinewood mill village must have shuddered. That "rabble" assumedly included himself, along with scores of white people who, like him, had participated either as manufacturers, managers, clerks, or workers in the first act of the modernization of the South and whose ideas and outlooks had been shaped and transformed by that very process.

NOTES

1. James Montgomery's most famous work is *A Practical Detail of the Cotton Manufacture of the United States of America* (Glasgow: John Niven Jr., 1840). On northern opinions, see, for example, Richard Hildreth, *Despotism in America: An Enquiry into the Nature, Results and Legal Basis of the Slaveholding System in the United States* (1840; reprint, Boston: John P. Jarrett, 1854), 141, and Andrew Preston Peabody, *Position and Duties of the North with Regard to Slavery* (Newburyport, N.H.: Charles Whipple, Abel Whitton Printer, 1848), 5.

2. James Montgomery, "Why Southern Factories Fail," *DeBow's Review* 26 (1859): 95–96.

3. This idea, as expressed in Alfred D. Chandler Jr., *The Visible Hand: The Managerial Revolution in American Business* (Cambridge, Mass.: The Belknap Press of Harvard University Press,

1977), has been challenged by Steven D. Lubar, "Corporate and Urban Contexts of Textile Technology in Nineteenth-Century Lowell, Massachusetts: A Study of the Social Nature of Technological Knowledge" (Ph.D. diss., University of Chicago, 1983).

4. Although the two terms were used interchangeably, that of "manager" was more common in the iron industry, and that of "superintendent" prevailed in textile manufacturing.

5. Three years earlier, Wilkins had been among the incorporators of a textile mill, the Lexington Manufacturing Company.

6. O. M. Mather, "Aetna Furnace," Hart County, Kentucky (1816–185?), The Filson Historical Society, Louisville, Kentucky (hereafter FHS), n.p., 3.

7. Mather says that this sum roughly corresponded to the salary of state governors "in the early days of the Commonwealth," ibid., 4.

8. Whether Lockerbee was a guest lecturer, or a shareholder in the enterprise who was about to take over the general management of the new factory, remains unknown. "To the Directors and Stockholders of the Sanders Manufacturing Company," Lexington, February 14, 1818, Sanders Family Papers, FHS.

9. Ibid. In the northeastern textile industry, "agents" were usually in charge of controlling the behavior and work performance of the operatives as well as production, while "superintendents" provided the technical support connected with the operation of the machinery. In his study of Athens, Georgia, Michael Gagnon identifies as factory agents people who, through the purchase of company stock, obtained title to handle the commercial aspects of an enterprise. "Transition to an Industrial South: Athens, Georgia, 1830–1870" (Ph.D. diss., Emory University, 1999) [electronic version, 2001], 108.

10. "To the Directors and Stockholders," Sanders Family Papers, FHS. The now classical reference work on operatives' patterns of resistance to factory discipline is Jonathan Prude, *The Coming of Industrial Order: Town and Factory in Rural Massachusetts, 1810–1860,* 2nd ed. (Amherst: University of Massachusetts Press, 1999).

11. Up until the 1840s, the corporate form of enterprise was adopted only for the purpose of pooling large amounts of capital, but companies continued to be handled as if they were "extended" partnerships. During the 1850s, this situation began to change, giving rise to a true and proper circulation of the companies' stock.

12. Based on the 1832 *Report* compiled by Secretary of the Treasury Lewis McLane, Alfred Chandler found that textile enterprises showed the highest level of capital investment, immediately followed by iron-making and iron working-related enterprises; *Visible Hand,* ch. 2. The Boston Manufacturing Company at Lowell was begun with a capital of $100,000, which was increased to $600,000. In the South, the capital of the Graniteville Manufacturing Company was worth $300,000, and that of the Saluda Factory in South Carolina, $100,000. *DeBow's Review* 10 (1851): 461, 678; 11 (1851): 319. Information for the state of Tennessee reveals that the level of initial investment in both textile and iron manufacturing averaged around $100,000 between the late 1830s and the early 1850s, with upward trends for major corporate enterprises, regardless of their manufacturing vocation. *DeBow's Review* 9 (1850): 431–32; 10 (1851): 461; *Acts passed by the General Assembly of the State of Tennessee* (Nashville: The State, 1838–60); U.S. Census, Manuscript Returns (hereafter MCR), 1850, Manufactures, Tennessee.

13. The diversity of skilled and semi-skilled capacities needed at an antebellum ironworks can

be glimpsed from the records of the Hurricane Iron and Mining Company, Hickman County, Tennessee, Account Book, 1840, University of Tennessee Libraries, Knoxville, Special Collections (hereafter UTK). For a description of the working of a southern—and American—ironworks, see my essay "Invisible Woman: Female Labor in the Upper South's Iron and Mining Industries," in Susanna Delfino and Michele Gillespie, eds., *Neither Lady Nor Slave: Working Women of the Old South* (Chapel Hill: University of North Carolina Press, 2002), esp. 286–90.

14. "Statement of machinery and hands employed," Sanders Manufacturing Company, February 1818, Sanders Family Papers, FHS.

15. "Gallery of Industry and Enterprise: Charles T. James of Rhode Island," *DeBow's Review* 9 (1850): 675.

16. George Davidson Todd, "The First Cotton Factory in the West," Todd Family Papers, FHS, n.p., 6–7, 28, 34–36. The factory operated successfully from December 1790 until 1841.

17. Michele Gillespie, "Building Networks of Knowledge: Henry Merrell and Textile Manufacturing in the Antebellum South," in Susanna Delfino and Michele Gillespie, eds., *Technology, Innovation, and Southern Industrialization: From the Antebellum Era to the Computer Age* (Columbia: University of Missouri Press, 2008), 97–124, 124 (quotation); Gagnon, "Transition to an Industrial South," 104–5.

18. The invention of the air-boiling process to make steel—the equivalent of the Bessemer process—by William Kelly, occurred in Kentucky. On technology in antebellum America, see Delfino and Gillespie, *Technology, Innovation, and Southern Industrialization*, 1–17.

19. North of the Kentucky-Tennessee state line, the core of the iron industry was located in the counties of Caldwell, Trigg, and Lyon. In Tennessee, it comprised those of Dickson, Montgomery, Stewart, and Hickman.

20. Mather, "Aetna Furnace," 8–12, FHS. The number of slaves owned by Holderman was derived from the 1827 tax list for Hart County.

21. The case of Cumberland Furnace illustrates the point. Founded in the 1790s by Colonel James Robertson of North Carolina, its ownership turned over to Richard Napier, another North Carolinian and Robertson's son-in-law. Between 1804 and 1817, it was owned and operated by Montgomery Bell, then by Anthony W. Vanleer, in partnership with Daniel Hillman from 1833. "Cumberland Furnace, Dickson Co., ca. 1792–ca. 1942," Small Collections, Tennessee State Library and Archives, Nashville (hereafter TSLA); Buena C. Daniel, "Cumberland Furnace: The First Ironworks in Middle Tennessee," typescript, Land between the Lakes Project, J. Milton Henry Collection (hereafter Henry Collection), b. 7, f. 4, TSLA. In 1850, both Tennessee and Kentucky ranked high at the national level in the production of raw and forged iron, and Kentucky ranked second in that of rolled iron. U.S. Census, 1870, vol. 2 (Washington, D.C.: Government Printing Office, 1872), 602–8.

22. J. Winston Coleman Jr., "Old Kentucky Furnaces," *The Filson Club History Quarterly* 31 (1957): 255; "Tennessee Rolling Works, Lyon Co., KY"; deed from A. J. and Martha Porter to Daniel Hillman, Trigg County, February 20, 1851, Henry Collection, TSLA; *One Century of Lyon County History* (Eddyville, Ky.: Lyon County Historical Society, 1985), 52, 54.

23. In 1850, William C. Napier owned 99 slaves; Anthony W. Vanleer, 153; and Woods, Stacker & Co., 350. In 1860, Woods, Lewis & Co. reported the ownership of 418 slaves. MCR, 1850 and 1860, Slave Schedules, Dickson, Hickman, Montgomery, and Stewart counties, Tennessee.

24. "Tennessee Rolling Works, Lyon Co. Kentucky," Henry Collection, TSLA.

25. This company should not be confused with Cumberland Furnace. In 1833, the property of the Cumberland Iron Works included 18,000 acres of land on which two furnaces and forges and a rolling mill were located. Ten years later, it comprised more than 50,000 acres, with the addition of two furnaces and related forges. James Woods to John Bell, September 4, 1852, Polk-Yeatman Collection, Henry Collection, b. 9, f. 6, TSLA.

26. In 1842, the company took the name of Stacker, Woods & Co. "Indenture between R. and J. Woods, Joseph Woods, John and Jane Bell, Samuel Stacker, and James Yeatman, November 12, 1842," Cumberland Iron Works, Papers, 1842–1888, Small Collections, V-K-2, f. 4, TSLA. In 1852, Henry C. Yeatman entered the partnership by acquiring one-sixth of the interest therein. The company was later reorganized under the title of Woods, Lewis & Co., and three more furnaces were built. In 1859, H. C. Yeatman's interest in the concern was worth $41,047.89. James Woods to John Bell, September 4, 1852, Polk-Yeatman Collection; James Woods Jr., to Henry C. Yeatman, October. 29, 1859, Polk-Yeatman Papers, b. 51, f. 2, TSLA. Originals in the Southern Historical Collection, Chapel Hill, North Carolina (hereafter SHC). Joseph H. Parks, *John Bell of Tennessee* (Baton Rouge: Louisiana State University Press, 1950), 115.

27. Among the largest companies were Cobb, Phillips & Co.; Newell, Irvine & Co.; Lewis, Irvine & Co.; Brien, Ledbetter & Co.; and Jackson, McKernan & Co. Some ironmasters, including Alabama-born Thomas Kirkman, A. W. Vanleer's son-in-law, and the Napiers, preferred, however, to conduct an independent business. Tennessee General Assembly, *A Geological Reconnaissance of Tennessee*, Appendix to Senate and House Journals, 1855–56, Supplement to the Appendix (Nashville: The State, 1856), 34–35.

28. Following a strategy adopted in Pennsylvania, from the 1830s Tennessee and Kentucky ironmasters tried to impose a tighter control over production by increasing managerial efficiency. Paul Paskoff, *Industrial Evolution: Organization, Structure, and Growth of the Pennsylvania Iron Industry, 1750–1860* (Baltimore: Johns Hopkins University Press, 1983), 25. The same exigency was felt by New England textile manufacturers who, during the 1830s, separated managerial responsibilities into three essential capacities: the treasurer, the agent, and the superintendent. See Frances W. Gregory, *Nathan Appleton: Merchant and Entrepreneur, 1779–1861* (Charlottesville: University Press of Virginia, 1975), 258.

29. Goodrich was also son-in-law of another substantial Middle Tennessee iron manufacturer. W. Jerome D. and David L. Spence, *A History of Hickman County, Tennessee* (Nashville: Gospel Advocate Publishing Company, 1900), 221, 310; Jill K. Garrett, "Historical Sketches of Hickman County, Tennessee," n.d., n.p., 41, UTK, 100–101.

30. Mockbee was the son and nephew of, respectively, John B. and Thomas D. Mockbee. Originally from New Jersey, his mother's family—the Baxters—owned at least four furnaces in Montgomery County, and were partners in the property of another in Hickman. Ursula Smith Beach, *Along the Warioto: A History of Montgomery County, Tennessee* (Clarksville: Clarksville Kiwanis Club and the Tennessee Historical Commission, 1964), 122; MCR, 1850, Population Schedules, Dickson County, Tennessee; Robert E. Corlew, *A History of Dickson County, Tennessee* (Nashville: The Historical Commission and the Dickson County Historical Society, 1956), 87–88. W. L. Cook, "Furnaces and Forges," *Tennessee Historical Magazine* 10 (1925): 191–92.

31. Andrew Erwin Jr. to George Erwin, April 1, 1833, June 1, 1849; Andrew Erwin to George Erwin, August 2 1837, George Erwin Papers, FHS. Correspondence from George Erwin to his family between 1832 and 1837 is postmarked "Dover Furnace."

32. William Yeatman to George Erwin, December 16, 1844, Erwin Papers, FHS.

33. Don F. Adams, "Report on the Peytona Furnace, 1847–1862," typescript, Henry Collection, b. 7, f. 6, TSLA; MCR, 1860, Population Schedules, Stewart County, Tennessee.

34. MCR, 1850 and 1860, Population Schedules, Stewart, Hickman, Dickson, and Montgomery counties, Tennessee.

35. Testimonies of William Kelly's employees before the Commissioners of Patents, March 10–16, 1857, Henry Collection, b. 7, f. 4, TSLA.

36. Although the Civil War interrupted the operation of many ironworks in the Upper South, causing some to permanently shut down, a number of superintendents were able to resume their old jobs thereafter and continued their career paths to higher managerial roles. For instance, Robert B. Stone was rehired at Cumberland Furnace at the end of the conflict and worked his way up to become general manager, a position he held until 1889. *Goodspeed's History of Tennessee* (1887; reprint, C. and R. Elder Booksellers, 1972), 1355; Cook, "Furnaces and Forges," 190; MCR, 1860, Population Schedules, Dickson County, Tennessee.

37. Previously owned by Henry Fulenwider in partnership with his cousin Robert H. Burton, the company was reorganized and incorporated by the North Carolina General Assembly in 1839. In his position as the original co-owner of the ironworks, Fulenwider was to act "as agent and superintendent." Besides Coreran, two more people (John Webster and Alfred Ransom) were hired to act as clerks at the furnace and forge, respectively. "Stock Holders Journal of the High Shoals Manufacturing Company," August 1, 1840, and November 10, 1842, William Preston Bynum Papers, SHC.

38. Although the position of "bookkeeper" is today perceived as more prestigious than that of a mere "clerk," no clear-cut distinction seems to have applied to the antebellum times. Montgomery, "Why Southern Factories Fail," 96.

39. Tennessee-born Norman Brandon, a manager in the employ of McKernan, reported $4000 worth of real estate and $310 worth of personal property to the 1860 census taker; B. S. W. Wicks, also a native Tennessean employed at an ironworks, possessed real estate valued at $3000; and Edward Ellis, a manager, reported $1000 of personal property. MCR, 1860, Population Schedules, Dickson, Montgomery, and Stewart counties, Tennessee; Iris Hopkins McClain, *A History of Stewart County, Tennessee* (Columbia, Tenn.: by the author, 1965), 45, 47; Beach, *Along the Warioto*, 122.

40. MCR, 1860, Population Schedules, Montgomery and Stewart counties, Tennessee.

41. In other areas of the Tennessee iron district, bookkeeper H. C. Lockhart reported $500 worth of real estate and $3000 of personal property, but Pennsylvania-born Henry McClelland only a personal property valued at $200, thus suggesting a lack of correlation between origin and remuneration level. MCR, 1860, Population Schedules, Dickson, Hickman, Montgomery, and Stewart counties, Tennessee. As for the textile industry, Michael Gagnon's examples from Clarke County suggest that clerking in a factory could at times be an effective springboard to proprietorship; "Transition to an Industrial South," 113–17. Of course, in both the iron and tex-

tile industries, clerking could be one way to train the sons of manufacturers in the managerial perspective. These figures are consistent with the findings of Robert A. Margo who, in *Wages and Labor Markets in the United States, 1821–1860* (Chicago: University of Chicago Press, 2000), indicates exceptionally high remuneration levels for white-collar positions in the South Central states—actually the highest among the several sub-regions of the country—and increasingly higher than those prevalent in the South Atlantic states between 1820 and 1860. At the close of the antebellum era, the average monthly wage for such professionals was $49.19 in the Northeast, $53.34 in the Midwest, $43.76 in the South Atlantic states, and $69.61 in the South Central ones; Margo, *Wages and Labor Markets in the United States*, tab. 3A.7.

42. Stewart County, Tennessee, Deed Book 18:129–30, Articles of agreement, December 17, 1853, February 18 and December 4, 1854; Deed Books 18:435 and 19:172–73, Henry Collection, b. 7, f. 5, TSLA. The 1850 census for Stewart County does not include property values.

43. Trigg County Deed Books M:208–10, N:530–32, Henry Collection, TSLA.

44. MCR, 1860, Population Schedules, Stewart County, Tennessee.

45. "Article of partnership between William and Robert Blair, Charles Meek, and Addison Threadway," October 20, 1858, Thomas A. R. Nelson Papers, Calvin McClung Historical Collection, Lawson-McGhee Library, Knoxville, Tennessee. The Blairs do not seem to have either owned or employed slaves at the Pleasant Valley Ironworks. For a full account of the history of the Embreeville Ironworks, see Susanna Delfino, "'To Maintain the Civil Rights of the People': The Tribulations of Duff Green, Iron Manufacturer in Civil War East Tennessee," *Journal of East Tennessee History* 72 (2000): 49–61.

46. MCR, 1860, Population Schedules, Washington County, Tennessee.

47. These figures are consistent with the findings of Margo, *Wages and Labor Markets in the United States*. "Stock Holders Journal of the High Shoals Manufacturing Company," November 10, 1842, William Preston Bynum Papers, SHC.

48. U.S. Census, *The Ninth Census, 1870* (Washington, D.C.: Government Printing Office, 1871), 567–68. Counties of Hardin, Hickman, Lawrence, Lewis, and Wayne.

49. Garrett, "Historical Sketches of Hickman County," 24–25; Samuel L. to Frances (Fanny) Graham, May 29, 1852, Eleanor Graham Collection, Small Collections, TSLA.

50. *Ninth Census*, 577. British visitor James Silk Buckingham reported that the southern textile industry witnessed females of both races "working together without repugnance or objection." See Michele Gillespie, "'To Harden a Lady's Hand': Gender Politics, Racial Realities, and Women Millworkers in Antebellum Georgia," in *Neither Lady Nor Slave*, 261–84, esp. 274.

51. *Early sales and ownership of lots in Lawrenceburg, Lawrence County, Tennessee* (Lawrenceburg, Tenn.: Lawrence County Historical Society, 1970), 36, 62, 75. *Goodspeed's History of Tennessee*, 749. The Crescent Mills, operated by William Simonton, and the Crowson Mills, often called Sykes Mill, were built in 1852. Simonton owned forty slaves, and the Parkes several dozens of them. MCR, 1850, Slaves Schedules, 1850, Lawrence and Wayne counties, Tennessee.

52. Gagnon, "Transition to an Industrial South," 112.

53. William Parkes to Thomas Parkes, December 6, 1846, Hope Factory Letters, TSLA.

54. Peter Seales to Thomas Parkes, February 21, 1849, ibid.; MCR, 1860, Population Schedules, Lawrence County, Tennessee. Sykes reported $1500 worth of real estate and $7000 of personal property.

55. Following the definition of tasks and responsibilities in use in New England, the general manager of a textile mill was called a "superintendent." At lower managerial levels, "superintendents" were those in charge of the machinery, while "agents" were primarily concerned with the work performance of factory hands in its relation to production levels.

56. Precise information concerning Hope Factory is unavailable; from one letter we can infer, however, that its hands were partly white and partly slave. Glen Factory employed nineteen family-owned slaves. MCR, 1850, Slaves Schedules, Lawrence County, Tennessee. Daniel Gustine to Thomas Parkes, October 24, 1849 (quotation), Hope Factory Letters, TSLA.

57. Seales to Parkes, February 21, 1849, ibid. Misspellings in original.

58. Gustine to Parkes, October 24, 1849, ibid.

59. Agreement between William B. Lenoir and Presley L. Amos, October 17, 1851; "W. B. Lenoir's statement of slaves owned," Lenoir Family Papers, UTK.

60. Michele Gillespie, *Free Labor in an Unfree World: White Artisans in Slaveholding Georgia, 1789–1860* (Athens: University of Georgia Press, 2000), 100, 118–29; Gagnon, "Transition to an Industrial South," 101–6.

61. The case of Hickman County, Tennessee native John Brown is illuminating in this regard. In the early 1870s, as a youth of eighteen, Brown entered the service of the Grahams' textile mills at Pinewood, where his sister already worked. He began as a card stripper but then learned the blacksmith trade, machinist trade, loom operation, and little by little "how to run all the departments in the factory." When the foreman retired, owner Samuel Graham hired Brown to supervise the weave room and eventually named him superintendent of the entire factory, under the general management of Graham's own son. *Dickson County Herald,* August 12, 1938, in Jill K. Garrett, "Historical Sketches of Dickson," n.d., n.p., 58, UTK.

62. Rockford Manufacturing Company Papers, 1852–1856, Ledgers, UTK; Inez E. Burns, *History of Blount County, Tennessee: From War Trail to Landing Strip, 1795–1955* (Nashville: Benson Printing Co., 1957), 224–26.

63. MCR, 1850 and 1860, Population Schedules, Blount County, Tennessee. In 1860, Arthur A. Kennedy reported $17,000 of real estate and $6000 of personal property and his father, $56,000 in real estate and a personal property valued at $30,000. For comparable examples from Georgia, see Gagnon, "Transition to an Industrial South," 103–4, 116–17.

64. James Montgomery, "Why Southern Factories Fail." Georgia manufacturer Henry Merrell confirmed this fact in his autobiography. Gillespie, "Building Networks of Knowledge," 113–14; Gagnon, "Transition to an Industrial South," 112.

65. MCR, 1860, Population Schedules, Lawrence County, Tennessee, Lincoln and Richmond counties, North Carolina; *Raleigh Register and North Carolina Gazette,* February 7, 1840. New Yorker Joseph G. Gibbs, age twenty-eight, and Tennesseans A. J. Hill and N. F. Cherry, age twenty-six and twenty-nine, respectively, were all "factory superintendents" in Lawrence County. In North Carolina, one Mr. Spears was a superintendent in Richmond County, while native North Carolinians E. S. Gould and James Ray were, respectively, a "superintendent" and a "factory manager" in Lincoln County.

66. Gillespie, "Building Networks of Knowledge," 101–2.

67. Twenty dozen thread were worth $2.00. Joseph Brittain to William B. Lenoir, August 1, 1850, Lenoir Manufacturing Company Papers, UTK.

68. *DeBow's Review* 9 (1850): 430; MCR, 1860, Population Schedules, Baldwin and Muscogee counties, Georgia. Gagnon, "Transition to an Industrial South," reports a similar range of property values for Clarke County. Some anecdotal evidence hints at the fact that the gap between northern and southern salaries may not have been wide. In 1845, the son of Thomas G. Carey, the treasurer of the Hamilton Manufacturing Company of Massachusetts, replaced the clerk who had recently resigned from his job. On that occasion, one of the company's directors, William Appleton, objected to the "large" salary of $1200 for such a neophyte in the business as young Carey was. Gregory, *Nathan Appleton*, 260. Considering the differential existing between North and South in terms of cost of living, annual salaries in the order of approximately $1000 were remarkable down South. There, the high status of white-collar workers must have been enhanced by the widening gap between their incomes and those of common laborers that occurred during the antebellum period. According to Margo's calculations, in the 1850s the white-collar to common labor wage ratio was of 2.07 in the country as a whole, but was lowest in the Northeast (1.90) and highest in the South Central states (2.50). The data provided by Margo for the antebellum period (*Wages and Labor Markets in the United States*, 156–57, 181) are in line with the findings of Claudia Goldin and Lawrence Katz.

69. Gillespie, *Free Labor in an Unfree World*, ch. 4.

70. Thomas M. Doerflinger, *A Vigorous Spirit of Enterprise, Merchants and Economic Development in Revolutionary Philadelphia* (Chapel Hill: University of North Carolina Press, 1986); C. P. Kindleberger, "Commercial Expansion and the Industrial Revolution," in Stanley L. Engerman, ed., *Trade and the Industrial Revolution, 1700–1850*, 2 vols. (Celthenam, U.K.: Edward Elgar Publishing, 1996), 1:1–38.

6

Three Faces of the Southern Middle Class
The Aikin Brothers in the Old Southwest

ANGELA LAKWETE

hree brothers from South Carolina fueled the flush times of the Old Southwest, injecting entrepreneurial vigor into the expanding middle class of northern Alabama and Mississippi. The oldest, William A. Aikin, manufactured cotton gins near Huntsville, Alabama; the middle brother, Cyrus S. Aikin, invested in commercial firms in Columbus, Mississippi; and the youngest, John G. Aikin, practiced law in Tuscaloosa and Mobile and lumbered in nearby Stockton. Aggressive businessmen, they mirrored the European middle class of the early nineteenth century, pursuing wealth through industrial and commercial endeavors rather than agriculture, and exploiting new technologies and markets. Wealthy southerners, they mirrored the planter class in their ownership of enslaved African men and women, using them in the factories and firms they owned. Engaged in the political process, the brothers vied for public office but held none. Despite their wealth and moneyed associations, William died bankrupt in 1840 and Cyrus penniless in 1842. John spent much of his professional life settling William's estate. John had achieved recognition for his 1833 *Digest of the Laws of the State of Alabama* but maintained a modest life until his second marriage in 1844. The number of enslaved people he owned jumped from three in 1840 to fifty in 1860, theoretically pushing him into the planter class. His self-identification as a lawyer, his ownership in 1860 of a steam saw mill, and his absence from the agricultural census support his inclusion in the middle class. Never aspiring planters, the Aikin brothers exemplified the complexity of the antebellum southern middle class and the diversity of the southern economy.

Historians have long recognized the presence of merchants, manufacturers, and professionals in the southern economy but until recently most have underestimated their influence. In his 1965 study of the Cotton South,

The Political Economy of Slavery, Eugene Genovese identified merchants and manufacturers as critical but subservient to the plantation economy. He characterized merchants as sycophants who aped planters and shunned industry. Manufacturers he characterized as class traitors because they exploited rather than rejected slavery, defying the presumed free-labor mandate of capitalism. Planters invested in industry but, he argued, to contain rather than to expand industrialism. In concluding that slavery underdeveloped the South, Genovese sparked a productive debate.[1] Scholars since have questioned the compatibility of slavery, industrialism, and class formation, seeking to understand the nature of southern society and the individuals and ideas that shaped it.

Jonathan D. Wells shifted the debate in 2004 with a monograph on the making of the southern middle class. He argued that a self-conscious middle class that emerged by the 1850s drew on the northern middle class for ideals and institutions, and adapted to both southern culture and slavery. So successful was southern adaptation, Wells argued, that it threatened the northern free-labor model and contributed to the sectional tensions that led to civil war. He found that middle-class southerners reestablished social ties with their northern peers soon after the war and resumed the modernization they had begun earlier.[2] William and Cyrus had died in the 1840s; John, seven months after Appomattox. Had they lived, the brothers surely would have demonstrated the same commitment to the South, to slavery, and to modernization, as did the people in Wells's study. The Aikins add an empirical layer to Wells's analyses and shift the focus of middle-class formation to the Old Southwest.

The backdrop of the Aikin brothers' careers was the Old Southwest, a region created by cessions of tribal and state lands to the national government and organized by the land ordinances of 1784, 1785, and 1787. From it Mississippi Territory was formed in 1798, bounded on the west by the Mississippi River, on the east by the Chattahoochee, and on the north by the Tennessee. In 1808, the governor of the territory formed Madison County and designated Huntsville, a settlement on a tributary of the Tennessee, as the seat. In 1817 Congress carved Alabama Territory out of the eastern half of Mississippi Territory and in 1819 awarded it statehood. The movement of European Americans and enslaved African Americans into the territories escalated after the War of 1812, aided by the appropriation of Creek lands and systematic Native American removal. Daniel Dupre studied the settlers, speculators, and slaves who populated Madison County in the wake of the removals. Most came from the Carolinas, like the Aikins, but others moved from Georgia and other southern states. They came to make their fortune planting cotton and providing services to the cotton economy. Dupre focused on the latter, the merchants who dominated Huntsville society. Many were also industrialists, operating cotton gins and grist and saw mills. Some planted; most owned enslaved individuals whom they used on their farms and in their firms. They were developers, forming partnerships to establish port towns and steamboat lines. Through them, Dupre tracked not the decline of republicanism but its reconciliation with capitalist market relations in Huntsville before 1840.[3]

The merchant-ginners Dupre studied were the first industrialists in Huntsville. They provided an essential service in a cotton economy, processing the seed cotton delivered by planters for shipment and sale to textile manufacturers in the United States and abroad. Merchants hired or owned a skilled ginner who operated a water- or steam-powered cotton gin, a machine that separated the fiber from the seed. Other workers packaged the fiber into standardized bales with a screw or steam press, then wrapped and warehoused the bales until shipment. Most merchants assumed ownership of the cotton and issued planters credit determined by the quality of cotton and the market price. Owners of capital and issuers of credit, merchants were among the wealthiest men in Huntsville. LeRoy Pope, first among them, led the powerful Georgia faction. Founder of the Huntsville Planters and Merchants Bank, incorporated in 1816, he had worked as a merchant-ginner for Phineas Miller, Eli Whitney's business partner, in Petersburg, Georgia, in the 1790s. In Huntsville he promoted the interests of fellow merchant-ginners like David Moore, who sat on the bank's board. Moore became a justice of the peace and later state representative, an office he held through 1844. Merchant-ginner William I. Adair was a director not of Pope's bank but of the Muscle Shoals Canal Company incorporated in 1827.[4] He also joined Moore in land development projects. With their investments in industrial and commercial infrastructure, middle-class men like these powered the regional economy.

Manufacturers followed merchant-ginners and millers into northern Alabama, supplying necessities and luxuries to area residents. Shortly before statehood, they began peppering newspapers with advertisements that heralded industrial expansion. Announcing new businesses in 1818 were tanner

James Allsup, wood turner James Lynch, saddler Andrew Cross, shoe maker Ebenezer Darbey, and the tailoring firm of J. L. & Sloss & Company. Charles Cabaniss advertised his "Cotton Spinning Factory" and George Lynes his saddlery business. Henry Pope (unrelated to LeRoy) operated a tobacco factory selling "common and Santo Domingo sigars." In 1819, a mill and handstone grinder offered his services along with a pump maker from Philadelphia.[5] Huntsville attracted manufacturers and artisans throughout the period, who in turn nurtured a population of skilled white, free black, and enslaved men and women.

Territorial-era notices published in Madison County newspapers identified enslaved artisans attached to durable and non-durable goods firms suggesting their use in mixed-race shops. "Runaway" notices from the 1810s and 1820s identified among others Anthony, a carpenter; Matt, a shoemaker; and Peter, a blacksmith, who may have been a freedman. "For hire" notices included those from sawyer Robert H. Rose, who hoped to hire out his enslaved sawyer, and from miller J. J. Winston hiring out "to the highest bidder" six experienced enslaved millers. "For sale" notices emanated from industrialists selling assets and slaves to settle accounts, like that from a tanner who advertised the sale of his enslaved tanners along with his tan yard. Charles Cabaniss, who advertised his cotton yarn factory in 1818, may have hired or owned enslaved operatives; the factory expanded under different ownership in 1824, adding power looms and incorporating in 1832 as the Bell Factory, with a documented history of using enslaved workers.[6]

Newspaper notices only suggested what business records, diaries, and other primary sources confirmed: Enslaved artisans and laborers constituted the productive core of the southern middle class. From Robert Starobin in 1970 on industrial slavery generally to Diane Barnes in 2008 on artisans in the Upper South city of Petersburg, Virginia, scholars have used similar sources to study the prevalence of mixed slave and free labor in mills, mines, and factories and to examine the implications. Focused on the artisans in cities in the Lower South state of Georgia, a 2000 study by Michele Gillespie found that the planters who hired out enslaved artisans, and the manufacturers who employed them, limited the wage-earning potential of white artisans. The 1830s was a turning point for Gillespie, before which the possibility of white artisans' achieving planter status was attainable and after which it became increasingly unlikely. Middling journeymen could no longer afford slaves, suffered from competition with them, and were powerless to legislate against them. Gillespie and Barnes concurred that antebellum journeymen became permanent wage laborers but never formed an articulate working class. Neither did they in the Old Southwest, where merchants, makers, and manufacturers exerted the same pressures on state and local legislatures to protect the employment of enslaved and free black labor. Throughout the South, enslaved artisans enabled middle-class formation.[7]

As they detailed the use of an enslaved labor force, notices in local newspapers documented the arrival of cotton gin manufacturers. Like the merchant-ginners who provided an essential service in Huntsville's cotton economy, manufacturers provided the essential machine. Advertising in 1818 were James Hendrick, "late from South Carolina," with a shop just west of Huntsville, and Henry Gaines, a cotton gin and press maker located in Meridianville, just north of the city. In April 1819, William W. Gaines announced the opening of his "gin making and screw cutting" business in Meridianville, possibly in conjunction with Henry Gaines, perhaps a relative. William T. Crenshaw opened his Huntsville factory in May 1819 and was still in business at the time of the 1850 census. Thomas W. Kemp and Mathias Munn commenced their gin-making partnership in late May 1819, humbly soliciting "a share of the public patronage."[8] William A. Aikin avoided the crowded Huntsville market, settling in Triana, a new commercial town founded by merchant-ginners. Just south of Huntsville, it was close to labor markets, convenient to cotton planters, and located on the Tennessee River, a major commercial waterway.

William joined a community of Huntsville merchants when he moved to Triana in the early 1820s. He strengthened his ties through marriage in 1825 to Elizabeth S. Noble, the daughter of a prominent member. They had five daughters and one son. In the same year, in the pages of the *Southern Advocate*, a "Planter" nominated him for state representative. Although he never held the office, the nomination reflected the high regard of his peers. Five years later, the 1830 census documented him supporting a household of twenty-six, including nineteen enslaved men and women. In 1836, he fought in the Second Creek War at the rank of brigadier general.[9] When his associates addressed him as "Colonel" or "General," they used the title deferentially not gratuitously. By the 1840 census, his household had increased to thirty-three and now included twenty-five enslaved men and women. But William was no planter. To the 1840 federal census marshal he reported twelve "persons" employed in manufacturing, taken from among the thirteen working-age men he owned.

Although he may have begun his career as a merchant, William made his fortune as a cotton gin manufacturer. His water-powered factory demonstrated a commitment to technological innovation, and his sales network revealed an understanding of the cotton gin market. Like large southern cotton gin makers, William made and marketed inexpensive copies of northern gins; like them he also made gins of his own unique, branded design. He was, however, the only southern cotton gin manufacturer in the 1820s and 1830s who developed a network of sales representatives in Mississippi, Tennessee, and northern Alabama that rivaled that of the popular Massachusetts cotton gin manufacturer Eleazer Carver.

William contracted factors and merchants to act as sales agents in prominent commercial centers envisioning a regional—not merely local—market. Targeting large Mississippi Delta planters, his agents took orders and payments; received, distributed, and installed the gins; and arranged for repairs. In the process they promoted the Aikin brand, using their familiarity with planters to inform their advertising strategies. M. B. Sellers worked out of Warrenton, Mississippi. Aware of the influx of Carolina planters, he emphasized William's South Carolina roots in an 1821 notice. E. B. Clarke worked out of Natchez and knew that his clients favored large, fast gins. In an 1821 notice he emphasized the size and performance of the Aikin gin, claiming it turned out "in the best order from 5 to 6,000 wt per day." A. Glass, who also operated out of Warrenton, emphasized novelty, announcing in an 1822 notice the availability of Aikin gins now built on "a new plan."[10] William's sales agents through their frequent notices identified his southern origins, his technological expertise, and his commitment to innovation, introducing him to a selective and informed planter clientele throughout much of the Old Southwest.[11]

Ironically William chose Huntsville's *Democrat,* founded in 1823 in opposition to the city's Whig newspaper *Southern Advocate,* to explain his advantages. He addressed cotton planters throughout the South in a notice he himself wrote and published on June 6, 1824. After announcing a new partnership he had formed with his brother Cyrus, and the expansion of the Triana

Cotton Gin Factory, he described his new product line. He continued to make the branded Aikin gin, which he had modified "with many important alterations and improvements," and he also now offered "Carver's model" made with Carver-branded parts. He assured readers of his "long experience" in the business and informed them of his recent trips to Mississippi and Louisiana to examine the latest gins, likely Carver's. He pledged that "no labour or attention will be spared that may be necessary to give entire satisfaction to planters." The concluding paragraph on configuration options gave credibility to the accommodations he promised.[12]

The next year he published a longer notice in the *Southern Advocate*. Addressing the "Planters of North Alabama" specifically, William extended appreciation to those "disposed to patronize the mechanics of their own section [rather than] those abroad," referring to Carver and other Massachusetts gin makers. Affirming their support, twenty-seven planters from northern Alabama counties attached their names as Aikin's satisfied customers. William concluded the essay with an appeal to journeymen gin makers, carpenters, and apprentices, communicating prosperity to potential customers.[13]

Responsible for some of the prosperity was Thomas B. Murphy, a merchant with whom William operated in partnership as Murphy & Aikin. One warrant issued by the firm in 1825 against a delinquent customer and one reference William made in the 1825 newspaper notice, described above, regarding the termination of his "mercantile engagements," were the only direct evidence of William's career as a merchant.[14] The men may have dissolved the firm, but they maintained a relationship until William's death in 1840. The receipts that Murphy submitted along with entries from the W. A. & C. S. Aikin Account Book, preserved in William's estate case files, revealed day-to-day operations of the Triana factory. Mechanics machined gudgeons, heavy cast iron cylinders that held gin saws and brushes; they turned whirls and repaired doffing brushes. They refurbished inks, the small cast iron containers that held lubricating oil for the gin's cylinders. They repaired and repainted flues, the ducts that carried cotton fiber from the gin to the lint room. They made coffins, including one ordered by Murphy for a "negro's child." William's mechanics made iron screws and repaired wagon wheels and broken saddles, but most frequently they forged horseshoes.[15] Rich in operations details, the receipts merely hinted at staffing. They mentioned by name only two enslaved mechanics: Booker, a carpenter, and Henry, a skilled breaster whom William paid for overwork in 1838; and only one white artisan, prominent watchmaker David T. Knox, who worked for Aikin in 1839.[16]

William A. Aikin never exerted a monopoly in the gin industry either locally or regionally. In addition to competition from Massachusetts gin makers, local gin makers vied for market share. For example, William W. Gaines moved from Meridianville to Triana in the 1820s, having formed a partnership and expanded his business. With the new resources he offered mill gearing, specialty gins, and Carver gin copies. He eventually left Triana for Vicksburg, Mississippi, where he established a large foundry and gin factory in 1832.[17] Joseph Carothers and Archibald Rison formed a partnership in Huntsville in 1835 but dissolved it to establish other firms.[18] In 1850, the North Carolina-born Carothers, in business with his sons, operated a modest gin and repair shop, while the Tennessee-born Rison owned a gin shop, real estate, and four enslaved men. By 1860, Carothers was out of business, but Rison ran a steam-powered gin factory, claimed $20,000 in real and personal estate, and owned seven working-age men.[19] Aikin may never have met these younger men; his career had peaked when theirs were forming.

William's effusive advertisements of the 1820s faded to cryptic one-line notices in the late 1830s, foreshadowing a decline in his enterprise.[20] He continued making gins, filling orders from Mississippi factors and local merchants, and placing orders for gin saws and other supplies with hardware merchants in Huntsville and Florence, Alabama, and Philadelphia. In 1838 and 1839, he hired additional artisans to build and repair gins and engaged the services of a boat to deliver them. Yet doctors' invoices in the probate records suggest that William also battled illness. William routinely engaged physicians Michie and Wilkinson to treat family members and slaves, but visits and prescriptions increased during late 1839.[21] In 1840, he requested the services of physician Albert Russell perhaps for a second opinion of an unnamed illness. On July 22, 1840, Dr. Russell visited him "in consultation" but returned on July 25 and stayed overnight. In a deposition Russell was identified as treating William "during his last illness" and may have been with him when he died sometime that month.[22]

William, in his late forties, may have anticipated the outcome of his illness; in February 1840, he had executed a power of attorney, appointing his brother and business partner Cyrus S. Aikin his "agent and attorney."[23] Overriding William's wishes, the court named his brother John administrator. John, then a lawyer in Mobile, assumed guardianship of William's children, secured Elizabeth's dower rights, and discovered that William, despite his assets and thriving business, was deeply in debt. John turned to Cyrus for help, giving him power of attorney.[24] But in 1840 Cyrus was struggling with his own debt obligations in Columbus, Mississippi. John worked alone settling the estate, gathering together the fragments that remained of William's life.

The affidavits, depositions, receipts, and inventories that John submitted to the court documented William's twenty-year career as a cotton gin manufacturer. They also revealed his business relationships, beverage preferences, and reading habits. His library included a copy of Oliver Goldsmith's 1774 *A History of the Earth and Animated Nature,* Aaron Burr's 1837 *Memoirs,* and runs of *American Turf Register.* He carried a gold lever watch and furnished his home with elegant trappings, including a mahogany china press and a "Yankee Clock." He invested in the Triana Female Academy and possibly sent his daughters there. He also spent beyond his means, jeopardizing the welfare of his wife, children, and enslaved families. Following court orders, John hired out and sold William's slaves. Elizabeth kept her housekeepers and their children. Cyrus hired William's gin makers Henry and Booker, Booker's family, and four other mechanics, including Jordan then twenty-one, whom William had acquired in 1828 through marriage. Local merchants hired or bought those remaining.[25] John collected debts and sold cotton gins, tools, and household goods, but the payments scarcely diminished William's liabilities. Debt, however, did not impinge on William's middle-class status.[26] In his occupations and associations, if not in fiscal responsibility, he embodied the burgeoning southern middle class.

William's younger brother Cyrus S. Aikin may have begun a career as a manufacturer but made his reputation as a merchant. A partner in numerous mercantile firms, the president of the Columbus and Tombigy Transportation Company, and co-vice president of a local State Rights Whig organization, Cyrus achieved a degree of social distinction that his reckless investments and chronic indebtedness jeopardized.[27] Like John, Cyrus was a lawyer, but where he read law is unknown. Like William he never planted. Like his brothers he owned slaves but far fewer. Census records indicated his ownership of eighteen enslaved people in 1830 but only one young woman, probably a house-maid, in 1840. He supported a local school, in his case the Franklin Academy, a sixteenth-section or public school in Columbus, Mississippi.[28] Unlike William, who was anchored in Triana, Cyrus moved frequently, shifting residences among Huntsville, Tuscaloosa, Columbus, and finally Paducah, Kentucky. Cyrus was the prodigal brother who pursued opportunities where he found them. More so than William or John, he exploited the flush times of the 1830s.

After moving from South Carolina with his brothers, Cyrus lingered in the Huntsville area. In 1824, he formed a partnership with William enabling the expansion of the Triana Cotton Gin Factory. Cyrus may have stayed to help William in the business and to learn the fundamentals of cotton gin manufac-turing. In 1827, he traveled to Tuscaloosa to settle the estate of their father and move their mother and sister into his Tuscaloosa home. In 1833, he returned to Huntsville to marry Mildred "Milly" Spicer Noble, possibly the sister of William's wife Elizabeth. An advertisement published in Huntsville's *Southern Mercury* that year suggested that Cyrus had remained active in the Triana fac-tory.[29] That changed when he moved to Columbus, Mississippi, and opened a cotton gin factory there.

"New Gin Stand Factory" headed the announcement Cyrus placed in the Columbus *Democrat* in December 1836. It explained that the new partnership of "C. S. Aikin & Company" continued a previous firm Cyrus operated with Columbus merchant George L. Estes. The notice situated Cyrus within a com-munity of merchant-manufacturers and signaled that he had quickly secured access to capital and credit networks. It also marked the beginning of a pattern of confusing and questionable partnerships he formed and soon dissolved. Indeed, the firm of C. S. Aikin & Company may have manufactured few gins. It closed two years later when Estes withdrew.[30] By then the men had already formed partnerships with other colleagues, creating a tangle of business and credit relations that informed their careers.

Cyrus's career as a Columbus manufacturer began with one Estes; his ca-reer as a merchant began with another, William J. Estes, a lawyer and clerk of the circuit court. Estes was the principal in W. J. Estes & Company, the suc-cessor of Estes, Gibbs & Company, an auction, warehouse, and shipping firm. Estes added a grocery when Cyrus joined him in July 1837. Six months later, in January 1838, Cyrus left him to join John C. Glass in a "New and Fancy Dry

Goods Establishment."[31] The partnership ended when Cyrus formed another with William H. Gibbs in October 1838. They offered the services of "Auction, Commission, Receiving & Forwarding Agents" in the building "formerly oc-cupied by "C.S. Aikin." They used the services of Eugene B. Drake as auction-eer. Drake, a lawyer and merchant, was also the editor of the *Southern Argus*. Aikin & Gibbs lasted until October 1840, when Thomas W. Brown replaced Gibbs and the firm became Aikin & Brown. The "Receiving, Forwarding, and Commission Merchants, and General Agents" were located on a "steam-boat landing."[32] The firm planned to offer shipping services but the plan hinged on the success of a steamboat company, formed in 1838 and barely afloat in 1840.

The men with whom Cyrus formed the evanescent mercantile partner-ships were among the thirty-three men who organized the Columbus and Tombigby Transportation Company (CTTC) in 1838 and incorporated it in 1839. The articles of incorporation stipulated two officers, a president, elected by stockholders, and a cashier, appointed by a board of ten directors. In 1839, the stockholders elected Cyrus president and the directors appointed Eu-gene Drake cashier. The articles outlined the company's two goals: to operate steamboats on the Tombigbee River and to make river improvements to fa-cilitate navigation.[33] The Tombigbee, a critical cotton waterway, originates in northeastern Mississippi and ends in southwestern Alabama, where it flows into the Alabama River, forming the Mobile River, which flows into Mobile Bay and the Gulf of Mexico. Along its shores lay the bustling cotton ports, in-dustrial centers, and middle-class seedbeds of Aberdeen and Columbus, Mis-sissippi; Demopolis and Gainesville, Alabama; and, most important to the company directors, the city of Mobile, second only to New Orleans in cotton shipments. They pinned their hopes for profitability on shipping out bales of cotton and receiving the assortment of goods they advertised for sale in the columns of the city's weeklies.[34]

The merchant-directors capitalized the firm at $500,000 and offered stock shares in $100 increments sold for "specie, or the notes of specie-paying banks" or for a "pledge of real estate, or an estate for a term of years," secured either by "trust deeds or mortgages or both." Fourteen of the original thirty-three investors paid in specie; the remaining nineteen used the trust deed or a mortgage, borrowing money on property to pay for company stock. The articles mandated that the cashier of the Columbus and Tombigby Transportation Company negotiate the transactions. Investors made a down payment of a stipulated percentage of the total share package in exchange for a loan to cover the cost of the shares, using real estate as collateral.[35]

The trust deed required payment of a regular installment, but the company was free to change the frequency and amount upon notification in the newspaper. If the borrower failed to make the installment payment, the articles empowered the company to sell the pledged real estate at public auction to recover the funds. The CTTC published the names of defaulters in "trust sale" notices in the *Southern Argus*. The trust deed thus privately legitimized the loan while the trust sale publicly proclaimed the debt. Yet what seemed like humiliations unfolding in the pages of the weeklies were in many cases collegial exchanges. Another company investor often bought the property being auctioned and typically allowed the original owner to continue using it. When lenders completed their payments, the company authorized either a "release" or "quit claim" deed, which returned all rights and privileges of the property to the original owner. As contentious as the arrangements seemed, they were transactions that retained elements of republican reciprocity and mirrored the cyclical realignment of the city's small businesses.

Cyrus's election by stockholders may have reflected his social or financial status, but in the process of funding the firm he ensnared himself in a web of deeds that threatened both. A deed that documented his debt relationships was struck in July 1837, when he, William J. Estes, and Benjamin Estes borrowed $3000 from the Tombigby Rail Road Company.[36] In another deed made in September 1837, Cyrus and William J. Estes lent $200 to a borrower who used Franklin Academy leased lots as collateral. Then in January 1838 Cyrus borrowed $15,999.84, mortgaging his home. As part of the transaction his wife Milly forfeited her dower rights. In February of the same year, William J. Estes borrowed $8000 from Cyrus, mortgaging the Estes home and requiring Estes's wife Sarah Ann likewise to forfeit her dower rights.[37] Two days later Cyrus transferred to Estes the Franklin Academy leased lots he acquired in a defaulted loan. Nowhere in the deeds were the purposes of the loans mentioned, but the men likely applied the funds to their firms or to the upstart CTTC. More critically, the deeds illuminated the debt obligations that bound merchant families.[38]

Cyrus's obligations deepened when he borrowed to buy shares in the CTTC. On April 12, 1838, he authorized three loans in three trust deeds, two in

Columbus and one in Huntsville, for a total of $8500 in CTTC stock. To secure the Columbus loans he mortgaged property he had bought from Estes; for the Huntsville loan he used his interest in the Triana Cotton Gin Factory. As did all trust deeds, these included a clause warning the borrower that default would result in the sale to the highest bidder of "the [pledged] lot or parcel of ground with all the appurtenances thereof . . . to satisfy and fully pay off the amount required to be paid by said Company."[39] The third party on all of the deeds was John Crusoe, identified as the "Superintendent of the Columbus and Tombigby Transportation Company," an office not stipulated in the articles of incorporation. Nominally Cyrus remained president, but his authority appeared compromised.

By the end of 1838, CTTC had raised enough money to begin staffing and equipping the company. Directors addressed staffing first, advertising for ten men to buy and then for twenty-five enslaved steamboatmen to hire.[40] They next planned to buy steamboats but found funds short. The articles allowed them to call "for additional installments" after publishing a thirty-day notice informing stockholders. In the wake of the notice, a spate of trust sales ensued. By July 1839, the company had raised enough money to solicit bids for "two first rate Steam Boats."[41] The bids seemed to signal financial stability, yet organizationally the company faltered. In August 1839, George Vaughn, a founding stockholder, replaced Cyrus as president of the CTTC, and between 1840 and 1841 three different men occupied the critical office of cashier.[42] Cyrus's name, which had earlier peppered the newspapers in connection with Whig Party politics, various grocery and warehousing firms, and the Columbus and Tombigby Transportation Company, had faded from print.

Debt now dogged Cyrus. Although he had repaid a $3000 loan in January 1839, he had also borrowed $965 from a Franklin Academy trustee. In May, he borrowed $1150 from his brother William and, in June, $5000 from the Bank of the CTTC, using his warehouse, gin factory, and a Franklin Academy leased lot as collateral. Then, in November 1839, the *Southern Argus* published a trust sale notice naming him as a defaulter. He had not met his obligation for a trust deed he executed in 1838, and his warehouse and factory were threatened with sale.[43] Following customary practice, he continued to occupy both until February 1841, when the Lowndes County sheriff issued two writs of *fieri facias,* executing the sales. One writ authorized the sale of Cyrus's former gin factory to CTTC stockholder Erasmus L. Acee and Cyrus's current business partner Thomas W. Brown. The other writ authorized the sale of the warehouse co-owned by Cyrus and Brown to a different trustee of the Franklin Academy.[44]

In February 1841, as bankruptcy loomed, Cyrus registered fourteen transactions in the Columbus land office, acquiring a total of 1202 acres in Lowndes, Neshoba, and Webster counties in Mississippi. In every case he was the assignee of his former business partner Benjamin Estes, who was himself the assignee of a third party who paid cash for the property.[45] The apparent owner of the property, Cyrus may not have had access to it; he did not use it to defray his debt. A deed he signed in August 1841 that transferred his "real and personal estate, debts, dues, and demands" to William's estate, left him still indebted for it.[46] Amid the land acquisitions and debt transfers, Cyrus suddenly left Columbus. Only later was it discovered that he had gone to Paducah, Kentucky, a city on the Tennessee and Ohio rivers, poised to become a center of steamboat trade. It was a place where a man of Cyrus's talents could perhaps start over. Unfortunately, Cyrus died there sometime in July 1842 at roughly the age of forty.[47] Not until 1843 were Cyrus's remains and property returned to his wife Milly, in Huntsville. All that she received were a "watch, papers, and money," and a buggy and horse.[48]

Like William, Cyrus died without a will but, unlike him, left no estate for John to settle. The fragments that remained of Cyrus's life were the trust deeds that documented his debt and the newspaper advertisements that announced his partnerships and politics.[49] Reckless in business, Cyrus nevertheless characterized an era when opportunities in the expanding economy created cohorts like his, who with selfish as well as civic motives fueled the expanding regional and national markets. Mediating capitalist relations with republican comity, Cyrus and his associates reinforce Dupre's characterizations of the region and the era. In occupation and aspiration, if not in deportment, they epitomized the businessmen of a modernizing southern middle class.

John Gaston Aikin lived a private life yet of the three brothers left the most public legacy. He read and practiced law in Tuscaloosa and achieved recognition in 1833 as the compiler of the second *Digest of the Laws of the State of Alabama*. He married twice. In 1825, he wed Temperance Miles, with whom he had five sons and two daughters. They lived modestly, owning no slaves in 1830 and two women and an infant in 1840. Sometime in the early 1840s, tragedy struck the family and he somehow lost Temperance and the children. During that time he moved to Stockton, in Baldwin County, near Mobile, where he had kept an office since 1839. In 1844, he married Clarissa (or Clara) A. Kennedy, the daughter of a wealthy Mobile planter.[50]

Through his second marriage John gained a modest allotment of land and a considerable number of enslaved individuals. In 1850, he owned fifty improved acres in Stockton, and grew corn but no cotton according to the agricultural census schedule. At the time he owned seventeen people, thirteen of them working-age men. By the 1860 census, he owned fifty people, nineteen of them working-age men. Now his name appeared not in the agricultural but the industrial schedule. John owned a steam saw mill, which he capitalized at $70,000. Other Baldwin County lumbermen sawed pine logs, but he processed cypress exclusively. Prominent Natchez lumberman Andrew Brown also specialized in cypress and, like other southern lumbermen, relied on slave labor for all but the most skilled jobs.[51] John may have as well. He reported employing in his mill twelve men who may have been men he owned. Before he began lumbering, however, law dominated John's life.

The only brother commemorated in a biographical dictionary, John ironically left virtually no documents providing the details of his life. Even his year of birth is contested. Chiseled into his tombstone in the Stockton Memorial Cemetery is the year 1800, while historian and biographer Thomas M. Owen reckoned it 1803 and the 1860 manuscript census indicates 1808.[52] Owen recorded that John attended the University of Alabama and read law at Yale College, but there is no evidence he did either. He likely read law in Tuscaloosa under the eminent jurist Robert Emmett Bledsoe Baylor. Baylor moved from Kentucky in 1820 and served in the Alabama legislature from 1824 to 1825. The men shared a law practice, and the senior Baylor may have used his influence to secure legislative assignments for John. In 1827 the General Assembly asked John to preside over the Senate "for a few days" in the absence of the secretary of state. In 1833 it commissioned him to prepare the second digest of the laws of the state. [53]

Required by all state constitutions, the decennial digests summarize laws, arrange them topically, and cross-reference them in a compact volume. Not a literary assignment, the digest commission nevertheless placed John in the company of esteemed jurists and writers. As the second compiler of the state digest he followed Harry Toulmin, a founding settler of the state, who compiled the first digest in 1823.[54] Alexander B. (A. B.) Meek, who is mistakenly associated with John's 1836 revision, authored the 1841 supplement. Meek and Aikin may have been colleagues. Like John, Meek was born in South Carolina and moved to Tuscaloosa in the early 1820s. In the Alabama legislature for twenty years, Meek was also an essayist, poet, and editor of the *Southron,* a journal founded to promote southern letters. It is possible that the Meek and Aikin families migrated together and that "F. W. Meek," who made claims on William's estate, was related to A. B.

A. B. Meek and John G. Aikin shared interests in law and literature, but differed notably in their social credentials. That they were both lawyers from South Carolina may have provided a pretext for social exchange. John may have contributed to Meek's *Southron,* possibly under a pseudonym not yet deciphered. Their differences, however, may have thwarted friendship. While Meek graduated from the University of Alabama and fought in the Creek War of 1836, John neither graduated nor fought. Those details, coupled with the mysterious loss of John's first family, may have instilled suspicions that limited his social advancement. The legislature never awarded John an office yet, significantly, it commissioned him to publish its signature text.

For John the digest was an opportunity to display his prose and to dispel suspicion. He did both in an "Introductory Notice," a long, formal, and defensive essay that revealed as much about the author as it introduced the text. In it John painstakingly explained the editorial review process to which the digest had been subjected. The commissioners and the judiciary committee of the House had scrutinized the text and their approval validated his "unremitting diligence" and rendered any apologies "for any mistakes or deficiencies" unnecessary. He defended his exclusion of certain laws and inclusion of others, blaming critics for failing to appreciate the function of a digest and wanting a history instead. Had he followed their advice, he wrote, the work would have been "unfit for general use." In the conclusion, he generously thanked the legislature and the commissioners, among whom was Baylor, his law partner. They in turn lavishly praised the work. The ultimate honor they bestowed was reprinting the 1833 introduction in John's 1836 revision.[55]

By then John had made plans to leave Tuscaloosa. He had established a law office in Mobile in 1839 and would have known that the state capital would relocate to Montgomery within the decade. When John appeared in the 1842 Mobile city directory, William and Cyrus had died and he was immersed in settling William's estate.[56] He continued his law practice in Mobile and established a residence in Stockton, a town on the Tensaw River, with packet service to Mobile. Sometime after his marriage to Clarissa in 1844, he moved William's widow Elizabeth and her six children from Triana to a home near his own and may have supported them.[57] Evidence has yet to confirm if he maintained professional associations in Tuscaloosa or continued a literary relationship with Meek in Mobile. He ensconced himself in Stockton and died in relative obscurity in 1865.

Like his brothers, John died without a will. His 1833 digest, its 1836 revision, and the hundreds of estate case filings he submitted in settlement of William's bankrupt estate attest to his competence and persistence, but reveal nothing of his personal or political associations. The federal census schedules of 1860 positioned him among the wealthiest men in Baldwin County with a combined personal and real estate of $196,000. Origen Sibley, a planter who owned a saw mill, was only slightly wealthier with a combined estate of $200,000. Yet wealth alone does not determine social class. In a county populated by timbermen and turpentine makers, oystermen and stock tenders, flatboat men and steamship masters, John was the rare lawyer.[58] His identification as a lawyer in the 1850 and 1860 federal census suggest that he capitalized on the distinction, maintaining a modest practice as he settled William's estate and managed his saw mill. The evidence, although scant, indicates that John was a professional not a planter and, although inhabiting the upper extreme of wealth, was nevertheless a member of the southern middle class.

The evidence of the three Aikin brothers substantiates much of the new scholarship. As middle-class southerners, they juggled slavery and capitalism, exploiting the cost benefits of wage and slave labor to provide goods and services in expanding markets. In the process, they limited the economic mobility of white artisans and appropriated the labor of enslaved artisans. They were, however, not simply a grasping Marxist bourgeoisie. They invested in internal improvements and supported public libraries and schools, bolstering their class but benefiting southern society generally. Porous middle-class communities reinforced their perspectives and ambitions. Communities of manufacturers and merchants attracted William A. Aikin to the Huntsville area.

His visibility and success in turn attracted others, expanding the industrial sector. Cyrus S. Aikin joined a community of Columbus merchants who collaborated in Whig politics and cooperated in ambitious development projects, increasing commercial opportunities as they reinforced social relations. In Tuscaloosa and Mobile, John G. Aikin inhabited communities of lawyers and politicians. They wrote and defended the laws that enabled the manufacturers and merchants of Alabama to form partnerships and incorporate and to hire whom they wished.

While much of the brothers' lives confirms current scholarship on the middle class, much also complicates it. William owned twenty-five people in 1840 and died bankrupt. Cyrus owned one young woman in 1840 and died virtually penniless two years later. John owned three people in 1840 but fifty in 1860 and an estate valued at $196,000. The indebtedness of William, the insolvency of Cyrus, and the wealth and slaveholdings of John did not nullify their middle-class inclusion. If not wealth but occupation, associations, expectations, and choices determine middle-class membership, then the brothers met the standard. Manufacturer, merchant, and professional, the Aikins represented three incarnations of the southern middle class and three perspectives on the economic development of the Old Southwest.

NOTES

1. Eugene D. Genovese, *The Political Economy of Slavery: Studies in the Economy and Society of the Slave South* (1965; reprint, Middletown, Conn.: Wesleyan University Press, 1989), 19–20, 181, 187, 207–8.

2. Jonathan Daniel Wells, *The Origins of the Southern Middle Class, 1800–1861* (Chapel Hill: University of North Carolina Press, 2004), 6–12, passim.

3. Daniel S. Dupre, *Transforming the Cotton Frontier: Madison County, Alabama, 1800–1840* (Baton Rouge: Louisiana State University Press, 1997), 3, 5, 12, 39, 216.

4. *Huntsville Gazette*, December 21, 1816; *Huntsville Republican*, October 13, 1817, March 20, 1819, April 24, 1819; Dupre, *Transforming the Cotton Frontier*, 174–75; Alabama Legislative Act 91, To Incorporate the Muscle Shoals Canal Company, January 11, 1827. http://www.legislature.state .al.us/misc/history/acts_and_journals/ 1826/acts/Acts_88–90.html [accessed May 24, 2010].

5. *Madison Gazette*, May 10, 1814; *Huntsville Republican*, September 9, 1817, September 30, 1817, October 28, 1817, November 25, 1817, January 27, 1818; *Alabama Republican*, February 17, 1818, March 10, 1818, January 2, 1819.

6. *Huntsville Republican*, September 9, 1817–August 15, 1819; *Alabama Republican*, February

17, 1819; *Huntsville Democrat,* January 27, 1824; U.S. Census, 1860, Industrial Schedule, Madison County, Alabama. The firm owned its ninety-three hands.

7. Robert S. Starobin, *Industrial Slavery in the Old South* (New York: Oxford University Press, 1970), 137–45; L. Diane Barnes, *Artisan Workers in the Upper South: Petersburg, Virginia, 1820–1865* (Baton Rouge: Louisiana State University Press, 2008), 6, 37, 197–98; Michele Gillespie, *Free Labor in an Unfree World: White Artisans in Slaveholding Georgia, 1789–1860* (Athens: University of Georgia Press, 2000), 34, 37, 69, 109, 112–13, 138; Wells, *Origins of the Southern Middle Class,* 15–16, 183–85, 208–9; Seth Rockman, *Scraping By: Wage Labor, Slavery, and Survival in Early Baltimore* (Baltimore: Johns Hopkins University Press, 2009), 7, 47, passim. Rockman studies the mixed-race labor sites that characterized the menial trades.

8. *Alabama Republican,* April 18, 1818 (Hendrick); July 4, 1818 (Henry Gaines); May 15, 1819 (W. W. Gaines); June 5, 1819 (Kemp and Munn); May 8, 1819 (Crenshaw).

9. *Southern Advocate,* May 6, 1825. Aikin may have earned the rank of brigadier general before the Second Creek War. He served in the 1st Brigade, 1st Division of the Alabama Militia in 1818. See Territorial Militia and Civil Service, 1818; Indian War 1836, Microfilm M870634, MIL-2A, Alabama Department of Archives and History, Montgomery, Alabama.

10. *Port-Gibson Correspondent,* April 24, 1821 (Sellers); *Mississippi Republican,* July 9, 1821 (Clarke); *Port-Gibson Correspondent,* July 11, 1822 (Glass).

11. Power of Attorney, February 3, 1840, Deed Record Book I, pp. 573–74, Lowndes County Court House, Columbus, Missouri (hereafter LCCH). William authorized Cyrus to oversee sales in Mississippi, Louisiana, and Arkansas, in addition to Alabama; on Eleazer Carver, see Angela Lakwete, *Inventing the Cotton Gin: Machine and Myth in Antebellum America* (Baltimore: Johns Hopkins University Press, 2003), 78, 90–94.

12. *The Democrat,* June 6, 1824.

13. *Southern Advocate and Huntsville Advertiser,* May 27, 1825.

14. Complaint, Thomas B. Murphy and William A. Aikin, April 1825, Circuit Court Loose Papers, County Court Records Room, Huntsville-Madison County Public Library, Huntsville, Alabama (hereafter HMCPL); William may have remained a member of the firm Picket, Banks &c. See Deposition, Lawrence S. Banks, January 8, 1844, Estate Case File 335, HMCPL.

15. Thomas B. Murphy to William A. Aikin, Account, April 10, 1830, "Transcribed from W. A. Aikin Account Book," September 28, 1833; Account of Robertson Brewer, February 1835, Estate Case File 335, HMCPL.

16. William A. Aikin to David T. Knox, May 7, 1841, Estate Case File 335, HMCPL. Knox was also a noted silversmith. See E. Bryding Adams, ed., *Made in Alabama: A State Legacy* (Birmingham: Museum of Art, 1995), 305; William A. Aikin, Will Book No. 4, pp. 250–51, filed April 14, 1828; Inventory, Sales, Rents & Hirings, compiled 1840, filed 1841 by John G. Aikin, Estate Case File 335, HMCPL.

17. *Southern Advocate,* July 8, 1825; John H. Moore, *The Emergence of the Cotton Kingdom in the Old Southwest: Mississippi, 1770–1860* (Baton Rouge: Louisiana State University Press, 1988), 211.

18. *Southern Advocate,* January 3, 1837, notice dated March 23, 1835.

19. Joseph Carothers, Archibald Rison, U.S. Census, 1850 and 1860, Free Population, Slave, and Industrial Schedules, Madison County, Alabama.

20. For example, see *Manchester Herald and Yazoo Advertiser,* March 15, 1834.

21. Michie and Wilkerson, Receipt, August–December 1839, submitted July 3, 1841, Estate Case File 335, HMCPL.

22. Filing, July 22, 1840, Estate Case File 335, HMCPL.

23. Power of Attorney, February 3, 1840, Deed Record Book I, pp. 573–74, LCCH.

24. John G. Aikin, Affidavit, October 5, 1840; A Report of the Debts and Liabilities of William A. Aikin, July 5, 1841, Estate Case File 335, HMCPL.

25. William A. Aikin, Inventory, Sales, Rents & Hiring, made 1840, recorded 1841 by John G. Aikin, Admin., Estate Case File 335, HMCPL; William A. Aikin, April 14, 1828, Will Book No 4, pp. 250–51, Estate Case File 335, HMCPL.

26. Bruce H. Mann, *A Republic of Debtors: Bankruptcy in the Age of American Independence* (Cambridge, Mass.: Harvard University Press, 2002), 256, 260.

27. *Southern Argus,* December 11, 1838.

28. The Land Ordinance of 1785 reserved the sixteenth section of each township for the support of a public school through the sale and lease of lots.

29. Orphan Court Minutes, 1824–1831, p. 278, Oct. 3, 1827, Tuscaloosa County Court House, Tuscaloosa, Alabama. William, Cyrus, and John were joined at the settlement by another brother James and a sister Jane; *Southern Mercury,* July 6, 1833.

30. *Columbus Democrat,* January 28, 1837, April 22, 1837; *Southern Argus,* December 18, 1838.

31. *Southern Argus,* July 4, 1837, January 30, 1838 (quotation).

32. *Southern Argus,* September 29, 1840, October 28, 1840.

33. Laws of the State of Mississippi, Ch. 147, "An Act to Incorporate the Columbus and Tombigby Transportation Company" (Jackson, MS: B. D. Howard, 1839), Sec. 2, Mississippi Department of Archives and History (hereafter MDAH); *Southern Argus,* November 6, 1838; the CTTC's spelling of the Tombigbee River follows nineteenth-century usage.

34. A typical list of offerings appeared in the *Southern Argus,* February 4, 1839. In individual advertisements of two or three lines, merchants simply named the products they had for sale. For example, in one notice Aikin & Gibbs listed "50 sacks Rio and Java coffee"; in another they listed "50 barrels brown New Orleans sugar." All merchants did likewise. Franklin & Brother, for example, sold Carolina hoes in one listing and "Champaign Brandy" in another.

35. CTTC, Articles of Incorporation, Sec. 2, 6, 7. I have assumed that original stockholders paid in full for stock if I have not been able to link them to CTTC trust deeds and if the *Southern Argus* did not publish their names as defaulters.

36. Trust Deed, William J. Estes & Others to H. W. Cater and the Tombigby Rail Road Company, July 30, 1837, Deed Record Book 8, pp. 23–24, LCCH. Across the page was written "April 12th 1838, Satisfied in full, [illegible name], President, Tombigby Rail Road Co."

37. Deed, Matthew Hopkins to William J. Estes and Cyrus S. Aikin, September 5, 1837, Deed Record Book 8, p. 228; Deed, Cyrus S. Aikin to Henry Newell of Pickens County, Alabama, January 10, 1838, Deed Record Book 9, pp. 278–79; Deed, William J. Estes to Cyrus S. Aikin, February 21, 1838, Deed Record Book 9, pp. 58–59, LCCH.

38. Mann, *Republic of Debtors,* 15, 19, 232. Although he covers an earlier period, Mann's explanation of mortgage instruments and debt relations applies here.

39. CTTC, Articles of Incorporation, Sec. 14; Indentures, Cyrus S. Aikin to Ovid P. Brown and William P. Puller, Trustees, April 12, 1838, Deed Record Book 9, pp. 311–16, LCCH; Indenture, Cyrus S. Aikin to Ovid P. Brown, William P. Puller, and John Crusoe, April 12, 1838, Deed Record Book R, pp. 139–41, Madison County Court House, Huntsville, Alabama (hereafter MCCH).

40. *Southern Argus,* January 8, 1839, dated December 11, 1838; December 25, 1838.

41. CTTC, Articles of Incorporation, Sec. 14 (first quotation); *Southern Argus,* August 18, 1840; notice dated August 10, 1840 (second quotation).

42. Trust Deed, William A. Hicks to Ovid P. Brown and William P. Puller, August 5, 1839, Deed Record Book 12, pp. 78–81, Chauncery Court Records Office, LCCH.

43. Quit Claim Deed, January 25, 1839, Deed Record Book 10, pp. 470–71; Trust Deed, January 28, 1839, Deed Record Book 10, pp. 463; Trust Deed, May 1, 1839, Deed Record Book 10, pp. 603–4; Trust Deed, June 7, 1839, Deed Record Book 10, pp. 662–64, LCCH; *Southern Argus,* November 5, 1839.

44. Writ of *Fieri Facias,* Pryor M. Grant to Erasmus L. Acee and Thomas W. Brown, February 1, 1841, Deed Record Book 16, pp. 522–23; Indenture, *Fieri Facias,* Pryor M. Grant to Eli Abbott, February 1, 1841, Deed Record Book 16, pp. 528–29, LCCH.

45. Cyrus S. Aikin, February 27, 1841, U.S. General Land Office Records, http://www.ancestry.com [accessed May 25, 2010].

46. Release Deed, January 1, 1843, pp. 79–80, Deed Record Book U, MCCH. The release deed referred to the August 12, 1841 trust deed. Cyrus undoubtedly borrowed more money than the sums in the deeds I located. In June 1840, he borrowed $8998 from William. John wrote on the reverse of the promissory note that Cyrus had repaid only $1348 before his death. See Receipt, June 8, 1840, Estate Case File 335, HMCPL. Many thanks to attorney Katherine Marie Klos of Akridge & Balch, Auburn, Alabama, for reviewing the deeds and land records.

47. Minutes of the Orphan Court, vol. 8, p. 485, August 1, 1842, MCCH. The entry dates Cyrus's death because it orders John G. Aikin, as administrator of William's estate, to compensate for the security that Cyrus, now deceased, could no longer provide.

48. Deposition, Lawrence S. Banks, October 24, 1861, Estate Case File 335, Folder No. 1, HMCPL.

49. "Great State Rights Whig Meeting," *Southern Argus,* December 11, 1838.

50. Jordan R. Dodd and Norman L. Moyes, eds., *Alabama Marriages, Early to 1825: A Research Tool* (Bountiful, Utah: Precision Indexing, 1990), 2; U.S. Census, 1830 and 1840; *Mobile Directory, or Strangers' Guide for 1839 by Thomas C. Fay* (Mobile: R. R. Dade, 1839), 44.

51. U.S. Census, 1850 and 1860, Free Population, Slave, Agricultural, and Industrial Schedules, Baldwin County, Alabama; John H. Moore, *Andrew Brown and Cypress Lumbering in the Old Southwest* (Baton Rouge: Louisiana State University Press, 1967), 12, 27, 113, 130–31.

52. Either 1800 or 1803 are more probable years of birth; they put him in his twenties when he married and began his legal career. Thomas M. Owen, *Dictionary of Alabama Biography,* 1978 ed., s.v. Aikin, John Gaston; Thomas W. Palmer, comp., *A Register of the Officers and Students of the University of Alabama, 1831–1901* (Tuscaloosa: The University, 1901), 253.

53. William R. Smith, *Reminiscences of a Long Life; Historical, Political, Personal, and Literary* (Washington, D.C.: W. R. Smith, 1889), 71; Owen, *Dictionary of Alabama Biography,* s.v. Aikin,

John Gaston; Alabama Senate Journal, 1826 Annual Session, January 3, 1827, http://www.legislature
.state.al.us/misc/history/acts_and_journals/1826/senate-journal/Jan_3.html [accessed May 24,
2010]; John G. Aikin, *A Digest of the Laws of the State of Alabama* (Philadelphia: Alexander Towar,
1833). The General Assembly paid John the following year; Act No. 147, Compensating John G.
Aikin for Certain Services, Approved 18 Jan. 1834, *Acts of the General Assembly of the State of
Alabama* (Tuscaloosa: May and Ferguson, 1834), 182.

54. Harry Toulmin, *A Digest of the Laws of the State of Alabama* (Cahaba, Ala.: Ginn & Cur-
tis, J. & J. Harper, Printers, 1823).

55. Aikin, *Digest of the Laws of the State of Alabama,* iii–v; John G. Aikin, *A Digest of the Laws
of the State of Alabama,* 2nd ed. (Tuscaloosa: D. Woodruff, 1836).

56. *Mobile Directory,* 44. John appeared in the next extant directory: *Mobile Directory, or
Strangers' Guide for 1842 by R. P. Vail* (Mobile: Dade & Thompson, 1842), 9.

57. U.S. Census, 1850, Free Population and Agricultural Schedules, Baldwin County,
Alabama.

58. U.S. Census, 1860, Free Population Schedule, Baldwin County, Alabama.

7

Born of the Aristocracy?

Professionals with Planter and Middle-Class Origins in Late Antebellum South Carolina

JENNIFER R. GREEN

I received a letter from brother John, my favorite brother and the man, who if any I model after[;] . . . you will love him for my sake Carrie and certainly for his own," nineteen-year-old Micah Jenkins wrote his fiancée about his oldest brother, describing John "of noble men the noblest." Four years later, when the brothers had families of their own and intertwined financial worlds, Micah wrote John: "No one can appreciate more than I the kindness and love which have made you more a father than a brother to me. . . . As Guardian and friend I have needed no other stimulus to manly exertion, than the desire to win your respect and esteem."[1] This South Carolinian identified 1855 to 1859, the years following their father's death and the ones in which John helped him start a school, as their closest. Micah's devotion to John illustrates more than family affection, however. Their relationship also provides a window onto the ways in which a professional class developed out of and alongside agriculturalists in the late antebellum South. Before the Civil War, Micah ran Kings Mountain Military Academy and middle brother Edward worked as a physician, while John ran plantations on Edisto and Mussleborough Islands. The older brother, thus, received considerable status from his (inherited) agricultural holdings, whereas the younger men were a part of the increasing number of professionals that surged in the region after 1840.

The first Jenkins son, named John after his father, was born around Thanksgiving 1824, at Old Hill, the family's plantation on Edisto Island. He became a successful South Carolinian, assuming the place his father's status and wealth granted the eldest son. The patterns of his life most closely followed those of the elite planter class. His father owned approximately 1300 acres (including unimproved land on 2 plantations) and just under 100 slaves. John Jenkins Sr.

bought another nearly one thousand-acre plantation (doubling his acreage) shortly before he died, when his oldest son was thirty years old. John Jr. had already been managing the estate, as the father's apparent illness put John's education and potential law career on hold around 1845.[2] John's primary employment was as a planter on the family land, what accounts labeled the "Estate," and which remained intact for at least five years after the father's 1854 death. John served in the South Carolina legislature from 1850 to 1852 and sat in the 1860 secession convention, where he joined his uncle Joseph and Micah's father-in-law. He gained prestigious connections from his status and reputation; for example, he was on friendly terms with Congressman Laurence M. Keitt, who joked with Jenkins about finding "an Edisto 'lassie'" to wed.[3] While Keitt may not have found an Edisto Island bride, John did, wedding Marcelline Murray in November 1851 or 1852.[4]

Given the prestige of plantation ownership, the career choices of the younger Jenkins brothers (and many similar young men) reflected the changing times and planters' family structure in accommodating professions. John gave up his career as a lawyer to run the family plantations, which could possibly have provided sufficient funds for the younger brothers to remain in agriculture. In 1856, for example, accounts recorded the estate's cotton sales at $7588 (and John's individual account earned $846 from cotton and $1900 from a "Check on Rail Road Bank"); yearly income of $8000 to $10,000 compared favorably to $515 for a clerk's salary or $1000 to $2500 for a professor's salary in the 1850s South. With three sisters also sharing the estate, a straight division of the plantations might have been impossible.[5] More likely, the Jenkins family preserved land and its associated status to maintain class stability. Without land, second son Edward selected a medical career and youngest son Micah became a military educator.

The second Jenkins son Edward, born in 1831, attended South Carolina College and then the state medical college in Charleston, the second of six medical schools started in the antebellum South. His generation found itself in a region altered by the development of the market economy, soil exhaustion, the evolving economy and ideology surrounding slavery, industrialization, and professionalization, to name a few of the major developments in the first half of the nineteenth century. In the words of one scholar, the market revolution limited "traditional routes to becoming a head of household through slave ownership and farming." Young southerners coming of age in those decades found very different circumstances and opportunities than their fathers had.[6] Growing numbers of planter younger sons appeared to accept the changes—young people everywhere usually accepted and embraced modern ideas more than their parents—and even when unsettled by them or worried about their personal prospects, they entered professions to find social stability (and avoid downward mobility).

The Jenkins brothers suggest a way in which planters' sons could adapt to professional careers. Each younger son found himself successively lower than his older brother in the social hierarchy: John was a planter; Edward, classically trained at a university, worked as a physician and received professional prestige from that socially acceptable occupation; Micah graduated from a state military school, practiced a professional career of moderate status (education), and as his business succeeded, hoped to purchase a plantation to move into a dual career. Sons' birth order launched them into a decreasing hierarchy of prestige, occupational status, and education and increasingly placed younger planters' sons into circumstances similar to those of the emerging middle class.

Indeed, these brothers illuminate the fluid class boundaries in the late antebellum South and highlight the emerging middle class's relationship to the plantation elite. The picture that emerges is a world in which planter ideology dominated but the concurrent acceptance of professions infiltrated their ideology. This changing worldview and occupational structure have become increasingly accepted in historical scholarship, but the distinctions between planters with professions and middle-class professionals still need clarity. Scholars, including myself, have asserted the differences—in status, economic situation, ideas of manhood and honor, slave and land ownership—between the planters and the emerging southern middle class. While economic and social demographics separated the social classes from each other, members of the antebellum middle economic rank tried to separate themselves from those groups below them and potentially from those above them. The emerging middle class was, by definition, in the "middle" of the white social structure, most clearly located between planters and yeomen (and clearly possessing higher status than laborers and African Americans). The southern middle class was employed in non-manual and primarily professional and nonagricultural occupations. Middle-class southerners possessed sufficient resources to have access to goods, but also had clear limits on their wealth. They began to demonstrate similar traits in their developing class awareness, especially in their social organization and values. Building on Jonathan Daniel Wells's southern middle class of urban commercial and professional men and incorporating rural professionals into the class, the group can be counted as greater than 10 percent of the southern population by 1860. This small but growing constituency of merchants, industrialists, teachers, doctors, and other non-manual workers fits into the social structure of white southerners between James Oakes's dual-career planters and Michele Gillespie's artisans cum manufacturers. How scholars decide between the labels of emerging middle class, small planter, and plain folk (whom Samuel Hyde Jr. identifies as agricultural members of the middle class) needs continued specificity, as Hyde himself suggests.[7]

Elite young southerners entered the professions of law and medicine, working alongside middle-class professionals.[8] Young men of both groups increased the number of physicians in the 1840 and 1850s, with an especially large spike in the 1850s, when physicians became 49 percent of southern professionals according to the 1860 census. Many of those newly minted doctors graduated from elite state universities in the South, which suggests the status of the occupation had increased alongside its professionalization, as seen in the formation of the American Medical Association in 1847. As more men entered professions, they slowly increased their occupations' status. By putting their sons or brothers into professions, planters encouraged professionalization, even if unintentionally. Some planters supported the growth of an industrial economy and society (with slavery, of course, and, same as all nineteenth-century Americans asserted, particular limits).[9] How much an occupation indicated men's shared class status, or shared values, needs to be further explored; individual Jenkins brothers' choices and the professionals' continued (personal and monetary) connection to their planter relations illuminate the complicated process of class formation in the Old South. Put simply, if the emerging middle class of the 1850s consisted in large part of professionals, did it include those professionals born of the planter class?

Identifying the social position of men like Edward and his brother Micah, born in the South Carolina planter aristocracy but employed as a military school superintendent, helps show the differences and similarities of professionals in the two classes. First, young men selected and entered careers with different class-based resources. Second, planter support of their professional kin illuminates the significant planter assets in comparison to those of the middle class. The prevalence of dual and agricultural careers among planters, third, contrasted middle-class occupational mobility. The increase in professional occupations, however, contributed to the continued prevalence of southern values in both groups; specifically, men of both classes possessed ambition but a final distinction between the value placed on planters' status versus that of nonagricultural occupations separated professional men with different class backgrounds.

Edward Jenkins's languid movement into his career and the number of options he had illustrate the clear advantages an elite son had over a middle-class youth in selecting his profession. In 1853, twenty-two-year-old Edward finished medical school and then continued his medical education in Paris, surely participating in the elite gentlemen's European tour. Taking European medical courses was not uncommon in the 1850s for young doctors who could afford it and would have been the path of those seeking (or possessing) elite status. Medical schools started professionalizing in the 1840s but had no standard curriculum and often offered only a one-year course; apprenticeship completed a young man's training.[10] Early on, Edward explained to John that France would not cost an extreme amount, as lectures were inexpensive. Unfortunately, he quickly suffered a series of calamities from the theft of $100 to typhoid fever. He took time to accustom himself to the language and did not appear to have overly applied himself to school. "Having commenced my Medical studies I am somewhat busy," Edward declared that November.[11]

By January 1854, Edward needed more cash and had begun to consider his future practice. He had spent the $700 in cash and credit line that John had provided and even borrowed money from a friend, a debt now totaling $400. He shared these concerns with John and not with their mother, to whom he wrote the day before he wrote his brother.[12] Clearly John controlled the family purse, an unsurprising situation within the family and gender expectations of the era.

In the same letter, Edward outlined different options for his medical future. Although he would "prefer to settle among my family and friends, that is on Edisto," Edward specifically wanted to avoid curtailing another doctor's "profession and means of support," which implies that he saw his career somewhat differently than as a means of support, that he accepted an ethical code that said one doctor should not compete with an existing practice, or that he acknowledged competition limited the viability of multiple practices in many areas. He asked John to help find him a position or to contact the local physician to do so. If family connections fell through, Edward then proposed St. Louis as the best place to settle because the city's population provided "that the opportunity is open to all and merit generally wins the day." A St. Louis practice would necessitate surgical training, which he proposed to pursue in Berlin or Vienna. "In which case [St. Louis,] I should be obliged to accept your kind offer, My Dear Brother, to the extent of enabling me to finish my studies," Edward reminded his older brother of the financial realities his career choices entailed.[13]

These plans came into question when the cotton market made family finances tight in early 1854 and, by June, Edward prepared to return home. He explained to his father that he appreciated his family financing his time in France, but "I fear that the embarrassment to which the furnishing of that sum has, and will give rise, will rend those benefits dearly bought." Yet the market sufficiently revived for John to send him $700 in August and suggest that he remain in Europe. Edward arranged for a subscription to the Charleston *Mercury* and told John, "You must pay for it out of my next remittance."[14] Family money supported the numerous permutations in preparation of his career.

Upon returning from France, Edward began his career as a doctor. He returned to South Carolina in 1855 and married cousin Isabella Jenkins of St. Paul's Parish that December. In early 1856, Edward brought his bride to Yorkville and joined an existing medical practice.[15] Early in his career, he struggled, securing a $1500 loan, an amount equal to a college professor's annual salary, while complaining that he could not even afford to keep a horse. He tried to find a specialty, prescribing drugs and moving into eye surgery. Throughout the 1850s, Edward focused on his professional career and apparently relied on that income for his livelihood; the cotton factors who managed all the family accounts recorded no income except that which he or John transferred into the account.[16]

Edward Jenkins demonstrated the slow entry into a career that a middle-class young man could not have afforded. Middle-class young men worried when they did not have a position upon graduating from school. "I am solely dependent upon my salary, not only temporarily but as the means whereby I may be able to prosecute my studies and carry out my intention of becoming a physician," nineteen-year-old William Finney complained soon after his military school graduation. Fatherless Finney needed to work as a teacher in order to become a doctor, very unlike Edward who enjoyed a European sojourn. An alumnus of Micah's alma mater, the South Carolina Military Academy (SCMA), described his mother having to teach for the family's survival and his own subsequent entry into teaching.[17] In contrast, Edward relied more on what educational historian Lawrence Cremin described as the Old South's "three significant educative relationships" of kin, role model, and employer.[18] Edward sought kin connections for an employer and possible role model, whereas middle-class men lacked those planter resources and more often relied on formal education and on a teaching salary to obtain that education.

Despite choosing a different path and occupation, Micah also reflects the resource differences between a middle-class youth and a planter's son. The youngest Jenkins brother arrived at Old Hill a full eleven years after his oldest brother John in December 1835 and entered SCMA in 1851. While the two oldest boys trained in the classical languages of Latin and Greek and entered expensive higher education, Micah received a practical education grounded in sciences and dedicated to promoting teaching careers. As did many families, the Jenkinses provided for the education and training of all members of the younger generation, even when it required sacrifice and often meant less schooling for the youngest ones. One of the many elite southerners who went north for university education, John attended Princeton University; arriving in the 1840s, however, put young John in the declining years of the trend as southerners increasingly turned to their region for education. Indeed, both of his younger brothers would attend schools in the South. The oldest two boys followed the pattern of South Carolina planter education: lowcountry men were the southerners most likely to attend school in Europe; when those youth went North, Princeton was the most frequently chosen university; and South Carolina College was, unsurprisingly, the most commonly selected southern institution. That university remained one of the most elite schools in the nation, rejecting curricular reforms that encouraged broader access to secondary education, reforms that had already begun infiltrating the region. These educational reforms promoted a non-classical curriculum and, as one byproduct, military schools; military institutes, such as the state-funded SCMA, which opened in 1842, served as cheaper and more vocational training. While some antebellum men equated military academies with "collegiate education" (even without conferring bachelor's degrees), the schools clearly had lower status than the classical education of state universities.[19] Micah's family must have accepted the limits on his career that a non-classical education meant and the status that SCMA provided its youngest boy.

While Edward was in Paris, Micah graduated from the Citadel, one of the SCMA campuses. No correspondence described why he enrolled in that school instead of the elite colleges that his brothers attended. His status as a martyred Confederate general—this organizer of the Palmetto Sharpshooters was killed in the confusion at the Wilderness in May 1864—has meant that extant collections and historical attention primarily represent interest in his wartime exploits. Micah's biographers suggest his love of the military as the reason he attended the state military academy, but without direct evidence, the reason could as easily have been monetary or vocational.[20] The Citadel encouraged a professional trajectory. Its graduates primarily entered white-collar professions, as 1857 graduate Henry Moore's record of the careers of the antebellum graduates indicates: "48 were teachers, 27 physicians, 20 lawyers, 16 civil engineers and architects, 15 farmers, 12 merchants, 9 ministers of the Gospel, 2 city officials, 3 editors, 1 railroad official, [and] 7 were dead."[21] Micah served as a teaching assistant as a senior and graduated valedictorian of his 1854 class. He joined the majority of his peers as an educator when he and classmate Asbury Coward started Kings Mountain Military Academy (KMMA), a preparatory school and one of the growing number of southern schools, in Yorkville, South Carolina, in January 1855.

On the cusp of his career choice, Micah applied to his older brothers, as Edward had also done. Micah solicited the guidance of family members, who apparently encouraged him into the law. Edward's brotherly advice to Micah on his "choice of a profession" was that teaching "would, perhaps, be the best method of commencing" a literary career. Edward ambitiously assumed Micah sought and would attain the goal of "most literary men," a professorship. Not attempting to dissuade his younger brother from teaching, Edward did qualify, "But I must say that I agree with the rest of the family in desiring you to make choice of the law." Micah's decision could wait, Edward felt, since he was young, but once a choice was made, it seemed to have a finality to it. "Remember that your <u>future</u> hangs on <u>your</u> <u>decision</u>," he declared.[22] His view suggests that once a man entered a profession, that identification stayed with him and encouraged or restricted his mobility according the status of the selected profession. Although planters' sons could use the time that family resources allowed them to decide on a profession, it is apparent that occupation was as important a marker of status for the elite and their progeny as it was for emerging middle-class professionals.

The status that the professional Jenkins brothers found in their occupations was supported and gained with assistance from the plantations their family owned. Both Edward's and Micah's start in professions illustrates how money followed those choices in a planter family. The family clearly supported the professional choices of the younger sons, providing both financial and moral support. Regardless of region and class, family was the cradle of a young man's life choices. The Jenkinses were no exception. Scholars of the northern middle class have well developed this conception, and families had at least equal significance in the Old South.[23] In this family, John necessarily had to be involved with the establishment and early years of KMMA as Micah and his business partner Coward were not yet twenty-one years old. "I am but too sorry that my business connections are so limited, as to cause me to turn to you with the trouble at all. But I forget that as an '<u>Infant</u> of tender years' such is obliged to be the case," Micah apologized in the school's first year.[24] John, unsurprising given the circumstances, took the lead in many of the financial transactions over the next five years. He made financial contacts and contracts in Micah's name (and at Micah's behest). In August 1859, months before his twenty-fourth birthday, Micah finally assumed full legal responsibility for his financial contracts.[25] John's assistance and financing indicated his support of Micah's professional choice, and monetary exchanges in the family demonstrate the sustenance of both young professionals: money to start and expand their careers. The resources that the estate provided to Edward and Micah were beyond those available to most members of the emerging middle class.

Micah used his greater than middle-class resources as his school, KMMA, succeeded in quick order. Within the first year, the cadet corps jumped from forty to seventy. Jenkins and Coward felt secure enough to arrange for a new building, each contributing $5000. The enormous sum approximated the sales price of the Jenkins family plantation sold in 1855 and five years of either's professional salary. Micah justified the debt: "Our prospects are such as warrant, the step proposed."[26] He wrote to John about getting an advance on his share of their father's estate paid out in annual installments. "I would prefer to borrow and assume the debt to be paid off as I proposed above, without parting with any property that may fall to my share."[27] Micah willingly went into debt for new barracks to expand his school; his optimism about the repayment of the loans, however, verged on naïveté. "I trust and hope that the money may be obtained without disembarrassment, and further trouble to you," he explained to John even as he reported that they were compelled "to add onto one building and buy furniture for $500; this should end our outlay." In addition to family expenditures, Micah owed Dr. Bailey $6000, and a $2000 loan was recorded to the estate on May 7, 1856, and one to Edward for $807.[28] Four years later Micah acknowledged that he had not, as of that date, repaid any of a $6000 loan, half of which was coming due. He could not afford such large sums of cash—five to ten times the average income for a white-collar clerk or teacher—yet his willingness to incur them shows his commitment to the enterprise and his professional career. It also suggests the family resources he knew he could fall back on. The significance of planter support should be clear. The start of KMMA resembled that of numerous schools started by southern middle-class educators in the 1840s and 1850s. However, its rapid expansion, influx of capital, and insertion of classics into the curriculum (taught by Jenkins family friend and Edisto local Cato Seabrook, who had received the classical education of his elite family) belie its founder's higher than middle-class status and resources.

Throughout the ebb and flow of the relationship, money was integral to the brothers' exchanges. Although nominally the family patriarch after his father's death, John made few personal payments to either of his brothers. Jenkins family financial relationships revolved primarily around their father's estate. The estate made direct payments to each son as cotton income came in. While John received steady cash payments of $275 to $580 between 1855 and 1860, the younger brothers each received large amounts of cash as part of their inheritance and recouped very little in subsequent years.[29] Edward's European trip and resettlement cost the estate more than $1100 (and as much as $3000) by 1855, and Micah received at least $4000 from the estate in 1855 and 1856. Then, between 1858 and 1861, Edward received no direct payments from the estate and Micah, only $56.90 in 1860.[30] Edward's relocation to Yorkville in 1855 facilitated the social and financial connections between the younger siblings; Micah paid Edward $200 in August 1856, accepted a $500 loan from him 2 months later, but also line-itemed him almost $300 (minus "little debts I have settled for him"). Family finances were never completely separate.[31]

This money aided the professional Jenkinses at the same time that it clearly set them and similarly positioned men apart from the emerging southern middle class. James Oakes identifies the necessity to struggle and lack of financial security as significant differences between planters and those slave owners who remained in the middle class.[32] It likewise reflects a divergence between planters (elite to small) and the nonagricultural middle class. The ability to purchase goods, as well as access education, separated the upper class from the middle class regardless of region.[33] While both planters and the middle class incurred debt, the meaning and ability to pay off debt would have been very different between the classes. Planters, even Oakes's middle-class slaveholders for that matter, possessed resources superior to those of the average middle-class man and, by definition, possessed human property, which in itself conveyed prestige. Even when lacking cash, planters and their offspring had access to loans, such as the one Legare and Colcock agree to arrange for John in 1854 or the one Micah arranged with planter neighbor Dr. Bailey.[34]

The resources of time, kin, and wealth were incongruous between planter- and middle-class professionals. Thus, the former created dual careers for themselves and the latter built the status of and encouraged the professionalization of their occupations. Edward Jenkins's first suggestion when he looked to establishing his medical career was to enter practice with Dr. Bailey, who apparently owned a plantation and a medical practice on Edisto. A map of Edisto in the 1850s indicates a Bailey with a plantation near the Jenkins's family estate and numerous financial exchanges, including the $6000 barracks loan, connected the Jenkins brothers to a Dr. Bailey. That man appears to have had a dual career, as physician and planter; he even appears to have engaged in the common practice of money lending between planters, a prevalent source of income.[35] William Scarborough's extensive study of elite planters describes approximately 20 percent of them as having some type of dual career, usually commercial occupations. Considering small slave owners, Oakes attributes the use of dual careers to enhancing upward mobility as the "defining characteristic of middle-class slave owners."[36] Thus, the highest ranks of southern society were primarily agricultural, although some of those men also worked in a nonagricultural occupation.

Young men just starting in their careers often did not possess the land to have a dual career that included agriculture. If from a landowning family, their fathers were usually still alive (and kept possession of the family lands) or that plantation went to the oldest son.[37] Members of the emerging southern middle class usually possessed no land. Thus, younger men and especially middle-class youths from military schools, like Micah's alma mater, were more likely to engage in sequential careers rather than dual careers. They moved between white-collar jobs to find the most lucrative and prestigious one, such as parlaying a clerkship or teaching into a law career. Men similar to William M. Tennent Jr., Citadel valedictorian three years after Micah, taught a few years until he passed the bar in January 1860. Indeed, nearly half of military academy alumni educators left teaching for other careers.[38] Micah, as a third son, followed the professional young men both of the aristocracy and of the emerging middle class.

The Jenkins brothers' experience reflects a final difference in the complexity of class differentiation and formation. Southerners, regardless of class, shared characteristics and, as the antebellum years passed, professionals of middle-class and planter origin valued regional and professional traits. Occupation created similarities between men in the learned professions, whether their origins were planter stock or middle class; it is unsurprising that like-minded men chose the same careers and that the demands of the career molded them. Specifically, they ambitiously dreamt of professional success because they accepted the legitimacy and status of the professional occupations in which they worked (and usually of other professions). In distinct ways, however, the goals of men of the two classes reflected their class origins. While members of both groups surely had a similar drive to raise themselves in the southern male hierarchy, their ideals of status increasingly differed as the years advanced.[39]

By the 1850s, some southerners, even some planters, accepted professional values. After Micah started his school in 1855, his father's elder brother Joseph E. Jenkins sent two thoughtful letters that detailed the older generation's judgment. (The opinion of John Jenkins Sr. was unavailable, as he had already passed away.) This planter clearly promoted the idea of entrepreneurship: "Were I twenty years younger, that is to say forty three instead of sixty three; I would come up to you to see the Jenkins who has had the energy, and enterprise to rouse himself from his lair, and shaking off the tramels of cotton corn and potatoes, declare himself a man resolved to effect for himself, that independance which results from ones own exertions—to seek out a path for himself, of reputation and wealth, in fine to make his name known and felt as of some importance. The very attempt is an honor, and let there be no fear as to the success."[40] The elder Jenkins clearly endorsed Micah's career choice of education, specifically praising it over agriculture. At the same time, however, he used the language of the traditional southern elite. He described the "honor" of his nephew's pursuits and the "reputation" that they would bring the young man; this centrality of southern honor and its public face reflected southern elite ideals. He also promoted the more professional values of nonagricultural occupation, individualism, and energy.[41] The compliments equated Micah's profession with planting or law. The praise of Micah's independence, however, contrasted the uncle's description of his own son's career: "I put him under Attorney Genl Bailey for the study of law."[42] The status of a teaching career and Micah's semi-independence show the acceptable hierarchy of sons— these things were accepted for third-born Micah though not necessarily for his cousin, an eldest boy—and reflect the rise of professional approval among elite South Carolinians.

All three Jenkins brothers had ambition for their careers and for success in the larger world. John maintained the largest two plantations and entered legislative service, although he never expressed personal ambitions to his younger brothers in extant letters. Edward certainly sought professional advancement, notoriety, and wealth when he presented his prospects for his own career and for those of his brothers. "Besides, Brother John, if you aim at political distinction, which I believe and hope you do, the Law is the best stepping stone," Edward counseled.[43] Young Micah was as overtly ambitious as his elder brother. When asked about Micah for a memorial, two former Citadel classmates characterized Jenkins as "ambitious." His friend and colleague Coward commented, "Was he ambitious? Yes; he was full of an ambition free from all sordid or selfish taint—an ambition for high achievement in the cause of humanity and country."[44] Although much of Coward's praise focused on military accomplishments and moved into the prosaic hyperbole of nineteenth-century rhetoric, Micah's expanding his school, choosing Carrie Jamison as a wife, and pursuing his career demonstrated his ambition. His actions also show the distinct vision of status that an elite son held as opposed to his middle-class contemporaries.

In early 1855, even as nineteen-year-old Micah began to make plans to settle down, he still aspired to greater success. He started the military school at Kings Mountain and, within a year, doubled the size of the student body and buildings with loans and family money. He validated his choice by stressing the dignity of teaching, "Do you think that I would be content to aim no higher than my present position. Tis true, most honorable, and fortune and reputation I am morally certain can be made, but is this all?"[45] He entered the profession of teaching, which was gaining in stature but never achieved the highest status, and acknowledged some would not think him well settled. One of Jenkins's former Citadel classmates, John P. Thomas, provides an interesting parallel to Micah. Thomas's father stopped practicing medicine in 1834 and relied on his plantation; apparently he was a planter who moved up the social hierarchy to end his dual career. The son graduated from the Citadel the year Micah arrived and became a military educator; Thomas's younger brother taught (and died) at KMMA. The Thomas brothers mirrored the pattern of most military school alumni and middle-class men: they taught rather than start a school as it was safer and no capital was needed, and maintained the approximately 90 percent nonagricultural rate among Citadel alumni.[46] Likewise, 1846 Citadel alumnus W. J. Magill went on to teach at Kentucky Military Institute and advanced to the position of commandant of the Georgia Military Institute (GMI) by 1860; J. M. Richardson (Class of 1852) taught at both GMI and Hillsboro Military Academy in North Carolina. Micah Jenkins, in contrast, acted the entrepreneur, developed his school, and used family money to attempt to regain his foothold in the agricultural elite.

Even the social position of Micah's fiancée reflected his ambition and its plantation focus. At the young age of nineteen, he informed his brother of his engagement to eighteen-year-old Caroline "Carrie" Jamison. Her father, David F. Jamison, was a planter (comparable to John Jenkins Sr., with 76 slaves and 2000 acres in 1860) with a dual career as a former lawyer and legislator in the Barnwell district of South Carolina. He was also the senator who intro-duced the bill for SCMA, attended the Southern Rights Convention of 1852, and chaired the South Carolina secession convention. Interestingly, however, Micah's professional leanings mix yet again with his class status; the Jamison family possessed a long line of professional men: David Jamison's father had been a doctor as was the man married to his father's eldest sister. Carrie's grandfather moved into plantation ownership with land from his marriage (same as Old Hill entered the Jenkins family with the boys' mother).[47] Despite the families' encouraging their waiting, the couple wed on July 3, 1856, and had a fruitful life with four sons living at KMMA.

Over the next four years, Micah fulfilled his ambition via professional av-enues and continued to employ family resources. After Edward returned from France, Micah dispatched a letter to John that detailed "our" starting a phar-macy.[48] He also commenced studying law, although in an apparently cursory way: "by myself," he noted in April 1855. "I have resumed the study of law, and intend to prosecute it with vigor this session, I do not expect to do much at it next session," Micah told Carrie nine months later.[49] Biographer James Swisher claims Micah studied law with Yorkville lawyer William Wilson to appease John, but at least by 1859 Micah presented his own reasons for look-ing for a different source of income. He was twenty-three years old with two young sons and thousands of dollars in debt. The mention of law had slipped from his letters between January 1856 and 1859, interestingly, the same years he felt the closest connection to John, as indicated in this essay's opening. Those were years when Micah worried about paying off his debts, calculating doing so through his profession of teaching, until 1859, when his plans turned to purchasing a plantation. "I have commenced in earnest the study of law. I am much, much worried about my debts and prospects for the future and must redouble my efforts to advance," Micah informed his brother about the pos-sibilities of purchasing land in Yorkville.[50] It is important to note that Micah pursued financial gain primarily through professions (maintaining the school into which he had put so many years and dollars and also discussing the law) and later selected agriculture.

Although their connection to plantations is clear, the younger Jenkinses wrote with the distance from agricultural concerns that only nonagricultural men could feel. In a society where community evaluation of family name could be everything, John must have felt the pressure to maintain the standing of his family in a way the younger, and nonagricultural, brothers did not. Micah and Edward expressed concern about John's state of mind about the land, rather than concern about the condition of the land itself. "I hope your mind is relieved as to the state of the crop," Micah told John. Six months later, he reiterated his disconnection to the family land: "It is with deep regret that I notice no improvement in the sales of cotton and still see your advertizement for the sale of the [family home] 'Old Hill' unanswered. I fully appreciate your difficulties and consider it my greatest grief that I can do nothing but give my best wishes and hopes."[51] The professional brothers thought only remotely about the crops, while John actually worried about them. John's congratulations to Micah on the birth of a son, for example, included a worry about caterpillars destroying the cotton crop and a note about the price of a parcel of land.[52] Simply put, professionals Micah and Edward were more detached from the land than John was.

Thus, although some values crossed class lines, a closer examination of particular traits reveals disparities, especially in the views of manhood and of status. While the younger generation of the planter class contemporary with the Jenkins brothers increasingly entered professions, they found the occupations in juxtaposition to the male ideal they learned in antebellum elite colleges, according to Stephen Berry. He asks, "How could they be contented clerks and mechanics—as their Yankee brethren seemed to be—when their expectations for themselves ran always towards energy and éclat?" The elite southern ideal of manhood remained distinct from the development of the market. Middle-class men, sharing some characteristics across the nation, found no such disjunctions because their education usually promoted professional values; military education such as SCMA forced young men to accept "mundane" routine. Alumnus Micah dreamt of better careers, but neither solely "éclat" nor the traditional elite manhood of mastery.[53] He suggests both the desire for what Berry called southern elite "éclat" and also a fundamental acceptance of routine.

Of even greater variation than manhood was the vision of status and success held by professional sons of the elite and of the developing middle class. Young elites used education and wealth (specifically their fathers' land and slaves) to enter professional occupations in hopes of leveraging those jobs to gain their ideal of status. They often wanted to maintain planter status wherein mobility was achieved through land and slave ownership. Below the ranks of planters, men such as Oakes's "middle-class slaveholders," combining their agricultural lives with a classical education and professional occupation, hoped to acquire more slaves and land and to rise into the planter class. This goal of slave and land ownership (and mastery, the cultural value that they encouraged) was central to the planter and dominant southern definition of mobility and status. Slave owners and their kin generally accepted this elite model of success; in contrast, the emerging middle class sought professional status and wealth. They could not benefit from the patrimony and/or advances that money and position gave the young men born into the aristocracy.[54] Some middle-class men emulated planters, craving their status and the possessions that provided that status. Others (consciously or not) redefined social status, created social mobility via professionalization, and distanced themselves from the elite. Men with the latter beliefs remained in professions and were disconnected from the land. The former group believed the learned professionals to be of lower but acceptable status, whereas the latter found its highest status in managerial and professional options. Here rests a critical distinction between men with connections to planters (with or without nonagricultural jobs) and men of the emerging middle class (who may or may not have owned slaves): By the late antebellum years, men in the middle social position worked to improve the status of their rank rather than to move into plantations.

Overall, Micah never broke away from his family or his class background. He defined himself professionally and spent years building his school (and his reputation in Yorkville). However, by 1859, he illustrated dominant elite ideology, looking into plantation ownership. He suggested reorganizing or disbanding his father's estate so that he could purchase a local plantation. "I would have no responsibility rest upon any but myself," he asserted, "nor would I for an instant desire what was not justly mine or what could be objected to, or unfair any of you [sic]." Micah hesitated over John's "adverse opinion" but indicated he would buy the land if sold at a "nominal price." Micah was not alone in parlaying professional profit into a plantation. That path followed the standard southern ideal of mobility and status. James Legare, cofounder of the cotton factor firm that held the Jenkins family money, himself used the profits from his mercantile business to purchase a large plantation with hundreds of slaves in the 1850s.[55] In the end, Micah gave up the plantation he discussed, purchased a 300-acre farm near Yorkville, and sent for family-owned slaves from Edisto to work it. He embraced this status, increasing the number of slaves he owned to twelve in the 1860 census, although the brothers' combined slave ownership remained almost constant between 1854 and 1860. This fact suggests a reallocation of enslaved property within the estate.[56]

The case study of the Jenkinses complicates some of our assumptions about southern professionals and the emerging middle class. Micah's years working as a military educator—a solidly middle-class status occupation—and then, just before the war's outbreak, move to agriculture and slave ownership from his family estate ended up appearing very different from the career trajectory of a middle-class professional. Men of this transitional generation—growing up at the same time as professional occupations increased and the middle class emerged—call into question a direct and uncomplicated equating of professional with middle class.

Indeed, southerners such as the Jenkins brothers indicate that all professionals did not have identical characteristics and that occupation cannot be the sole definitional criterion for social class. Professionals in planter families suggest how difficult it can be to separate the planter elite and the emerging middle class. Scholars need to seek clear criteria for class identification, and the continued exploration of segments of the middle class and of the group's formation aid this work. Existence in the middle social position, thus "middle class" between elite and poor, and their location in the occupational structure, predominantly non-manual and nonagricultural work, encouraged the development of social arrangements (especially family and associations) and values in many members of the group; middle-class men promoted education, professionalism, and self-discipline whether they lived in the North or the South.

Given these criteria members of that class would rarely have been born of the aristocracy. The slow entry into a profession and the options available illustrate a central schism between planters' sons (consider the evidence of Edward Jenkins) and middle-class offspring. The money and connections that supported planter sons meant, furthermore, that they possessed a greater access to goods than middle-class individuals. The reliance on agricultural careers among planter kin, even if dual careers, opposed the middle class's white-collar focus. The larger connection of the emerging southern middle class to agricultural careers remains open for continued investigation.

Finally, the Jenkins men did not solely see their lives as professionals, as many members of the emerging middle class did. In fact, they indicate just how slow and overlapping the process of class development was. Success for the middle class came from ambition and professionalization, whereas among plantation families the vision of success was primarily status and wealth brought by land and slave ownership. The entry of planters' sons into professions both supported the development of the emerging middle class and concurrently reinforced the master-class dominant model of mobility. The Jenkins family suggests that planters and the developing middle class were not antagonistic and confirms that a legitimacy for professions was emerging in the Old South, certainly by the 1850s.

The Jenkinses indicate the shared values and also the differences in those values between classes in the late antebellum South. The social and occupational structure that privileged planters was the dominant model, but the growth in professionalization and numbers of professionals encouraged what scholars have identified as middle-class ideals. Even more specifically, middle-class professionals built their status on a respect for knowledge (whether legal, medical, or scientific) not a respect for family, land, and slave ownerships; indeed, this valuation of specialized knowledge was central to the national process of professionalization. Elite values could and did coincide with those of the professional middle class: marriage, lucrative and prestigious careers, and community reputation. Edward and Micah were "ambitious" young men, but Micah's goals and definition of status more closely followed those of the master class than those of the emerging middle class. Men's family backgrounds—especially the resource disparity of the classes—show the complicated picture of professionals and the middle class in the late antebellum South.

NOTES

1. MJ to [Carrie Jamison], May 10, 1855 (first and second quotations), Micah Jenkins Papers, South Caroliniana Library, University of South Carolina, Columbia (hereafter SCL); MJ to JJ, August 29, 1859 (third quotation), John Jenkins Papers, SCL. In these endnotes, the Jenkins brothers are identified by initials.

2. EJ to JJ, October 7, 1853, John Jenkins Papers, SCL. John Jenkins Sr. owned forty-five slaves in the 1850 census and ninety-eight in the official postmortem inventory of May 25, 1855. "Inventory and Appraisement of the Goods and Chattels of John Jenkins Sr. of Edisto Island Planter deceased," *Inventories, Appraisements and Sales Records,* pp. 282–83, South Carolina Department of Archives and History (hereafter SCDAH). Ted Weaver, "The Future's Promise: The Civil War Correspondence of Micah Jenkins" (M.A. thesis, Clemson University, 1996), 11; John Donald Duncan, "Pages from Froissart: The Ante-Bellum Career of Micah Jenkins" (M.A. thesis, University of South Carolina, 1961), 35; James J. Baldwin III, *The Struck Eagle: A Biography of Brigadier General Micah Jenkins, and a History of the Fifth South Carolina Volunteers and the Palmetto Sharpshooters* (Shippensburg, Pa.: Burd Street Press, 1996), 4, 10.

3. L. M. Keitt to JJ, July 12, 1853, John Jenkins Papers, SCL.

4. http://janesgenealogy.info/sc_colleton/lee-marr.html [accessed January 30, 2008]. John's marriage is recorded in 1859 but chronology (and the fact that a son was born in 1854) suggest that the correct date is either 1851 or 1852.

5. Entries for Estate of John Jenkins Sr. and John Jenkins Jr., Legare and Colcock Account Books, South Carolina Historical Society (hereafter SCHS). Robert A. Margo, *Wages and Labor Markets in the United States, 1820–1860* (Chicago: University of Chicago Press, 2000), 45, uses the designation "white-collar labor" in the South Atlantic region (Maryland, Virginia, the Carolinas, Georgia, and Florida); Colin B. Burke, *American Collegiate Populations: A Test of the Traditional View* (New York: New York University Press, 1982), 48.

6. Steven M. Stowe, *Doctoring the South: Southern Physicians and Everyday Medicine in the Mid-Nineteenth Century* (Chapel Hill: University of North Carolina Press, 2004), 8–9; Peter S. Carmichael, *The Last Generation: Young Virginians in Peace, War and Reunion* (Chapel Hill: University of North Carolina Press, 2005), ch. 2, 37 (quotation); Jonathan Daniel Wells, *The Origins of the Southern Middle Class, 1800–1861* (Chapel Hill: University of North Carolina Press, 2004).

7. Oakes, *The Ruling Race: A History of American Slaveholders* (New York: Vantage Books, 1982); Gillespie, *Free Labor in an Unfree World: White Artisans in the Slaveholding Georgia, 1789–1860* (Athens: University of Georgia Press, 2000); Wells, *Origins of the Southern Middle Class;* Samuel C. Hyde Jr., "*Plain Folk* Reconsidered: Historiographical Ambiguity in Search of Definition," *Journal of Southern History* 71 (November 2005): 803–30.

8. In the antebellum period, elite southerners were planters, based on the status conferred on that occupation; differences certainly existed within the ranks of planters (usually identified as small, middling, and elite). Thanks to Jennie Goloboy at the Society for Historians of the Early American Republic Annual Meeting, July 19, 2009, for pointing out the need to clarify elite versus planter.

9. Recent scholars, including Jonathan Daniel Wells, Tom Downey, Chad Morgan, and Bruce Eelman, have described the planter support for such development.

10. Stowe, *Doctoring the South,* 21–25.

11. EJ to JJ, August 12, 1853, October 7, 1853, November 11, 1853, John Jenkins Papers, SCL.

12. EJ to Mother, January 12, 1854; EJ to JJ, January 13, 1854, John Jenkins Papers, SCL.

13. EJ to JJ, January 13, 1854, John Jenkins Papers, SCL.

14. EJ to JJ Sr., June 18, 1854 (first quotation); EJ to Sister, August 27, 1854; EJ to JJ, August 8, 1854 (second quotation), John Jenkins Papers, SCL.

15. Duncan, "Pages from Froissart," 22–23.

16. EJ to JJ, April 2, 1856, April 15, 1856, John Jenkins Papers, SCL; Edward Jenkins entry, Legare and Colcock Account Books, SCHS. Edward paid for guano in 1857 but not previously or subsequently so he may have owned land.

17. William Finney to Francis H. Smith, November 20, 1848, Preston Library, Virginia Military Institute Archives (hereafter VMI Archives); Victor Manget, unpublished memoir, The Citadel Archives and Museum (hereafter CIT).

18. Lawrence A. Cremin, *American Education: The National Experience, 1783–1876* (New York; Harper and Row Publishers, 1980), 365.

19. Recommendation letter, [1841] (quotation), Carlton Munford student file, VMI Archives; William Kauffman Scarborough, *Masters of the Big House: Elite Slaveholders of the Mid-Nineteenth-Century South* (Baton Rouge: Louisiana State University Press, 2003), Table 3, 68; Michael Sugrue, "South Carolina College: The Education of an Antebellum Elite" (Ph.D. diss., Columbia University, 1992). On southern education, see Jennifer R. Green, *Military Education and the Emerging Middle Class in the Old South* (New York: Cambridge University Press, 2008).

20. On Jenkins, see E. T. Crowson, "Jenkins, Coward, and the Yorkville Boys," *Alumni News* (Winter 1974–75), CIT, 3–4; James K. Swisher, *Prince of Edisto: Brigadier General Micah Jenkins, C.S.A.* (Berryville, Va.: Rockbridge Publishing Co., 1996), 4, 23–24; Baldwin, *Struck Eagle*; John P. Thomas, *Career and Character of General Micah Jenkins, C.S.A.* (1903; reprint, Charleston: The Citadel Christian Heritage Series, 2002).

21. Henry Moore, unpublished memoir, typescript, 1899, CIT. His findings closely match extant data.

22. EJ to Bunch [MJ], June 21, 1854, John Jenkins Papers, SCL. Emphasis original. A similar point is made in Samuel Garland to Samuel Garland Sr., January 12, 1848, Virginia Historical Society.

23. Cremin's model suggests families' dominance in career choice and placement (although it appears to stress elite families); Jane Turner Censer, *North Carolina Planters and Their Children, 1800–1860* (Baton Rouge: Louisiana State University Press, 1984); Mary P. Ryan, *Cradle of the Middle Class: The Family in Oneida County, New York, 1790–1865* (New York: Cambridge University Press, 1981); Steven M. Stowe, *Intimacy and Power in the Old South: Ritual in the Lives of the Planters* (Baltimore: Johns Hopkins University Press, 1987), esp. Part I, ch. 3.

24. MJ to JJ, August 30, 1855, John Jenkins Papers, SCL.

25. MJ to JJ, August 16, 1856, August 8, 1859, John Jenkins Papers, SCL.

26. MJ to Brother [JJ], March 22, 1855, Micah Jenkins Papers, Folder 1, Rare Books, Manuscript and Special Collections Library, Duke University. MJ to JJ, August 14, 1855, August 30, [1855], John Jenkins Papers, SCL.

27. MJ to JJ, August 30, [1855], John Jenkins Papers, SCL.

28. MJ to JJ, January 22, 1856 (first quotation), October 20, 1856 (second quotation), John Jenkins Papers, SCL. Misspelling in original.

29. Over the years, John sold a plantation inherited through his mother for $5467 to pay debts and a bond for $4420. Both transactions indicate the patrimony and resources available to these young men. Legare and Colcock to JJ, January 26, 1854, John Jenkins Papers, SCL; Account books, SCHS.

30. EJ to JJ, January 13, 1854; MJ to JJ, April 2, 1856, John Jenkins Papers, SCL.

31. MJ to JJ, August 16, 1856, October 20, 1856, John Jenkins Papers, SCL.

32. Oakes, *Ruling Race,* 62–65.

33. See, for example, Stuart M. Blumin, "The Hypothesis of the Middle-Class Formation in Nineteenth-Century America: A Critique and Some Proposals," *American Historical Review* 90 (1985): 299–338.

34. Legare and Colcock to JJ, January 26, 1854, John Jenkins Paper, SCL; Account books, SCHS.

35. Scarborough, *Masters of the Big House,* 222.

36. Scarborough, *Masters of the Big House;* Oakes, *Ruling Race,* 58; http://www.edistomuseum .org/map.asp [accessed May 25, 2008].

37. Joan E. Cashin, *A Family Venture: Men and Women on the Southern Frontier* (New York: Oxford University Press, 1991), ch. 2, finds that southern men usually inherited at the age of twenty-seven.

38. W. M. Tennent papers, SCL. I discuss careers and networking in greater depth in *Military Education and the Emerging Middle Class in the Old South.*

39. Stowe, *Intimacy and Power;* see, for example, Craig Thompson Friend and Lorri Glover, eds., *Southern Manhood: Perspectives on Masculinity in the Old South* (Athens: University of Georgia Press, 2004).

40. Joseph E. Jenkins to MJ, [1856], Micah Jenkins Papers, SCL. Misspelling and missing punctuation in original.

41. Numerous texts well describe southern honor and elite culture, especially Bertram Wyatt-Brown, *Southern Honor: Ethics and Behavior in the Old South* (New York: Oxford University Press, 1982), and Kenneth S. Greenberg, *Honor and Slavery: Lies, Duels, Noses, Masks, Dressing as a Woman, Gifts, Strangers, Humanitarianism, Death, Slave Rebellions, the Proslavery Argument, Baseball, Hunting, and Gambling in the Old South* (Princeton: Princeton University Press, 1996). Scarborough, *Masters of the Big House,* finds that elite planters valued professional traits that aided in their success.

42. Joseph Jenkins to MJ, January 22, 1856, John Jenkins Papers, SCL.

43. EJ to JJ, October 7, 1853, John Jenkins Papers, SCL.

44. Thomas, *Career and Character,* 11 (first quotation), 4 (second quotation).

45. MJ to [Carrie Jamison], May 10, 1855, Micah Jenkins Papers, SCL.

46. Moore, memoir, CIT; *Official Register of the South Carolina Military Academy* (Charleston: R. W. Gibbes, 1860), 21–24; John Peyre Thomas, *The History of the South Carolina Military Academy* (Charleston: Walker, Evans and Cogswell Co., 1893), 258–69; *Alumni Register,* CIT. Only living class members are included in statistics.

47. MJ to JJ, March 20, 1855, Micah Jenkins Papers, Duke University; Duncan, "Pages from Froissart," 32; Swisher, *Prince of Edisto,* 17; http://bellsouthpwp.net/j/a/jamison_clan/p20.htm [accessed January 30, 2008].

48. MJ to JJ, February 24, 1856, February 27, 1856, John Jenkins Papers, SCL.

49. MJ to JJ, April 22, 1855, January 27, 1856 (quotation), John Jenkins Papers, SCL.

50. MJ to JJ, July 4, 1859, John Jenkins Papers, SCL. Swisher, *Prince of Edisto,* 11.

51. MJ to JJ, August 16, 1856 (first quotation); MJ to JJ, February 14, 1855 (second quotation),

John Jenkins Papers, SCL. Micah's letter to John did not mention the ongoing legal procedures about Old Hill; three days earlier the court had awarded Edward guardianship of Micah and his younger sisters so that the family could receive a judgment to sell the plantation; Bill #115, *Charleston Equity Bills*, 1855, SCDAH.

52. JJ to MJ, July 27, 1857, Micah Jenkins Papers, SCL.

53. Berry, *All that Makes a Man: Love and Ambition in the Civil War South* (New York: Oxford University Press, 2003), 35. On manhood, also see Friend and Glover, *Southern Manhood*, and Nicholas L. Syrett, *The Company He Keeps: A History of White College Fraternities* (Chapel Hill: University of North Carolina Press, 2009).

54. Oakes, *Ruling Race*, x, 52–57, 62–65.

55. MJ to JJ, August 8, 1859 (quotations), John Jenkins Papers, SCL; Scarborough, *Masters of the Big House*, 230.

56. "Inventory and Appraisement," U.S. Census, 1860, Slave Schedules, SCDAH.

8

Navigating "the Muddy Stream of Party Politics"
Sectional Politics and the Southern Bourgeoisie

FRANK TOWERS

li Yates Reese, a minister as well as the newspaper editor and book publisher for the Baltimore Conference of the Methodist Episcopal Church (MEC), had a complicated relationship with politics. In 1853, Reese won election as a Whig to the Baltimore city council; four years later, he served as a school commissioner for the anti-immigrant and anti-Catholic American Party (also called Know Nothings because of their origins as a secret society). In addition to party activism, Reese worked for nonpartisan temperance societies that sought a legislative ban on making and selling alcohol. Yet, despite this political engagement, Reese criticized political parties, including his own, as corrupters of public life. Outraged at local Know Nothings' reliance on street gangs as election-day muscle, Reese editorialized that "the muddy stream of party politics is, in this country, too generally suffered to taint the pure fountain of justice . . . Hold your opinions—vote your sentiments—but beware of party strife and bitterness."[1]

This call to participate in politics while avoiding partisan excess extended to the sectional conflict that, in 1845, prompted a majority of proslavery conferences to form a breakaway southern branch of the MEC. The slavery issue was especially delicate for Reese's Baltimore Conference, whose jurisdiction straddled the Mason-Dixon Line. The Baltimore Conference remained in the national MEC, which barred slaveholders from preaching but allowed them as church members. Reese maintained a "conservative and nonpartisan" editorial stance on all political issues, especially slavery and sectionalism, but neither he nor his church could avoid calamity during the secession crisis of 1860–61. In 1861, the Baltimore Conference split into antislavery, proslavery/pro-Union, and proslavery/pro-Confederacy factions in reaction to a new MEC ban on association with slaveholders. The schism, which also ruined the Conference's publishing house, came on top of the death of Reese's wife one year previous. Adding to these woes, friends noticed that Reese was "disturbed by the Civil War in the country." Although under the care of a worried sibling, on September 14, 1861, Reese ended his life by slashing his throat.[2] Politics alone do not explain Rees's suicide, but they surely contributed to the despair prompted by his family and business misfortunes. In this light, Reese's warning about the "muddy stream of party politics" foreshadowed how the secession crisis, a fundamentally political process, derailed the middle-class reform vision suggested in his earlier activism.

Reese's concerns about political morality were not unique to his social experience but they had a special resonance with other middle-class values such as devotion to work and profit on the one hand, and promotion of domestic home life as a sanctuary from the corruption of the market on the other. Middling Americans' interest in social reform drew them to elections and government, but their "pursuit of upper- and middle-class respectability" pushed them away from the social mixing and compromise of conscience that mass politics required.[3] In the slave states, this ambivalence sheds light on the fiery 1861 conclusion to antebellum southern political history. At their extreme, antiparty sentiments led the already troubled Reese to his demise. More commonly antipartyism made the Old South's businessmen and professionals receptive to radical solutions, like secession or a war to suppress it, because those proposals also promised to do away with party politics as they knew it. For the South's middle-class Unionists, criticizing the corruption of political parties, or at least of the rival to one's own party, proved an ideological stumbling block to combating secession because fire-eating disunionists used the same arguments to make their case against northern majority rule.

Determining the extent of middle-class southerners' political involvement matters for understanding their impact on the outcomes of southern politics and the meaning of their oft-voiced disdain for party business and electioneering. However, the political ideas and actions of the southern bourgeoisie have been obscured by the historiographic dominance of studies that emphasize sharp differences in sectional politics. For the South, such an interpretation posits that honor culture and stronger communal (as opposed to individual) moral standards discouraged the self-reflection on the individual's relationship to public order that led the northern bourgeoisie to question the virtue of party politics. According to Bertram Wyatt-Brown, "Northerners . . . made contracts, obtained loans, and settled debts by institutional means . . . rather than by personal relationships . . . in the South, the yeomanry often sought help . . . from wealthy landowners with an unspoken understanding about who should receive the farmer's vote when the squire's name appeared on the ballot." In this rendition, the personalism of slave society overrode the contractual, individualism present in "the new language of the middle-class" emerging in the North.[4]

In an attempt to reconsider this sharp contrast between sectional political cultures, this essay investigates the politics of the southern middle class, which, as recent scholarship has demonstrated, developed a worldview and cultural practices that deviated significantly from those of their region's agricultural majority. For the purposes of this essay, the southern middle class refers to white families headed by (mostly male) workers who earned their livelihoods from nonfarm and non-manual labor but who did not rank in the top bracket of southern wealth holders. In affirmative terms, these were businessmen and professionals of moderate means. The middle class comprised perhaps one-tenth of the total white population and was concentrated, and more influential, in cities and towns.[5]

In light of their antiparty rhetoric, it is somewhat surprising that non-manual, nonagricultural workers held more than twice as many public offices as their share of the white southern population. This claim rests on the predominance of lawyers in all levels of partisan politics. Most mid-nineteenth-century lawyers relied on courtroom trials for their income and looked to politics as a way to publicize their names and speaking talents. Moreover, their work at county courthouses put them in daily contact with elected officials, and the government funded several jobs that only lawyers could fill, such as state's attorneys and judges. Despite comprising less than one percent of the South's white population in the 1850s, lawyers held 23 percent of the section's state legislative seats. On the other hand, many of these professional politicians had amassed great fortunes that put them at the top of the South's wealth pyramid. If considered by income as well as occupation, the proportion of middle-class officeholders approximated their share of the total white population.[6]

Despite showing that southern middle-class men like Reese were active in the party system, notwithstanding their denunciations of it, regional data on officeholding obscure differences in middle-class politics that corresponded to the dynamics of country, town, and city. Middle-class southerners, no matter their occupation, tended to be more politically active in urban places. In the countryside planters and yeomen far outnumbered professionals and businessmen, and the rural middle class tended to follow rather than lead public opinion. The urban South presented more opportunities for middle-class political leadership because planters and farmers had less influence there and because all urbanites shared the middle class's interest in government aid to economic diversification. In towns, middle-class men often controlled local government and just as often split their support between competing parties. Despite partisan conflict, town politics were relatively pacific because their smaller proportions of enfranchised workers prevented wage earners from using government to advance a class agenda at odds with that of the bourgeoisie. In the few cities large enough to host a sizeable white working class, the middle class added containing labor militancy to its agenda. Forced to make a public case for their interests versus those of white workers, middle-class politics in the big cities provided the fullest articulation of the southern bourgeoisie's ambivalent attitude toward party competition and mass democracy.

Because businessmen and professionals usually worked in urban settings, which had the necessary infrastructure of courts, transportation depots, and schools, it was in rural counties that planters truly ruled southern politics, holding the important local judicial offices and usually running with minimal opposition for legislative seats. For example, in 1850 three-fifths of the adult white men (an approximation of the eligible voters) in Prince Edward County, Virginia, a typical rural county in the state's southeastern tobacco belt, farmed for a living, while only one-tenth practiced a white-collar profession. These demographics militated against a politics that elevated any occupation above agriculture. Instead, the rural middle class tended to identify with their agricultural neighbors and the rural electorate divided along lines of kinship and neighborhood.[7] In a social world where community opinion could make or break a career, fitting in outweighed potential gains from campaigning for a candidate or party hated by one's neighbors. For these reasons, Augustus Garland, a young attorney starting out in the village of Washington, Arkansas, a bastion of the American Party, opted for the Know Nothings notwithstanding Democrats' predominance statewide.[8] When villagers like Garland lobbied for government aid to railroads, banks, and industry they usually had the support of neighboring farmers who also wanted access to transportation, credit, and manufactures. As historians Darrett and Anita Rutman observe for Georgia, "townsmen and villagers were not out to change the slave and staple nature of their society . . . Their intent was simply to serve their own aspirations within the society as they found it."[9]

Middle-class political activism increased in relation to population density. In larger towns—defined on the low end by the census designation of urban as a place with at least 2500 people and on the upper boundary by 10,000 residents—middle-class southerners often held top posts in local government. While absent in many rural beats, party divisions thrived in towns, and elections were closely contested. In Vicksburg, a settlement of 4600 in 1860 located in rich river-bottom land of Warren County, Mississippi, winning candidates rarely polled more than 60 percent of the vote, whereas candidates running elsewhere in the county usually won by landslide margins of 80 percent or more.[10] Vicksburg's closer contests reflected the greater tolerance for disagreement among white-collar voters and the absence of a single notable planter or other dominant political family in town.

On the other hand, the dynamics of the town electorate and the relationship between towns and their agricultural neighbors made for a restrained style of party competition in which bourgeois leaders practiced a politics of respectability that kept class conflict out of the electoral arena. Towns were less likely to develop an insurgent working-class politics because manual workers, the majority of the urban male population, comprised disenfranchised African Americans (enslaved and free) and unnaturalized immigrants.[11]

Although able to override the political aspirations of local workers, town businessmen and professionals could not openly defy the will of their more numerous rural neighbors. When town merchants and manufacturers lobbied state governments for measures that countered agrarian wishes, they tried to paper over differences with the countryside. Town businessmen's pursuit of expanded credit, which inflamed farmers' worries about speculative frenzies and inflated land values, typified middle-class disclaimers of urban-rural differences. Mindful of rural objections, Wilmington, North Carolina voter Miles Castor told his congressman that the existing commercial bank "will not discount paper to be paid in full. That is no accommodation to farmers and not much to merchants. . . . [Another bank] will assist the farmers as well as the merchants and what will benefit one will also benefit the other for the farmer and merchant is all the same." Similarly, stockholders in the Bank of Hamburg asked the South Carolina legislature to renew the institution's charter and argued that the lending facility had been "of great service and utility, not only in furnishing commercial facilities . . . but also in promoting the agricultural and manufacturing interest." When lobbying planter-run state legislatures, merchants and manufacturers downplayed their differences with the agricultural South.[12]

The best way for middle-class townsmen to demonstrate political solidarity with rural planters was to defend slavery at every opportunity. Because southern politicians fought to outdo each other in demonstrating their proslavery credentials, support for slavery was truly bipartisan. Similarly, the middle class adapted proslavery to the work of nonpartisan voluntary associations. For example, in 1849, lawyers and manufacturers in the upcountry South Carolina town of Spartanburg struck a Committee of Vigilance and Safety to suppress abolitionist mailings, and, in 1853, a vigilance committee in Tuscaloosa, Alabama, called abolitionists "enemies of God and Man, deserving severe punishment," and promised to "use all means to ferret out, confine, and bring punishment" to anyone spreading abolition tracts. The same middle-class southerners who formed proslavery committees also used voluntary associations to lobby for public schools, humane penitentiaries, and temperance laws, all modeled on northern precedents and opposed by planters who saw in these measures "a formal centralized power immune to their personal authority." Townsmen's nonpartisan proslavery activism counteracted planter suspicions that bourgeois reformers meant to overthrow the social order.[13]

Within their town boundaries, middling southerners sometimes stood up to planter intervention in their affairs. For example, in 1843, grocers and merchants in Tallahassee, Florida, defeated Mayor Francis Eppes, a friend of the planters who had imposed draconian restrictions on commerce in order to police slaves and poor whites gathering at groceries and taverns. Eppes's severe limits on middle-class enterprise prompted Tallahassee's voters, the majority of whom were petty proprietors and professionals, to force his resignation.[14]

These challenges had less success in countywide politics. In Warren County, Mississippi, home of Vicksburg as well as several very wealthy planters, including future Confederate president Jefferson Davis and his brother Joseph, the issue of flood protection demonstrated where power lay when town and country came into conflict. Building levees along the Mississippi River protected towns lining its banks, but strong earthworks cost money and raised water levels on downstream plantations. Town petitioners failed to persuade county government to finance levees. Among their foes were the Davis brothers. Instead of relying on government the Davises ordered their slaves to construct a flood barrier that protected the plantations and left middle-class townsmen to fend for themselves.[15]

Like other prosperous slaveholders, Warren County planters regarded many government initiatives as either irrelevant to their labor needs, as in the case of public education, or as needless duplication of projects, like levee building, that they carried out with their enslaved labor. To be sure, some wealthy slaveholders also supported and, in the case of Kentucky's Henry Clay, led the Whig Party that advocated an "American System" of government-funded improvements. However, even Whig planters worried about an agenda that might create a powerful, urban-based middle class and a political culture governed by bourgeois tastes.

The influence of this antibourgeois sentiment on party fortunes manifested itself in Alabama, a state that shared in the late antebellum railroad and town boom that swept the Cotton South. In the 1850s, Alabama's cities and towns grew at double the rural rate, and the nonfarm share of the workforce increased to 30 percent. Growth concentrated in the northern hill counties, where mining, iron, and textile industries were starting up. Initially, parties competed to hasten "progress" with new prisons, asylums, and a public school system. In so doing, according to one historian, legislators' "efforts tended to reflect the values of the booming urban environment and of the wider Victorian world. Thus the government in trying to please an obviously restless constituency [the urban middle class], became more and more active" so as to "terrify a people steeped in the precepts of Jackson." Whig and Democratic support for government-led social reform fueled rural resentment against both parties that ultimately benefited secessionists who stoked white southerners' greatest fear of big government activism: abolition.[16]

Just as town growth produced an agrarian backlash against middle-class political ambitions, the expansion of cities generated a parallel bourgeois reaction against working-class-influenced party politics. Cities simultaneously afforded the middle class its greatest political influence and fostered its stron-gest challenge from white workers. In 1860, the South boasted fifteen urban places of more than ten thousand people, which qualified them as cities in mid-nineteenth century America. Three southern cities—Baltimore, New Or-leans, and St. Louis—housed more than 150,000 people and ranked among the nation's 10 largest.

While not the sole power in city government, middle-class men were well represented. In Baltimore, the South's largest city, high-status professionals (lawyers, merchants, bankers) comprised more than one-third of a sample of 219 men holding minor political office (below federal, state, and citywide positions). In the 1850s, shopkeepers, teachers, commodity dealers, and other low-status professionals made up 35 percent of the minor officeholders. Ar-tisans were one-fourth of that group, and no semi-skilled or unskilled wage earners appeared in the sample. Among high officeholders the presence of petty proprietors and clerks diminished. The top rank of white-collar workers held four-fifths of these positions.[17] The same pattern of three- to four-fifths of elected city officials having white-collar occupations held in smaller cities such as Louisville, Charleston, Norfolk, and Savannah.[18] As with state legisla-tors, many of these white-collar officeholders came from the city's economic elite instead of its middle ranks yet, although not always in charge, the middle class had significant access to city government and generally shared cultural and economic aspirations with the wealthy men who held the top offices.

This influence gave the middle class access to municipal tax and bond revenue to finance internal improvements that it hoped would diversify the southern economy. City governments devoted considerable portions of their budgets to transportation projects, especially the expensive railroads of the 1850s. Cities also dredged harbors, cleaned streets, and built waterworks, schools, jails, and hospitals. Although city bourgeoisie outstripped townsmen in enacting their mutual vision of economic and social progress, both groups met their limits when they took on agrarians in state government.

Constitutional reform, a process carried out in several southern states around 1850, demonstrated the urban middle class's need for agrarian allies to enact change at the state level. With the help of upcountry yeomen, city politi-cians succeeded in reapportioning state legislatures according to population and loosening rules for bank charters. These victories alarmed some planters but pleased others, like Henry Wise, a conservative from Virginia's Eastern Shore, who "advocated the white basis and universal suffrage as the only safe protection for slave property." In Virginia, which retained property qualifications for voting until 1851, Wise and like-minded slaveholders agreed to broaden suffrage and equalize apportionment representation in order to remove a potent source of class resentment against the eastern tobacco magnates.[19]

Although reformers agreed on democratization, the alliance between cities and farmers fell apart over economic legislation. Instead of giving more money to railroads and industry, new constitutions in Maryland, Kentucky, Virginia, and North Carolina capped state indebtedness and sometimes banned state funding of internal improvements. Opponents of public works spending viewed it as zero-sum game, in which cities gained at the expense of the countryside. At Kentucky's 1849 constitutional convention, a farm delegate said that Louisville wanted state funding for roads "Because it will contribute to her aggrandizement. She does not do it from disinterested motives." The financial dreams of middle-class politics often foundered on the shoals of agrarian mistrust of government power and urban growth.[20]

Blocked by rural voters at the state level, the urban middle class battled workers in city politics. In the smaller cities of the South, white workers' challenges to the bourgeoisie focused on competition with slave and free black labor, which they sought to curtail via local legislation. For example, mechanics in Petersburg, Virginia, resolved "inasmuch as free negroes are not allowed to be Doctors, Lawyers, Merchants or Tradesman [they should have] no more right to compete with our employment by undertaking mechanical arts." Moreover racial restrictions on industrial trades threatened middle-class plans to adapt slavery to manufacturing, a movement well under way in Upper South cities that relied on leasing slaves from rural planters. Urban employers preferred black workers, free and slave, because their legal condition inhibited their ability to strike and barred them from voting for pro-labor politicians. In each test of the South's racially divided labor market, urban politicians denied white labor's demands and instead sided with middle-class employers and planters who benefited from slave hiring. As with town proslavery voluntary societies, the urban bourgeoisie's support for slave hiring helped counteract planters' unease with other aspects of their political agenda.[21]

The working-class challenge to the southern bourgeoisie was strongest in the largest cites of the South. In the 1850s, white workers in Baltimore and New Orleans fought elite municipal rule through the vehicle of the anti-immigrant American Party. Taking power in 1854 in Baltimore and a year later in New Orleans, Know Nothings initially united middle-class ex-Whigs and working-class renegade Democrats. Native-born workers and the bourgeoisie shared an interest in public improvements that helped business and created jobs, expanded urban political representation in state government, and, for different reasons, restricted immigration. Know Nothing politicians coordinated these themes in a call to "reform" party politics that drew credence from the new party's distance from the Whigs and Democrats and from its origins in the world of nonpartisan secret societies.

The subsequent history of the urban South's Know Nothing regimes demonstrated the fundamental tension between middle- and working-class definitions of reform. For the middle class, reform meant an end to party corruption by reducing government patronage, restriction of alleged immigrant voter fraud, and improved public morals through sabbatarianism and temperance. For working-class Know Nothings reform meant more places for their kind in government, curbs on immigrant job competition, ten-hour day laws, and police neutrality during strikes. The coalitions came apart by the late 1850s as labor gained more influence in the insurgent parties, and workers and employers fell out over municipal assistance to those thrown out of work by the Panic of 1857. In 1858, New Orleans Know Nothings elected as mayor Gerard Stith, a printer who led a strike against immigrant competition. In 1857, Baltimore's Know Nothing police aided striking railroad workers and a year later they helped nativist gangs take the jobs of free black ship's caulkers. As workers gained strength in the American Party, middle-class reformers turned to more drastic antiparty alternatives.[22]

In both cities, middle-class voters drifted toward nonpartisan reform movements that trumpeted their freedom from party attachments but that nonetheless cooperated with the planter-run Democratic parties influential in state government. At its organizing meeting, the New Orleans' Vigilance Committee declared that "For the present the ordinary machinery of political justice is suspended."[23] In Baltimore, the City Reform Association told voters, "while, therefore, we earnestly desire to see the present administration of the city wholly gotten rid of . . . that desire is altogether secondary to the paramount anxiety which we feel for the suppression of partisan municipal government altogether."[24] New Orleans Know Nothings defeated the Vigilantes largely because they retained control of the police, whereas in Baltimore, the Democratic-controlled state legislature took over municipal policing and reined in Know Nothing gangs, which facilitated a Reform Association victory in the 1860 elections. Indicative of middle-class perceptions, Julius Obendorf, a young German Jewish clerk, described "The great Reform Victory" in Baltimore as "an election of unparalleled fairness [in which] the decency and respectability of the city triumphed over the rowdy elements."[25]

Despite the variations between country, town, and city, some common themes ran throughout southern middle-class politics. No matter where they lived the southern bourgeoisie promoted moral reform, economic diversification, and slavery. Furthermore, whether they were professional politicians or alienated bystanders who never voted, middle-class southerners agreed that party politics was corrupt. Antipartyism found adherents in all classes and regions of antebellum America, but in the hands of the southern bourgeoisie it became a rationale for not only reforming politics but also for distinguishing themselves as a class.

The middle class of the late antebellum South put new meanings onto the familiar contrast between statesmen and spoilsmen that Americans inherited from the republican political culture of the eighteenth century. After the Revolution, Federalists and Jeffersonians worried about demagogues fomenting rebellions from below and tyranny from above. The South's agrarian republicans regarded land ownership's financial independence and household mastery's patriarchal benevolence as the sources of civic virtue that enabled true statesmen to resist government's temptations to seek wealth and power.[26] Unlike rural classical republicans, middle-class southerners focused on new dangers present in social modernization. Cities, markets, cheap entertainments, and even mass politics allowed clever dissimulators—typified by the confidence man—to advance by manipulating language and presenting false accounts of themselves to the public. Simultaneously, parties resembled an emerging bureaucratic order that prized conformity and compromise over independence and adherence to principle.[27] To combat these corruptions, middle-class southerners looked to evangelical religion and new gender identities rather than ownership of land and mastery of dependents.

Indicating the pull of their new cultural world, middle-class southerners invoked metaphors of sexual propriety to criticize party politics. South Carolinian David Gavin, an attorney-turned-planter and a virgin bachelor, weighed his revulsion at sexual "licentiousness" against his doctor's advice that "it is not healthy to live single or without intercourse between the sexes." Gavin saw democratic politics through the same moral framework that made him uneasy about sex. He would not run for office because "it is sickening to a good, or even a moral man to see how elections are managed or conducted now, a candidate stands little or no chance who does not flatter, deceive and bribe." Like many middling southerners Gavin gravitated toward the Know Nothings for their promise to rise above ordinary political practice. "The American party is now abused by the dirty politicians and the democratic or mob-o-crat-ic party," Gavin wrote, but only because Know Nothings were "the true advocates of free government, and the true opponents of bribery and corruption in elections."[28]

William C. Cooke, a Virginian who moved to Hannibal, Missouri, to make a career as a lawyer, shared Gavin's understanding of politics as a form of seduction. In 1848, Cooke wrote to John Coles Rutherfoord, a college friend and a rising star in the Virginia Democratic Party, to denounce politics. "Political distinction," he wrote, "has wonderful fascinations for men of ardent fancies," but it exacerbated ambition's tendency to destroy good character. "[T]he blaze that ornaments at the same time consumes him. It is the most troubled of all turbulent lives. He may sow good grain but will reap nothing but thorns. God save me from politics."[29]

Cooke's antiparty attitudes persisted even after he ran for public office. In 1851, Cooke won election to a Hannibal judgeship. First gushing about the job's salary and career exposure, Cooke then worried about playing on the "seductive fields of politics." "I am not so sure," he wrote, "that we would not all be better off if we would confine ourselves within the modest limits of our businesses, and instead of cultivating the tricks of politicians, endeavor to preserve and perfect the traits of the Gentleman." Cooke's choice of metaphors, a contrast between the modesty of gentlemen and the seduction of politics, resonated with the emerging bourgeois distinction between the moral sanctity of the private sphere and the corruption of public spaces. It is noteworthy that Cooke also agonized about his frequent visits to prostitutes and his desire to break with sin. The binary moral divide that middle-class southerners drew between sexual virtue and vice provided a ready metaphor for comprehending their unease with the demands of party politics.[30]

By the 1850s, white southerners perceived the growing power of antislavery politicians in the North as the greatest threat to the country. Sharing this view, middle-class antipartisans characterized the Free Soil and, later, Republican parties as the most egregious examples of political corruption. Commenting on the 1848 presidential election, Cooke called Free Soil nominee Martin Van Buren "a miserable wretch of a 'free negro' white man, one of those 'Northern men' whose 'Southern principles' the omniscience of the 'Democracy' perceived, as they now perceive the same qualities in his successor [Lewis Cass] in jugglery." Although unenthused about Whig Zachary Taylor, Cooke supported him "because I believe him the only candidate that the South can trust on the subject of slavery, and that in my mind is the all-absorbing question of the day." A self-described "man who loathes 'politics,'" Cooke framed his diatribe against Free Soilers and Democrats through an antipartisan lens that mistrusted professions of political integrity.[31]

Hostility to northern party politics often linked the rise of antislavery to the dynamics of the northern electorate, in which slavery's absence gave manual labor more voting power. John L. Buchanan, a clerk-turned-educator from southwestern Virginia, furthered Cooke's critique of free-soilers by connecting party corruption with mass suffrage: "It is this battling, this *warring*, this STORMING of parties that tends to work the masses of the people into a rabid multitude—an infuriated mob—in whose hands their own welfare cannot be trusted." As did Cooke, Buchanan blamed northern free-soil politicians for the worst excesses of partisanship. "If the violence of party conflicts continues to increase," he described a more ferocious version of Reese's muddy stream in 1854, "and the remorseless spirit of Northern aggression continues to advance, the hot vapors that will rise up from the turbulent sea of human passion, will gather into a fiery storm-cloud of desolation."[32]

Antipartisan proslavery formed the theme of several novels written by John Beauchamp Jones, a Baltimore editor and occasional party activist. In 1842, Jones edited the administration newspaper for President John Tyler, a Virginia Whig who alienated his party brethren by rejecting their economic agenda and refusing to put party interests before his own.[33] In the mid-1850s, Jones backed the Know Nothings. During the Civil War he worked for the

Confederate bureaucracy, where he compiled his widely read memoir, *A Rebel War Clerk's Diary.* The consistent theme in these attachments was the antiparty stand taken by Tyler Whigs, southern Know Nothings, and the Confederacy.[34]

In *The Adventures of Colonel Gracchus Vanderbomb,* published in 1852, Jones satirized mass democracy's tendency to inflame sectional conflict. Patterned on the Whigs' disastrous presidential nominee Winfield Scott, whom southerners rejected for equivocating on sectional issues, the novel's namesake railed against abolition when in the South and castigated slaveholders when in the North. Jones depicted the crowds in both sections as ignorant mobs that Vanderbomb won over by flattering majority rule and promising an incoherent mix of protective tariffs, Cuban annexation, and free land. In a parody of partisan self-interest, Vanderbomb's "policy . . . is to please everybody, and to reap the greatest amount of popularity in the shortest amount of time." For Jones the southerner, the true villain of the story is not Vanderbomb, but rather his campaign advisor Numerius Plutarch Kipps, described as "a true Yankee . . . [who] had the faculty, not only to adapt himself to circumstances, and to the dispositions of those from whom he desired to receive benefits, but likewise to reap the greatest possible advantage from his servility." Kipps bribes editors, lies to everyone, and pushes Vanderbomb to ignore his own moral doubts.[35]

In 1859, as the sectional crisis intensified, Jones produced *Border War!* a novel that tried to envision a proslavery Union through the means of enlightened partisanship. Jones's heroes use modern political practice to keep together a diverse coalition of supporters. President George Washington Randolph, a Virginian, possesses integrity—he has a "firmness of purpose and decision of character"—but deceives when needed. His sidekick, Wiry Willy, is a party hack with an ethical core. A friend tells Randolph that "Willy, being once a politician, takes sometimes one side and sometimes the other; but in whatever he does, I can see a good motive . . . he can serve you better than any of the violent partisans. . . . You may have the most perfect reliance on his honor and judgment." While Randolph and Blount, commander of the Southern Unionist army, are planters, other protagonists like Willy lack strong identification with the South, land, and notable families: a New York City gang leader guards Randolph's daughter; a Pennsylvania senator proves that "all the Northern people are not fanatics"; and Missouri frontiersmen outsmart abolitionist militia. Jones struggled to balance condemnation of partisanship's contribution to the sectional crisis with his scenario for preserving the Union through established institutions and veteran leaders.[36]

As Jones's contorted plot and his ultimate decision for the Confederacy indicate, the realities of sectional politics mitigated against a southern Unionism that embraced enlightened partisanship. Instead, middling southerners' antiparty idiom pushed them away from compromise and toward secession or war, ironically turning middle-class moderates' push to make politics respectable into an accelerant to sectional conflict rather than an obstacle. During the secession crisis, southern Unionists occasionally played up resentment of planters by characterizing the issue as a struggle between "honest yeomen" and what a Tennessean called the "purseproud nabobs of cottonocracy." Such arguments did better with urban workers and small farmers in homogeneous border-state counties than with middle-class southerners accustomed to combating labor militants in cities and anti-tax/anti-improvement yeomen in state legislatures. Instead, on class grounds, secession had some subtle attractions for the South's petty proprietors and aspiring professionals. As Jacqueline Jones says of Savannah, secession's fire-eaters criticized "the baneful effects of an excess of 'democracy' dominated by nonslaveholding white men," chief among which was the opportunity for manipulating poor voters that mass suffrage offered to unscrupulous demagogues.[37] This secessionist attack on mass politics had two arguments that appealed to middle-class southerners: defeating incipient working-class political machines and enacting an antipartisan, proslavery vision of democratic politics.

Alabama orator William Lowndes Yancey echoed the middle-class critique of mass democracy as an obstacle to individual integrity, but even more than some middling southerners, fire-eaters like Yancey linked the excesses of mass political parties to the North's social order. "The northern man surrenders his individuality—See one of them and you have before a type of all," Yancey said in 1856. "He will smother in his heart every individual suggestion of propriety and duty . . . His conscience is that great Public Opinion which thinks for him and decides for him." As these remarks suggest, the secessionist arguments about sectional differences resonated with middle-class concerns about preserving individual conscience and integrity.[38]

The same bourgeois critique of northern democracy drove T. R. R. Cobb's case for disunion in the Georgia secession convention. Cobb castigated the "miserable demagogues and political leaders of the North, in their party excitement, bidding for this Abolition vote. Without real sympathy for the movement, we find them vying with each other in pretended zeal." Cobb characterized the Republican constituency as a rabble: "Look at its cohort and see their mottled ranks—free negroes and boot-blacks, coachmen and domestics, infidels and free-lovers, spiritual rappers and every other shade of mania and folly. Scan all its long list of speakers or voters as far as we can see them, and where is the man you would ask into your table, or with whose arm you would walk through your streets. *And yet these are our rulers.* . . . Let me rather have a king . . . or an aristocracy." Cobb's attack on northern democracy highlighted its disregard for respectability by citing Republicans' "mottled ranks" as the kind of class mixing that bourgeois southerners disdained. Building on this theme, Cobb advised the assembled legislators to act independently of a popular referendum on secession. "[S]elected as you are to represent the wisdom and intelligence of Georgia: wait not till the grog-shops and cross-roads shall send up a discordant voice from a divided people but act as leaders in guiding and forming public opinion."[39] Cobb appealed both to planters' aristocratic pretensions and to middle-class respectability.

Cobb was uniquely situated to speak to both upper- and middle-class southerners. His father was an absentee planter who ran a 6000-acre, 150-slave estate in east-central Georgia from a comfortable home in the town of Athens. Thomas Cobb's older brother Howell led the state Democratic Party and served in James Buchanan's cabinet. Educated as a lawyer, Thomas exploited family connections to win a minor office in the Georgia legislature and held several patronage appointments in state government. Not unlike Reese, Cobb abhorred the party system's compromise of individual conscience and integrity even though, similar to many professionals, he was attracted by the career advancement that politics offered. "I am done with politics," he wrote in 1844, "I see the cup is sparkling, but the dregs I must drink with it . . . are misery disappointment and hate." In another echo of Reese, Cobb's devout evangelicalism added to his fear that party activism corrupted one's morals. Caught between his interests in the family business and a personal desire to keep clean of party corruption, Thomas told his brother that "[any]thing honest and honourable of interests you may demand of me[.] General partisanship for the present I must eschew."[40] In 1861, Cobb advocated secession as a nonpartisan measure that would elevate southern politics by rescuing it from the corruption of mass democracy and party demagogues.

Cobb's argument before the Georgia legislature aimed at both upper- and middle-class listeners who shared in the pursuit of moral and intellectual refinement. Edmund Ruffin, perhaps Virginia's best-known fire-eater and a proponent of scientific agriculture, played to this same sentiment when he tried to persuade readers that slavery protected democracy. According to Ruffin, "In the great cities of the North and especially in the learned professions and scientific pursuits, there are more of highly educated and scientific professional men, than are to be found in the Southern States. But even of these shining lights of learning and science, but few . . . are entrusted with political offices and duties, by the votes of their fellow citizens." Ruffin blamed this perceived exclusion of urban professionals on the North's enfranchisement of its working masses that, as the largest voting bloc, overruled the more enlightened bourgeoisie. "In all questions which self-interest or sectional aggrandizement is supposed to be involved, the highest intellectual power must be governed by the power of numbers," lamented Ruffin.[41] Fire-eaters played on middle-class fears that social modernization might falter by creating conditions, like strict majority rule, that denied rewards for individual talent and effort. Therefore, secessionists argued, an advanced, meritocratic society could only be realized in a slaveholding political order that culled the working masses from the electorate.

Not all middle-class southerners agreed. Until the late 1850s they, like most southerners, generally opposed secession, but the crisis of 1860–61 drew a substantial portion toward disunion. The rise of the Republican Party, partisan conflict in the big cities, and political and economic pressure exerted by secessionist majorities in the Lower South turned some middling southerners toward the Confederacy. In concert with these forces, antiparty rhetoric helped to push middle-class moderates off the fence and into rival camps.

For politicians from the bourgeoisie, such sentiments did not mean abandoning old party hatreds but rather folding earlier antipartisan arguments into a more extreme rhetoric of political nationalism, wherein one's foes were not simply misguided and venal but, far worse, traitors. In Knoxville, the largest town in Unionist East Tennessee, William "Parson" Brownlow, a diehard

Whig, conflated partisan difference with sectional allegiance when he said that "this vile, designing, corrupt and abominable Democracy are [sic] responsible for" secession and that the Confederacy was "a revival of corrupt Southern Democracy" pursuing power behind a mask of proslavery unity. Other Unionists pushed this attack to assert that the crisis justified a complete end to partisan give-and-take. J. Morrison Harris, a Baltimore lawyer and Know Nothing congressman, argued that "he who rises above the trammels of politics and party will find that he has achieved a greatness more enduring, infinitely, than he ever could have done within the lower sphere of his partisan operations."[42]

Urban secessionists used the same antipartisan theme in behalf of their cause. In Baltimore's 1860 presidential campaign, Harris's foe Frank Key Howard, a pro-Breckinridge Democrat editor later arrested for anti-Union activities, wrote that "the Bell Everett party [the Constitutional Unionists] is . . . the discarded and defeated Know-Nothing faction." Given the hidden party ambitions of Unionists, Howard concluded that "the plainest duty of the people of Maryland" was to "defend the principles for which the South now contends." For secessionists affiliated with the Whigs and Know Nothings, who outside of a few pockets were in the minority, suppressing partisanship rebutted Democratic suspicions. For example, Cumberland County North Carolina editor Edward Hale, who had for most of his career been a zealous Whig, co-authored a town meeting's resolution "that the exigencies of the times require every loyal son of North Carolina to bury past political animosities, and forgetting past political contests to unite hand and heart in resistance to sectional rule."[43]

For urban middle-class voters, the conflation of party and sectional loyalty transformed local partisan rivals into enemies of the nation and turned an antebellum rhetoric of party corruption into a black-and-white, loyal-or-disloyal wartime political culture that made little allowance for southerners' fluid affiliation to the Union and Confederacy. Missing in their calls to put national allegiance above the need to compromise was another principle, perhaps one that prized keeping political conflict within orderly boundaries such as those worked out by antebellum parties, which could have moderated the stark choice of Confederacy or Union.

Secessionists' adoption of bourgeois reform rhetoric counts as one of many ironies of southern history. Although the Confederacy came to be associated with the defense of anti-modern traditions, such as slavery and agrarianism, its creators pioneered good-government rhetoric that flourished in the Progressive era and after. Secession's modern-minded reform rhetoric was more than a concession to middle-class values. It also reflected a tentative convergence between the South's ruling planter class and its emerging middle class around the transatlantic discourse of Victorianism that originated in Britain, the metropolitan center of nineteenth-century modernity. Like other imports, Victorianism came to America through its major ports cities, especially New York, Philadelphia, and Boston. Few southern yeomen visited the urban Northeast, but many middling southerners did so on business and while there they imbibed the latest trends in bourgeois culture. The planter elite also traveled, but they spent their time with their wealthy counterparts in the urban Northeast and Europe. Reading and consumption reinforced both classes' appreciation for the culture of modernity.[44]

Yet while the language of Victorianism used by middle- and upper-class southern whites was similar, the purposes of transatlantic modernity that each pursued were quite different. For the planter elite, cosmopolitanism fit into a vision of a modern commercial nation-state based on slavery and led by the owners of human property.[45] For the South's middle class, a proslavery nation-state had less allure than did the more attainable bourgeois ideals of domestic privacy and career advancement. Prosperity within the Union benefited the middle-class version of southern Victorianism, whereas the grander vision of the planter secessionists seemed more viable free from a union with the antislavery North. Although some middling southerners stood strong for the Union, many more in the seceding states cast their lot with their planter-class patrons and waged a war that destroyed their dreams of "increasing wealth, rapid urbanization, and an expanding manufacturing base."[46] Ironically, it was the affinity between middle- and upper-class southern political culture that undercut the ability of the southern bourgeoisie to articulate and defend a Unionist alternative to secession.

NOTES

1. Quotations in Baltimore *Methodist Protestant,* October 25, 1856; Henry Slicer Journals, September 16, 1861, Henry Slicer Papers, United Methodist Historical Society, Lovely Lane Museum and Library, Baltimore. Also see *Baltimore American,* November 9, 1846, October 13, 1853, and February 5, 1857; Baltimore *Sun,* April 3, 1852.

2. Edward J. Drinkhouse, *History of Methodist Reform, Synoptical of General Methodism, 1703–1898* (Baltimore: Methodist Episcopal Church, 1899), 447–49; Homer L. Calkin, "The Slavery Struggle, 1780–1865," in *Those Incredible Methodists: A History of the Baltimore Conference of the United Methodist Church,* ed. Gordon Pratt Baker (Baltimore: Baltimore Conference, 1972), 212, 216–18 (quotation 217).

3. Stuart M. Blumin, *The Emergence of the Middle Class: Social Experience in the American City, 1760–1900* (New York: Cambridge University Press, 1989), 257 (quotation); Glenn C. Altschuler and Stuart M. Blumin, *Rude Republic: Americans and their Politics in the Nineteenth Century* (Princeton: Princeton University Press, 2000), 8.

4. Bertram Wyatt-Brown, *The Shaping of Southern Culture: Honor, Grace, and War, 1760s–1880s* (Chapel Hill: University of North Carolina Press, 2001), 65 (quotations); William H. Pease and Jane H. Pease, *The Web of Progress: Private Values and Public Styles in Boston and Charleston, 1828–1843* (Athens: University of Georgia Press, 1991), 81–82; Anne C. Rose, *Victorian America and the Civil War* (New York: Cambridge University Press, 1992), 218; Wallace Hettle, *The Peculiar Democracy: Southern Democrats in Peace and Civil War* (Athens: University of Georgia Press, 2001), 24.

5. Jonathan Daniel Wells, *The Origins of the Southern Middle Class, 1860–1861* (Chapel Hill: University of North Carolina Press, 2004), 8, 10; Jennifer R. Green, *Military Education and the Emerging Middle Class in the Old South* (New York: Cambridge University Press, 2008), 19–20.

6. Calculated from Ralph A. Wooster, *The People in Power: Courthouse and Statehouse in the Lower South, 1850–1860* (Knoxville: University of Tennessee Press, 1969), 35; Wooster, *Politicians, Planters, and Plain Folk: Courthouse and Statehouse in the Upper South, 1850–1860* (Knoxville: University of Tennessee Press, 1975), 34.

7. Christopher J. Olsen, *Political Culture and Secession in Mississippi* (New York: Oxford University Press, 2000), 111, 127; Martin Crawford, *Ashe County's Civil War: Community and Society in the Appalachian South* (Charlottesville: University Press of Virginia, 2001), 52–53.

8. Beverly Nettles Watkins, "Augustus Hill Garland, 1832–1899: Arkansas Lawyer to United States Attorney General" (Ph.D. diss., Auburn University, 1985), 7.

9. William G. Shade, "Society and Politics in Antebellum Virginia's Southside," *Journal of Southern History* 53, no. 2 (1987): 163–93; Darrett B. Rutman and Anita H. Rutman, *Small Worlds, Large Questions: Explorations in Early American Social History, 1600–1850* (Charlottesville: University Press of Virginia, 1994), 266–67.

10. Christopher Morris, *Becoming Southern: The Evolution of a Way of Life, Warren County and Vicksburg, Mississippi, 1770–1860* (New York: Oxford University Press, 1995), 144.

11. Ira Berlin and Herbert G. Gutman, "Natives and Immigrants, Free Men and Slaves: Urban Workingmen in the Antebellum American South," *American Historical Review* 88, no. 5 (1983): esp. 1177–78; Morris, *Becoming Southern,* 144; Steven Elliott Tripp, *Yankee City, Southern Town: Race and Class Relations in Civil War Lynchburg* (New York: New York University Press, 1997), 258–59.

12. Miles Castor to Thomas McDowell, October 2, 1852, Thomas David Smith McDowell Papers, Southern Historical Collection, University of North Carolina (hereafter SHC). Tom Downey, *Planting a Capitalist South: Masters, Merchants, and Manufacturers in the Southern Interior, 1790–1860* (Baton Rouge: Louisiana State University Press, 2006), 153.

13. William J. Cooper, *The South and the Politics of Slavery, 1828–1856* (Baton Rouge: Louisiana State University Press, 1978); Bruce W. Eelman, *Entrepreneurs on the Southern Upcountry: Commercial Culture in Spartanburg, South Carolina, 1845–1880* (Athens: University of Georgia Press, 2008), 85, 98, 106, 109; John W. Quist, *Restless Visionaries: The Social Roots of Antebellum Reform in Alabama and Michigan* (Baton Rouge: Louisiana State University Press, 1998), 69 (third quotation), 309 (first and second quotations).

14. Edward E. Baptist, *Creating an Old South: Middle Florida's Plantation Frontier before the Civil War* (Chapel Hill: University of North Carolina Pres, 2002), 229–30.

15. Morris, *Becoming Southern,* 143–44.

16. J. Mills Thornton III, *Power and Politics in a Slave Society: Alabama, 1800–1860* (Baton Rouge: Louisiana State University Press, 1978), 292–93, 302 (quotation), 360–64.

17. Lists of politicians gathered from local newspapers and tracked in Manuscript Census Returns, U.S. Census, 1850, Schedule 1, Population schedule, Baltimore City, Maryland, and U.S. Census, 1860, Population schedule, Baltimore City, Maryland.

18. Altschuler and Blumin, *Rude Republic,* 90; Alexander I. Burckin, "The Formation and Growth of an Urban Middle Class: Power and Conflict in Louisville, Kentucky, 1828–1861" (Ph.D. diss., University of California, Irvine, 1993), 676; Brian E. Crowson, "Southern Port City Politics and the Know Nothing Party in the 1850s" (Ph.D. diss., University of Tennessee, Knoxville, 1994), 288–89.

19. Michael F. Holt, *The Rise and Fall of the American Whig Party: Jacksonian Politics and the Onset of the Civil War* (New York: Oxford University Press, 1999), 687; William G. Shade, *Democratizing the Old Dominion: Virginia and the Second Party System, 1824–1861* (Charlottesville: University Press of Virginia, 1996), 282 (quotation).

20. Shade, *Democratizing the Old Dominion,* 279; Burckin, "Formation and Growth of an Urban Middle Class," 349 (quotation).

21. L. Diane Barnes, *Artisan Workers in the Upper South: Petersburg, Virginia, 1820–1865* (Baton Rouge: Louisiana State University Press, 2008), 44, 70, 111 (quotation); Wells, *Origins of the Southern Middle Class,* 182–83.

22. Frank Towers, *The Urban South and the Coming of the Civil War* (Charlottesville: University of Virginia Press, 2004), ch. 4.

23. Mary P. Ryan, *Civic Wars: Democracy and Public Life in the American City during the Nineteenth Century* (Berkeley: University of California Press, 1997), 146.

24. Baltimore *Daily Exchange,* October 10, 1860.

25. Julius Obendorf to Aaron Friedenwald, October 14, 1860, Friedenwald Papers, Jewish Historical Society, Baltimore.

26. Kenneth S. Greenberg, *Masters and Statesmen: The Political Culture of American Slavery* (Baltimore: Johns Hopkins University Press, 1985), 20; Bertram Wyatt-Brown, *Southern Honor: Ethics and Behavior in the Old South* (New York: Oxford University Press, 1982), 35, 45–46, 69; Olsen, *Political Culture and Secession in Mississippi,* 5, 8.

27. David Brion Davis, *The Slave Power Conspiracy and the Paranoid Style* (Baton Rouge: Louisiana State University Press, 1969), 28; Karen Haltunnen, *Confidence Men and Painted Women: A Study of Middle-Class Culture in America, 1830–1870* (New Haven: Yale University Press, 1982), 34; Rose, *Victorian America and the Civil War,* 194; Kimberly K. Smith, *The Domin-*

ion of Voice: Riot, Reason, and Romance in Antebellum Politics (Lawrence: University of Kansas Press, 1999), 219.

28. David Gavin Diary, vol. 1, September 29 (first quotation), October 25, November 5 (third quotation), 1855, October 13, 1856 (second quotation), SHC.

29. William C. Cooke to John Coles Rutherfoord, October 9, 1848, John Rutherfoord Papers, Rare Book, Manuscript, and Special Collections Library, Duke University, Raleigh, North Carolina.

30. Cooke to Rutherfoord, September 11, 1845, April 18, 1851.

31. Ibid., October 9, 1848.

32. Peter S. Carmichael, *The Last Generation: Young Virginians in Peace, War, and Reunion* (Chapel Hill: University of North Carolina Press, 2005), 43 (first quotation), 115 (second and third quotations).

33. Holt, *Rise and Fall of the American Whig Party,* 129.

34. Armistead C. Gordon Jr., "John Beauchamp Jones," in *Dictionary of American Biography,* ed. Dumas Malone, 20 vols. (New York: Scribner's, 1933), 10:182–83.

35. John Beauchamp Jones, *Adventures of Colonel Gracchus Vanderbomb of Sloughcreek in Search of the Presidency* (Philadelphia: A. Hart, 1852), 22, 32, 74–75, 93, 98–99, 125–26.

36. J. B. Jones, *Wild Southern Scenes, a Tale of Disunion! and Border War!* (Philadelphia: n.p., 1859), 19 (third quotation), 23 (first quotation), 51–52 (second quotation).

37. Robert Tracy McKenzie, *Lincolnites and Rebels: A Divided Town in the American Civil War* (New York: Oxford University Press, 2006), 69; Jacqueline Jones, *Saving Savannah: The City and the Civil War* (New York: Alfred A. Knopf, 2008), 95.

38. Eric H. Walther, *William Lowndes Yancey and the Coming of the Civil War* (Chapel Hill: University of North Carolina Press, 2006), 192.

39. Quoted in William W. Freehling and Craig M. Simpson, *Secession Debated: Georgia's Showdown in 1860* (New York: Oxford University Press, 1992), 16–17, 19–20, 29–30.

40. William B. McCash, *Thomas R. R. Cobb (1823–1862): The Making of a Southern Nationalist* (Macon, Ga.: Mercer University Press, 1983), 5, 7, 19 (first quotation), 23 (second quotation).

41. Edmund Ruffin, *Consequences of Abolition Agitation* (Washington: Lemuel Towers, 1857), 12–13.

42. Brownlow quoted in McKenzie, *Lincolnites and Rebels,* 67–68; J. Morrison Harris, *State of the Union . . . January 29, 1861* (n.p., n.d. [1861]) in James Morison Harris Papers, Maryland Historical Society, Baltimore. See also Daniel W. Crofts, *Reluctant Confederates: Upper South Unionists in the Secession Crisis* (Chapel Hill: University of North Carolina Press, 1989), 52–53.

43. Towers, *Urban South and the Coming of the Civil War,* 160; Harry L. Watson, *Jacksonian Politics and Community Conflict: The Emergence of the Second Party System in Cumberland County, North Carolina* (Baton Rouge: Louisiana State University Press, 1981), 315.

44. Wells, *Origins of the Southern Middle Class,* 67; Michael O'Brien, *Conjectures of Order: Intellectual Life and the American South, 1810–1860,* 2 vols. (Chapel Hill: University of North Carolina Press, 2003), vol. 1, chs. 2–3.

45. Nicholas and Peter Onuf, *Nations, Markets, and War: Modern History and the American Civil War* (Charlottesville: University of Virginia Press, 2006), 223–24, 252–53, 325.

46. Wells, *Origins of the Southern Middle Class,* 67, 162.

The Human and Financial Capital of the
Southern Middle Class, 1850–1900

MARTIN RUEF

> In all other countries there is a natural connection and dependence between the
> rich and the poor . . . when the middle class only is examined, it may appear to
> belong either to the upper or the lower sphere, according to the point from which
> it is viewed. Not so here. The line is marked. On one side lies the planter class,
> on the other the poor. Individuals may pass over the line, but the transition is
> abrupt. There are no intermediate resting-places.
>
> —MILTON CLAPP, *Southern Quarterly Review*

lthough the concept of the middle class is a central term in the social
science lexicon, the process of middle-class formation has typically
been ceded to historians as a subject of scholarly inquiry. As recently
as the early 1990s, a review by Melanie Archer and Judith Blau suggested that
social science theories have largely treated the emergence of a middle class as
a residual phenomenon, instead favoring a "two-class" model that emphasizes
tensions between the elite and a laboring proletariat.[1] Like Clapp, the editor of
the *Southern Quarterly Review* who denied the existence of a southern middle
class during the antebellum period, social scientists have often fallen back
on dichotomized conceptions of class history. While recent treatments have
enriched our theoretical understanding of the foundations of class, social scientific analysis of middle-class emergence has arguably made only limited
progress beyond the classic statement of C. Wright Mills in *White Collar*.[2]
Contemporary scholars seeking an account of the rise of the middle classes
will find most of them in community-based social histories, focusing on specific urban contexts or institutions that were supportive to the development
of a petit bourgeois consciousness. Influential studies include Stuart Blumin's
work on middle-class formation in the large seaboard cities of the northeast-

ern United States, Leonore Davidoff and Catherine Hall on the creation of 'middling' institutions in Britain, Lynne Feldman on the painstaking effort of blacks to carve out a middle-class community in segregated Birmingham, and C. Vann Woodward on the rise of an entrepreneurial class in the urban New South.[3]

This historical scholarship has offered rich insights into middle-class organization and culture, but takes a slightly different perspective than that adopted by sociologists and economists. Following E. P. Thompson's pioneering study of the English working class, a common emphasis in historical studies concerns the appearance of a self-interested class consciousness or a perception on the part of others that a class does (or does not) exist. In certain respects, this privileges the opinions and behaviors of historical observers. In contrast to this conceptualization of class-for-itself (or, in Marx's terms, "Klasse-für-sich"), quantitative social scientists tend to be inclined toward descriptions of class-in-itself ("Klasse-an-sich"), offering summaries of characteristics that may be linked systematically to a class, apart from self-awareness or self-promotion.[4] In this sociological conception, class formation is ultimately dependent on awareness of position, but meaningful distinctions in the objective relationship of individuals to the means of production (via investments in human and financial capital) typically constitute a precondition to such awareness. It is in this spirit that this essay considers the financial and educational correlates of middle-class existence in the South during the latter half of the nineteenth century.

As a research site, the South offers several critical advantages to students of social stratification. First, the South witnessed a particularly dramatic institutional transition between an agrarian system of chattel slavery, dominated by large landowners, and a purported "New South," with a nominal basis in a free labor market. As Woodward has argued, "the 'victory of the middle classes' and 'the passing of power from the hands of landowners to manufacturers and merchants,' which required two generations in England, were substantially achieved in a much shorter period in the [American] South." Second, this historical setting also permits us to revisit the thriving debate on occupational (or disaggregate) versus aggregate conceptions of class. Proponents of an occupational conception have suggested that a new class map is needed to track the processes of socialization, recruitment, and closure that occur around occupational categories at the site of production. Advocates of aggregate, particularly Marxist, conceptions of class counter that occupations merely constitute a technical relationship to production and that a broad understanding of exploitation—rather than individual life chances—hinges on the different relationships of large class groups to productive assets. The argument advanced here is that both conceptions offer empirical insights into the process of class formation, albeit with divergent conclusions in the case of the southern middle class.[5]

Drawing on census micro-data, this essay will suggest that the middle classes—when defined on an occupational basis—exhibited considerable heterogeneity in literacy and financial assets during the latter half of the nineteenth century. At the same time, aggregate analyses of financial and human capital within two factions of the middle class (an "entrepreneurial" and a "bureaucratic" group) indicate that these class positions were already differentiated from yeoman farmers, planters, and laborers during the antebellum era. Moreover, the entrepreneurial middle class became more delineated during the postbellum period, differentiating itself from bureaucratic middle-class elements and ultimately controlling more assets on a per capita basis than any other major class in southern society. Paralleling these trends at the individual level, the opportunity structure of the entrepreneurial class also became more clearly defined in the postbellum era. While antebellum shopkeepers, artisans, and professionals had no better access to financial institutions than common laborers on average, the entrepreneurial class became spatially concentrated in counties with banks and money lenders after the Civil War. The essay concludes by linking these developments in class structure more generally to contemporary and historical debates about the emergence of a middle class and a New South.

CONCEPTIONS OF THE MIDDLE CLASS

A central dilemma in the literature on middle-class formation is that there is not *one* middle class, but many middle classes. Archer and Blau, for instance, identify four distinctive occupational groups that appear in the literature on the history of the middle class, including skilled artisans, retailers and shopkeepers, a petite bourgeoisie of (non-retail) business owners, and the "new" non-manual white-collar class of clerks, managers, officials, and other employees of bureaucratic organizations. To this list, one might add the established professions of the nineteenth century—such as physicians, lawyers, and civil engineers—as well as quasi-professionals—such as teachers, nurses, journalists, and the like.[6] Although all of these occupational groups could lay claim to being part of the middle classes, it is not immediately evident what basis of social commonality is shared among them. Are the historical boundaries of the middle class marked by income and status? By education and cultural capital? Or by self-conscious efforts to associate and organize in view of shared collective interests?

To simplify matters somewhat, this essay begins with a basic differentiation of the middle classes into two groups: one defined by a propensity toward small business proprietorship (the "entrepreneurial" middle class) and another defined by a propensity toward non-manual employment in large organizations (the "bureaucratic" middle class). Viewed historically, the entrepreneurial middle class subsumes master artisans, small manufacturing proprietors, independent professionals, service proprietors, and storekeepers. The bureaucratic middle class includes clerks, white-collar employees, military and government officials, quasi-professionals, and salespeople. Farm proprietorship and employment are conventionally excluded from both definitions, thus distancing the middle classes from yeoman farmers, agricultural laborers, and slaves, as well as the landed gentry that dominated the antebellum South.

The division between the entrepreneurial and bureaucratic middle classes offers a number of empirical benefits to students of stratification. From a disaggregate perspective on class, it is relatively straightforward to employ detailed occupational information to delineate membership in each group. Moreover, records on business ownership allow analysts to evaluate the validity of definitions that hinge on particular subsets of occupations; for example, records can differentiate between a manufacturing proprietor with his own business and the laborers who are employed in his enterprise. From an aggregate perspective on class, the two groups enjoy a distinctive—though some would argue, transitory—relationship to capitalist production. In contrast to the landed gentry and owners of large industrial enterprise, the entrepreneurial middle class employs little or no wage labor, yet may exercise substantial control over financial and/or physical capital.[7] Likewise, members of the bureaucratic middle class do not employ wage labor directly, but exercise considerable control over their own activities (and, potentially, those of others) by virtue of their human capital. The clear organizational requirements of the entrepreneurial class (small, independent business enterprise) and bureaucratic class (larger nonagricultural organizations, typically with substantial administrative functions) allow us to explore the institutional preconditions of both with some precision.

CORRELATES OF MIDDLE-CLASS FORMATION

Literacy is considered to be a basic historical correlate of middle-class existence. Small entrepreneurs had to be literate in order to write orders for goods, manage inventories, extend credit, and enter into contracts. Independent professionals required literacy for their schooling and to keep up with the latest developments in law, medicine, or engineering. Bureaucratic professionals, by definition, were expected to follow and generate systems of written organizational rules. In the middle classes, perhaps the only exception to this pattern was found among skilled artisans and proprietors of small manufactories. Even in these occupations, enterprises benefited considerably from the human and cultural capital of literate owner-managers.[8]

Although the technical functions of literacy and numeracy come to mind most readily, historians and sociologists have also called attention to their rhetorical function for the middle classes. Newspapers and the periodical literature represent an important source of bourgeois ideas and solidarity in early capitalist societies. Advocacy for literacy and education can even become a *cause célèbre* among the middle classes, especially when it is opposed—as it often was in the antebellum South—by a landed gentry. Aside from its function as an enabler of middle-class enterprise, education offers a way to demarcate and legitimate the position of the petite bourgeoisie between a lower class of common laborers and an upper class of agrarian elites. Numeracy entails similar rhetorical advantages. For instance, the use of double-entry bookkeeping as an accounting method does as much to legitimate the trade of a merchant, as it does to ensure the valuation and verification of profit. This holds true, especially, when the audiences for such accounts are themselves members of literate and numerate classes.[9]

On the American South, there is some debate among historians as to the impact of literacy on the emergent middle class during the second half of the nineteenth century. In Jonathan Daniel Wells's thesis of antebellum class formation, the founding of schools, academies, and colleges exploded in the three decades *prior* to the Civil War, a rich literary culture emerged (especially among middle-class women), and intellectual exchange between North and South solidified class solidarity across sectional divisions. Similarly, Jennifer R. Green has found that the military schools that developed in the South during the 1840s and 1850s often served as a "launching pad for the professional careers of nonagricultural, non-elite" men, particularly through their vocational and scientific training. Historians have documented earnest attempts at public schooling in the antebellum era, even in areas—such as South Carolina— where such efforts were ultimately thwarted.[10]

Other scholars have been less sanguine about educational opportunities during the antebellum period. Edward Ayers notes the weak tradition of public schooling in the antebellum South—for blacks and whites—and lack of political support for educational institutions. In this perspective, one of the heralded accomplishments of the New South was the school reform that began in the 1880s and the matching improvements in educational expenditures and literacy.[11] As of yet, however, the historical record has been unclear as to whether this expansion in educational effort served to differentiate the middle class *in particular* (on the basis of human capital investments) or contributed to the educational uplift of *all* factions of southern society.

Along with literacy, systems of banking, credit, and a money economy constitute another basic institutional support to the middle class. Historically, small proprietors have relied on credit for loans, trade finance with suppliers or importers, and transactions with commission merchants. While the fortunes of a few large enterprises—and the bureaucratic middle class they employed—were tied to distant banks or wholesalers, the viability of most small entrepreneurs and managers depended on local financial infrastructure. Comprising part of a larger nineteenth-century movement in favor of "internal development," members of the middle classes were especially vocal proponents for bank creation.[12]

The character of capital allocation among the entrepreneurial middle class distinguished them from the landed gentry and yeoman farmers in agrarian society. Much of the economic well-being of farm proprietors was vested in physical capital, such as land, livestock, agricultural implements, farm structures, and, in the Old South, human property. The capital allocation of the small entrepreneur, on the other hand, required more flexibility. Liquid assets or short-term credit were needed among shopkeepers, master artisans, and physicians to maintain store inventories, procure raw materials, stock medical supplies, and the like. The existence of monetary exchange and banking greatly simplified these transactions.

In contrast to other institutional changes following the Civil War, the problems posed by financial reconstruction were not necessarily conducive to a thriving middle class. During the antebellum era, the cotton planter and his intermediaries were at the center of an elaborate financial network, linking banks, wholesalers, importers, and manufacturers. With the collapse of this system in the 1860s, the South faced severe shortages of credit and currency. A short-lived boom occurred in private banking, but the banking services available for the duration of the century were greatly reduced in scale compared to their level in 1860. Compounding these difficulties, postbellum debate about monetary standards (for example, gold versus greenbacks) generated profound uncertainty about the nature of monetary exchange. In this environment, the middle class itself—and rural storekeepers, in particular—became key financial intermediaries, passing goods and credit from wholesalers to family farmers through a consignment system.[13] These developments suggest that the monetary liquidity of the middle class in the postbellum era should be distinct from other classes in southern society, though, as in the case of literacy, there has been no systematic investigation of statistics on the financial capital of this group.

DATA AND MEASURES

The primary data for this essay are taken from the five censuses spanning the period from 1850 to 1900.[14] Analysis focuses on class composition in the Lower South, including the states of Alabama, Georgia, Louisiana, Mississippi, and South Carolina. The sampling frame is limited to this region for a number of reasons. As noted above, some historians, including Woodward, have suggested that a thriving middle class first emerged in the Lower South in the decades after the Civil War. By comparison, Blumin times the formation of a middle class in the more industrialized Northeast to the three decades before the Civil War, and Whig Party activism in the Upper South created conditions that were conducive to antebellum middle-class emergence. From a research design perspective, the nineteenth-century Lower South thus offers the most nascent stage of middle-class emergence covered by available micro-data. In addition, this region also experienced the most pronounced pattern of institutional change between the antebellum and postbellum periods. The transition between chattel slavery and a free labor market triggered many of the institutional antecedents of middle-class development, though the magnitude of these changes varied widely across different urban and rural areas in the Lower South. This context thus yields a natural experiment in which to explore the human and financial capital of an emerging middle class.[15]

Using a 1 percent random sample of the free population in the Lower South, as well as an oversample of African Americans in 1860 and 1870, the initial data set includes 251,845 person records. Since this study defines middle-class membership on an occupational basis, I generally restrict attention to individuals who were in the labor force and did not reside in group quarters (for example, correctional facilities, mental institutions, and poorhouses). To ensure comparability between the antebellum and postbellum eras, I also limit empirical analyses of human and financial capital to white adults, ages twenty and older. The resulting sample comprises 32,923 individuals between 1850 and 1900.

Selected measures from the micro-census records provide evidence for the evolution of human and financial capital among the southern middle class. I define middle-class membership on an occupational basis (see detailed list on page 210). Individuals are considered to be members of the *entrepreneurial middle class* when they (a) are likely proprietors of small independent businesses or partnerships; and (b) derive their income from nonagricultural pursuits. Historically, this subsumes artisans, proprietors of small manufactories, independent professionals, service proprietors, shopkeepers, and wholesale merchants. The definition excludes factory operatives and apprentices in the trades, who are classified as common laborers. It also excludes individuals often employed in cottage industry (for example, potters and basket-makers), as well as the construction trades (carpenters, masons, etc.), since these occu-

Artisans and Manufacturing Proprietors
Baker
Blacksmith
Boat Maker
Book / Newspaper Publisher
Bookbinder
Boot / Shoemaker
Brewer or Maltster
Butcher
Clock / Watchmaker
Confectioner
Cooper
Distiller / Refiner
Dressmaker
Engraver
Gilder / Goldsmith
Gun / Locksmith
Harness / Saddlemaker
Jeweler
Marble / Stonecutter
Mechanic or Machinist
Miller
Printer / Lithographer
Shipwright
Tailor
Tanner
Upholsterer
Wheelwright
Other Artisan or Proprietor†

Clerk or White-Collar Employee
Banker / Broker
Bookkeeper / Accountant
Clerk
Manager / Company Official
Other White-Collar Employee

Independent Professionals
Architect
Dentist
Engineer (Civil)
Lawyer
Physician
Veterinarian

Military or Government Employee

Quasi-Professionals
Actor / Artist
Auctioneer
Author
Barber
Clergy
Designer / Draughtsman
Journalist
Musician
Nurse / Midwife
Photographer
Teacher
Undertaker
Other Quasi-Professional

Salesperson

Service Proprietor
Billiard- or Bowling Saloon Keeper
Boarding-House Keeper
Hotel Keeper
Livery-Stable Keeper
Restaurant Keeper
Saloon Keeper

Storekeeper or Wholesaler
Commercial Broker
Trader or Dealer (any set of goods)

† Includes makers of agricultural implements, artificial flowers, blinds, brooms, brushes, cabinets, candles, carpets, carriages, cars, cordage, doors, hats, organs, patterns, pianos, pumps, sails, sashes, shirts, soap, steam boilers, stoves, tinware, tools, trunks, and woodenware.

pations tended to be associated with self-employment but not proprietorship of "brick-and-mortar" enterprise.

Members of the *bureaucratic middle class* are defined as either (a) non-manual employees of large organizations, such as banks, railroads, insurance companies, the military, or government; or (b) service-sector employees who are differentiated from common laborers, but have not attained the autonomy of independent entrepreneurs. In particular, the latter part of the definition differentiates between the established professions (medicine, law, engineering, and the like), which afford their occupants an opportunity for independent practice that places them in this essay's entrepreneurial category, and the quasi-professions (teaching, nursing, and ministry), which tend to position their occupants as employees of organizations or congregations and locates them in the bureaucratic group.[16]

I assess human capital via the census measure for *literacy*, referring to the ability to read or write in some language (not necessarily English). *Monetary liquidity* is assessed as the extent to which the assets of a respondent are invested in stores of wealth aside from real estate (for example, stocks, bonds, jewelry, or promissory notes).[17] Availability of real asset data is limited to the censuses from 1850 to 1870, while personal asset data is limited to 1860 and 1870.

The essay also considers the opportunity structure available to individuals who sought banking or educational institutions. Geographic access to financial capital is measured by the number of banks or money lenders located in the same county as a respondent. Using J. Smith Homans's *Bankers' Magazine and Statistical Register* and Robert G. Dun's *Reference Book*, I identify each national, state, and private bank in the counties of the Lower South.[18] I consider access to education via a county-level measure of the percentage of the school-age population (ages six to nineteen) who have attended a school, college, or university within the last year. For the sake of comparability with the individual-level data, this measure is derived from micro-census data on white children and adolescents in the Lower South.

RESULTS

Drawing on micro-census records, Table 1 summarizes the human and financial capital of the southern middle class in the antebellum and postbellum eras,

TABLE 1 Human and Financial Capital of Occupational Groups in the Lower South†

	ANTEBELLUM PERIOD (1850–60)			POSTBELLUM PERIOD (1870–1900)		
	Literacy Rate (%)	Value of Real Estate ($)	Value of Other Property ($)	Literacy Rate (%)	Value of Real Estate ($)	Value of Other Property ($)
Entrepreneurial Middle Class	95.91	1,874.78	3,858.44	95.42	1,578.14	1,113.88
Artisans and Manufacturing Proprietors	93.26	428.60	833.92	93.65	5,97.05	259.50
Independent Professionals	99.55	4,756.74	6,546.14	98.08	2,672.17	1,350.81
Service Proprietors	96.00	1,437.33	1,929.57	94.67	2,127.50	575.00
Storekeepers and Wholesalers	98.99	3,134.03	8,372.34	96.75	2,140.36	2,108.12
Bureaucratic Middle Class	99.54 *	1,182.85	2,212.13	97.40 *	490.30 ***	253.68 ***
Clerks and White-Collar Employees	100.00	8,18.92	1,259.05	97.70	441.21	205.19
Military and Government	96.43	737.68	2,440.00	95.62	703.44	608.36
Quasi-Professionals	99.60	603.57	1,676.37	96.82	519.69	245.03
Salespeople	—‡	—‡	—‡	99.04	—‡	—‡
Farm Proprietors	85.80 ***	2,662.05 *	6,286.43 ***	81.94 ***	1,268.40	671.54 ***
Laborers	87.18 ***	217.65 ***	283.73 ***	76.62 ***	158.71 ***	81.99 ***
Agricultural Laborers	85.56	258.14	377.34	72.59	54.15	66.34
Manufacturing Laborers and Apprentices	93.79	468.94	540.98	87.44	308.84	130.29
Service Laborers	85.07	74.60	113.23	76.23	306.06	90.11

| F-Test (across classes) | 67.63 *** | 21.90 *** | 48.20 *** | 349.16 *** | 30.90 *** | 53.45 *** |
| Total Sample Size | 8,929 | 8,956 | 5,157 | 23,994 | 5,901 | 5,901 |

Source: Integrated Public Use Microdata Series (IPUMS), 1% Samples (excluding 1890).

† For purposes of comparability, all samples are limited to white adults, age twenty and older.

‡ Less than twenty observations in these cells.

* p < .05; ** p < .01; *** p < .001 (two-tailed tests, comparisons to entrepreneurial class)

comparing the resources maintained by this group with those held by farm proprietors and by common laborers.[19] During the antebellum period, the entrepreneurial middle class was only weakly differentiated from its bureaucratic counterparts on these dimensions. Given bureaucratic reliance on systems of written rules, employees of large enterprises and quasi-professionals tended to be significantly more literate (99.5 percent) than small proprietors (95.9 percent). But these factions of the middle class cannot be distinguished on the basis of average financial capital, considered in terms of real estate or other assets. Owing to the high level of asset variance within each group, the differences reported in the table ($1875 versus $1183 for real estate and $3858 versus $2212 for other property) are not statistically significant.[20]

With respect to laborers and farm proprietors, the southern middle class occupied a predictable position in the status hierarchy. On average, members of the middle class were more literate than both laborers and farmers, possessed less land and other property (including slaves) than the yeoman farmers and planters, and owned more property than the laborers. On the basis of this distribution of human and financial capital, it seems appropriate to speak of an objective position for "middling sorts" during the antebellum era, consistent with qualitative evidence on class formation before the Civil War. However, this class position would have necessarily combined a diverse set of occupations, owing to the weak differentiation of capital among entrepreneurial and bureaucratic elements at the time.

In the postbellum era, the distinctive positions *within* the middle class became more apparent. The entrepreneurial and bureaucratic middle classes were now clearly differentiated, with the small proprietors controlling more land and liquid assets in pursuit of entrepreneurial profit and non-manual employees exhibiting a higher level of literacy in the service of large enterprise. With the demise of chattel slavery, the financial resources of the entrepreneurial class also placed them above farm proprietors in mean liquid assets ($1114 versus $672, $p < .001$) and marginally higher in real estate assets ($1578 versus $1268, $p \approx .06$). Statistically, this process of class differentiation is reflected to some extent in F-tests for the micro-census data, which compute the ratio of between-class variability over within-class variability (see Table 1).[21] During the antebellum period, these ratios were already high (more than 67 for literacy and between 20 and 50 for material wealth), suggesting that the distinctions among classes explained much of the variation in human and financial capital. The sole exceptions, in this regard, were the entrepreneurial and bureaucratic factions of the middle class, which remained undifferentiated in terms of material wealth. Considering the data after the Civil War, on the other hand, the F-test ratio for literacy jumps to a value approaching 350 and the test statistic increases for material wealth as well (falling within the range of 30 to 50). In contrast to its antebellum birth as a vague component of the "middling sorts," the entrepreneurial class appeared to achieve a cohesive class position in postbellum southern society. On average, members of the postbellum entrepreneurial class also amassed more assets than any other major occupational class.[22]

The unique structural position of the postbellum entrepreneurial class becomes even clearer when we consider the relative components of wealth among the groups (see Table 2). In contrast to agricultural producers, laborers, and the bureaucratic middle class, nonagricultural proprietors required substantial liquid assets in order to maintain store inventories and pay employees. Even during the antebellum period, this resulted in the lowest relative level of real estate holding (33 percent as a percentage of all assets) of any southern social class. Still, differentiation on this dimension from other classes (with the exception of laborers) was limited at the time. After the Civil War, the entrepreneurial middle class continued to display the most limited reliance on real estate as a store of wealth and was now significantly different on this measure

TABLE 2   Real Estate as a Percentage of all Property Value among Classes in the Lower South[†]

	ANTEBELLUM PERIOD (1860)	POSTBELLUM PERIOD (1870)
Entrepreneurial Middle Class	32.8	58.6
Bureaucratic Middle Class	38.8 *	65.9 **
Farm Proprietors	35.6	65.4 ***
Laborers	41.3 ***	65.9 ***
Total Sample Size	5153	5895

Source: Integrated Public Use Microdata Series (IPUMS), 1% Samples

† For purposes of comparability, all samples are limited to white adults, age twenty and older.

* $p < .05$; ** $p < .01$; *** $p < .001$ (two-tailed tests, comparisons to entrepreneurial class)

(p < .001) than farm proprietors, laborers, and the bureaucratic class, which all held around two-thirds of their assets in land and physical structures.

Aside from wealth and educational attainment, a full assessment of financial and human capital should also address the opportunity structure that individuals are confronted with. In Table 3, I consider the geographic access that members of different classes had to banking and schooling, based on their physical distribution across counties in the Lower South. During the antebellum era, the middle classes were somewhat fragmented with respect to organizational infrastructure. Owing to their importance in the urban economy, members of the bureaucratic middle class tended to be close to financial institutions. However, the location of the entrepreneurial middle class, which arguably had the greatest need for capital and credit, was far less propitious. Averaging less than one and a half banks in their county of residence, small business proprietors and professionals had a significantly lower chance of having a bank nearby than common laborers and most white-collar employees. In this respect, they fared better only than farm proprietors, who tended to migrate to underdeveloped areas during the antebellum period.[23] With respect to education, on the other hand, members of both middle classes were located in areas exhibiting significantly higher rates of school attendance than laborers, yeoman farmers, and planters.

As in the case of individual-level attributes, the statistics for the postbellum period reveal a shift for the entrepreneurial middle class. On average, the organizational density of financial institutions was now the highest in the counties of residence of business proprietors, even exceeding that of the bureaucratic middle class by a small, but statistically significant, margin. Whereas the average middle-class entrepreneur was confronted with a bank monopoly or duopoly during the 1850s, the number of local financial institutions for this class tripled in the postbellum era, yielding more opportunities for loans and capital accumulation. This development is particularly telling when coupled with evidence that a decline in local bank monopolies was linked with a convergence of interest rates during the same period.[24] More generally, the F-test for the postbellum census micro-sample suggests a more definitive separation between all major classes with respect to geographic proximity to banks and money lenders. With respect to schooling, the bureaucratic middle class appeared to enjoy the most advantageous ecological position in the postbellum era, though school attendance in counties settled by members of the entrepreneurial middle class continued to be comparatively high.

It is difficult to trace the effects of this opportunity structure on individual outcomes, though there is some evidence in the historical census as to how it served to perpetuate class status across generations. Pooling the data from 1850 until 1880, we can readily identify the higher rates of school attendance and literacy among the children of household heads who occupied middle-class positions. In nineteenth-century southern households headed by members of the bureaucratic or entrepreneurial middle classes, some 15 percent of school-age children were attending school during the year that the census was conducted and, during the postbellum period, 75 percent of those children over nine years of age were literate.[25] By contrast, in households headed by members of other classes, only 10 percent of their children were attending school at the time of census collection and 49 percent of the older children (age ten-plus) were literate. Although the data do not permit a more fine-grained investigation into the intergenerational transfer of human capital, it seems clear that members of the middle class were able to pass educational privilege on to their offspring, potentially sharpening class boundaries over time.

DISCUSSION

When did a coherent middle class emerge in the Lower South? Early in the twentieth century, the historian John Spencer Bassett argued that, "the rise of the middle class has been the most notable thing connected with the white population of the South since the war . . . everywhere trade and manufacturing is almost entirely in the hands of men who are sprung from the nonplanter class." Recent historical treatments suggest a more nuanced picture, with evidence pointing to a rich middle-class culture and record of community activism in the antebellum era.[26]

In this essay, I have sought to examine these claims by focusing on the human and financial capital of different occupational groups during the latter half of the nineteenth century. My point of departure is a sociological conception of "class-in-itself," which defines it not just as an aggregate of occupations, but also as a social relationship to a means of production. This social relationship entails control over (or access to) monetary resources, land, human

TABLE 3 Access to Banks and Schools among Occupational Groups in the Lower South†

	ANTEBELLUM PERIOD (1850–60)		POSTBELLUM PERIOD (1870–1900)	
	# of Banks in County	% of Children Attending School in County	# of Banks in County	% of Children Attending School in County
Entrepreneurial Middle Class	1.49	44.53	4.65	43.63
Artisans and Manufacturing Proprietors	1.29	43.55	5.28	43.83
Independent Professionals	0.75	46.24	2.32	39.63
Service Proprietors	2.72	45.98	4.45	48.24
Storekeepers and Wholesalers	2.12	45.21	4.91	44.05
Bureaucratic Middle Class	2.22 ***	45.35	4.31 *	45.21 ***
Clerks and White-Collar Employees	3.11	46.44	5.42	45.27
Military and Government	2.74	43.41	4.08	43.70
Quasi-Professionals	1.25	44.59	3.31	44.15
Salespeople	—‡	—‡	2.13	48.98
Farm Proprietors	0.08 ***	40.66 ***	0.33 ***	39.23 ***
Laborers	1.74 **	42.44 **	2.48 ***	40.04 ***
Agricultural Laborers	0.26	41.69	0.53	37.69
Manufacturing Laborers and Apprentices	1.22	41.91	3.00	42.94
Service Laborers	2.56	43.15	5.48	42.12

F-Test (across classes)	287.00 ***	23.55 ***	638.82 ***	116.86 ***
Total Sample Size	3,799	8,937	23,995	23,962

Sources: For banks, Homans (1850) and R. G. Dun and Co. (1870–1900). For schools, IPUMS (1850–1900) sub-sample of white children, ages six to nineteen.

† For purposes of comparability, all samples are limited to white adults, age twenty and older.

‡ Less than twenty observations in these cells.

* p < .05; ** p < .01; *** p < .001 (two-tailed tests, comparisons to entrepreneurial class)

capital, and labor. In this conception, a class exists objectively when it exhibits a distinct profile of skills and capital assets and engages in social relationships on the basis of that profile.

Applying this definition, I have found qualified support for both the antebellum and postbellum theses of middle-class emergence. In the decade before the Civil War, the Lower South's "middling sorts" were already fairly distinct from common laborers and farm proprietors in their level of literacy, real estate holding, and personal assets. However, their monetary liquidity and access to financial institutions were not yet fully aligned with the requisites of their class position. Nor were the internal divisions between the entrepreneurial and bureaucratic elements of the middle class clearly drawn at the time. By contrast, the entrepreneurial middle class in the New South was wealthier and more clearly differentiated from other middle-class elements than it had been in the mid-nineteenth century. By most standards, the fortunes of the entrepreneurial group had improved, placing it near the top of the southern status hierarchy in education, assets, and access to organizational infrastructure. These dimensions increasingly accounted for variance across broad classes of southern society, rather than variability within them.

The quantitative analyses offered in this essay have a number of methodological limitations. The measures of human and financial capital in the historical census records are fairly rudimentary. For instance, a more refined analysis of education might differentiate between various levels of schooling or trace the educational trajectories required for an individual in southern society to become a bona fide member of the "middling classes." Qualitative approaches— such as those represented in other essays within this volume—may be better suited to tackle these dynamics of middle-class emergence in the nineteenth century. The temporal frame of the analysis presented here is also limited by the availability of micro-census data, which presently do not predate 1850. Insofar as the early stages of middle-class emergence in the South occurred in the preceding decades, this essay may be missing a crucial period of antebellum class formation and differentiation.

While the statistics offered in this essay offer some insights into the southern middle class as a class-*in-itself*, they have little to say about this group as a class-*for-itself*. Nevertheless, there is considerable qualitative evidence to suggest the emergence of a self-conscious middle class, both before and after the Civil War.[27] In the closing decades of the nineteenth century, newspaper boosters were especially vocal in spreading the gospel of a New South that was built with the sweat of urban entrepreneurs and values of the middle class. Although the journalist Henry Grady, editor at the *Atlanta Constitution* during the 1880s, was perhaps the most vocal of these proponents, his ministry was soon carried forth by other journalists, as well as southern politicians such as Joseph E. Brown and Benjamin Hill. Along with a myriad of young southern progressives, these postbellum writers and politicians helped create the "New South Creed," an ideology of racial harmony and economic progress rooted in the leadership of a petite bourgeoisie.[28] Despite the persistence of Jim Crow and the relatively small number of entrepreneurs in the South, the creed was widely accepted as fact by 1900, sustaining the appearance of a vibrant middle class as a then-dominant feature of southern society.

NOTES

Epigraph: Milton Clapp, "The Prospects and Policy of the South," *Southern Quarterly Review* 10 (1854): 446.

1. Melanie Archer and Judith Blau, "Class Formation in Nineteenth-Century America: The Case of the Middle Class," *Annual Review of Sociology* 19 (1993). For other sociological critiques of dichotomous conceptions of class, see M. S. Hickox, "The English Middle-Class Debate," *British Journal of Sociology* 46 (1995), and Hayward D. Horton, Beverlyn L. Allen, Cedric Herring, and Melvin E. Thomas, "Lost in the Storm: The Sociology of the Black Working Class, 1850 to 1990," *American Sociological Review* 65 (2000).

2. C. Wright Mills, *White Collar: The American Middle Classes* (New York: Oxford University Press, 1951). Recent perspectives on neo-Marxist and occupational conceptions of class are reviewed by Erik Olin Wright, *Class Counts: Comparative Studies in Class Analysis* (Cambridge: Cambridge University Press, 1997); David Grusky and Jesper Sørensen, "Can Class Analysis Be Salvaged?" *American Journal of Sociology* 103 (1998); and Kim Weeden and David Grusky, "The Case for a New Class Map," *American Journal of Sociology* 111 (2005).

3. Stuart Blumin, *The Emergence of the Middle Class: Social Experience in the American City, 1760–1900* (New York: Cambridge University Press, 1989); Leonore Davidoff and Catherine Hall, *Family Fortunes: Men and Women of the English Middle Class, 1780–1850*, rev. ed. (London: Routledge, 2003); Lynne Feldman, *A Sense of Place: Birmingham's Black Middle-Class Community, 1890–1930* (Tuscaloosa: University of Alabama Press, 1999); and C. Vann Woodward, *Origins of the New South, 1877–1913* (Baton Rouge: Louisiana State University Press, 1951).

4. E. P. Thompson, *The Making of the English Working Class* (New York: Pantheon, 1963). The distinction between the subjective awareness of class position and its objective manifestation

is especially central to Marxist analysis of class consciousness; see Iring Fetscher, "Class Consciousness," in *A Dictionary of Marxist Thought,* ed. Tom Bottomore, 2nd ed. (Oxford: Blackwell, 1991), 89–91.

5. Woodward, *Origins of the New South,* 140–41. The occupational conception of class has been advanced, in particular, by Grusky and Sørensen, "Can Class Analysis Be Salvaged?" and Weeden and Grusky, "The Case for a New Class Map." An early Marxist critique is offered by Erik Olin Wright, "Class and Occupation," *Theory and Society* 9 (1980) and a more recent one by the same author in "The Shadow of Exploitation in Weber's Class Analysis," *American Sociological Review* 67 (2002).

6. Archer and Blau, "Class Formation in Nineteenth-Century America." Other discussions of the diversity in the middling classes can be found in Burton Bledstein and Robert Johnson, eds., *The Middling Sorts: Explorations in the History of the American Middle Class* (New York: Routledge, 2001). For an early and influential treatment of the social position of the professions, see Harold Wilensky, "The Professionalization of Everyone?" *American Journal of Sociology* 70 (1964).

7. Howard Aldrich and Jane Weiss, "Differentiation within the United States Capitalist Class: Workforce Size and Income Differences," *American Sociological Review* 46 (1981).

8. The issue of artisanal literacy was raised more than a century ago by W. E. B. DuBois, who noted that illiterate black artisans faced considerable obstacles in learning their trades during the antebellum era; see his *The Negro Artisan: A Social Study* (Atlanta: Atlanta University Press, 1902), 15. The problem of illiteracy only became more acute in the postbellum period, when, as Roger Ransom and Richard Sutch have written, "the skilled freedmen probably found illiteracy a major obstacle to pursuing artisan trades independently," given the need to keep books and communicate with distant suppliers or customers. Ransom and Sutch, *One Kind of Freedom: The Economic Consequences of Emancipation,* 2nd ed. (Cambridge: Cambridge University Press, 2001), 35.

9. On the historical role of newspapers and periodicals in middle-class culture, see Mary Ryan, *Cradle of the Middle Class: The Family in Oneida County, New York, 1790–1865* (Cambridge: Cambridge University Press, 1981). On the role of numeracy and accounting skills, see Bruce Carruthers and Wendy Espeland, "Accounting for Rationality: Double-Entry Bookkeeping and the Rhetoric of Economic Rationality," *American Journal of Sociology* 97 (1991).

10. Jonathan D. Wells, *The Origins of the Southern Middle Class, 1800–1861* (Chapel Hill: University of North Carolina Press, 2004); Jennifer R. Green, "Networks of Military Educators: Middle Class Stability and Professionalization in the Late Antebellum South," *Journal of Southern History* 73 (2007): 39 (quotation). See also Jennifer R. Green, "'Practical Progress is the Watchword': Military Education and the Expansion of Opportunity in the Old South," *Journal of the Historical Society* 3 (2005); Bruce Eelman, "'An Educated and Intelligent People Cannot Be Enslaved': The Struggle for Common Schools in Antebellum Spartanburg, South Carolina," *History of Education Quarterly* 44 (2004).

11. Edward Ayers, *The Promise of the New South: Life after Reconstruction* (Oxford: Oxford University Press, 1992). The possibility of educational uplift into a middle class was embraced by black leaders, in particular, whether as a means of expanding the ranks of skilled artisans and small proprietors or developing the "talented tenth" of college-educated freedmen; see W. E. B.

DuBois, *The Souls of Black Folk* (Chicago: A. C. McClurg, 1903). Owing to difficulties in antebellum and postbellum census comparability, though, this essay limits its attention exclusively to the white population in the South.

12. Martin Ruef and Kelly Patterson, "Credit and Classification: The Impact of Industry Boundaries in 19th Century America," *Administrative Science Quarterly* 54 (2009); David Carlton and Peter Coclanis, "Capital Mobilization and Southern Industry, 1880–1905: The Case of the Carolina Piedmont," *Journal of Economic History* 49 (1989); Wells, *Origins of the Southern Middle Class.*

13. On the importance of rural merchants as financial intermediaries, see Ransom and Sutch, *One Kind of Freedom,* 121–25. On the postbellum monetary debate, see Bruce Carruthers and Sarah Babb, "The Color of Money and the Nature of Value: Greenbacks and Gold in Postbellum America," *American Journal of Sociology* 101 (1996).

14. Steven Ruggles, Matthew Sobek, Trent Alexander, Catherine A. Fitch, Ronald Goeken, Patricia Kelly Hall, Miriam King, and Chad Ronnander, *Integrated Public Use Microdata Series: Version 3.0* [machine-readable database] (Minneapolis: Minnesota Population Center, 2004). The data from the integrated public use micro-data series (IPUMS) include the censuses for 1850, 1860, 1870, 1880, and 1900. Most of the 1890 federal census records were destroyed by fire and therefore do not yield usable micro-data.

15. Woodward, *Origins of the New South;* Blumin, *Emergence of the Middle Class.* For discussions of antebellum middle-class formation in the Upper South, see Wells, *Origins of the Southern Middle Class,* and Ralph Wooster, *Politicians, Planters, and Plain Folk: Courthouse and Statehouse in the Upper South, 1850–1860* (Knoxville: University of Tennessee Press, 1975). On local variations in the rise of the postbellum middle class, see Don Doyle, *New Men, New Cities, New South: Atlanta, Nashville, Charleston, Mobile, 1860–1910* (Chapel Hill: University of North Carolina Press, 1990).

16. On the difference between professions and quasi-professions, see Wilensky, "The Professionalization of Everyone?" Using census data, it is unfortunately not possible to draw more fine-grained distinctions, such as those cases where quasi-professionals are able to exercise greater autonomy as organizational founders (for example, teachers who start their own schools), as opposed to working as employees.

17. For 1870, the census itemization for "personal estate" was "to be inclusive of all bonds, stocks, mortgages, notes, live stock, plate, jewels, or furniture, but exclusive of wearing apparel." The 1860 itemization added the value of slaves.

18. J. Smith Homans, ed., *Bankers' Magazine and Statistical Register* (Boston: Wm. Crosby and H. P. Nichols, 1850); Robert G. Dun (and Company), *The Mercantile Agency Reference Book (and Key), Containing Ratings on Merchants, Manufacturers and Traders Generally, Throughout the United States and Canada* (New York: Dun, Barlow & Company, 1870, 1880, 1900). Using this definition, a bank can be a financial institution that is chartered by the state or federal government or an unchartered private entity (for example, moneylenders who extend credit but lack the legal ability to create deposits). The latter organizational form was especially active in the years immediately after the Civil War, when financial collapse led to a shortage of credit.

19. Note that data on literacy are available for the full time span (1850–1900).

20. In particular, the probability (p) values at the bottom of the table indicate when a difference between a statistic and the mean for the entrepreneurial middle class is unlikely to have occurred by chance alone (owing to sampling error). Thus, a single asterix denotes that there is less than a 5 percent chance that a given difference occurred due to sampling error, two denote that there is less than a 1 percent chance, and three denote that there is less than a 0.1 percent chance.

21. Although the F-tests may be compared across the antebellum and postbellum eras, the averages in the body of the table are not strictly comparable. Census question wording for literacy changed between 1860 and 1870, with one question in 1860 identifying those who could not read *and* write and two separate questions in 1870 identifying those who could not read *and* those who could not write. This difference in question wording appears to lower the literacy rate artificially following the Civil War. Question wording for personal assets also changed, since the value of "other property" included slaves in the antebellum period.

22. Remnants of the old planter elite continued to dominate the peak of the wealth distribution in 1870. Of the top 0.01 percent of all wealth holders in the Lower South (irrespective of age, employment, or race), about 42 percent were active planters with large landholdings and 19 percent were retirees or widows with large landholdings.

23. Donald Schaefer, "Locational Choice in the Antebellum South," *Journal of Economic History* 49 (1989).

24. John James, *Money and Capital Markets in Postbellum America* (Princeton: Princeton University Press, 1978).

25. The data for 1850 and 1860 only consider literacy rates for adult "children," age twenty or older. Consequently, they are not comparable to the postbellum measure of child literacy and are omitted from discussion here.

26. John Spencer Bassett, "The Industrial Decay of the Southern Planter," *South Atlantic Quarterly* 2 (1903): 112–13; also in Woodward, *Origins of the New South.*

27. For exemplary treatments of the antebellum and postbellum phases of class formation, see Wells, *Origins of the Southern Middle Class,* and Doyle, *New Men, New Cities, New South,* respectively.

28. Paul Gaston, *The New South Creed: A Study in Southern Mythmaking* (New York: Knopf, 1970). Canonical examples of the creed can be found in Joel Harris, *Life of Henry W. Grady, Including His Writings and Speeches* (1890; reprint, Whitefish, Mont.: Kessinger Publishing, 2004).

Reconstructing the Southern Middle Class
Professional and Commercial Southerners after the Civil War

JONATHAN DANIEL WELLS

In September 1866, the *New York Sun* lamented the collapse of southern commercial activity in an editorial that was reprinted in a Georgia newspaper. "The remarkable business activity which sprung up all over the South immediately after the conclusion of the war," the editorial read, "was regarded as a sure indication of the speedy prosperity of that desolate section." Such prosperity, however, was merely an illusion, according to the paper. "Unfortunately, time has proven that the wonderful business activity of the South was spasmodic, unnatural and transient . . . Trade is dull, money is scarce, times are hard, and a despondent feeling generally prevails."[1] Such sentiment was common among northern and southern businessmen in the immediate post–Civil War period, as tales of woe and despair filled the columns of newspapers and consumed considerable ink in the personal letters of postbellum southerners.

Although the collapse of the southern plantation economy in the aftermath of the Civil War has been well documented by modern scholars, much less is known about the trials and tribulations of commercial and professional men and their families. Scholars have done well to delve deeply into the postwar circumstances of the freedmen and freedwomen and their masters, and the picture that has emerged after many decades of work is one of racial violence, economic dislocation, social upheaval, and political turmoil. Largely missing from this picture, however, is the story of middling white southerners, among the least understood of all nineteenth-century Americans.

Complicating matters further, there were varied responses to Reconstruction within the South. All cities and towns did not experience the war or its aftermath in precisely the same ways. As Don Doyle has found, cities of the New South struggled with a range of postwar problems. While Atlanta and

Nashville prospered after Appomattox and took off economically in the 1880s, Charleston and Mobile languished.[2] Part of the reason for the differences in postwar urban recovery had to do with the level of destruction suffered during the war, but it seems a determined cohort of boosters was also a necessary ingredient for revitalization. Leading the boosters of the New South were the same middle-class southerners who had championed economic and cultural progress before the Civil War.

In contrast to the historical depiction of the former slaves who struggled mightily to make their way in the New South and the planters who lost all in the destruction caused by advancing Union troops, middle-class southerners would seem likely to have fared much better in the aftermath of the Civil War. After all, such men and women would have the most to gain by the region's move toward a more modern, industrialized, and urban future. As the South jettisoned the baggage of an economy focused so sharply on cotton, and since the region was forced against its will to abandon slavery, the path appears to have been opened to a New South dominated by a class of commercial and professional southerners. This southern middle class stood to benefit most from the destruction of the Old South and the onset of a new economic and social reality. As C. Vann Woodward argued in *The Origins of the New South*, in the postwar period men "of middle-class, industrial, capitalist outlook, with little but a nominal connection with the old planter regime" would seize the reins of political and economic power by joining forces with northern capitalists.[3] Indeed, reformers such as Henry Grady symbolize the very term "New South," providing an ideological foundation for a more modern region that valued cultural progress in the form of public schools and libraries, a more diversified economy that welcomed industry alongside agriculture, and a society unburdened by the debilitating weight of slavery.

As scholars have also pointed out, even as the New South left slavery behind, new forms of racial violence and economic subjugation took root in the postwar period. The terrorizing of former slaves by paramilitary groups like the Ku Klux Klan, the trap of sharecropping and tenant farming, and the continuing dominance of the economic and power structure by many of the same Confederates who led the region into war are also part of the prevailing Reconstruction narrative. The story of Reconstruction, however, cannot be complete without an understanding of those southerners who were neither former slaves nor former planters. Just as the antebellum southern middle class allows us to see the society and culture of the Old South in a new light, an assessment of the postwar southern middle class offers a similar opportunity to reexamine Reconstruction through the experiences of professional and commercial interests. How well did they fare in the midst of devastation and humiliation? How did other southerners react to middle-class calls for economic and cultural reform?

Examining middle-class southerners in the years after the war offers insight into the precarious nature of business and professional life in the region. For, far from prospering in the early stages of the New South, these southerners suffered from economic woes, suspicion, and vigorous opposition from southerners of other classes. In fact, middle-class southerners faced a postwar southern culture that seemed wholly antithetical to the values and ideology promulgated by the middle class in the antebellum period. For example, the elaborate links and associations that had been so important to the antebellum culture and trade of both sections, and had led to the rise of a southern middle class before the war, were not easily rebuilt. Indeed, in the decade following Lee's surrender, middling southerners found themselves floundering, criticized as never before, attacked for the very practices and ideas around which they formed a class identity. As a result, a class that before the Civil War had forged a distinct and coherent consciousness faced a significant crisis of legitimacy when the fighting ceased. In what might have been a moment of ascendance, when the southern middle class could say with justification that it had warned against the disaster of war and had been right to question secession, middling southerners confronted significant challenges to their vision for the region's future. This essay explores those challenges in the immediate aftermath of the war. Far from a period when the southern middle class emerged triumphant from the ashes of the war, the late 1860s and 1870s were years in which a previously self-conscious class of southerners struggled to regain its identity and legitimacy.

In the immediate aftermath of the war, the crisis of legitimacy experienced by the southern middle class continued and intensified. First, the associations formed between northerners and southerners were not reestablished as quickly or as easily as all had hoped. Almost as soon as it became clear that the Confederacy might suffer defeat, middle-class southerners attempted to reunite with their northern counterparts and their efforts to restore trading relationships with northern firms began early. For example, the Savannah chamber of commerce petitioned President Abraham Lincoln in January 1865 to allow the city to restore relationships "as early as convenient."[4] Northern firms sent letters as well as agents themselves to assess the postwar state of their clients. One of New York's most prominent suppliers to southern merchants, Charles Leverich & Co., corresponded with clients throughout the postwar South and relied on such communication to acquire information about local conditions. The Leverich Papers, as well as the papers of other New York firms, contain hundreds of letters from late 1864 and early 1865 from southerners seeking desperately to reestablish business relationships.[5]

In the midst of the frenzy to reconnect with antebellum business associates, southerners who before the war had called for economic diversification in the region renewed their calls for southern manufacturing and industry. Chief among these advocates was James D. B. DeBow, whose antebellum magazine proved a tireless advocate for the cause of expanding southern industry. Right after the war, *DeBow's Review* resumed its push. In a representative essay, DeBow asserted that "*We have got to go to manufacturing to save ourselves. We have got to go to it to obtain an increase in population. Workmen go to furnaces, mines, and factories—they go where labor is brought.*"[6] DeBow also advocated an increase in immigration to the region, from both the North and abroad, to provide the necessary labor force for this expansion.

The well-documented postwar financial difficulties experienced by southern merchants made attempts to reconnect with northerners even more problematic. One Texas merchant wrote in 1865 that "Our country is in a state of anarchy . . . murders and stealing is the order of the day here."[7] Richard Arnold, a Savannah doctor, complained in February 1865 that in his city "bank capital has been swallowed up in the vortex of Confederate currency; her immediate railroads have been damaged to an extent which will require a large amount of labor and capital to repair; and the productive powers of the country at large are . . . entirely prostrated."[8] Yet, for many southerners, the state of the region provided a chance to prove that, although they were suffering, opportunities could also be had. As a contributor to *DeBow's Review* put it, "Our young men have lost their slave property . . . [but] let them show the world that they can maintain their standard and station in society by other means. They can assume the management of a mine, of a forge, of a mill, of a factory, of a vessel."[9] The magazine optimistically called for the reemergence of the pro-business fervor that had prevailed in the 1850s.

Despite such optimism, in the late 1860s it was hard to see in which direction the local economies were heading from month to month. Frequently in postwar southern newspapers essayists might express great optimism but their columns would regularly be followed in the same paper several weeks later by tales of doom and despair. For example, the Savannah *Daily Herald* reported in March 1866 that there was "in some minds the apprehension that a financial panic is at hand . . . It is obvious to all that if the present condition of affairs grows worse . . . the panic will soon become general."[10] Yet less than two months later its sister paper reported that "We anticipate for Savannah a brighter future than she has ever yet realized."[11] The uncertainty of political reconstruction and the lingering problems with reestablishing links to northern businessmen made the economic future extremely uncertain. With little firm or reliable information to go on, middle-class southerners alternated constantly between pessimism and optimism, riding a roller coaster of economic anxiety.

Middle-class anxieties were only exacerbated when measures designed to aid economic recovery actually created new tensions within the class itself. The Federal Bankruptcy Act passed in 1867 attempted to help middle-class southerners with debt relief. As one Mississippian argued, the law was designed to help "merchants, bankers, and traders" and others in "this useful class of the community" to meet their obligations to northern and southern creditors.[12] Personal property exemptions were clearly aimed at those in middle-class professions, such as the exemption of books worth up to $250 for doctors and lawyers. Yet, this was also a fight that divided the southern middle class, for many of the creditors were in fact small commercial firms. As scholar Elizabeth Lee Thompson has shown, two of every three creditors in and around Charleston were partnerships and almost all of those were either merchants or professionals. Only one in three creditors was a planter.[13]

New tensions within the middle class added to the economic hardships and sense of defeat and humiliation that southerners experienced after the war, a combination that was so overpowering that the immediate postwar culture itself created a climate that was antithetical to the middle class agenda of economic and cultural reform. Indeed, some southerners seemed to revel in the destruction and privation from which their region suffered. Despair had so consumed their outlook that the pursuit of business and prosperity became subjects impossible to consider. "Prosperity" became for many an anathema, a cruel word worthy of condemnation. As Albert Taylor Bledsoe wrote in the *Southern Review* in early 1869, "This generation of the South . . . has but one mission; the sublime mission, namely, to bear its awful lot with quiet resignation to the will of Heaven . . . remembering the time-honored adage, that 'Adversity makes men; prosperity, monsters.'"[14]

This was the context in which the southern middle class sought to reestablish its class identity: the very notion of pursuing prosperity in the midst of such trauma created suspicion. The prosperity and boosterism that we now associate with the term "New South" was far off on the horizon for many southerners in the late 1860s and early 1870s. Southerners identified themselves with suffering and loss, and their Protestant faith had taught them much about the virtues to be gained through distress. A contributor to *DeBow's Review* claimed that "adversity is a stern school, but it is the gymnasium of great souls."[15] Resignation was for many southerners an entirely acceptable and legitimate way to deal with the crisis. It is not too much to say that many southerners felt that there was little choice but to embrace their pain. Indeed, some argued that the South would lose its identity in the pursuit of wealth. "The danger," warned Virginia's Edward A. Pollard, is that southerners would "lose their literature, their former habits of thought, their intellectual self-assertion, while they are too intent upon recovering the mere *material* prosperity . . . But there are higher objects than the Yankee *magna bona* of money and display, and loftier aspirations than the civilization of material things."[16] Pollard told the readers of his newspaper that cultural preservation was more important than the pursuit of profit, a claim that middle-class southerners rejected.

Protestant criticism of materialism, which manifested itself in attacks on "Mammonism" before the Civil War, resonated even more strongly in the midst of postwar misery. Historian Kenneth Moore Startup has documented considerable opposition to materialism, commercialism, and greediness among southern clergymen, who often associated the pursuit of profit with merchants. In fact, Startup argues persuasively that Protestant clergy interpreted the financial panics of 1819, 1837, and 1857 as appropriate divine punishment for the region's greed. So it might not be surprising that many postwar observers similarly interpreted the suffering caused by the war as retribution for slavery and the pursuit of wealth. "Famine, pestilence and war," one Alabama minister asserted in a letter to his merchant brother, "are all the scourges which God employs to chastise guilty nations." North Carolinian Samuel Wilson agreed: "I own that we were sinners and deserved severe correction from God for our sin." Of course, such materialism could be equated with the conquering North in the minds of many southerners. As the Reverend B. M. Palmer lamented in an 1872 address at Washington and Lee University, "The spirit of materialism . . . is the angel of pestilence dropping the seeds of death from its black wing whenever it sweeps . . . and making [people] depend upon the interest and caprice of large capitalists."[17]

But it was not just merchants who faced this suspicion in the postwar period; town lawyers too experienced a backlash. There is a long history of antipathy toward lawyers in Western culture, but this hostility was not as apparent in the antebellum South as it was after the war. Like their middle-class merchant counterparts, town lawyers were accused of cunning and conniving, of harboring a willingness to lie and cheat to turn a profit. One Atlanta lawyer described his colleagues this way: "They drummed up cases and sought clients with as much avidity as a Chatham street clothier would seek customers."[18] In such characterizations, views of lawyers paralleled views of southern businessmen. One essayist, for example, claimed that "the suspicions concerning this class of professional men" was based upon those who "consider them as unscrupulous in the courtroom, mystifiers of the law, perverters of the truth, and the fast friends of knaves of many description."[19] Reactions against the bar grew even stronger when it became apparent that many lawyers were aiding the postwar North. An attorney in Florida, for example, was chastised for representing northern creditors as a collection agent and investigator.[20] Stories about such "spies" and "traitors" in their midst only intensified southerners' existing misgivings about lawyers.

Physicians came in for their share of attacks for hiding their lack of medical knowledge under a cloak of professionalism. One southerner was asked what the letters "M.D." stood for and "he replied that he did not know for 'sartain,' but thought it meant *Modest Dunce*."[21] Doctors had been held in high esteem throughout much of the South in the mid-nineteenth century, as historian Steven Stowe has found.[22] But in the postwar reexamination of the value of professional men to society, doctors were tossed in with lawyers and merchants. As one Virginia commenter complained in 1867, "Are we under the new order of things, as we were under the old, to be overstocked in Virginia with professional men? . . . We have now more lawyers, doctors, and other non-producers than are needed. There are enough to last for twenty or thirty years . . . Most of them will be poor but proud gentlemen as long as they live."[23] Nineteenth-century Americans doubted the training and skill of physicians, much as they denounced the lawyer's willingness to bend the truth and the merchant's devotion to profit.

At the same time that middle-class professionals were being assailed, southerners exalted the virtues of the small farmer, harkening back to prewar sentiments that would contribute to later lamentations for the Lost Cause. While southern reformers claimed that the Old South and its myopic defense of slavery and cotton were to blame for the region's plight, others argued that a return to the basics of small farm life would save the region from descending into Yankee-like materialism and financial ruin. "I venture to say," wrote a Baltimore farm supporter in 1868, "that twenty merchants fail in business to one farmer, and this ought to open the eyes of young men with small capital going into business."[24] In the postwar reassessment of what caused the war and thus the South's ruin, farmers were quick to blame the region's supposed softness and penchant for leisure. According to a Richmond newspaper in 1867, before the war "labor was not honored . . . Almost every young man of any pretensions studied law or medicine . . . or, if the son of a merchant, to merchandise. Only those who had no choice between pursuits became mechanics or artisans."[25] Hard work and a return to rural values were the keys in the eyes of such southerners. Indeed, many reasserted the old denunciations of the city as antithetical to virtuous living. As one observer warned, "Stay away from the city as from an evil genius! Here are libraries and societies and learned men, it is true; but these are hard to reach and enjoy; the learned men are busy and reserved; the societies are either very exclusive or very common; the libraries are of practically little value, save to mere readers."[26] Such sentiments became an important ideological foundation for associations of farmers that would later sweep the South and West. As North Carolina's Michael Shoffner put it in 1873, "We think here that what we call middle men are making more money off of us Farmers than they should and therefore we will form ourselves into an association for the purpose of protection."[27] The farmers' revolt of the late 1800s was brewing, and merchants were among the revolt's key targets.

Agricultural newspapers and magazines urged young southern men to consider agriculture as a profession. "Agriculture," one southerner observed in 1867, "is free from many of the corroding and heart-sickening cares which fall to the lot of the merchant, lawyer, and physician."[28] A rural Georgian, who signed his contribution to an Atlanta paper with the telling moniker "One Eye," even questioned the manhood of southern young men who opted for professional or commercial careers rather than farming. "We allude to the great *mania* of Southern parents for transforming their sons into lawyers, doctors and merchants. . . . Gentlemen of leisure should now come forth from their downy couches, and rise with the morning's sun . . . Our fast, fashionable, pretty, smart, and promising boys, should lay aside their cigars, and endeavor to invest more *sense* in their heads than *cents* on their backs."[29] The thinly veiled implication, of course, is that *real* men work with their hands, awaken early in the morning, and (presumably) avoid downy couches at all costs. Middle-class southerners thus had to confront not only postwar economic difficulties and attacks on their character, but they also had to contend with attacks on their masculinity. In these attacks, farmers were conflating the planters and their penchant for leisure with what they saw as the nonproductive professional classes.

In the eyes of many, professional and commercial southerners were suspect for another powerful reason. Despite the postwar miasma, many middle-class southerners sought to establish the roots of a new South that would one day emerge from the economic devastation of the war, and in pursuing this vision free from slavery and from a singular dependence on cotton farming, spokesmen for the middle class were often perceived by fellow white southerners as prominent advocates of liberal reforms. As historian Hyman Rubin notes in his book *South Carolina Scalawags,* many white southern Republicans were men of middling means who had opposed secession before the war. Radicals like South Carolina's Simeon Corley, a tailor who had argued against secession and war, preached racial equality, including universal suffrage, after the war.[30] While Corley's liberalism was certainly an exception, other professional and commercial interests believed a New South required new ideas, even on matters of race. James Alex Baggett found similarly in his study that many scalawags had opposed secession and the war and continued to harbor reformist views during Reconstruction. Men such as Louisiana's Anthony Dostie, a dentist, were active during the war as Unionists and then joined the Republican Party when the fighting ceased.[31]

Middling southerners were also well represented among postwar southern Republicans, a fact that did much to increase suspicion among other whites. Like the Whigs before them, the postwar southern Republicans led the calls for economic and cultural reform. As Carl Degler has noted, in South Carolina, Alabama, and Texas a high percentage of Radical Republicans were "business or professional men." And in another study, of 140 active Republicans identified in Mississippi, 12 were physicians.[32] Before the war, many middle-class southerners favored the Whig Party due to its support for internal improvements such as banks and railroads and its greater friendliness toward cultural and intellectual progress like public schools and libraries. Calvin Wiley, the leading advocate of public education in antebellum North Carolina, for instance, was a leading southern Whig. Similarly, after the war, significant southern middle-class support for the Republican Party was due in no small part to that party's stated positions in favor of postwar expansion of industry and manufacture, as well as its progressive approach to governmental activism in supporting education. Samuel F. Phillips delivered a Fourth of July oration in Concord, North Carolina, in 1870 that tied the Republican Party to the prosperity and peace that he hoped would become the hallmark of the New South. Highly critical of the Ku Klux Klan (KKK), which in his mind had "led to gross outrages upon the person, to assassination, and to a reign of terror," Phillips argued that the Republican Party was the vehicle through which southerners should create a new order. "It is for that reason," Philips proclaimed to his audience, "that I co-operate with the Republican Party. It seems to me that all quiet men who wish to establish a foundation upon which the fabric of private fortune, for themselves and their children, may be erected, will be apt to do so too. Industry cannot flourish but with an assured peace."[33] To the dismay of Democratic white supremacists, pro-business Republicans favored putting aside racial grudges for the sake of creating a climate conducive to business.

Not all who advocated a New South based on a prosperous and growing middle class favored progressive approaches to remaking society. In fact, many argued that removing the freedmen and exiling them to Africa or the North would facilitate the erection of a bourgeois Republic. At the end of the war, the Houston *Tri-Weekly Telegraph* newspaper created its version of a utopian New South, one that conspicuously left out the former slaves. By removing the freedmen from the South, "the country will be peopled by a white population, and society will be organized and established." The paper acknowledged that "there will still be large proprietors probably, but in connection with them will rise up that strength and glory of a country—a prosperous, strong-charactered, intelligent, and refined middle class—a population that can vote as well as labor, and intelligently and healthfully represent the wealth of the country in its legislative councils."[34] This was the view of many pro-business Democrats: a rebuilt New South could only prosper under white dominance.

In general, though, many postwar professionals and merchants were more open-minded when it came to expanding the rights of the freedmen. A writer in *DeBow's Review,* the nineteenth-century South's leading commercial magazine, advocated an open mind when it came to the former slaves. The freedmen "should be treated with the greatest possible kindness . . . [and] every reasonable effort should be made to alleviate their condition, to elevate them in the scale of civilization . . . [and] to educate them for their new situation."[35] Others interested in the development of manufacturing in the region called for ways to attract northern and European immigrants to the South.[36] One should not overestimate the progressiveness among middling southerners, for few of them backed black suffrage or other similarly radical notions. But in the eyes of their southern neighbors, who associated radicalism and racial equality with the abolitionist North, any hint of progressive ideas emanating from the middle class rendered such men suspect.

Despite such negative views of the middle class from their fellow southerners, there were many in the region who continued to trumpet the virtues of a healthy middle class. Indeed, references were often made to the "healthy" or "happy" middle class that is the "bulwark" of any stable society. Georgia's *Macon Weekly Telegraph* newspaper claimed that the generally content middle class rendered them less likely to succumb to a range of maladies. "Hysteria," the paper noted, "occurs more frequently among the very rich and the very poor, the happy middle class being most free from it." In fact, in such discussions about culture one can discern subtle critiques of the upper class, evidence not only of a class consciousness but also of significant mistrust between the classes. "The young women of the richer classes, pampered and coddled, whose whims and wants have been served without stint or opposition, often pass into hysterical conditions without any special determining cause."[37] The *Weekly Telegraph* similarly argued that suicide was much less likely among the middle class. "Many have observed," the paper declared in an editorial in 1886, "that suicides . . . occur chiefly among the very poor or very rich, the larger portion being with the former. The middle class, and by that is meant the laboring well-to-do respectable people of all occupations, is not a fruitful source of suicidal tragedies." Here the newspaper repeated a trope common throughout the nineteenth-century North and South: that the middle class was largely content, stable, and working too hard to succumb to self-pity. The middle class, in its busy, hardworking routine, did not have time to daydream or ponder that which might lead to depression. Recounting the case of one young gentleman, the paper noted that "very recently a young man in a neighboring city was found dead with a bullet through his brain. He had been reared in comfort . . . [but] from occupation to occupation he drifted, losing gradually fortune, usefulness, character, friends, resolution and self-respect." Interestingly, it was the lack of usefulness that really doomed this formerly wealthy man, for as the columnist concludes, "there is a strong, healthy lesson in these extremes, which meet at the grave, the idle poor and the idle rich."[38] Importantly, such values had long been an integral part of middle-class ideology.

While some editors attributed the virtues of hard work, usefulness, and stability of character to the middle class, other southerners, particularly those rural and agrarian interests who distrusted the commercial and professional occupations, continued to pin vices such as luxury, a penchant for leisure, and idleness on the southern middle class. Even in the late 1870s, the same southerners who idealized small farmers questioned the value of the middle class. "Our public schools," complained one Georgian, "now give to the children of the poor, and to the great middle class, and education that includes ornamental and many other branches . . . They want situations in stores, banks, or professions. These places are filled. There is no demand for clerks or lawyers . . . If an advertisement calls for a young man to fill a situation in an office or store, a troop answers the call . . . No one wants to *work* who can get his living by his *wits.*"³⁹ Clearly, within a society in the midst of its own gradual transformation from a rural to an increasingly urban economy, there existed no consensus on the meaning and characteristics of the middle class. Whereas by the late antebellum period southerners had largely agreed that the term "middle class" was reserved for professionals such as physicians, lawyers, teachers, and others, as well as for commercial occupations such as merchants, shopkeepers, and small-scale entrepreneurs, that consensus on the meaning of middle class was lost in the trauma of war. And similarly, while antebellum southerners could agree that there were benefits to society in having an industrious middle class, even that sentiment was under siege in the postwar South. While some observers like DeBow continued to highlight the virtues of the middle class, others, particularly those of a rural and agrarian mindset, saw an opportunity to question once again the very notion that an energetic, prosperous, educated, and entrepreneurial middle class brought much benefit to society at all.

These agrarian and urban interests conflicted in other ways as well. In contrast to traditional, agrarian mistrust of foreign influences, postwar middle-class southerners vigorously and persistently called for more immigration from the North and Europe to the South. Aware that the antebellum flood of European immigrants helped to spur the economic growth of northern cities and speed the processes of industrialization and urbanization, southern businessmen in particular advocated new and far-reaching plans to encourage immigration and migration as soon as Robert E. Lee surrendered at Appomattox. Agents and land companies eagerly promoted the new opportunities in the former slave states just as they had advertised Boston and New York to Europeans. The Southern Land Company of New York published brochures and pamphlets that promised "farms and homes for the people." Emigrants, one booklet promised, had "an opportunity to secure a good farm and a home in a [North Carolina] settlement, at less cost than the rent of an ordinary tenement in the cities."⁴⁰ Immigration, particularly the influx of workingmen who could provide the necessary labor to promote southern industrialization, was deemed essential to the future prosperity of the region. One Georgia observer claimed that without immigration and a reduction of taxes, "the present rapid progress of the country to an extinction of the middle class, and a grand division between capitalists and paupers, will be increased to railway speed."⁴¹

These same southerners, however, were also fully cognizant that the region's reputation for aristocracy, lackluster interest in modernization, and general lassitude in business would harm their attempts to draw new people to the former slave states. The postwar resurgence of the KKK, many in the South knew, would hamper attempts to facilitate population growth. In a speech to Republicans in Smithfield, North Carolina, in 1870, Robert M. Douglas chastised fellow whites for ignoring the effects of racial violence. "You talk of the injury done to the State by Radical extravagance and corruption," Douglas admonished his audience, "when you know that your acts of violence and midnight assassination have done more to ruin its credit than any possible amount of extravagant appropriation." Douglas, son of Stephen A. Douglas and a future justice of the North Carolina Supreme Court, stated boldly that as long as this "Kukluxism continues the emigrant will shun the State like he would the den of a moccasin; and the capital we need so much to improve our magnificent country, will seek some safer channel of investment."[42] Those like Douglas interested in a truly New South advocated reforms that would sever the region from its violent past, especially the view of the region expressed by the North. Here southerners like Douglas mirrored the antebellum southern middle-class concern for how the region was viewed by outsiders. Antebellum advocates for an end to dueling, for the erection of public schools and libraries, and for greater attention to industrialization were constantly comparing North and South and lamenting the latter's backwardness. The prewar southern middle class often unabashedly held up northern cities like New York and Philadelphia as models for their own region to follow. In calling attention to the negative perception of the New South and its racial violence, Douglas made clear that the South had to reform itself in fundamental ways if it was to attract laborers from the North or Europe.

The New South and its middle class largely carried over prewar ideas regarding gender roles. Before the war, a few middling southern women could be seen in important roles as editors and authors, and even occasionally as proprietors themselves. Antebellum southern women read the same periodicals, like the widely popular *Godey's Lady's Book*, as their northern sisters. Although scholars have often emphasized the differences separating northern and southern women, recent research has evinced little difference between northern and southern notions about gender.[43] The middle classes in the antebellum and postbellum North and South shared a great deal culturally, especially notions about domesticity and the proper sphere for women in society. In both sections after the war a small but vocal minority of men and women spoke in favor of the expansion of women's rights, including suffrage. Northern activists were echoed by leading southern voices like newspaper editors Eliza Nicholson, Ellen J. Dortch, and A. B. Stark. Such female journalists became a leading force in the southern middle class along with popular postwar authors like Mary Edwards Bryan and Sherwood Bonner.

Harkening back to sentiments routinely heard in the 1820s and 1830s, postwar American women were contrasted with their degraded counterparts in Old Europe. "The typical American woman," declared the Columbus [Georgia] *Daily Enquirer*, "the woman of the great middle class, does almost everything that is worth doing in this country."[44] An especially powerful trope that spanned the nineteenth century was the admonition to middle-class women to avoid extravagance and luxury. In contrast to the materialism of the upper class, southern class ideology stipulated that middle-class women demonstrated virtue by resisting such temptations. As the *Daily Enquirer* maintained in an 1870 editorial, "Let our ladies dress neatly and becomingly, but not to a degree to impoverish and cripple those upon whom they are dependent—and our word for it, there will be less envy and more charity extant; for really it is the poor and middle classes who must suffer, in their attempts to imitate the examples of the more wealthy and fortunate."[45]

By the 1880s, a decade similar in many ways to the prosperous and dynamic 1850s, the southern middle class would begin to regroup to play leadership roles in the economic and political rebuilding of their region. Not only were the 1880s years of vigorous economic and cultural change, but by this time the middle class had also begun to assume greater visibility in leading local and state governments. As Don Doyle found, about one-third of the leaders of postwar Nashville and Atlanta "were descended from the small antebellum middle class of merchants, lawyers, physicians, schoolteachers, and clergy."[46] But in the late 1860s and 1870s, the road to prosperity and political power for the southern middle class was not at all clear. Commercial and professional southerners suffered not just from the obvious economic dislocation that followed the Confederacy's surrender, but they also faced more amorphous challenges to their legitimacy. Thus, the nineteenth-century evolution of the middle class can hardly be described as a smooth one from coherent antebellum social class to the triumphant leaders of C. Vann Woodward's New South. Between the 1860s and the 1880s, the southern middle class faced powerful tests of its most fundamental values and ideology.

By the 1880s, a new African American middle class of commercial and professional interests also emerged within the urban South. Rising literacy rates and expanded opportunities provided African American men and women with means to economic advancement, even in the face of the crushing violence and intimidation of Jim Crow and the KKK. Southern black men became shopkeepers, barbers, merchants, and manufacturers, while black women entered new fields such as teaching and journalism. As Leslie Brown has found in *Upbuilding Black Durham,* southern towns and cities harbored an increasingly complex black social structure that is in need of further study.[47]

Within the decade of the 1880s too one can readily observe the sharpening of class consciousness, the hardening of boundaries between classes, and new and more intense forms of class conflict. Southerners were at the heart of these battles among the working, middle, and upper classes. Yet without acknowledging that an awareness of class, and even varying degrees of class conflict, has always been a part of southern history, the Grange and populist movements seem strangely out of character for the region. Without coming to terms with and understanding the distrust and anger between southerners of different means, the fights that would erupt at the end of the nineteenth century appear out of context. Even the class struggles of the 1880s were tied to the middle class. The Socialistic Labor Party, as reported the *Dallas Morning News* in 1885, believed that the modern economy "destroys the middle class and creates two separate classes of individuals, the wage worker and the bosses."[48] Despite a scholarly and popular reputation as a homogeneous time and place, the nineteenth-century South was wrought with class conflict that sometimes flared above the surface and sometimes remained an undercurrent, but was almost always nearby, lurking for an opportunity to reach its potential power.

NOTES

1. Savannah *Daily News and Herald,* September 19, 1866.

2. Don H. Doyle, *New Men, New Cities, New South: Atlanta, Nashville, Charleston, Mobile, 1860–1910* (Chapel Hill: University of North Carolina Press, 1990).

3. C. Vann Woodward, *Origins of the New South, 1877–1913* (Baton Rouge: Louisiana State University Press, 1951), 20. See also John B. Boles and Bethany L. Johnson, eds., *Origins of the New South: Fifty Years Later* (Baton Rouge: Louisiana State University Press, 2003), and James L. Roark, *Masters without Slaves: Southern Planters in the Civil War and Reconstruction* (New York: W. W. Norton & Co., 1977).

4. Resolutions of the Savannah Chamber of Commerce, January 24, 1865, quoted in Harold D. Woodman, *King Cotton and His Retainers: Financing and Marketing the Cotton Crop of the South, 1800–1925* (Columbia: University of South Carolina Press, 1968; reprint), 238.

5. While the Leverich Papers are particularly rich in documenting the persistent attempts by southerners to sell cotton in the immediate postwar period, evidence for the extensive North-South correspondence in late 1865 and early 1866 can be found in the Tobias, Hendricks & Co. Papers, New-York Historical Society. In fact, northern cities competed with one another to gain preeminence in the southern trade. As one Philadelphia businessman declared in January 1866, "The business community [here] is moving to counteract what they consider the false position of Philadelphia [in] allowing all the foreign and southern trade to be carried on through New York." See Charles King to John A. King, January 12, 1865, King Family Papers, New-York Historical Society. A. Brighton of New Orleans wrote in June 1865, for example, that "Our city is filling up rapidly with her returning citizens who are preparing to go to work again." See A. Brighton to Charles P. Leverich, June 14, 1865, Box 11, Folder 1, Leverich Family Papers, New-York Historical Society. Other correspondence originated from bigger cities like Memphis and Charleston and smaller towns like Cokesbury, South Carolina.

6. DeBow quoted in Paul M. Gaston, *The New South Creed: A Study in Southern Mythmaking* (New York: Knopf, 1970), 25.

7. John C. McGammon to Joseph A. Gaston, December 31, 1865, Gaston-Strait-Wiley-Baskin Papers, South Caroliniana Library, University of South Carolina, Columbia.

8. Richard D. Arnold to W. H. Baldwin, February 8, 1865, in Richard H. Shyrock, ed., *Letters of Richard D. Arnold, M.D. 1808–1876* (Papers of the Trinity College Historical Society, 1929), 113.

9. "Exodus," *DeBow's Review* 5 (December 1868): 1060.

10. Savannah *Daily Herald,* March 28, 1866, 2.

11. Savannah *Daily News and Herald,* May 26, 1866, 1.

12. *Davis v. Armstrong,* 7 F.Cas. 109, 110 (DCND Miss. 1869), quoted in Elizabeth Lee Thompson, *The Reconstruction of Southern Debtors: Bankruptcy after the Civil War* (Athens: University of Georgia Press, 2004), 29.

13. Thompson, *Reconstruction of Southern Debtors,* 26, 100. Even within the region, however, there was a great deal of variation in the level of economic hardship. Doyle, *New Men, New Cities, New South.* Areas that had successfully hidden cotton during the war brought the bales out after the fighting and commanded high prices. One New York agent estimated that some 2 million bales were stored away by the summer of 1865. Woodman, *King Cotton,* 236.

14. Albert Taylor Bledsoe, "The Sumter and Alabama," *Southern Review* 5 (January 1869): 226.

15. W. W. Boyce, "The South: Its Duty and Destiny," *DeBow's Review* 1 (January 1866): 75. "The overflowing prosperity which invited luxury and repose before the war," argued another essayist in *DeBow's Review,* "influenced the mistaken belief that the people of the South were deficient in

the sterner virtues which combat adversity." "Editorial Notes and Clippings," *DeBow's Review* 3 (April–May 1867): 489.

16. Edward A. Pollard, *The Lost Cause: A New Southern History of the War of the Confederates* (New York: E. B. Treat, 1866), 751, quoted in Gaston, *The New South Creed*, 156.

17. Kenneth Moore Startup, *The Root of All Evil: The Protestant Clergy and the Economic Mind of the Old South* (Athens: University of Georgia Press, 1997), 26–27, 33. Eugene V. LeVert to Francis John LeVert, November 18, 1865, LeVert Family Papers, Southern Historical Collection, University of North Carolina (hereafter SHC). Samuel Wilson to Lawson Wilson, May 29, 1868, Leonidas Glenn Papers, SHC. "The Present Crisis," *Southern Review* 12 (January 1873): 4–5.

18. Raphael J. Moses Autobiography, SHC, 100.

19. "The Legal Profession," *Southern Review* 5 (April 1869): 324.

20. Thompson, *Reconstruction of Southern Debtors*, 50.

21. John Smithry, "Hedging Again," *Southern Cultivator* 28 (February 1870): 46.

22. Steven M. Stowe, *Doctoring the South: Southern Physicians and Everyday Medicine in the Mid-Nineteenth Century* (Chapel Hill: University of North Carolina Press, 2004).

23. "Our Young Men and the Pursuits of Life," *Southern Planter and Farmer* 1 (March 1867): 89.

24. "Profits of Farming," *The American Farmer* 3 (July 1868): 16.

25. "Professional Students and Mechanics in the South," *Richmond Whig*, reprinted in *The American Farmer* 1 (April 1867): 326. Such a state of affairs, the paper argued, was bound to produce disaster: "The mistaken notion prevailed that labor was degrading—a delusion that, more than all other things combined, retarded the growth and development of Virginia."

26. "Don't Come to the City," *Southern Planter and Farmer* 3 (March 1869): 152.

27. Michael Shoffner to his uncle of the same name, May 19, 1873, Michael Shoffner Papers, SHC.

28. J.E.W., "Agriculture as a Profession," *Southern Planter and Farmer* 1 (May 1867): 232.

29. "One Eye," "What We Must Do," *Southern Cultivator* 25 (June 1867): 172. Emphasis original.

30. Hyman Rubin III, *South Carolina Scalawags* (Columbia: University of South Carolina Press, 2006), 18–19.

31. James Alex Baggett, *The Scalawags: Southern Dissenters in the Civil War and Reconstruction* (Baton Rouge: Louisiana State University Press, 2003), 112. Baggett, however, does not argue strongly for a class interpretation of Republican Party membership.

32. Carl N. Degler, *The Other South: Southern Dissenters in the Nineteenth Century* (New York: Harper & Row, 1974), 196–97.

33. "Speech of Mr. Samuel F. Phillips, at Concord, Cabarrus County, July 4th, 1870," n.p., 6.

34. "Possibility," *Houston Tri-Weekly Telegraph*, July 24, 1865, 4.

35. W. W. Boyce, "The State of the Country," *DeBow's Review* 1 (February 1866): 136.

36. For example, see "How to Induce Immigration to the South," *DeBow's Review* 1 (February 1866): 214–15.

37. "Hysteria a Malady," *Macon Weekly Telegraph*, March 4, 1887, 4.

38. "Where Extremes Meet," *Macon Weekly Telegraph*, November 2, 1886, 2.

39. "Educating too Much," *Macon Weekly Telegraph*, August 6, 1878, 3. Emphasis original.

40. "The North Carolina Hyde Park Settlement" (New York, 1869), cover.

41. "Foreign Immigration Southward," *Macon Weekly Telegraph,* November 20, 1868, 2.

42. "Speech of Col. Robert M. Douglas, of Washington, D.C., Delivered at a Republican Mass Meeting Held at Smithfield, N.C., July 12th, 1870," 10.

43. Elizabeth Fox-Genovese, *Within the Plantation Household: Black and White Women of the Old South* (Chapel Hill: University of North Carolina Press, 1988), argues that a gender ideology developed differently in the South because the region never experienced the division between work and home experienced in the antebellum North. For a different view, see Jonathan Daniel Wells, *The Origins of the Southern Middle Class, 1800–1861* (Chapel Hill: University of North Carolina Press, 2004), 111–32.

44. "The Woman Who Bets," *Columbus Daily Enquirer,* May 26, 1887, 3.

45. "Extravagance in Dress," *Columbus Daily Enquirer,* February 10, 1870, 3.

46. Doyle, *New Men, New Cities, New South,* 93.

47. Leslie Brown, *Upbuilding Black Durham: Gender, Class, and Black Community Development in the Jim Crow South* (Chapel Hill: University of North Carolina Press, 2008).

48. "Socialistic Sentiment," *Dallas Morning News,* October 9, 1885, 2.

Manufacturers and Rural Culture in the
Reconstruction-Era Upcountry

BRUCE W. EELMAN

I n April 1875, an upcountry newspaper correspondent reported on a recent
visit to the Bivingsville textile factory and village in Spartanburg County,
South Carolina. Bivingsville had brought together the best of the rural
world and the emerging machine age. The reporter surveyed the nice homes
of the operatives, the factory itself, "the store, workshops, and last but not
least the tasteful residences of the proprietors, to which add the blended harmony of falling waters and the busy hum of machinery . . . a scene where art
and nature have combined to make life pleasant and profitable."[1] This happy
blending of modern industry with rural society was a common theme in public campaigns to promote manufacturing in the southern upcountry during
Reconstruction. The era would be an important one for manufacturers who
looked to expand their operations while attempting to craft a social environment receptive to industrial change.

Much good recent work has focused on the activities of a burgeoning
middle class in the antebellum era and important scholarship has been done
on the boom in middle-class business during the post-1880 era of the New
South.[2] Far less work has looked at the activities of the middle class in the
Reconstruction era. Some of the best scholarship on the Reconstruction South
has understandably centered on the transition from slavery to free labor and
racial violence.[3] Yet if more and more scholarship confirms the existence of
an active middle class in the antebellum era, it is important to have a fuller
understanding of the activities of this class between the end of the Civil War
and the New South of the late nineteenth century. My work represents one
attempt to broaden the conversation through a study of middle-class industrialists in the upcountry region of North Carolina and South Carolina during
Reconstruction.

The Reconstruction era represents an important chapter in southern middle-class formation as political and social upheaval offered a complex combination of opportunities and challenges. The erosion of planter control expanded the role of cotton merchants who helped foster trading centers in the South.[4] In the case of middle-class manufacturers, the shift away from large plantations and increasing urbanization provided incentive to increase operations with the prospect of reaching new markets. In addition to expanding production, Reconstruction-era industrialists also looked to redefine and control norms in social behavior in accordance with middle-class ideals. Such efforts would clash with long-established cultural traditions. Therefore, this examination of upcountry manufacturers seeks to make a wider contribution to the study of class formation and the contested development of social structure.

This study focuses on Gaston County and Lincoln County in North Carolina and the counties of Anderson, Greenville, and Spartanburg in South Carolina. Each of these counties maintained white majorities and, prior to the Civil War, slaves represented between 25 and 35 percent of the population. Yeoman farmers dominated the landscape with planters representing less than one half of 1 percent of the white population in all of the selected counties.[5] Industrial activity, although limited in comparison to later years, was nevertheless established in the upcountry by 1860. Beginning in the late 1700s, enterprising businessmen first exploited the iron ore of the region, building foundries in a number of upcountry communities in both North Carolina and South Carolina. Following the War of 1812, New Englanders established many of the early textile mills, seeing the virgin waterways of the southern upcountry as a better alternative to the increasing competition in their native region.[6]

By 1860, the upcountry counties of Anderson, Greenville, and Spartanburg operated twelve of South Carolina's seventeen total textile factories, representing about 35 percent of the state's capital investments in the industry. Gaston and Lincoln counties maintained just four of North Carolina's thirty-nine textile operations in 1860, but were nevertheless the center of upcountry cotton manufacturing.[7] Many of the state's textile mills were to the east, either as part of Edwin Holt's operations in Alamance County or centered near Fayetteville in Cumberland County. By the late antebellum period, upcountry textile factory owners looked to extend their economic reach beyond local or even regional markets. Accomplishing this would require no less than a revolution in the socioeconomic world of the upcountry. Manufacturers like Simpson Bobo and Gabriel Cannon of Spartanburg and Vardry McBee of Greenville pushed for rail lines to connect with outside markets and suppliers. They also supported the creation of more banks in the region for greater access to credit. In addition to these financial and infrastructural changes, public schooling and temperance reforms were viewed as critical to establishing a cultural climate suited to an increasingly diversified commercial and industrial economy. Throughout the antebellum era, these efforts faced challenges from an existing rural culture that viewed dependence—whether on employers or on outside market forces—as a threat to freedom.[8] Compulsory schooling or control over access to alcohol could be additional signs of eroding independence. However, industrialists did not challenge one of the central institutions of southern society. Slavery, they argued, would thrive alongside white wage labor as slave work would provide the raw materials for factories and the factories would offer new opportunities for poor whites.[9]

During the Civil War, industry in the upcountry and throughout the South thrived in response to wartime needs. Iron factories that had been on the decline due to competition from anthracite regions of the Northeast experienced a brief resurgence in supplying munitions to the Confederacy. Many textile firms also prospered both on the open market and in response to government demand for army clothing. In 1864, Thomas Tate's Mountain Island mill and Jasper Stowe's factory were both producing 8000 cotton products per month in Gaston County. In 1863, the Bivingsville textile factory in Spartanburg was "so extended that neither the machinery nor operative force [were] adequate to supply it."[10] Even as the Confederacy disintegrated, some industrialists recognized business opportunities. In April 1865, John Bomar of the Bivingsville factory told his agents to buy up cotton from planters who were desperate to sell at any price as Sherman's troops threatened to advance on the region. "Cotton is the first thing to [be] burn[ed] by the Yankees when on Raid," he wrote an agent, "& this is becoming a matter of alarm to the planter and it will induce many to sell to get it out of the way."[11]

At war's end, whites throughout the South faced severe economic struggle, having lost an estimated 76 percent of the region's 1860 gross worth. In August 1866, a Greenville, South Carolina resident reflected the mood of many farmers in the region when she commented on the poor condition of crops and saw "nothing but suffering & starvation staring us in the face." Plantation owners also experienced substantial loss, particularly due to the disappearance of approximately $2.4 billion of capital invested in slaves.[12]

Although faced with initial losses, especially in Confederate bonds, textile factory owners fared better. This was particularly the case with those who had established strong businesses prior to the war. The Lineberger Manufacturing Company in Gaston County, North Carolina, offers an example. Founded in the 1850s, the firm was valued by creditors at $30,000 in 1860. By 1866, the company's worth had increased to $50,000 and would continue to expand through the 1870s. Mountain Island, Gaston's first textile factory, also emerged from the war in strong financial health. The company's founder, Thomas R. Tate, decided to close the factory for the first few years of Reconstruction, not out of necessity, but out of an apparent desire to conserve the family's wealth while waiting for raw cotton prices to fall. Creditors estimated Mountain Island's worth at $100,000 in 1866 and found Tate to be an entirely "reliable" credit risk. Following the elder Tate's death in the early 1870s, his sons reopened the factory in 1873 with "improved & modernized" equipment. Mountain Island would enjoy success into the late nineteenth century. John Phifer's cotton factory in Lincoln County, North Carolina, jumped from an already robust value of $100,000 in 1869 to $200,000 by 1872. The Pendleton Manufacturing Company in Anderson County, South Carolina, was "a v[er]y strong money making concern" in the late 1860s and early 1870s. As early as 1866, both the Bivingsville and Crawfordsville textile mills in Spartanburg were installing new machinery to expand operations. Jasper Stowe's South Point factory in Gaston County was one of the few exceptions to textile success in the immediate postwar upcountry. Stowe had accumulated debts prior to the Civil War that left him "considerably in debt & embarrassed." These old debts put Stowe's factory in a "failing condition" through the late 1860s and resulted in insolvency by late 1870.[13]

The financial worth of some of these factory owners might suggest that they were more comfortably upper class. However, their focus on commercial careers, town building, internal improvements, thrift, and institutional changes kept them more closely aligned with middle-class values rather than the aristocratic style of wealthy planters. In addition, as sociologists Melanie Archer and Judith R. Blau argue, the composition of the nineteenth-century middle class shifted depending on time period and geographic location. Historians have demonstrated that merchants and industrialists were critical in southern antebellum middle-class formation.[14] Following the Civil War, both small-scale and larger-scale manufacturers continued to promote middle-class values.

Efforts to diffuse middle-class ideals through the broader populace, however, faced unique challenges during Reconstruction. In looking to forge a successful postwar industrial economy, middle-class businessmen had to accommodate traditional southern community standards, especially regarding race. Native white frustrations of loss—economic, military, and cultural—gave rise to the violent resistance of the Ku Klux Klan and similar organizations. The Carolina upcountry was particularly bloody since most communities sustained a white majority but were faced with the political control of black and white Republicans.[15] For middle-class merchants and manufacturers, the Ku Klux Klan was at one and the same time useful and disruptive to their goals. Like most white southerners, upcountry industrialists often supported the ouster of Republicans and reaffirmation of the inferiority of free blacks. Benjamin F. Perry, a prominent Greenville lawyer and South Carolina governor during Andrew Johnson's administration, had long been a supporter of industry, education, and other signs of modernization. However, Perry clung tightly to social and cultural traditions regarding race. Viewing white and black Republicans as responsible for the economic ruin and social degradation of the South, Perry saw "no hope of any change until the negroes die out & the white race has a majority." The Klan, he argued, was not political, but rather "for the protection of property & the prevention of crime." As such, "They were a terror only to evil doers. Good negroes & good white people had no apprehension of them."[16]

Some industrial managers were reputedly linked to Klan activity as well. Witnesses testified to congressional investigators that Spartanburg factory owners Gabriel Cannon and Simpson Bobo had threatened or intimidated some blacks and white Republicans in the county. Black Republican H. H. Foster stated that Cannon made threatening remarks at a freedmen's meeting. "We own the lands; you live on them," Cannon allegedly remarked, "[y]ou eat our bread and meat, and if you vote for our enemies, the radicals, you will get your earth, two by six; you will go like the Indians, and your bones will whiten our hillsides." When the Klan visited white Republican John Genobles, they threatened his life unless he consented to renounce his political affiliation on the Spartanburg courthouse steps at the next sales day. Genobles testified that on sales day, Bobo stopped the sheriff's sale and forced Genobles to reject Republicanism.[17] Although Cannon and Bobo denied these accusations, a loose affiliation with Klan activity would allow these entrepreneurs to end local Republican control and thus serve their political goals. Additionally, such affiliation could strengthen the ties between businessmen and poorer rank-and-file Klan members and allow manufacturers, merchants, and professionals greater local leverage in pursuing their economic plans. However, most manufacturers likely charted a course similar to Alamance's Edwin Holt who, according to historian Bess Beatty, "wished to neither condone nor expose Klan violence."[18]

For all of Perry's claim that the Klan was not political, it is clear that for most business leaders and politicians in the upcountry, the ability to remove Republicans from office was the primary appeal of the Klan. David Schenck, a lawyer and former Klan leader in Gaston and Lincoln counties, told congressional investigators that the Klan was originally a political society but had been taken over by "the lower orders of life." Schenck thought most of the violence was centered on the county's iron factories, where white "coalers" were "always in broils with the negroes," many of whom chopped wood for the factories.[19] Increasing violence and nationwide attention to Klan activities ran counter to the goals of middle-class business interests, especially industrialists looking for outside investment. Despite having reputedly threatened black Republicans, factory owner Cannon grew alarmed at reports of Klan violence toward black railroad laborers. Like many involved in manufacturing, Cannon also invested in railroad ventures and complained that Klan activity "operates very seriously on all business."[20] Even the day-to-day business of delivering finished goods to retailers could be disrupted. In May 1868, John Bomar and Company, a textile firm in Spartanburg, appealed to the commander of the Second Military District for permission to carry firearms since "their goods are hauled by agents to different parts of N. & S. C. [and] agents don't feel safe to travel without protection."[21]

The Federal Enforcement Acts of 1870 and 1871, along with President Ulysses Grant's suspension of habeas corpus in nine counties of the South Carolina upcountry, ceased most organized Klan activity, but by then the terrorism had silenced blacks and restored local politics to white Democrats.[22]

The decline in racial violence and the reassertion of the traditional racial order both served and hindered the goals of industrialists as had their potential support for the Klan. Despite some participation in the intimidation, middle-class businesspeople were embarrassed by reports of violent terrorism during the Klan's operations as they engaged in crafting the image of a New South. With organized Klan violence at an end, economic modernizers in upcountry communities looked to attract outside investment and emphasized the peace and stability of the region. New factories were also championed for the opportunities they would bring to local whites, thus continuing to distinguish their status from blacks. Newspapers became the primary industrial boosters in the early 1870s. "Manufactories of many kinds can flourish in Greenville," The Enterprise proudly announced. "No where in the United States are there better conditions of success. The climate is superior. The water power abundant even in the centre of the city and around about in all directions." Reporting that some northern towns had quadrupled their population just a few years after the arrival of factories, The Enterprise predicted even greater results for the South because labor was "as cheap or cheaper than at the North" and "living is cheaper."[23]

Publications championed textile mill managers and owners as heroes of the postwar South. A newspaper correspondent related a conversation he had with William Perry, who ran the Pendleton Manufacturing Company in Anderson County, South Carolina. Perry reported that the factory was "in fine operation, turning out more yarn than at any previous period, and the concern is paying ten percent per annum." The correspondent found Perry to be "a practical man of practical ideas, of large experience, and who deserves all the success he is meeting." In 1872, prominent Greenville resident Benjamin F. Perry authored an encomium to the recently deceased county industrialist William Bates. Perry praised Bates, a Rhode Island native, as the founder of the textile industry in Greenville. Here was the perfect example of the rewards of hard work. Although Bates had faced early financial setbacks, Perry observed that "instead of drowning cares in spirits, and idling his time away as a loafer, he went to work again, and finally achieved success by his indomitable energy and perseverance. No man who is industrious and sober need fear success in life, and without these virtues few, very few, can succeed in any business."[24]

Punctuality, hard work, and sobriety were emphasized repeatedly as keys to business success in the postwar upcountry. These values were essential to the middle-class culture embraced by manufacturers and merchants and were closely aligned with middle-class values in the North. However, these values also clashed in important ways with a deep-rooted rural culture. Although Mark Smith has argued effectively that antebellum planters relied on clock time for their operations, rural folk away from plantations were accustomed to working by seasonal rhythms rather than a factory manager's time clock.[25] In rural communities, alcohol served as a release from the daily grind, as a form of male social bonding, and as an important economic function.[26] The illicit distilling of alcohol was a significant business in the postwar upcountry. While alcohol production had been a part of the rural landscape since the antebellum era, the poor economic conditions of the postwar period led to a proliferation of family farm distilleries. In particularly isolated portions of upcountry counties, it was much more profitable to bring wagons of whiskey to market than bushels of corn. In estimating nineteenth-century prices, historian Wilbur Miller found that the same wagon hauling 20 bushels of corn worth $20 could haul 120 gallons of whiskey worth $150. During Reconstruction, poor farmers involved in illicit distilling violently defended their operations against federal revenue officers and did not look favorably on local temperance advocates either.[27]

Facing these socioeconomic challenges, middle-class manufacturers had to redefine elements of rural culture while convincing the region's white residents of the beneficial relationship between factories and farms. Local newspapers ran numerous testimonials both to the happy prospects of industry and to the integration of manufacturing and farming. Under the heading "How the Factory Helps the Farm," an article in *The Enterprise* queried, "We make cotton. Can we not also make a home market for it, and thus make the factory help the farm?" When Henry P. Hammett set out building a substantial cotton factory in Greenville County in 1873, he emphasized the proposed factory's positive impact on rural culture. The "intelligent and thrifty" farmers of the region would have a local market for their goods and the mill would benefit from buying "direct from the producers."[28] Holidays were opportunities to bring traditional farm communities and the mill villages together. One former mill worker from Mountain Island remembered celebrating July 4, 1875, "by having a Barbacue [sic] and Dance. The mill people furnished the bread, ice, lemons and sugar and the country neighbors furnished the sheep and beef. At the celebration we had one beef, six sheep, one hog barbecued and chicken pie and hash by the wash pot full." The celebration drew an estimated five hundred to six hundred people and offered middle-class business folks an example of the successful marriage of agrarian and industrial culture.[29]

However, a seamless connection between the white factory operative and the white farmer would require a public relations campaign to enhance the image of wage labor. An anonymous contributor to Greenville's *The Enterprise* wrote a series of articles on "The Laboring Class," looking to convince all readers that "Labor is honorable, to work is a divine command." The writer eschewed the development of a leisure class that scorned labor. There was only one way to economic and social progress: "Let your sons go to the workshops or plow, and your daughters to the loom or spinning wheel, and deck themselves in garments of their own handy-work; let them be educated, let their education and school books teach them the dignity of labor, and the worth of honest labor." A library was proposed so that laborers would expand their knowledge and fill their nonworking hours with cultural exercise. "It might be the means of keeping them away from the groceries, grogshops, billiard tables, card tables, gambling rooms, etc., and from places of the like, that would tend to draw their hard earnings from them." Mechanics were encouraged "to think that they are the backbone and capital of the country, and that their position in society is as good as any class of men on the face of the green earth." Nonfarm labor would grow ever more important as the upcountry made "rapid advancement as a manufacturing people." What mechanics lacked, the writer argued, was sufficient education. Schooling would bring greater skill and discipline. "You must let the school and workshop go together."[30] Schools and other sources of intellectual edification were important, then, because they could go a long way toward defusing middle-class culture throughout the populace. Curricula would emphasize hard work and punctuality while time spent in the classroom would be less idle time to spend in saloons.[31]

Educational reform was part of a much broader middle-class reform effort designed to modernize communities by eliminating obstacles to economic success such as alcoholism, crime, and poor infrastructure. Temperance was a critical reform for postwar manufacturers interested in a sober labor force.

The allure of strong drink was a growing concern in the early 1870s. Noting the "alarming increase of drunkenness and intemperance," *The Enterprise* applauded the corresponding growth in temperance organizations and urged their further expansion. Temperance was among the most important causes because it would "entail greater benefits upon public and private prosperity." The Greenville city council voted that it would no longer grant licenses to retail liquor.[32]

Greenville council member and former mayor Henry P. Hammett was a leading advocate for ending further liquor licensing. In the antebellum era, Hammett gained experience in the textile industry as a partner in the Batesville cotton mill. At war's end, the Batesville mill closed and Hammett served briefly in the state legislature and then in 1866 as president of the Greenville and Columbia Railroad. Like many postwar businessmen in the upcountry South, Hammett viewed rail lines as essential to developing the region's industrial capacity. Finding the challenges of financing and constructing the road nearly impossible, he resigned from the presidency in 1871 and was elected mayor of Greenville the next year. By 1873, Hammett was ready to reenter the industrial world and had selected a site on the Saluda River that would become one of the largest textile factories in the late nineteenth-century South. In order to achieve success, however, Hammett saw the need to reform the regional tradition of tippling and to foster a sober community. Hammett also worked to modernize the city of Greenville. He pushed to increase the street force charged with keeping streets clean and repaired and supported a city law that required livestock within the city be fenced.[33]

Although these social and economic reforms were promoted as the best means to bring an integrated network of prosperity to manufacturers and farmers alike, within the rhetoric supporting manufacturing lay evidence of both frustration and tension between traditional rural culture and evolving industry. In 1873, Francis DeLane began the *Lincoln Progress* newspaper in Lincolnton, North Carolina, because, he argued, "a county without a newspaper is comparatively unknown to the outer world, and its resources lie hidden in obscurity." In the antebellum era, Lincolnton's textile mills had been training grounds for future industrialists. Looking to that example, DeLane argued that postwar Lincolnton needed "capitalist-men who are able and willing to build up manufactories, improve our soil, and thus embrace the value of our lands and personal property. Then, and not before, will our people realize that they are living in a new era, and that peace and prosperity is bearing upon them." Similarly, in praising William Perry's management of the Pendleton Manufacturing Company, one observer noted that the "South now needs hundreds of thousands like him, of generous nature." In more than one instance, DeLane wrote of the need for people in the upcountry to "shake off the lethargy which has so long entrameled [sic] them."[34]

DeLane's call for capitalists to come to Lincolnton and his repeated reference to the "lethargy" of county residents reveals the continued struggles between the economic goals of town businesspeople and rural culture. In his account book, Jasper Stowe directly addressed the socioeconomic impasse to substantial industrialization in the Reconstruction South. Stowe had only recently gone out of business as a textile factory owner in Gaston County, North Carolina, due to massive debts incurred beginning before the Civil War. Stowe affixed much of the blame for his struggles and the overall challenges to manufacturing on rural culture. He blamed farmers for "the low estimate they place upon the business ability of their class." Stowe found that "farmers underrate [sic] their own and each others ability to perform duties outside of the plantation fence, and in a humiliating degree, subordinate themselves to other classes for agents to do that which in nine times out of ten, they can do better themselves." Instead, Stowe argued that there were "farmers of high ability to conduct large manufacturing establishments" in every county of North Carolina. Agrarian culture seemed to lead farmers to perform below their abilities "in all the affairs of life requiring intelligence." Stowe found this attitude to be a "cruel sacrifice of self-reliant manhood." Although Stowe acknowledged that a general manager of a factory did need to have intimate familiarity with each of the machines involved in production, the only raw talents required were "a good practical mind, fair intelligence and sound integrity." As evidence, he suggested that many of North Carolina's manufacturers had been farmers first and that "farmers of the same comparative ability are common in every county to conduct with the same success like establishments."[35]

Yet men such as Stowe sought to convince more than just a handful of farmers. Since to be successful factories needed the benefit of economies of scale, the "cooperation of a large number of small farmers" in financial support of industry would be necessary. The need for cooperation would perhaps be the greatest obstacle to reshaping commercial culture. "The farmers unfounded dread and hostility to cooperation and acting together," Stowe argued, "stands more in his way to wealth and usefulness, than the want of capital and all other causes besides." This inability to "act together in business industry as a means of power . . . in the history of rural character, has been the fatal barier [sic] that has stood so long in the farmers way to progress."[36] Stowe echoed the concerns of connecting manufacturers and farmers, same as Hammett had likewise promoted in Greenville.

While financial cooperation among many farmers was necessary to support factories, technological advancements were such that the required investments from each individual would not be great. Stowe maintained that "There never was a time in the history of the country when machinery of every kind could be purchased at rates so low as now, and the time is in every respect most opportune for patrons to open up the way to wealth." He then proceeded to provide a painstakingly detailed estimate for the costs and profits of both a hypothetical factory and of Gaston's Mountain Island factory. From his perspective, no rational business mind could ignore the clear profits to be derived from manufacturing.[37]

A central problem confronting the supposed symbiotic relationship between factory and farm was that textile manufacturers wanted raw materials at the lowest possible cost while selling their own finished product at the highest price point. The Phifer family of Lincolnton owned one of the more successful textile factories in the Reconstruction upcountry. C. Phifer observed with great interest the profits being made in the sale of Alamance plaids manufactured at Edwin Holt's Alamance Cotton factory. Phifer wrote to his brother George that the cloth was in "considerable demand for every day wear particularly [sic] for servants" and that Holt had "the reputation of making money." Phifer then advised him on the best way for textile factories to make money during Reconstruction. The key was to buy cotton from farmers when the crop was plentiful and prices low, and then wait until the crop grew scarce to sell finished cotton goods at higher rates. Phifer contended that he had done this in 1849 and made considerable profit. "Buy when there is a large crop and hold until a short crop comes along[,]" Phifer reiterated, "If I had persued [sic] this course several times in my life I could have made enough money to have done me."[38] Such a calculated profit-maximizing plan to buy crops low and sell high certainly seemed at odds with the public pronouncements of the mutual benefits to be shared by factory and farm.

Some local consumers of cotton products recognized the potential clash between their interests and the interests of manufacturers. A contributor to *The Mountaineer* newspaper in Greenville found that, despite economic hard times in the late 1860s, "there has not been a very great reduction in cotton goods for the reason that when the stock gets to a certain point, the mills stop running, on the same principle that the coal miners cease to mine black diamonds when the price falls near their standard of equality." However, the writer was encouraged by small signs of price reductions "notwithstanding the manipulations of the manufacturers, as those consumers who have had occasion to purchase will testify."[39] Such reference to the "manipulations" of textile mill owners suggested a financial selfishness antagonistic to the community's needs and reminiscent of antebellum southern assaults on greedy, Yankee manufacturers.

The potential for conflicts between industrial and agrarian interests grew with proposed state initiatives designed to foster greater industrial activity in the South. Republicans who controlled the southern state legislatures during Reconstruction supported government assistance to industry. In 1870, the South Carolina General Assembly passed an act whereby most taxes on cotton or wool manufacturing would be returned to investors. Three years later, Governor Franklin Moses recommended to the General Assembly that the state pay a five-year bonus to manufacturers equal to the amount of assessed taxes on money invested in manufacturing. For industrialists across the state, such a recommendation from the state's executive seemingly confirmed a shift to a more modern, diversified economy. Moses presented the plan, like many industrialists, as one that would bring prosperity to all sectors of the economy. The wages of agricultural laborers would increase, he reasoned, due to the greater demand for raw materials from factories.[40]

However, some farmers viewed Moses's proposal very differently. An angered resident near Greenville wrote a piece for *The Enterprise* newspaper under the heading "Gov. Moses vs. Agricultural Labor." Using the pseudonym "Senex," the writer attacked Moses's plan as "a direct tax for the benefit of the few monied [sic] aristocrats of the land." Senex argued that the farmer already faced the "heaviest tax that we have ever paid; and now this scheme is put on foot to tax him more to pay a bonus to manufacturers." What made the governor's recommendation so dangerous, the writer maintained, was that it looked to "use one class of constituents to oppress another class." Although *The Enterprise* printed the piece, the editors made clear that they embraced Moses's proposal because manufacturing was sorely needed for the state to be economically competitive.[41]

Despite the opposition of some to incentives for industry, the South Carolina legislature passed an act in December 1873 that offered ten-year tax exemptions for capital invested in the manufacturing of cotton, wool, paper, lime, iron, and farm implements.[42] By the mid-1870s, many upcountry textile manufacturers in both North Carolina and South Carolina expanded production. Abel P. Rhyne took over Gaston County's Lineberger Manufacturing Company in 1875 and was anxious to increase the machinery at his 1200 spindle cotton mill and become a major industrialist in the Reconstruction upcountry. Rhyne had "no doubt that manufacturing will pay if you will get good machinery but never get second hand machinery with the expectation of making any money."[43] The Lineberger family continued to operate another factory in Gaston County that creditors listed as "quite wealthy" and a "strong firm" in the mid-1870s. In Greenville, South Carolina, the business of McKenzie, David & Company looked to expand the McBee's Mills on the Reedy River, six miles south of Greenville city. The mills included a three and a half story factory building with 900 spindles and 20 looms and the company was looking to increase to a capacity of 2000 spindles and 50 looms. Under the leadership of Dexter Edgar Converse, the Bivingsville factory in Spartanburg underwent significant remodeling and expansion operating 5000 spindles and 120 looms by 1875. Converse also contracted with a New York commission house to solidify long-distance sales. A correspondent to the *Carolina Spartan* was most impressed by the "neat and comfortable houses" in the mill village and the factory's operation "with the regularity of clock-work."[44]

The newspaper correspondent's attention to the workers' "comfortable" homes and the mill's clock-work regularity reflected the tension between working-class opportunity and middle-class efficiency inherent in the emerging factory towns. Not surprisingly, factory managers highlighted job opportunities for plain folk, especially for those suffering during the economic crises of Reconstruction. When Henry Hammett proposed his cotton factory along

the Saluda River in Greenville County, South Carolina, he suggested the positive effects on whites who did not own their own farms. The opportunity to
labor in a factory would provide both material and moral uplift. He contended
that "There is an abundance of good material in the surrounding country for
operatives whose condition would be materially improved and their characteristics elevated by employment in such a mill; besides, they would become
producers and valuable members of society. The children too small to work in
the factory would have educational advantages and the families church privileges equal to those of the surrounding villages."[45] Yet Hammett's words reflect
a condescending attitude toward white wage laborers that would be common
among middle-class employers in the North and the South through the end of
the nineteenth century. They suggest that, without industry, those who would
be factory operatives were of poor character and were not valuable members
of society. The *Carolina Spartan* correspondent stated it more clearly after an
1875 visit to the Bivingsville factory village in Spartanburg County. In addition
to providing jobs for the otherwise idle, Bivingsville's schools and temperance
lodges brought a "civilizing influence" on the community that could be seen
in the "remarkably respectable appearance of the operatives."[46] Factories, then,
would take degraded people and teach them a "proper" culture. Both Allen
Tullos and Bess Beatty have noted that even in the antebellum era, emerging industrialists viewed the employment their factories offered as a way to
bring area residents out of "wretchedness."[47] Such an attitude continued into
the Reconstruction years and left little room for defining factory workers as
individuals with a culture distinct from the factory itself.

Although the post-Reconstruction period witnessed the impressive boom
in factory production that defined the New South, the decade following the
Civil War proved important as a bridge between the initial efforts of middle-
class manufacturers in the antebellum era and the textile magnates of the late
nineteenth and early twentieth centuries. Far from licking the wounds of war
and awaiting the political "redemption" of the South, upcountry manufacturers
looked to expand their business opportunities during Reconstruction. Equally
important were their efforts to replace or at least readjust elements of a traditional rural culture with middle-class values emphasizing punctuality, sobriety, formal education, and an acceptance of wage work. Despite a public campaign to unite the mutual interests of factory and farm, evidence of economic

and social clashes could be seen in the 1870s. In addition, the rhetoric to build up the image of wage laborers thinly masked the unequal relationship between factory management and operatives. These twin problems of factory-farm conflict and management-labor division would be central to the New South.

NOTES

1. *Carolina Spartan* (Spartanburg, S.C.), April 28, 1875.

2. Some recent examples for the antebellum era include Jonathan Daniel Wells, *The Origins of the Southern Middle Class, 1800–1861* (Chapel Hill: University of North Carolina Press, 2004); Frank J. Byrne, *Becoming Bourgeois: Merchant Culture in the South, 1820–1860* (Lexington: University of Kentucky Press, 2006); and Tom Downey, *Planting a Capitalist South: Masters, Merchants and Manufacturers in the Southern Interior, 1790–1860* (Baton Rouge: Louisiana State University Press, 2006). Definitive studies on the post–Reconstruction era begin with C. Vann Woodward, *Origins of the New South, 1877–1913* (Baton Rouge: Louisiana State University Press, 1951). Also see David Carlton, *Mill and Town in South Carolina, 1880–1920* (Baton Rouge: Louisiana State University Press, 1982), and Gavin Wright, *Old South, New South: Revolutions in the Southern Economy since the Civil War* (New York: Basic Books, 1986).

3. This scholarship is too voluminous to give complete attention to here. Some examples include Eric Foner, *Nothing but Freedom: Emancipation and Its Legacy* (Baton Rouge: Louisiana State University Press, 1983); Julie Saville, *The Work of Reconstruction: From Slave to Wage Laborer in South Carolina, 1860–1868* (New York: Cambridge University Press, 1997); Leslie Schwalm, *A Hard Fight for We: Women's Transition from Slavery to Freedom in South Carolina* (Urbana: University of Illinois Press, 1997); and George C. Rable, *But There Was No Peace: The Role of Violence in the Politics of Reconstruction* (Athens: University of Georgia Press, 1984).

4. On the role of cotton merchants in the postbellum South, see Harold D. Woodman, *King Cotton and His Retainers: Financing and Marketing the Cotton Crop of the South, 1800–1925* (Lexington: University of Kentucky Press, 1968), 246–333.

5. U.S. Bureau of Census, *Population of the United States in 1860* (Washington, D.C.: Government Printing Office, 1865), 360–61, 453; U.S. Bureau of Census, *Agriculture of the United States in 1860* (Washington, D.C.: Government Printing Office, 1864), 104–5, 237.

6. Ernest M. Lander Jr., "The Iron Industry in Antebellum South Carolina," *Journal of Southern History* 20 (August 1954): 337–55, and *The Textile Industry in Antebellum South Carolina* (Baton Rouge: Louisiana State University Press, 1969), 13–18.

7. U.S. Bureau of Census, *Manufactures of the United States in 1860* (Washington, D.C.: Government Printing Office, 1865), 426, 428, 552, 554, 556.

8. Lacy K. Ford Jr., *Origins of Southern Radicalism: The South Carolina Upcountry, 1800–1860* (New York: Oxford University Press, 1988), 226–27, 242–43; Bruce W. Eelman, *Entrepreneurs in the Southern Upcountry: Commercial Culture in Spartanburg, South Carolina, 1845–1880* (Athens: University of Georgia Press, 2008), 21–24, 56–69, 70–87, 108–12. On the importance of inde-

pendence in antebellum southern ideology, see Steven Hahn, *The Roots of Southern Populism: Yeoman Farmers and the Transformation of the Georgia Upcountry, 1850–1890* (New York: Oxford University Press, 1983), 86–91; Ford, *Origins of Southern Radicalism*, 49–51.

9. Downey, *Planting a Capitalist South*, 142–44. Also see Allen Stokes, "Black and White Labor and the Development of the Southern Textile Industry" (Ph.D. diss., University of South Carolina, 1977).

10. Harold S. Wilson, *Confederate Industry: Manufacturers and Quartermasters in the Civil War* (Jackson: University Press of Mississippi, 2002), 93–129, 293–94; *Carolina Spartan*, January 23, 1863.

11. John Bomar to "Dear Sir," April 12, 1865, South Caroliniana Library, University of South Carolina, Columbia, S.C. (hereafter SCL).

12. Douglas B. Ball, *Financial Failure and Confederate Defeat* (Urbana: University of Illinois Press, 1991), 300–301; M. F. Brooks to Ellen Leaphart, August 7, 1866 (quotation), Papers of the Janney and Leaphart Families, SCL.

13. On difficulties facing cotton mills in 1865–66, see Wilson, *Confederate Industry*, 236–43; North Carolina Credit Report Ledger, vol. 11, 473, 474; vol. 14, 44 (quotations), R. G. Dun & Co. Collection, Harvard Business School (hereafter HBS); Gustavus Galloway Williamson Jr., "Cotton Manufacturing in South Carolina, 1865–1892" (Ph.D. diss., Johns Hopkins University, 1954), 51. On mill expansion in North Carolina, see Richard W. Griffin, "Reconstruction of the North Carolina Textile Industry, 1865–1885," *North Carolina Historical Review* 41 (January 1964): 34–53. On mill expansion throughout the South in the late 1860s, see Wilson, *Confederate Industry*, 265–72.

14. Melanie Archer and Judith R. Blau, "Class Formation in Nineteenth-Century America: The Case of the Middle Class," *Annual Review of Sociology* 19 (1993): 21–22, 35–36. Especially see Wells, *Origins of the Southern Middle Class;* Byrne, *Becoming Bourgeois;* and Downey, *Planting a Capitalist South.*

15. On the Ku Klux Klan in the North Carolina and South Carolina upcountry, see Allen W. Trelease, *White Terror: The Ku Klux Klan Conspiracy and Southern Reconstruction* (New York: Harper & Row, 1971), 336–80.

16. B. F. Perry to A. P. Pettick, July 16, 1871, B. F. Perry Papers, SCL.

17. U.S. Congress, Joint Select Committee to Inquire into the Conditions of Affairs in the Late Insurrectionary States, *Testimony Taken by the Joint Select Committee to Inquire into the Conditions of Affairs in the Late Insurrectionary States* 42nd Cong., 2nd sess., no. 22, vol. 4:765–66, 800–804 (hereafter *KKK Testimony*).

18. Bess Beatty, *Alamance: The Holt Family and Industrialization in a North Carolina County, 1837–1900* (Baton Rouge: Louisiana State University Press, 1999), 114.

19. *KKK Testimony*, vol. 2, 392, 412–13.

20. Scott Reynolds Nelson, *Iron Confederacies: Southern Railways, Klan Violence, and Reconstruction* (Chapel Hill: University of North Carolina Press, 1999), 136.

21. Letter of J. Bomar and Company, May 28, 1868, Letters Received, Second Military District, 1867–1868, Box 23, National Archives, Washington, D.C.

22. Richard Zuczek, *State of Rebellion: Reconstruction in South Carolina* (Columbia: University of South Carolina Press, 1996), 98–99.

23. *The Enterprise* (Greenville, S.C.), September 27, 1871.

24. *The Enterprise*, October 14, 1871, April 24, 1872.

25. Mark M. Smith, *Mastered by the Clock: Time, Slavery, and Freedom in the American South* (Chapel Hill: University of North Carolina Press, 1997). For a good discussion of rural work routines in nineteenth-century America, see Jonathan Prude, *The Coming of the Industrial Order: Town and Factory Life in Rural Massachusetts, 1810–1860* (New York: Cambridge University Press, 1983), 15–17. Also see Allen Tullos, *Habits of Industry: White Culture and the Transformation of the Carolina Piedmont* (Chapel Hill: University of North Carolina Press, 1989).

26. On the importance of drinking in southern culture, see Bertram Wyatt-Brown, *Southern Honor: Ethics and Behavior in the Old South* (New York: Oxford University Press, 1982), 278–81, and William J. Rorabaugh, *The Alcoholic Republic: An American Tradition* (New York: Oxford University Press, 1979).

27. Wilbur R. Miller, *Revenuers and Moonshiners: Enforcing Federal Liquor Law in the Mountain South, 1865–1900* (Chapel Hill: University of North Carolina Press, 1991), 26–28.

28. *The Enterprise*, December 13, 1871, February 19, 1873.

29. "The Beginning of and the History of Mountain Island and the Industrial Life of Gaston County, N.C.," Robert Goodloe Lindsay Papers, Southern Historical Collection, University of North Carolina at Chapel Hill.

30. *The Enterprise*, June 5, 1872, December 4, 1872.

31. Manufacturers and other middle-class reformers in the antebellum North placed similar emphasis on punctuality and clean living in their push for common schools. See David Nasaw, *Schooled to Order: A Social History of Public Schooling in the United States* (New York: Oxford University Press, 1979), 44–48.

32. *The Enterprise*, March 26, 1873, April 17, 1872.

33. Tullos, *Habits of Industry*, 143–46; Shelene Collette Solomon, "'A Great Man Gone': Mill Village Paternalism and Henry Pinckney Hammett" (M.A. thesis, University of Charleston and The Citadel, 2001), 20–29; *The Enterprise*, February 19, 1873.

34. *The Lincoln Progress* (Lincolnton, N.C.), May 8, 1875, August 14, 1875; *The Enterprise*, October 14, 1871.

35. Jasper Stowe Account Book, Stowe Family Papers, Perkins Library, Duke University (hereafter DU).

36. Ibid.

37. Ibid.

38. C. Phifer to Geo. L. Phifer, March 10, 1872, Edward Phifer Collection, North Carolina Department of Archives and History, Raleigh, North Carolina.

39. *The Mountaineer* (Greenville, S.C.), September 14, 1870.

40. *The Enterprise*, February 26, 1873.

41. Ibid.

42. Francis Butler Simkins and Robert Hilliard Woody, *South Carolina during Reconstruction* (Chapel Hill: University of North Carolina Press, 1932), 291–92, 299.

43. A. P. Rhyne to G. W. Lawrence, December 23, 1876, Stowe Family Papers, DU.

44. North Carolina Credit Report Ledger, v. XI, 476, R. G. Dun & Co. Collection, HBS; *The Enterprise*, February 26, 1873; *Carolina Spartan*, June 30, 1875.

45. *The Enterprise,* February 19, 1873.

46. *Carolina Spartan,* April 28, 1875.

47. Tullos, *Habits of Industry*; Beatty, *Alamance,* 53–71; Bess Beatty, "Textile Labor in the North Carolina Piedmont: Mill Owner Images and Mill Worker Response, 1830–1900," *Labor History* 25 (Fall 1984): 485–503.

Of Culture and Conviction

African American Women Nonfiction Writers and the Gendered Definitions of Class

SONYA RAMSEY

> They tell her that it's true, that the upward way involves struggles to the end: and that hundreds have started and fallen; but if she'll only continue; the higher she goes, the stronger she'll get. They also tell of the many pleasures in the high circle, the many positions she can fill, and the advantages of obtaining good wages.
>
> —JOSIE BRIGGS HALL, 1905

I n her essay, "The Pinnacle of Fame," African American teacher and writer Josie Briggs Hall uses the metaphor of a ladder, offering seven "rungs" for young women to climb. These include a high aim, a fixed will, a firm hope, a strong resolution, charity, culture, and amelioration. In this 1905 work, Briggs Hall is attempting to provide young women with a systematic guide to achieving middle-class status. As the entrenchment of legal segregation and lynching engulfed the South at the turn of the century, African American leaders sought new methods to encourage racial advancement and economic prosperity in this dangerous environment. Along with the familiar theories of Booker T. Washington's accommodationism and W. E. B. Du Bois's promotion of political equality, black women activists such as Ida B. Wells also spoke truth to power as she challenged America to denounce lynching. While many are familiar with these prominent writers, activists, and leaders, other southern and southern-born black women, such as Virginia Broughton, in *Twenty Year's Experience of a Missionary,* Josie Briggs Hall, in *Hall's Moral and Mental Capsule,* and Madame Emma Azalia Hackley, in *The Colored Girl Beautiful,* told their stories or shared advice to advance the race and in particular African American women. These authors, often one generation removed from enslavement, formed the foundation of a rising black middle class of teachers and wives of professionals.[1]

As these teachers and former educators offered guides to direct the lives of their readers, their writings also conveyed a great deal about their own definitions of proper middle-class behavior. Historian Michele Mitchell has claimed that "advice literature was more than an attempt to create class values. Manuals, tracts and pamphlets were part of an effort by reformers to reproduce those values."[2] Several scholars of African American women's history such as Evelyn Brooks Higginbotham, Victoria Wolcott, Leslie Brown, Bettye Collier-Thomas, and Stephanie J. Shaw have insightfully explored the ways that African American women leaders attempted to dispel negative stereotypes and eliminate discrimination by demanding respectability as a strategy for progress, and this essay explores how three lesser-known writers promoted this philosophy, while also expanding its dictates to suggest that religious devotion mandated that one act in a proper way, pleasing to God and pleasing to the race. As Christian women, they also expressed a religious philosophy that directed young black women to assume traditional roles as wives and mothers, while also realizing their true potential as leaders. Although other historians have produced excellent studies discussing concepts of racial uplift, black community formation, and African American women living in large southern cities like Atlanta and Charlotte, the women featured in this essay resided in smaller towns or spent much of their lives traveling and working throughout the South as evangelists and artists. They took their lessons out of the classroom to share with young women across the South and the nation, but these writers' biographical insights also reflect their own personal struggles while living in a discriminatory society.[3]

These former educators promoted a model of the middle-class woman who was educated or self-taught, possessed the value of piety, kept a clean home, and maintained a proper appearance. Service to the race was also a primary requirement for social acceptance, despite the small but influential black middle class's attempts to forge a safe space by differentiating themselves from their poorer counterparts. In examining the writings of Broughton, Briggs Hall, and Hackley, we see that as these writers offered guidance and advice to the race, they also helped to construct an image of the religiously devoted, culturally refined, middle-class black woman in the South.[4]

The quest for educational access was one of the foundational freedoms sought by African Americans after slavery. As Christian missionary associations hired northern white and free black women to instruct the millions of freedmen in the basics of literacy and Christian religious doctrine, they sometimes faced an unwelcoming South that feared the power that they held within their primers. Many of these teachers lost their jobs during Reconstruction to white, southern teachers as cities began to open public schools and missionary associations began to focus more on developing higher education opportunities for African Americans. Ironically, while Reconstruction-era black Republicans pushed for the creation of state-sponsored public education, African Americans received a harsh blow with the establishment of substandard segregated black schools. As southern states continued to staff schools with local white teachers who held no connection to the African American community, parents in several cities organized to fight for black teachers. By the late 1870s, many of the newly created black normal schools, colleges, and universities began to graduate their first classes of young black men and women who were directed to go out and serve as teachers, ministers, and entrepreneurs. Blocked by race from entering other professional occupations, teaching became the best option for black women to enter the middle class.[5]

As these women matriculated through the halls of institutions of higher learning such as Fisk University in Nashville, Tennessee, or Tuskegee Institute in Tuskegee, Alabama, they learned that professionals had to serve as representatives of achievement in a world where black women encountered disrespect from the law, popular culture, and the larger society. Whether they studied at a black college or not, African American female teachers also realized their jobs would involve addressing the needs of students beyond academic training. These women attempted to represent a middle-class ideal, despite having to teach in old, broken-down buildings with insufficient supplies.[6]

In 1891, southern teacher, author, and feminist Anna Julia Cooper called for greater support of female higher education by explaining women's special role in the community. She explained, "We might as well expect to grow trees from leaves as hope to build up a civilization or a manhood without taking into consideration our women and the home life made by them . . . Let us insist then on special encouragement for the education of our women and special care in their training. Let our girls feel that we expect something more of them than they merely look pretty and appear well in society. Teach them that there is a race with special needs, which they and only they can help."[7] Cooper emphasized the importance of female education for the African American race and even for the development of African American "manhood." As was common, she focused on the female domestic role. Cooper and other black women leaders of the era thought that racial progress could only be achieved if women received educational opportunities so that they could help the less fortunate.

While other teachers such as Broughton, Briggs Hall, and Hackley shared Cooper's view and stressed the necessity for young women to gain educational opportunities, they also emphasized additional themes of religious devotion, moral responsibility, and cultural development. These women expanded the professional teacher's mandate to go forth and serve by sharing their experiences with the world through their writings. As women put pen to paper, they hoped to extend their ability to influence and shape the minds of young women outside the schoolroom; they also wanted to teach "class" as another tool in the arsenal of racial advancement.

Black women teachers, as members of the southern middle class, held exalted positions in the black community. Although economic success granted preliminary entry into the middle class, educational attainment was necessary to remain and gain acceptance. During segregation, female educators, much like their male counterparts, often assumed leadership roles in black communities. These black women writers' educational experiences prepared them for future careers in the public sphere.[8] One such woman was Virginia E. Walker, who became one of the first members of Fisk University's graduating class in 1875 and arguably the first black woman to graduate from a college in the South. Born in 1856 in Virginia, Walker came from an ambitious family. Her father purchased his family from slavery and later moved them to Nashville, where Walker studied in private schools. After graduating from Fisk, Walker took a teaching job in the Memphis public schools. She later married Julius Broughton, a local attorney and member of the state legislature, and became an active clubwoman. Although she was married, Virginia Broughton continued her career as an educator and climbed the ranks to become the principal of the North Memphis Grammar School. She later became a teacher at the Kortrecht Grammar School, which offered one year of secondary school and was the most prestigious African American school in the city. When the Memphis school board promoted a lesser-qualified man over her, she sued the board and won. She was later reinstated as head teacher (assistant principal).[9]

Broughton's calling to serve God drove her to become a missionary. Sister Joanna P. Moore, a white missionary working with the Women's Baptist Home Mission Society, invited Broughton to attend a meeting. Although she had no interest in becoming a missionary immediately after attending that initial meeting, it eventually changed her life. After recuperating from a serious illness, she found her calling and started splitting her duties by teaching during the week and traveling on the weekends to work as a missionary. After twelve years, Broughton left her Memphis teaching post to embark on a new career as a full-time Baptist missionary. Writing about herself in the third person, she explained, "As the mission work grew and it became necessary for Virginia to give up her schoolwork at a lucrative salary and give herself wholly to developing the missionary work of our women, it was somewhat of a struggle to give up a substantial, sure support to engage in a work of faith, with no visible means of support. Finally the struggle ended and Virginia sweetly surrendered." Broughton journeyed through Tennessee, Mississippi, and Missouri in unhealthy and unsafe conditions to start Bible Bands, women's groups dedicated to reading daily Bible devotionals.[10]

Broughton transferred her teaching and leadership skills from the public schools to the church. By establishing Bible Band classes, she not only expressed her religious devotion, she also empowered women and helped to create a new black feminist pedagogical theology. In 1907, Broughton published *Twenty Year's Experience of a Missionary.* Written in an almost novel-like fashion, Broughton's autobiography is not a formal behavioral or etiquette guide for "class" instruction; instead, it offered inspiration to young women who wished to have respectable religious careers as missionaries.

While Broughton dedicated her life to missionary work, Josie Briggs Hall, another southern teacher, also believed that she had a mission outside the classroom to serve her community by offering words of guidance and wisdom. Briggs was born in Waxahachie, Texas, four years after the end of slavery. Her mother died when she was eleven and she went to live with her older sister. She became a Sunday school teacher at her local Methodist church at twelve and later enrolled in Bishop College in Marshall, Texas. Unfortunately, she could not complete her degree and she left Bishop to teach in the public schools of Canaan, Texas, at age sixteen. In 1888, she married Fisk graduate and fellow teacher J. P. Hall, who later became principal of the Colored High School in Mexia, Texas. Despite being married and giving birth to five children, Briggs Hall continued to teach.[11]

After teaching for seventeen years, she decided that the best way to raise the moral standards of children was to counsel the parents. As Briggs Hall remarked, "I thought by teaching the parents the lesson of duty, I could admonish them to help save the youths of the race from destruction."[12] To facilitate her plan, Briggs Hall decided to write *Hall's Moral and Mental Capsule* because "I was confident of the fact that mere school education alone could not raise the race to the proper moral standard."[13] She framed her book of essays and poetry as a type of medical therapy, offering capsules of stern advice, which would cure African Americans by strengthening their character and helping them become productive and respected citizens. She claimed, "Tis true that as a race we are morally and intellectually weak. But I feel that many of the vices of our people are brought about from a lack of knowing how to find a remedy. Hence I have mixed and rolled a series of valuable ingredients together, the object which is two-fold, to make a better people and solve the Negro problem."[14]

While Briggs Hall severely chastised those she thought acted in morally unacceptable ways, Emma Azalia Hackley used the concept of beauty to guide young southern women who aspired to the middle class. Emma Azalia Smith was born in Murfreesboro, Tennessee, in 1867 and moved with her family to Detroit when she was three years old after incensed local residents threatened to destroy her mother's school for newly freed blacks. After living in Detroit for more than ten years, her father, Henry, the owner of a curio shop, left her emotionally unstable mother when Hackley was a teenager. As the family struggled to support itself and maintain an outward appearance of middle-class status, Hackley's prized music lessons were beneficial when she started performing in small concerts and parties to raise money for her music and French lessons and the care of her disabled little sister. After graduating from normal school in Detroit, she worked as an elementary school teacher and performed on the weekends. In 1884, after five years of dating, she eloped with Edwin Henry Hackley, an attorney and founding editor of the *Colorado Statesman* newspaper, and moved to Denver, where she became the first black woman to graduate from the Denver School of Music with a bachelor's degree in 1900. She started teaching at the Extension School of the Denver School of Music and began performing as a soprano soloist. She continued her work as a choir director and soloist after moving to Philadelphia. In 1901, she decided to leave the teaching profession and pursue a career directing choirs, coaching African American voice students, including a young Marian Anderson, and performing concerts that celebrated the Negro spiritual.[15]

In 1910, Booker T. Washington asked Hackley, now a well-known concert artist, to speak to a group of young women at Tuskegee Institute in Alabama about poise and class. For these students, who learned dressmaking as well as academic subjects, Hackley, adorned in the finest attire, was a regal and remarkable sight. Even as she instructed the young women about the proper behaviors of a middle-class lady, Hackley harbored memories of her own experiences as a financially struggling music student who had to perform concerts to support her dysfunctional family. Now, possessing a new stage name, Madame E. Azalia Hackley relied upon her college training to reinvent herself along with other black women teachers to become a prominent member of the middle class. As Tuskegee students listening to Hackley's lecture learned the necessary educational credentials for admittance into the black middle class, they sought the one element that academic books did not teach: how to be a respectable woman of class. Hackley wrote, "If I had a daughter I would desire that she should know these things and more, that she might be a beacon light to her home and the race. I send these thoughts to the daughters of other Colored women, hoping that among them there is some new thought worthy of a racial 'Amen.'" In 1916, she published a collection of her lectures called *The Colored Girl Beautiful* in which she offered advice relating to all aspects of a woman's life.[16]

Both Hackley's and Briggs Hall's guides reinforced a prevailing strategy for African American progress promoted by middle-class black women. Evelyn Brooks Higginbotham first coined the phrase the "politics of respectability" when she discussed the role of women in the black Baptist church. As African American women emerged from Reconstruction as newly freed people, they faced monumental obstacles as southern society attempted to reinforce and reestablish a racialized social order. By the century's end, thousands of black men could no longer vote due to changes in state constitutions. If they tried to assert their rights as citizens, blacks could face lynch mobs or the wrath of violent terrorist groups like the Ku Klux Klan. In response, African Americans turned inward to seek new avenues for progress. If white southerners did not deem blacks worthy of equality, then African Americans would strive to change the prevailing negative image by assuming an image of respectability. If black people could help each other become more moral and respectable, then they could cast off the stigma and negative stereotypes of slavery.[17] Thus, for the emerging African American middle class, cultural and behavioral traits were crucial.

As African Americans emerged from the mental and physical bonds of enslavement, religious participation likewise became one avenue for racial progress. Briggs Hall claimed that although blacks had to deal with the painful memories of slavery and racial discrimination in the present, if they followed the will of God, He would deliver them. She wrote, "But amid the distractions of life we must keep Christ before us, as did the children of Israel; and He will deliver us."[18] Hackley agreed, "The Negro undoubtedly brought about his own freedom through his own spirituality and faith, and the concentrated united thought of a whole people upon one subject—freedom."[19] Echoing the similar messages of these writers, Broughton's religious devotion gave her the opportunity to speak about the gospel, travel, gain leadership and become an influential writer.

As an educated member of the middle class, Broughton, in life and through her writing, constructed a new model for black women at the same time that she promoted a women-centered space for religious devotion. Broughton's independence as a missionary freed her from rigid church hierarchies, which often prevented black women from assuming leadership roles. Although prohibited from assuming ministerial roles or other positions of authority, educated black women often had important roles in the church working as charitable group leaders. For many southern African American middle-class women, educational achievement did not contradict their religious faith; it reinforced it. By forging a new path, Broughton expanded the role of women in the black church, where their religious authenticity could be influential in bringing others to Christ.[20] In her autobiography, *Twenty Year's Experience of a Missionary,* Broughton discussed how eager women were to participate in the Bible Bands. Through religious discussions, these groups promoted literacy and a middle-class standard of living. As Broughton wrote, "A general awakening in the study of the Bible followed these great meetings. Bible texts were repeated around firesides and at the dining-room tables . . . A general reform was evidently going on toward the development of the women and the betterment of the home and church life of the people." In Broughton's work, she identified specific behaviors that would mark a woman as not respectable or as not middle class. She thankfully reported that women in the Bible Bands "were giving up the vile habits of beer drinking and snuff dipping."[21]

All three writers, as well as other prominent black leaders of this era, promoted a sustaining faith that required adherence to strict moral and behavior codes. Women's contributions to the religious life of their community provided a measure of respect and authority that was equally as important as traditional education. By primarily addressing young middle-class women, these writers hoped to impart a new consciousness and sense of purpose among this group, which they could spread among the lesser educated in their communities. Higginbotham claimed that church participation also allowed working-class women without formal education to assume an image of respectability.[22]

These authors also promoted a concept of southern female uplift ideology that claimed that respectable women could live religiously and morally pure lives, regardless of class status. In a lecture to young working girls, Hackley asserted, "You the Colored working women, have the bone and the sinew of the race. A slip-shod, half-hearted working woman is a curse to the race, because she gives it a bad reputation. Put pride and joy in your work and let it reflect your inner self." Here Hackley was suggesting that the quality of one's work and the effort used to complete one's duties was worthy of respect despite the demeaning nature of the actual task. She also wished to remind them of their duty to counter destructive images of black women. Whereas the black middle class sought respectability as an avenue for racial advancement, participation in the church also enabled working-class black women opportunities to assume positions of power. However, this call to members of the working class also implied that they would be negatively affected the most if their peers did not act in respectable ways.[23]

As Briggs Hall explained, the critical words found in *Hall's Moral and Mental Capsule* might be hard to swallow.[24] Her harsh admonishments about lazy and degenerate blacks reflected less about the moral state of black America and more about her own internalization of negative stereotypes of African American sexuality. They also represented fears that the non-respectable behavior of the lower class would taint the middle class and hinder its aspirations to a higher class status. Briggs Hall's work was rife with disdain as she lamented, "A certain element of Negroes sometimes commit nameless crimes and a certain element of whites seem to think fire and oil are the best method of punishing them. However, it is claimed that when we as a race pay more regard to morals, and all of the higher virtues, we will be given an opportunity. These virtues will move out oppression, and they will have the good effect to keep the spirit of prejudice at low ebb so they claim."[25]

One could glean from Briggs Hall's work that the status of African Americans was entirely a result of their own immorality and laziness. Her reprimands epitomized the shortcomings in the promotion of respectability because she seldom acknowledged the impact of racism and abject poverty upon the lives of African Americans. She was not alone in this quality, as Higginbotham argues: "At times the rhetoric of the black Baptist women sounded uncannily similar to the racist arguments they strove to refute." Some prominent black women church leaders such as Nannie Helen Burroughs asserted that "proper and respectable" behavior proved blacks worthy of equal civil and political rights and made it possible for them to "demand what they can not hope to demand if they are boisterous and unclean."[26]

While black women often couched their discussion of the politics of respectability in spiritual terms, they also used it as a tactic to correct past historical injustices. During slavery, several concepts emerged to justify the rape of black women that suggested that they were immoral and sexually promiscuous. These stereotypes promoted the idea that the sexual abuse of black women was not a crime because they were always willing to have sex. In addition, the courts refused to admit the testimony of black women who accused their white attackers of rape or assault, making an already painful violation even more so. As black women entered the middle class and became professionals, they wished to free themselves from this stigma and gain respect. As southern society promoted stereotypes of the oversexed slave woman, the Jezebel, and the dangerous sexually deviant brute Negro, some African American leaders internalized these stereotypes and chastised African Americans who did not adhere to strict ideas regarding morality, behavior, and dress.[27]

For Briggs Hall the consequences for those who failed to live a virtuous life, built upon responsibility and respectability, were dire, personally and politically. She warned of the race's destruction unless its black women and men acted in moral and socially acceptable ways. As Briggs Hall claimed, "If impure women do not stay off the streets, trying to entice men and boys to enter the slums of debauchery; and if Negro men don't stop sitting on goods-boxes or beer kegs, with nothing to do but slander girls and talk politics, the politicians of the North and South will combine into a great force, and engulf us in a sea of proscription much deeper and wider than our present allotment."[28] To limit any further erosion of black rights and to promote race progress, she advised that there needed to be "a change in the moral status of the race." Countering white supremacist rhetoric that highlighted "uncivilized" behavior that demonized blacks, Briggs Hall and others instructed women of all classes to uphold the highest ideals of moral and chaste womanhood. For her, women were the key to the race's success: "Water cannot rise higher than its level, nor can a race rise higher than its women."[29]

Hackley did not condemn the race in such strong terms; instead, she provided a plethora of suggestions to encourage middle-class black women to be beautiful inside and out. In other words, Hackley advised girls that respectability requires sexual chastity. Whereas religious piety was paramount, black middle-class women also wished to counter over-sexualized images by promoting chastity and sexual restraint. After the positive response at the Tuskegee event, Hackley realized that there was a great need for lectures directed at young women. Filling that need, Hackley told the students how to carry themselves with poise and addressed a range of matters from dress to dating practices.[30]

In Hackley's expansive definition of beauty, a truly attractive woman was one who generated respect by acting in a responsible manner. Hackley maintained that "Control is culture, and culture is a beauty point. We must remove the stigma of loudness and coarseness that now rests upon the race." In a society in which so many negative portrayals of African American women permeated popular culture, to tell them ways to be beautiful was a radical idea. However, her use of the term "beauty" also emphasized the politics of respectability. In her chapter, "The Colored Girl Beautiful" she did not celebrate the actual appearances of African American women. Unlike other guides and popular women's magazines of the time, Hackley's creation of beauty required looking inward.[31]

Although visual beauty generated positive reactions in relationships and in society in general, black women had little to no protection against black and white men who viewed their bodies as beautiful or sexually desirable. For some black women, beauty caused them great emotional pain. Women, such as Hackley and Briggs Hall, attempted to construct a new image and definition of African American female beauty: one that led men and women to respect beauty as an outward manifestation of inner purity and respectability.

Hackley also suggested that young women should incorporate the teachings of Christ into their everyday lives. For her, spirituality was beauty; a truly beautiful girl expressed her spirituality by keeping a neat home and appearance. Hackley declared that "God is not only all that is perfect in cleanliness, order and harmony, but He is also all that is perfect in color and sound. God is in the body and all its parts."[32] Hackley maintained that a truly spiritual woman was quiet and did not get angry in public. Unlike Broughton, she did not push women to challenge the gender hierarchy of their communities. Instead, she encouraged them to develop feminine attributes of internal and external beauty, and to promote their moral authority in the home as well as in the larger society. While each of Hackley's book chapters focused on different themes, such as the "Religion of the Colored Girl Beautiful" and "Self Control," the underlying message was that black women should subscribe to a patriarchal view regarding behavior. If they integrated her advice into their daily lives, they would gain acceptance and respect from African American men, their middle-class female peers, and the larger society. Hackley declared that if women incorporated more spirituality in their lives, they would receive admiration and blessings. Historian Michele Mitchell explained that, "overall, not only did Afro-American advice literature provocatively insinuate that conduct reflected class and moral standing, its production reflected specific tensions, anxieties, and conflicts regarding gender and sexuality." Hackley's guide provided a script for young women to follow and a rationale that explained to overeager suitors as well as their peers the importance of remaining chaste. While African American women hoped the politics of respectability would alleviate discrimination from whites, both Hackley and Briggs Hall used these concepts to encourage young women to eliminate internalized negative stereotypical attitudes and see themselves as respectable women. These writings also illustrated the deep connection between status and morality among the nineteenth- and early twentieth-century African American middle class.[33]

For Hackley and other black women educators, living a virtuous life and practicing good manners could help young women obtain good jobs and eventually break down racial barriers. National black women's organizations also promoted these views. Hackley participated in several black women's organizations and clubs, such as the Denver Colored Women's League. Several scholars of African American club women such as Dorothy Salem, Stephanie Shaw, and Deborah Gray White have discussed the creation of the National Association of Colored Women (NACW) in 1896 and its rise and significance. The leaders of the clubwomen's movement created a new black feminist ideology that suggested that it was the black woman's responsibility to uplift the race.[34] Broughton, a member of several women's clubs including Memphis's Phyllis Wheatley Literary and Social Club, elaborated in a Memphis newspaper editorial: "The women now realize their responsibilities as never before, and from the weight of this realization they are organizing their forces to better prepare themselves to perform, in the best manner, every duty incumbent upon them, from the cellar to the garret; in the home; or their lot in the church and other religious organizations, and in the world." While some black clubwomen promoted this philosophy as the women's era, they also adhered to the politics of respectability by emphasizing that women had a special responsibility to create a proper home life.[35]

During the Progressive era, southern black clubwomen heard the national call for service by establishing segregated chapters of organizations such as the Woman's Christian Temperance Union, participating in suffrage associations, and serving in church missionary societies and clubs. Whereas white members of the General Federation of Women's Clubs, the Woman's Christian Temperance Union, or the United Daughters of the Confederacy were often successful in securing funding from their local and state governments, black women had to rely upon private donations from their own communities and benevolent donors to open homes for wayward boys and girls, elderly homes, and hospitals and support substandard, underfunded public schools. When most administrative positions in the schools were off limits, working to help one's community or performing service gave black women teachers opportunities to become leaders and a powerful platform to express their views and opinions.[36]

While African American clubwomen called for members to lead in the area of racial uplift, African American teachers thought that one of the best ways to ensure racial progress was to rebuild family life. Teachers such as Briggs Hall and Hackley also subscribed to the views of prominent educator and black spokesman Booker T. Washington, who promoted economic self-help and racial accommodation. These women incorporated his philosophies, along with the ideas of the leaders of the NACW, to encourage the formation of stable marriages. Briggs Hall warned young women of the dangers of marrying an unsuitable mate. She described four classes of women: the overworked, put-upon woman who married a worthless man who could not free her from hard labor; single mothers and women who had relationships with married men; lazy, immoral women; and wives of hardworking upstanding husbands. Yet, she applauded black women who were able to avoid the pitfalls of unsupportive family members, jealous peers, and objectionable men to secure an education and marry. For her and other southern black middle-class women, receiving a higher education and marrying a respectable man elevated them above the masses.[37]

During the Progressive era, prominent black women leaders also advocated for the vote despite southern white organizations' promotion of women's suffrage as a tool to ensure white supremacy. Historian Rosalyn Terborg-Penn claimed that black women wanted the right to vote not solely to have a voice as individual citizens, but as a way to serve the entire African American community. Nevertheless, while former Memphis teachers and activists such as Mary Church Terrell and Ida B. Wells Barnett marched for the right to vote, conservative women like Briggs Hall disagreed with such efforts. Briggs Hall emphasized her views in a poem she wrote entitled "Woman's Rights": "With me on Woman's Rights/You all may not agree./But I think her principal duty/Is that of housewifery;/For when she trains up a child in the right way/She has casted a vote in the right direction,/And that vote's as powerful/As if casted at an election."[38] She downplayed the importance of voting because she thought that promoting the role of women as wives and mothers was far more influential in shaping racial progress. She also argued that black mothers bore a special responsibility to ensure that their children would serve as proper representatives of the race. Presenting a similar view, Margaret Murray Washington, wife of Booker T. Washington, called for teachers to form mothers' clubs at a meeting of the NACW in Nashville in 1913: "Schoolteachers should come in contact with the children's parents, and if there is not a mothers' meeting organized in the community where they teach, they should call the mothers together and organize them. The subject: 'At what age shall I allow my daughter to receive company?'—Subjects like this and similar subjects, as, what our children should wear, what they should eat, and where they should go are discussed in this department. This helps to improve our homes."[39] Hackley also celebrated motherhood when she added, "the Colored mother beautiful carries a heavy burden—the weight of future generations of a handicapped, persecuted people; she may make a more beautiful race with the beauty that comes from beauty of character and right living."[40]

As Briggs Hall extolled the virtues of motherhood and marriage, she also used her position as the wife of a prominent local educator with five children to claim expertise in this area. While Broughton and Hackley both advocated religious devotion, their family lives were more complicated. For these women, exercising their calling took precedence over their marriages. For example, although Broughton felt that God had called her to become a missionary, she struggled with maintaining a balance between family and her religious work in the beginning of her career. When her husband reprimanded her for being away from home for long periods and asked, "When is this business going to stop? She replied, 'I don't know: but I belong to God first, and you next; so you two must settle it.'"[41] Although her husband eventually became supportive, it was harder to ignore the guilt she felt when she left her children behind to travel. Even though her daughter Selena died of complications from tonsillitis, Broughton realized after leaving a religious meeting to be with her sick daughter, "that she could stay home and sit by the bedside of her children and have all the assistance that medical skill could render, and yet God could take her children to himself if he so willed it." She then continued to do missionary work, trusting that God would protect her children.[42]

As a missionary, Broughton had a special role as a representative of her faith and her denomination. When she met with women and fellow believers, she could see how the church could better address the needs of its members. She and other religious workers helped the church become a living and breathing entity created not only to serve as a worship center, but also to improve the lives of its individuals by organizing separate women's conferences and associations. Broughton's foundation and experience as a teacher and principal provided her with the necessary skills to organize these groups, but her religious devotion and dedication enabled her to sustain her mission during adverse times. While other black women writers of this period discuss religion in a language of rules and behavior, Broughton used her faith to help women become spiritual leaders and promoted literacy.[43]

One of the things that she promoted as a missionary was a woman's ability and right to speak about the gospel. The role of the missionary, while promoting religious devotion and strict moral values, also enabled women to lead independent lives. However, a female serving as a religious leader did have its detractors. Although one would expect her book to expound upon her religious doctrine and discuss how she shared the teachings of Jesus, Broughton wrote her most revealing words to describe the opposition she encountered teaching women to read the Bible. As she gained more prominence and power within the Baptist church, Broughton explained, "Ministers and laymen, who looked with disdain upon a criticism that came from a woman, and all those who were jealous of the growing popularity of the woman's work, as if there was some cause of alarm for the safety of their own positions of power and honor, all rose up in their churches with all the influence and power of speech they could summon to oppose the woman's work and break it up if possible."[44]

This opposition seemed only to strengthen Broughton as she equated resistance to her mission as the work of the devil. She described how she relied on God to quiet her enemies, despite facing threats of violence and the destruction of her beloved Bible Bands. As a woman who spoke the gospel publicly, Broughton encountered stiff resistance from male church leaders who felt threatened. Her autobiography related shocking tales of near violent encounters she and her fellow female missionaries experienced. In one instance, Broughton revealed, "Another brother who opposed our work said, I would rather take a rail and flail the life out of a woman than to hear her speak in the church. As he spoke, not knowing what he said, God forgave him, brought him to the light, and he made an open confession of his fault."[45] While Hackley's sphere of influence was not religion, she considered promoting the Negro spiritual as a calling. She thought that by teaching spirituals, she could show America that African Americans could contribute to the artistic legacy of the United States. She also thought that she could help build the collective self-esteem of the race by promoting the richness of African American musical expression. She described her vision: "A missionary? There were religious missionaries: should not there be missionaries in music?. . .Yes, of course, to be really happy, to get the most of their lives, they must be made to know, appreciate, and sing their own song . . . And my people do have a song to sing. A song that has come from the soul of toiling hopeful people—the only song that America can call her own."[46]

Despite the varied lives these three writers led—missionary, moral educator, and cultural icon—they all promoted the idea that middle-class women should wear proper attire. Dress symbolized much more than one's fashion sense; it also identified one as a member of the middle class and deserving of respect and protection. Broughton, Briggs Hall, and Hackley all stressed the need for black women in the South to dress conservatively. Clothing not only reflected one's social status, but one's moral character as well. Broughton explained, "in the beginning of our organized missionary effort among the Negro women of Tennessee the following fundamentals were emphasized as necessary to our Christian development as women: First simplicity and cleanliness and neatness in dress and in our home furnishings." Wearing conservative clothes also separated middle-class women from those who had money but did not ascribe to the dictates of the middle class. Broughton also argued that African American women should discard "gaudy colors and conspicuous trimmings."[47]

For these writers, dressing conservatively was one way of dispelling stereotypes and of uplifting the race. Moreover, they thought that wearing immodest outfits indicated sexual availability; as Hackley declared, "They brought unwanted attention upon themselves." This mode of thinking or internalized sexism blamed black women for encouraging potential harassers or rapists. Some black middle-class women believed that they should deflect attention from their physical selves by portraying an outward modesty, countering stereotypes while also mimicking the conservative attire of some of their white counterparts.[48]

Although these writers promoted traditional beliefs, they did not lead conventional lives; they worked outside the home and placed their careers above all others, including their families. In *The Colored Girl Beautiful,* Hackley argued that women should seek husbands and serve as good wives. However, her own marriage disintegrated when she decided to become a professional musical artist and she later divorced. Although she also wrote about the proper care of children, she could not have children of her own. Instead, she focused her attention on her students.[49] Even Briggs Hall, the consummate promoter of married life, may have divorced, resulting in her move from Mexia, Texas, according to one scholar. These women promoted an ideal of respectability, but did not strictly adhere to their own teachings in their personal lives. Perhaps Briggs Hall could not live up to the standards she set for black women.[50]

As we review the writings of these women, we can reflect upon their differences in writing style and personalities, but several commonalities have emerged to suggest that these women's writings offered a window onto the attitudes and aspirations of black middle-class women in the South. While these women continued to redefine the image of black women, they were also striving to solidify their place in the middle class as African Americans found their place within the group. Even though the writers encouraged strong family values, they often personally abandoned traditional female roles to promote their own goals. In her twenty-year journey, Broughton worked to organize women's conferences, wrote religious articles, and taught religious instruction at the Women's Home Mission Society's Fireside School and A&M College, now Alabama A&M State University, in Normal, Alabama. After decades of working tirelessly to expand the role of African American women in the Baptist church, Virginia Broughton died in 1935.[51]

Prior to writing *The Colored Girl Beautiful,* Hackley wrote two other books on voice culture for music and voice teachers. In 1911, she opened the Vocal Normal Institute in Chicago and performed concerts to raise funds to operate the school. Although she insisted that the cost of *The Colored Girl Beautiful* be affordable, Hackley wrote the book to raise money for her school. Unfortunately, she could not raise enough funds and it closed in 1916. Undeterred, Hackley continued to organize folk song festivals in black schools and churches, and lectured to thousands of people across the South, dying in 1922.[52]

Briggs Hall continued to teach and organized the first black chapter of the Parent Teacher Association in Dallas, but she aspired to become a school administrator. After an attempt to open a junior college in Limestone County, Texas, proved unsuccessful, her dream became reality in 1916 when, with the help of white clubwomen and the Bureau of Social Welfare, she opened the Homemaker's Industrial and Trade School in Dallas to help black women become self-supporting. In her opinion, "Homemaking is a science to be learned, not a drudgery to be avoided," and she passed this belief on to her students. Following Washington's industrial education model, students took academic courses from grades one through six, and focused solely on domestic training from grades seven through twelve, enrolling in courses like laundering and interior decorating.

After graduation, students sought positions working for the Dallas elite and were fully equipped to manage their own homes. From its opening to its closing in 1928, the school awarded more than three hundred certificates. In 1919, Briggs Hall told a local newspaper that "This school was not organized for the purpose of profit to any individual and depends largely upon the public for support. It is one institution where colored servants can receive a proper training for the vocation they may choose to follow."[53] Briggs Hall died in 1935 in Dallas. While *Hall's Moral and Mental Capsule* promoted the merits of proper marriage as a way to ensure economic success, in later years, Briggs Hall endorsed philosophies of such prominent black women educators as Nannie Helen Burroughs, by insisting that women learn how to take care of themselves. This, in essence, reflected an underlying belief of black middle-class women who promoted the politics of respectability: that one should also know how to be independent. While all three women left the public school classroom, they continued teaching for the rest of their lives.[54]

At the same time as these writers promoted the politics of respectability in their efforts to serve as role models for southern African American women, their own personal stories reflect the dilemmas and pressures that black women placed upon themselves to uplift the race. Often describing their self-imposed responsibility as a burden, middle-class women often hid their own personal struggles to maintain class status. After the black troops returned from World War I ready to enact change and assert a new brand of militancy, the "Women's Era," so astutely promoted by black women activists, faded. These new strategies included working with civil rights organizations such as the National Association for the Advancement of Colored People (NAACP), where women, who had once headed their own groups, often filled secondary leadership positions. Their later teacher counterparts continued to uphold the belief that proper behavior and appropriate dress could be used to empower black women until the advent of the modern civil rights movement offered new and additional avenues for advancement.

NOTES

1. Josie Briggs Hall, *Hall's Moral and Mental Capsule: For the Economic and Domestic Life of the Negro, As a Solution of the Race Problem* (Dallas: Reverend R. S. Jenkins, 1905), 114 (quotation), note, 112; Virginia Broughton, *Twenty Year's Experience of a Missionary* (Chicago: Pony Press Publishers, 1907); Emma Azalia Smith Hackley, *The Colored Girl Beautiful* (Kansas City, Mo.: Burton Publishing, 1916). These texts hereafter are cited by author's last name.

2. Michele Mitchell, *Righteous Propagation: African Americans and the Politics of Racial Destiny after Reconstruction* (Chapel Hill: University of North Carolina Press, 2004), 139.

3. For more information about black women's experiences living in Atlanta and Charlotte, see Tera W. Hunter, *To 'Joy My Freedom: Southern Black Women's Lives and Labors After the Civil War* (Cambridge, Mass.: Harvard University Press, 1998), and Jeanette Greenwood, *Bittersweet Legacy: The Black and White Better Classes in Charlotte, 1850–1910* (Chapel Hill: University of North Carolina Press, 2001). *This is ambishous.*

4. For more information about black women's history and the politics of respectability, see Leslie Brown, *Upbuilding Black Durham: Gender, Class, and Black Community Development in the Jim Crow South* (Chapel Hill: University of North Carolina Press, 2007); Evelyn Brooks Higginbotham, *Righteous Discontent: The Women's Movement in the Black Baptist Church, 1880–1920* (Cambridge, Mass.: Harvard University Press, 1993); Stephanie J. Shaw, *What a Woman Ought to Be and to Do: Black Professional Women Workers During the Jim Crow Era* (Chicago: University of Chicago Press, 1996); Victoria W. Wolcott, *Remaking Respectability: African American Women in Interwar Detroit* (Chapel Hill: University of North Carolina Press, 2001); Bruce A. Glasrud and Merline Pitre, eds., *Black Women in Texas History* (College Station: Texas A&M University Press, 2008).

5. Sonya Ramsey, *Reading, Writing, and Segregation: A Century of Black Women Teachers in Nashville* (Urbana: University of Illinois Press, 2008). For more general information on black teachers in the South, see James D. Anderson, *The Education of Blacks in the South, 1860–1935* (Chapel Hill: University of North Carolina Press, 1988); Adam Fairclough, *A Class of Their Own: Black Teachers in the Segregated South* (Cambridge, Mass.: Harvard University Press, 2007).

6. Shaw, *What a Woman Ought to Be and to Do*, 74.

7. Anna Julia Cooper, "The Higher Education of Women," originally published in *The Southland* 2 (April 1891): 199–202, and in Elizabeth L. Ihle, ed., *Black Women in Higher Education: An Anthology of Essays, Studies, and Documents* (New York: Garland Publishing, 1992), 60.

8. Fairclough, *Class of Their Own*, 238.

9. Beverly Bond, "'Till Fair Aurora Rise': African American Women in Memphis, Tennessee 1840–1915" (Ph.D. diss., University of Memphis, 1996), 154, 163, 164. Although Virginia Broughton writes that her husband's first name is Julius in her autobiography, other scholars such as Elizabeth Higginbotham state that his first name was John.

10. Broughton, 124; Higginbotham, *Righteous Discontent*, 69–71.

11. Briggs Hall, v; Glasrud and Pitre, *Black Women in Texas History*, 117.

12. Briggs Hall, 4.

13. Ibid., 1.

14. Ibid., 6.

15. DeAnna Rose Patterson, "A History of Three African American Women Who Made Important Contributions to Music Education Between 1903–1960" (M.A. thesis, Bowling Green State University, 2007), 6–9; M. Marguerite Davenport, *Azalia: The Life of Madame E. Azalia Hackley* (Boston: Chapman and Grimes Publishers, 1947), 105–8.

16. Shaw, *What a Woman Ought to Be and to Do*, 90; Hackley, 11; Davenport, *Azalia*, 138–40.

17. For a full discussion of the politics of respectability, see Higginbotham, *Righteous Discontent*, 185–229.

18. Briggs Hall, 9.

19. Hackley, 4–6

20. Higginbotham, *Righteous Discontent*, 124–30.

21. Broughton, 32 (quotations).

22. Higginbotham, *Righteous Discontent*, 200.

23. Wolcott, *Remaking Respectability*, 8; Hackley, 150; Davenport, *Azalia*, 142–43.

24. Briggs Hall, 2.

25. Ibid., 17.

26. Nannie Helen Burroughs, *National Baptist Convention Twelfth Annual Session of the Women's Conference, 1912*, 281, and "Travelers' Friend," in *Du Bois Efforts for Social Betterment*, quoted in Higginbotham, *Righteous Discontent*, 203.

27. For more information about the impact of stereotypes upon enslaved African American women, see Deborah Gray White, *Arn't I A Woman: Female Slaves in the Plantation South* (New York: Norton, 1985).

28. Mitchell, *Righteous Propagation*, 112; Briggs Hall, 16.

29. Briggs Hall, 123.

30. Davenport, *Azalia*, 42.

31. Ibid., 46, 47.

32. Hackley, 129.

33. Mitchell, *Righteous Propagation*, 139; Henry Louis Gates Jr., "Trope of the New Negro and the Reconstruction of the Image of the Black," *Representations* 24 (Autumn 1988): 141.

34. Shaw, *What a Woman Ought to Be*, 8; Deborah Gray White, *Too Heavy a Load: Black Women in Defense of Themselves, 1894–1994* (New York: Norton, 1999); Dorothy Salem, "To Better Our World: Black Women in Organized Reform, 1890–1920," in Darlene Clark Hine, ed.,

Black Women in American History, vol. 14 (Brooklyn: Carlson Publishing, 1990); Stephanie J. Shaw, "Black Club Women and the Creation of the National Association of Colored Women," *Journal of Women's History* 3 (Fall 1991): 1–25.

35. Virginia E. Broughton, "Editorial-No Author Given," *Memphis Commercial Appeal,* February 14, 1895, quoted in Bond, "'Till Fair Aurora Rise,'" 166; Higginbotham, *Righteous Discontent,* 188.

36. Ramsey, *Reading, Writing, and Segregation,* 30; Glenda Gilmore, *Gender and Jim Crow: Women and the Politics of White Supremacy in North Carolina, 1896–1920* (Chapel Hill: University of North Carolina Press, 1996), 25.

37. Briggs Hall, 54–71, quoted in Mitchell, *Righteous Propagation,* 304; Briggs Hall, 124.

38. For more information about African American women's suffrage, see Rosalyn Terborg-Penn, *African American Women in the Struggle for the Vote, 1850–1920* (Bloomington: Indiana University Press, 1998); Briggs Hall, 155–57; Mitchell, *Righteous Propagation,* 135.

39. Anonymous, "Mrs. Washington to Women's Clubs," *Nashville Globe and Independent,* June 20, 1913, 1.

40. Hackley, 132.

41. Broughton, 46.

42. Ibid., 44.

43. Higginbotham, *Righteous Discontent,* 125.

44. Broughton, 34.

45. Ibid., 38, 39.

46. Davenport, *Azalia,* 108.

47. Broughton, 22; Higginbotham, *Righteous Discontent,* 202.

48. Hackley, 110.

49. Patterson, "History of Three African American Women," 10; Davenport, *Azalia,* 136, 127.

50. Paul Lucko, "Hall, Josephine Briggs," s.v. *Texas Handbook Online,* http://www.tshaonline.org/handbook/online/articles/HH/fhafw.html [accessed November 30, 2008].

51. Broughton, 111.

52. Patterson, "History of Three African American Women," 9.

53. Elizabeth York Enstam, *Women and the Creation of Urban Life: Dallas, Texas 1843–1920* (Commerce: Texas A&M University Press, 1998), 171.

54. "Club Women Endorse Industrial School," *Dallas Express,* February 15, 1919, quoted in Marie Delahoussaye "Healing With Verse" (unpublished paper, University of Texas at Austin, 1998), 9.

Middle-Class Masters?

T here was no more ardent defender of the southern way of life than Daniel R. Hundley. On the eve of the Civil War he published a book-length description of the *Social Relations in Our Southern States* that described in detail the various classes of men and women who together comprised southern slave society. Hundley was comprehensive. He began with a chapter on "The Southern Gentleman," included another on "The Southern Yeoman," and ended with one on "The Negro Slaves." But Hundley's second chapter, weighing in at more than fifty pages, surveyed "The Middle Classes." The "middle classes of the South," Hundley began, "constitute the greater proportion of her citizens, and are likewise the most useful members of her society." Into this stratum he placed many of the men and women who populate the essays in this book. "There are among them," Hundley explained, "traders, storekeepers, artisans, mechanics, a few manufacturers, a goodly number of country school-teachers, and a host of half-fledged country lawyers and doctors, parsons, and the like."[1]

But Hundley also included "farmers" and "planters" among the southern middle classes, and his references to "country" school teachers and "country" lawyers reinforce the point. "Since the South is mainly agricultural," Hundley explained, "perhaps the larger proportion of her middle classes are to be found among the tillers of the soil." Within southern rural society, the middle classes occupied a position in between the yeoman farmers and small slaveholders on the one side, and the planter aristocrats on the other. The middle-class southerner "is usually a slaveholder, owning from five to fifty negroes (sometimes more,) and generally looks after their management himself." Their homes were plain, their tables unrefined, their religion enthusiastic. In politics middle-class masters exercised a "healthy" influence, for it was at their insistence that primogeniture was abolished and the privilege of voting was extended to all white men. "Indeed, take them all in all," Hundley concluded, "and there is a striking similarity between the middle-class planters of the South, and the more well-to-do and intelligent farmers of New England."[2]

There are historians for whom Hundley's analysis makes no sense, and for whom the very subject matter of the essays in this volume is likewise misconceived. The middle class, to the extent that we can speak of it at all, appears only with capitalism, in an economy based on wage labor. For such scholars a slave labor system cannot by definition produce a genuine middle class. The businessmen, professionals, and industrialists who emerged in the Old South could only flourish as adjuncts of slave society. Of course the slaveholders needed merchants to market their cotton and rice, lawyers to settle their disputes and validate their claims, and teachers to educate their sons and daughters, and someone had to manufacture their cotton gins and sugar mills. But they were a stunted middle class whose social function was to serve the purposes of the slaveholders who *defined* southern society—a society that could not be bourgeois because it was not capitalist.

By contrast, the essays in this volume reflect a growing body of scholarship that traces the emergence of a genuine middle class within the antebellum South, the businessmen, doctors, intellectuals, and factory owners with economic interests, career paths, and cultural values all their own. Its members formed trade associations, they developed a professional ethos, and they did not simply use their professional careers as a stepping stone to slave ownership. Several of the authors focus on South Carolina, where an unusually aristocratic planter class initially disdained but ultimately accepted the emerging middle class. This reflects a general theme running through many of the essays: the economic and cultural chasm separating the slaveholders from the middle class. Notwithstanding its ties to the slave economy the southern middle class makes its way through these pages on its own rather than the slaveholders' terms.

But Hundley's analysis remains anomalous even in this volume. Most of the authors focus on a middle class that was based in cities and towns, thereby distinguishing it from the predominantly rural slaveholding class. What we have, then, is a debate between historians who see the southern middle class as dependent upon, and those who see it as largely independent of, southern slave society. Notice the assumption that both sides share: whether the professionals, merchants, and industrialists of the Old South were autonomous or subordinate to the master class, they were two distinct classes who either stood apart from or were antithetical to each other. But excluding the slave-holders from history of the middle class may obscure the possibility that there was something intrinsic to slave society that was conducive to the growth of a middle class. Subordination and independence are not the only ways to think about the relationship between slaveholders and the southern middle class.

Is it possible to appreciate the fundamental differences between slave-based and wage-based economies, but to do so in a way that can account for the emergence of a viable middle class within the Old South? It is possible, if you accept the premise that a bourgeoisie could flourish not merely in a capitalist society but wherever commerce was highly developed. Because southern slave society was intensely commercialized it could, in principle, generate a bourgeoisie, or at least bourgeois values, within itself.

The southern slaveholders embodied the bourgeoisie's glowing youth—. the early modern era of merchant capital. Feudalism had died but capitalism had not yet been born. It was in many ways a golden age for the independent proprietor, the farmer who owned his own land, the artisan who owned his own shop. These men—together with their domestic dependents, apprentices, indentured servants, and slaves—were the social ballast for the merchant capitalists who plied their trade across the oceans. The sixteenth and seventeenth centuries were also the time of the revolutionary bourgeoisie whose enemies were absolutist monarchs and arrogant aristocracies, but not yet a surly and demanding proletariat. Rejecting the ideal of an organically unified hierarchy, these bourgeois heroes gave us instead the separation of church and state, the division of the social from the political spheres of life, and the unbridgeable fissure of what came to be called race. They reversed the classical precept that work and family were the realms of necessity, that humans could find freedom only in the *polis,* and argued instead for the primacy of *society.* Work and family, not politics or the priesthood, were their preferred sources of human happiness. They gave us liberal republicanism, civil society, and racial slavery.

It is hard enough to pin down accepted definitions of liberalism, republicanism, and civil society. But "slavery" turns out to be an even more elusive term, and because of this the debate over southern middle class risks duplicating the logical flaws of the much longer-standing debate over slavery and capitalism. In both cases the theoretical apparatus sidesteps the basic scholarship on the definition of "slavery" and is instead devoted almost exclusively to clarifying the definitions of "middle class" or "capitalism." Slavery emerges in both debates as a largely negative entity. Capitalism means free labor, therefore, slavery can be defined as *not-capitalism*, or "unfree" labor. Similarly the middle class is the product of urban and industrial society, therefore, the slaveholders were *not* middle class. Both of these propositions may be true, but they are equally inadequate. No meaningful analysis of the relationship between slavery and capitalism, or of the middle class and the master class, can proceed if the terms of the debate never move beyond purely negative definitions that tell us not what slavery and the slaveholders *were* but only what they were *not*.

The definition of slavery is unnecessarily confused by the fact that slave plantations played host to a variety of very different social formations. In the earliest decades of settlement indentured servants were the main source of labor on southern plantations, and though the practice declined it did not disappear until well into the eighteenth century. Wage labor was also a familiar feature of southern plantations. Planters commonly entered into wage contracts with the managers, overseers, or foremen of their estates. The same was true of plantation tutors, who were paid wages to educate the planters' children. Sugar planters in southern Louisiana often hired immigrant wage laborers to dig the ditches or to beef up the workforce during the grueling cane harvest.

The master's family installed yet another social formation—domestic patriarchy—onto southern plantations. As soon as she got married a wife's property became her husband's, wives and children were his domestic dependents, and the power of the husband and father was enshrined in the laws of marriage and the family. At the same time, the legal severity of domestic patriarchy was tempered by the cultural value the slaveholders attached to the comfort and happiness of the domestic sphere. Slavery enhanced this culture of domesticity. As soon as the family acquired a slave or two the mistress withdrew from the field; a few more slaves allowed the children to go to school. Prosperity meant a college education for the sons and a shift from manual to managerial labor for the master himself. But notwithstanding the effect slavery had on the master's family, domestic patriarchy prevailed in the North as well as the South.

What distinguished the South, and the southern plantation, was the status of the slaves, who were neither indentured servants, wage laborers, nor members of the master's family. Instead, slaves were the master's property, defined, treated, and defended as such. Originally slaves were categorized as real estate, albeit with legal exceptions that made them easier to buy and sell. But with the development of capitalism the law of personal property grew in significance, and southern slaveholders took advantage of this legal development. They reformed the southern legal codes, shifting the slaves from the category of real to personal property. And it was the slaves' status—as moveable property that could be easily acquired, accumulated, or disposed of—that not only distinguished slaves from others on the plantation, but also distinguished southern slave society from northern capitalism.[3]

The Western European societies from which New World slaveholders emerged had unusually strong protections for the rights of property, and this was especially true of Great Britain.[4] The combination of strong common law traditions and a weak colonial state gave and Anglo-American masters virtually unrestrained dominion over their slaves.[5] For the masters there were great advantages to defining slaves as property. There were virtually no restrictions on who could own a slave—even children could become masters, along with anyone who could pay the price. And unlike marriage, the master could terminate his relationship with a slave at will, by means of a simple commercial transaction. Thus South Carolina's slaveholding legislators could rightly boast that they never permitted a marriage to be broken by a divorce, and never interfered with a master wishing to sell a slave. And unlike serfs, slaves were moveable. The ability to buy and sell slaves and to move them about easily made commerce in humans one of the defining attributes of slavery. All slave economies had slave trades, and the Old South was no exception.

In the lethal sugar-producing districts the slave trade was essential to replace the slaves who died so rapidly. But in the healthier cotton- and tobacco-growing regions the natural increase of the southern slave population made it possible for masters to count the annual increase in the number of slaves as an additional source of profit. The "advice to masters" offered by agricultural reformers was clear about this: the successful plantation not only produced a profitable cash crop, it also registered a healthy "increase" in the number of slaves. "A good crop means one that is good, taking into consideration everything," a Virginia planter explained in 1847, including "slaves, land, horses, stock, fences, ditches and farming utensils; all of which must be kept up and improved in value."[6] Efficiency experts aiming to maximize slavery's profits offered the most consistent and specific advice for treating slaves well. In the long run, they argued, a plantation would be more profitable—the cash crops more abundant and of higher quality, the increase in the number of slaves greater—if the slaves were well fed, properly housed, adequately clothed, and minimally beaten. One of the most telling observations in Erskine Clarke's study of the professional paternalist, Charles Colcock Jones, is that Jones's very few specific proposals for improving the treatment of slaves were identical to those made by the management experts whose professed aim was to enhance the profitability of slave farms and plantations.[7] It is a mistake to assume that paternalism was antithetical to commerce.

But it is always good to be reminded that commerce is not capitalism. Indeed, the extreme commodification of slaves exposed the difference, not the similarity, between northern and southern society. Slave labor may or may not have been less efficient than free labor, the accumulation of slaves as capital assets may have hindered southern economic development, but neither of these things made southern society less commercial than northern capitalism. On the contrary, the very fact that the slaves were capital assets that were bought, accumulated, and sold suggests that slavery was more rather than less commercialized than wage labor. In capitalist economies the commodification of labor is restricted to the sale of the worker's labor *power* whereas in the Old South the slaves were themselves commodities. As Marx put it, capitalism "demands that the owner of the labour power should sell it only for a definite period, for if he were to sell it rump and stump, once and for all, he would be selling himself, converting himself from a free man into a slave, from an owner of a commodity into a commodity."[8]

In the intense commercialization characteristic of slave society we can locate the origins of the southern middle class even as we differentiate that society from northern capitalism. For in truth any society with a high level of sustained commercial activity can generate a middle class of merchants, creditors, and shippers, and the slave societies of the New World were among the most highly commercialized the world had ever seen. Long before Frederick Winslow Taylor launched his campaign to make factory workers as efficient as bees, Thomas Jefferson and George Washington literally stood over their slaves carefully calculating the optimum amount of time a worker should devote to a particular task. Southern planters were buying watches and installing clocks at the same time the first textile factories were appearing in New England. William Kauffman Scarborough's monumental study of *Masters of the Big House,* the most thoroughly researched account of southern planters ever produced, demonstrates that even the most elite slaveholders cultivated the classic bourgeois virtues of thrift, sobriety, and hard work. This was not simply northern cultural hegemony at work; it was the logical product of a slave economy in which commodification penetrated deeply into the social fabric, more so than even capitalism would allow.[9]

So it is not enough to say that "commerce is not capitalism." If all that means is that slave labor was less efficient than free labor, it doesn't tell us much and may not even be telling us the truth. Instead, the commerce in slaves should help us appreciate that what the slave economy lacked was not capitalist efficiency but capitalist restraint. As Max Weber pointed out more than a century ago, it was the restraints that made capitalism dynamic. "Unlimited greed for gain is not in the least identical with capitalism, and is still less its spirit." On the contrary, Weber explained, "capitalism *may* even be identical with the restraint, or at least a rational tempering, of this irrational impulse."[10] If there was some basic weakness in the southern slave economy—a plausible but also a debatable proposition—the weakness resided not in the lack of a market but, on the contrary, in the lack of restraints on the market. By turning their workers into commodities the slaveholders rejected the boundaries capitalism placed on the market and in the process may have inhibited the southern economy's ability to develop.

The relative underdevelopment of the southern slave economy implied no resistance to commerce or the values that sustain it. Lax management of their farms and plantations could lead planters to financial ruin. The only planters who could afford to retreat into the leisurely life of fox hunts and endless socializing were those who hired good managers and overseers to handle the grubby business of making sure the plantations were running at a steady profit. Most slaveholders, including most planters, had no choice but to be diligent in their profession. They played hard, but they also worked hard. They raised their sons to the same values; they expected the same thing from their aspiring sons-in-law. These are the behaviors, the "bourgeois" virtues, that are likely to appear in any highly commercialized economy, the same virtues that flourished on the slave plantations of the New World.[11]

Robin Blackburn has argued that bourgeois civil society—with its patriarchal family structure, its privatized economy, and its zealous protection of the rights of property—was one of the preconditions for modern slavery.[12] Not surprisingly the slaveholders were famously protective of their economic independence, proud of their patriarchal authority over their wives and children, covetous of their property rights in their slaves, and determined to build and maintain a wall of separation between the government and their "private" economic and family lives. It made sense for the slaveholders to embrace the new and powerful distinction between the public and the private spheres of life do this, for as Jürgen Habermas has demonstrated, the modern public/private distinction was very much a product of "early finance and trade capitalism," the period in which "long-distance trade" generated unprecedented *"traffic in commodities and news."* In principle the public sphere was populated by men who stepped momentarily outside the confines of their "private" spheres—the patriarchal families that provided husbands and fathers with the economic independence they so valued and which became the material basis of the public sphere. If anything, the bourgeois distinction between the public and private spheres was, in Habermas's reading, threatened by the later development of capitalism.[13]

It should come as no surprise, then, that slaveholders produced some of the most compelling defenses of civil society America has ever produced. James Madison's arguments for the separation of church and state epitomized the bourgeois repudiation of an organically unified society. Similarly, Thomas Jefferson's faith in public opinion and the self-correcting nature of free expression reflected the early modern repudiation of arguments from authority. In truth, southern slavery flourished within a civil society founded upon the principles of free trade, "private" property, domestic patriarchy, the separation of church and state, and a critical press.

I have been painting in broad and bold strokes, so it's worth stepping back to add at least of few of the essential qualifiers. To say that slave society was able to produce an indigenous bourgeoisie is not to say that "bourgeois" is an adequate description of southern slave society. There was a culture of honor, there were aspirations to aristocracy, and there were crucial differences of time and space and equally important distinctions between established eastern planters and their frontier cousins, big planters from small slaveholders, the late eighteenth century from the mid-nineteenth century, and conservative Whigs from Jacksonian populists. The Old South was a big place with a host of competing tendencies. Southerners were committed to a free press but had no hesitation cracking down on antislavery sentiment. Theirs was a society torn by very real social divisions but which instinctively closed ranks in defense of property rights, whether in land or slaves. There were aristocratic impulses but there were structural elements that forever prevented southern slave society from becoming genuinely aristocratic. The slaveholders were no more successful at creating perfectly efficient slaves than Frederick Winslow Taylor would be in his effort to turn factory workers into automatons. Southern masters embraced a powerful bourgeois heritage, but it could never be fully realized because no slave society could ever absorb "self ownership" as one of its foundational principles.

The point is not that the slave South was merely bourgeois, but that it is wrong to assume that a master class and the middle class were fundamentally incompatible. That was Daniel Hundley's point, and it is not without merit.

JAMES OAKES
Distinguished Professor and Graduate School Humanities Chair
CUNY Graduate Center

NOTES

1. D. R. Hundley, *Social Relations in Our Southern States* (New York: H. B. Price, 1860), 77–81.
2. Ibid., 77–81, 84–85, 91.
3. The best guides to the centrality of property in the definition of slavery are M. I. Finley, *Ancient Slavery and Modern Ideology* (New York: Viking Press, 1980), 73ff.; Thomas Morris, *Southern Slavery and the Law* (Chapel Hill: University of North Carolina Press, 1996); David Brion Davis, *Inhuman Bondage: The Rise and Fall of Slavery in the New World* (New York: Oxford University Press, 2006), 27–47. Gavin Wright, *Slavery and American Economic Development* (Baton Rouge: Louisiana State University Press, 2006), is a profoundly important reexamination of the political economy of slavery that takes the slaves' status as "property" as the central issue to be addressed. Property was by no means the only salient aspect of slavery. There was also a

racial component that determined *who* was legitimately enslaved and thus treated as property. Yet property came close to the core of what slavery itself was, the thing that distinguished it from other forms of power. Orlando Patterson, *Slavery and Social Death: A Comparative Study* (Cambridge, Mass.: Harvard University Press, 1982), 21–27, sharply rejects this view, but David Brion Davis, cited above, argues persuasively for the restoration of the "chattel" principle as a central element of slavery.

There is a case to be made that "property" can be understood as a social relation. See especially Robert L. Hale, "Coercion and Distribution in a Supposedly Non-Coercive State," *Political Science Quarterly* 38 (1923): 470–94; Robert L. Hale, "Bargaining, Duress, and Economic Liberty," *Columbia Law Review* 43 (1943): 603–28; Felix S. Cohen, "Dialogue on Private Property," *Rutgers Law Review* 9 (1954): 357–87; C. B. MacPherson, ed., *Property: Mainstream and Critical Positions* (Toronto: University of Toronto Press, 1978), 1–13, 199–207; Jennifer Nedelsky, "Law, Boundaries, and the Bounded Self," *Representations* 30 (Spring 1990): 162–89; Joseph William Singer, "Sovereignty and Property," *Northwestern University Law Review* 86 (1991): 1–56; Duncan Kennedy, "The Stakes of Law, or Hale and Foucault!" *Legal Studies Forum* 15 (1991). For a useful overview and critique of this literature, see Stephen R. Munzer, "Property as Social Relations," in Stephen R. Munzer, ed., *New Essays in the Legal and Political Theory of Property* (New York: Cambridge University Press, 2001), 36–75. As Munzer points out, the literature on property as social relations is large and not internally consistent, but even if everyone agreed on what it means to say that property is a social relation, it would not follow that *all* social relations are property relations.

An alternative body of legal scholarship that defines property as a distribution of rights among persons with regard to the disposition of a thing has proven extremely useful for legal historians of slavery. The crucial statements of this view are Wesley Newcomb Hohfeld, *Fundamental Legal Conceptions as Applied in Judicial Reasoning* (1919; reprint, Westport, Conn.: Greenwood Press, 1978), and A. M. Honore, "Ownership," in A. G. Guest, ed., *Oxford Essays in Jurisprudence* (London: Oxford University Press, 1961), 107–47.

4. On the distinctive security of property rights as a partial explanation for the spectacular economic breakout of early modern Europe, see C. A. Bayley, *The Birth of the Modern World, 1780–1914* (Malden, Mass.: Blackwell, 2004), 60–61.

5. The freedom enjoyed by Anglo-American slaveholders to develop their own slave system has been remarked on in a classic study by Herbert Klein, *Slavery in the Americas* (Chicago: Ivan Dee, 1967), and more recently in a magisterial comparative analysis by J. H. Elliott, *Empires of the Atlantic World: Britain and Spain in America, 1492–1830* (New Haven: Yale University Press, 2006).

6. James O. Breeden, ed., *Advice Among Masters: The Ideal in Slave Management in the Old South* (Westport, Conn.: Greenwood Press, 1980), 39.

7. Erskine Clarke, *Dwelling Place: A Plantation Epic* (New Haven: Yale University Press, 2005), 150–51.

8. Marx, *Das Capital*, 1:168.

9. Mark M. Smith, *Mastered by the Clock: Time, Slavery and Freedom in the American South* (Chapel Hill: University of North Carolina Press, 1997); William Kauffman Scarborough, *Masters of the Big House: Elite Slaveholders of the Mid-Nineteenth-Century South* (Baton Rouge: Louisiana State University Press, 2003).

10. Max Weber, *The Protestant Ethic and the Spirit of Capitalism,* trans. Talcott Parsons (1958; reprint: Dover, 2003), 17.

11. James Livingston, "'Marxism' and the Politics of History: Reflections on the Work of Eugene D. Genovese," *Radical History Review* 88 (Winter 2004): 30–48. Livingston sees the bourgeoisie as a "transhistorical" class, one that has appeared throughout history in highly commercialized societies.

12. Robin Blackburn, *The Making of New World Slavery: From the Baroque to the Modern, 1492–1800* (London: Verso Books, 1997), 5–12.

13. Jürgen Habermas, *The Structural Transformation of the Public Sphere: An Inquiry into a Category of Bourgeois Society* (Cambridge, Mass.: MIT Press, 1991), 14 (first and second quotations), 15 (third quotation). The "structural transformation" to which Habermas's title refers was prompted by the decline of the economically independent household and the rise of wage labor. For Habermas capitalist development had a paradoxical effect. On the one hand, it undermined the material basis of the public sphere; on the other hand, the formal equality of capitalist social relations made the compromised public sphere "less ideological." Habermas speaks of the bourgeois world that gave rise to the modern public/private distinction as "early capitalism," but southern historians are more familiar with the term "merchant capital." See especially Eugene D. Genovese and Elizabeth Fox Genovese, *Fruits of Merchant Capital* (New York: Oxford University Press, 1983). In subsequent, more abstractly theorized versions of his argument, Habermas reformulated the threat capitalism posed to the public sphere in terms of a general process of rationalization marked by, among other things, the invasion of the "lifeworld" by the "system." See Jürgen Habermas, *The Theory of Communicative Action,* 2 vols., trans. Thomas McCarthy (Boston: Beacon Press, 1985).

CONTRIBUTORS

JOHN G. DEAL is an editor for the *Dictionary of Virginia Biography* (1998–), a multivolume reference work published by the Library of Virginia. His writings include more than thirty sketches for the DVB, an essay for the *Encyclopedia of the New American Nation* (2006), and an article in *Virginia Capitol Connections Quarterly Magazine* (2007).

SUSANNA DELFINO is associate professor of history and institutions of the Americas at the University of Genoa, Italy. She serves as the first vice president of the Southern Industrialization Project, an organization she helped to found. She co-edited, with Michele Gillespie, *Neither Lady nor Slave: Working Women of the Old South* (2002), the first two volumes of the series New Currents in the History of Southern Economy and Society: *Global Perspectives on Industrial Transformation in the American South* (2005) and *Technology, Innovation & Southern Industrialization* (2008), and with Michelle Gillespie and Louis M. Kyriakoudes, *Southern Society and Its Transformation* (2011).

DON H. DOYLE is McCausland Professor of History at the University of South Carolina and author of several books, including *The Social Order of a Frontier Community* (1978), *New Men, New Cities, New South* (1990), *The South as an American Problem* (1995, ed. with Larry Griffin), *Faulkner's County: The Historical Roots of Yoknapatawpha* (2001), *Nations Divided: America, Italy, and the Southern Question* (2002), *Nationalism in the New World* (2006, ed. with M. A. Pamplona), and *Secession as an International Phenomenon* (2010, ed.).

BRUCE W. EELMAN is associate professor of history at Siena College. He is the author of *Entrepreneurs in the Southern Upcountry: Commercial Culture in Spartanburg, South Carolina, 1845–1880* as well as articles and reviews in scholarly journals. An earlier version of the essay in this volume was presented at the Society for the History of Technology Conference in Lisbon, Portugal in 2008.

JENNIFER L. GOLOBOY is an independent scholar who has published essays about the early American middle class and edited a book on the social history of the Industrial Revolution. She would like to thank Jen Green, Jon Wells, Sally Hadden, Kirsten Fischer, John Howe, Christopher Clark, Megan Kate Nelson, Michael and Susan Goloboy, and Steve, Matthew, and Alexandra Sigmond. She also thanks the Gilder Lehrman Institute for funding her research at the New-York Historical Society and other New York City libraries.

JENNIFER R. GREEN is professor of history at Central Michigan University. She has published *Military Education and the Emerging Middle Class in the Old South* (2008) and articles in *Journal of Southern History*, *The Journal of the Historical Society*, and *Southern Manhood* (ed. Craig Thompson Friend and Lorri Glover). She thanks the College of Humanities, Social & Behavioral Sciences at Central Michigan University and the staff at the South Caroliniana Library.

SALLY E. HADDEN is associate professor of history at Western Michigan University. Her first book was entitled *Slave Patrols: Law and Violence in Virginia and the Carolinas* (2001). Her current book project on legal cultures in three eighteenth-century American cities has been supported by many grants, including a postdoctoral grant from the National Endowment for the Humanities. She thanks the editors, Jennifer Goloboy, Albrecht Koschnik, Claudia Mineo, John Wertheimer, and the staff of the South Carolina Historical Society. Earlier versions of this essay were presented to the American Society for Legal History and before the history department at Florida State University; comments offered at both venues have strengthened the final product.

ANGELA LAKWETE is associate professor in the department of history at Auburn University. Her first book, *Inventing the Cotton Gin: Machine and Myth in Antebellum America*, won the Society for the History of Technology's 2004 Edelstein Prize for Outstanding Book. She extends special thanks to colleagues Morris Bian, Bill Trimble, and Mike Hogan, who read and edited drafts, and to the editors of the volume for their constructive comments.

AMANDA REECE MUSHAL recently completed her doctorate at the University of Virginia and is assistant professor of history at The Citadel. Her research focuses on the role of honor among mercantile families in antebellum South Carolina. She would like to thank the staff at the South Caroliniana Library for their assistance and Jon Wells and Jen Green for their helpful comments on this essay.

JAMES OAKES is Distinguished Professor of history and holds the Graduate School Humanities Chair at the CUNY Graduate Center. He has produced three monographs—*The Ruling Race: A History of American Slaveholders* (1982; reissued 1998), *Slavery and Freedom: An Interpretation of the Old South* (1990), and *The Radical and the Republican: Frederick Douglass, Abraham Lincoln, and the Triumph of Antislavery Politics* (2008)—and numerous articles, essays, and review articles in major journals.

SONYA RAMSEY is an associate professor of History and Women's and Gender Studies at the University of North Carolina at Charlotte. She is the author of *Reading, Writing, and Segregation: A Century of Black Women Teachers in Nashville* (2008).

MARTIN RUEF is professor of sociology at Princeton University. His books include *The Entrepreneurial Group* (2010), *Organizations Evolving* (2006, with Howard Aldrich), and *The Sociology of Entrepreneurship* (2007, co-edited with Michael Lounsbury). An earlier version of this chapter was presented at the Cornell-McGill Conference on Institutions and Entrepreneurship and at the Harvard Business School. He is especially thankful to Howard Aldrich, Neil Fligstein, Jennifer Green, and Jonathan Wells for their insightful feedback on the initial drafts of the chapter.

FRANK TOWERS is associate professor of history at the University of Calgary. His publications include *The Urban South and the Coming of the Civil War* (2004) and the co-edited *The Old South's Modern Worlds: Slavery, Region, and Nation in the Age of Progress* (2011). He is currently researching connections between federal and grassroots proslavery politics.

JONATHAN DANIEL WELLS is associate professor of history at Temple University in Philadelphia. He is the author of *The Origins of the Southern Middle*

Class, 1800–1861 (2004), as well as a forthcoming study of black and white women journalists and editors in the nineteenth-century South. He has edited or co-edited four other books, including *Entering the Fray: Gender, Politics, and Culture in the New South* (2010).